*Fractured Europe: 1600–1721*

# *Blackwell History of Europe*
## General Editor: John Stevenson

The series provides a new interpretative history of Europe from the Roman empire to the end of the twentieth century. Written by acknowledged experts in their fields, and reflecting the range of recent scholarship, the books combine insights from social and cultural history with coverage of political, diplomatic and economic developments. Eastern Europe assumes its rightful place in the history of the continent, and the boundary of Europe is considered flexibly, including the Islamic, Slav and Orthodox perspectives wherever appropriate. Together, the volumes offer a lively and authoritative history of Europe for a new generation of teachers, students and general readers.

# Fractured Europe: 1600–1721

David J. Sturdy

Copyright © David J. Sturdy 2002

The right of David J. Sturdy to be identified as author of this work has been asserted in accordance with the Copyright, Designs and Patents Act 1988.

First published 2002
2 4 6 8 10 9 7 5 3 1

Blackwell Publishers Ltd
108 Cowley Road
Oxford OX4 1JF
UK

Blackwell Publishers Inc.
350 Main Street
Malden, Massachusetts 02148
USA

*British Library Cataloguing in Publication Data*

A CIP catalogue record for this book is available from the British Library.

*Library of Congress Cataloging-in-Publication Data*

Sturdy, D. J. (David J.)
  Fractured Europe, 1600–1721 / David J. Sturdy.
     p. cm. — (Blackwell history of Europe)
  Includes bibliographical references and index.
     ISBN 0–631–20512–8 — ISBN 0–631–20513–6 (pbk.)
1. Europe—History—17th century.  2. Europe—History—1648–1715.  3. Europe—Intellectual life—17th century.  4. Europe—Economic conditions—17th century.
5. Thirty Years' War, 1618–1648—Influence.  6. Great Britain—Politics and government—1603–1714.  I. Title. II. Series.

D246 S78 2001
940.2'2—dc21

                                                                                    2001001575

*Picture Researcher* Thelma Gilbert

Typeset in 10.5/12.5pt Galliard
by Kolam Information Services Private Limited
Printed in Great Britain by MPG Books, Bodmin, Cornwall

This book is printed on acid-free paper

To Isabel, Lucy and Ian

# Contents

# Illustrations

# Preface

When I was invited to write this book, the proviso was added that it should have a narrative structure. Excellent histories of the seventeenth century exist and continue to be published, but the vogue of recent years has been to organize them thematically. Such an approach has much to commend it, not least because it can unravel complicated episodes of history and identify their defining elements. Yet thematic history has its limitations. It can assume that readers already have a knowledge of the period in question, while the very process of treating themes discretely can militate against an understanding of their interconnections and development over time. Narrative history can preserve a sense of thematic clarity, while at the same time explicating the multifarious connections, interactions, and even accidents and contingencies which constitute the historical experience. Narrative history can convey a sense of the immediacy of the problems with which, in this case, seventeenth-century decision-makers had to wrestle, the powerful and complex influences which acted upon them, and the role of personality in deciding some of the great issues of the day.

The most important guiding principles underlying this present volume are as follows. First, it must cover the whole of Europe, not concentrate unduly on certain areas. Europe is taken to run from Ireland to the Ukraine, and from Scandinavia to Sicily; the Balkan provinces of the Ottoman Empire also are included. Britain and Ireland are integrated into the discussion, partly because we have, at last, abandoned the false division between British, Irish and European history (a glance through older books will demonstrate the

frequency with which European history was written with little reference to Britain and Ireland, and vice versa), but also because, towards
the end of the seventeenth century, Britain and Ireland were a major
force in the sphere of European international relations; correspondingly, the historical development of those islands was profoundly influenced by continental Europe.

A second principle is that the book should not confine itself to
political history, but should investigate the mutual connections between the great political, social, religious, economic and cultural
forces which were at work. Much of the material in this book is
organized around a political framework, but by no means exclusively
so; thus many pages are devoted to subjects in the visual arts and the
sciences. The argument is that, in the seventeenth century, regimes
of all types regarded the visual arts as powerful weapons to be
deployed in their service. Painting, sculpture and architecture both
reflected and helped to form the ideologies through which regimes
legitimated themselves. As regards the sciences (a word coming into
use in the 1600s, alongside the older 'natural philosophy'), the fundamental changes which were taking place, and to which the label
'Scientific Revolution' is often, if controversially, attached, likewise
had implications beyond the sciences themselves. They challenged
conventional thought in philosophy, religion and even politics, and
forced contemporaries to reassess their ideas in these domains.

A third principle is that a narrative history should also point out
some of the subjects which are the focus of present-day historiographical debate. There is a sense in which all the arguments and
propositions in this book are provisional: research continues apace,
new information is unearthed, and new perspectives are adopted; but
some subjects do occasion particular debates among historians, and a
narrative history should signal them either implicitly or explicitly.

Like all written history, narrative has to be selective. This means
that some themes are touched on tangentially rather than centrally.
Thus, overseas colonies are referred to only in so far as they had a
direct effect on Europe; the smaller states of Germany receive less
attention than would be the case in a history of Germany itself; social
and economic history likewise are included to the extent that they
are relevant to the broader arguments of the book. Readers who
desire more information on these and other topics should consult
the Further Reading section at the end of book.

Finally, a few words should be said about the structure of the
book, and the use of proper nouns. The main division is regional,

but there is a chronological break at 1660. This provides an opportunity to assess the condition of Europe and identify the principal historical trends up to that point. The story is taken up again in the second part of the book, and concludes with another review of major developments down to 1720. The chapter headings and section headings within chapters indicate the periods that they cover. These chronological references should be regarded as approximate and not exact, for the text of a particular passage might include material from before or after a given time scale. The use of proper nouns invariably presents problems to historians of this period: should the place-names of modern times be used or those of the early modern period; and should the names of historical figures be given in their 'native' form or in an anglicized version? Since the readership of this book is likely to be predominantly English-speaking, both 'native' and anglicized terms are employed: the criterion has been ease of understanding. A particular difficulty was the question of what to call the area now comprising the United Kingdom and the Republic of Ireland. For most of the period covered by this book, that area was 'the three kingdoms of England (with the principality of Wales), Scotland and Ireland'. This is an unwieldy phrase not inviting frequent repetition. On the other hand, although the words 'Britain' and 'British' are technically incorrect in many contexts, they do have the attraction of brevity, and for this reason are used in place of the longer formulation, unless one of the kingdoms is being discussed individually. Similar considerations arise with Spain, as is explained in chapter 4, and Switzerland, which strictly speaking was a geographical term, not a collective constitutional noun for the Swiss Cantons.

# *Acknowledgements*

Few, if any, scholars can claim to pronounce with authority on every facet of history, and having written this book I deny any pretensions towards omnicompetence. I therefore record with gratitude the assistance and advice of many people, some of whom read sections or all of the text and made comments which saved me from factual errors and suggested new or alternative lines of interpretation. In this regard I am indebted in particular to John Stevenson of the University of Oxford, the general editor of the series to which this volume belongs, Christopher Black of the University of Glasgow, Jeremy Black of the University of Exeter, Robert Evans of the University of Oxford, Lionel Glassey of the University of Glasgow, Robert Stradling of Cardiff University, and my colleagues at the University of Ulster, Keith Lindley and Raymond Pearson. For the maps and illustrations, I am grateful for the assistance of Gillian Coward of the Film and Sound Resource Unit in the University of Ulster. Staff at Blackwell have been unfailingly helpful and courteous; my thanks go especially to Louise Spencely, Tessa Harvey, Tamsin Smith and Leanda Shrimpton. I am also grateful to the copy-editor, Sue Ashton. My wife, Deirdre, read and corrected drafts of the manuscript. My love and thanks go to her.

The author and publishers would like to thank the following for permission to reproduce illustrations:

Fig. 1: Photo AKG London / Robert O'Dea.

Fig. 2: Photo AKG London / Stefan Drechsel.

Fig.  3:   Leiden University Library.

Fig.  4:   Photo AKG London.

Fig.  5:   British Library.

Fig.  6:   Photo AKG London.

Fig.  7:   National Maritime Museum, Greenwich.

Fig.  8:   © Ashmolean Museum, Oxford.

Fig.  9:   Science Museum / Science and Society Picture Library.

Fig. 10:   Bodleian Library, Oxford.

Fig. 11:   Nijmegen Museum, Commanderie van St Jan.

Fig. 12:   British Library.

Fig. 13:   photograph reproduced with the kind permission of the Trustees of the National Museums and Galleries of Northern Ireland, Ulster Museum.

Fig. 14:   Photo AKG London.

Fig. 15:   Novosti Photo Agency.

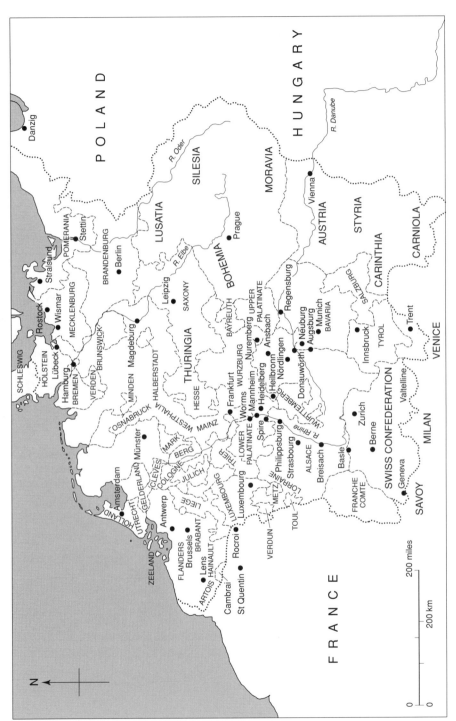

**Map 1**  The boundaries of the Holy Roman Empire in 1600

**Map 2** Italy about 1600

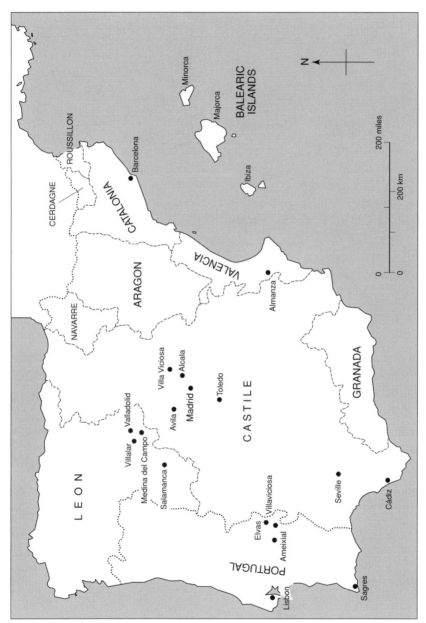

**Map 3**  Spain and Portugal in the seventeenth century

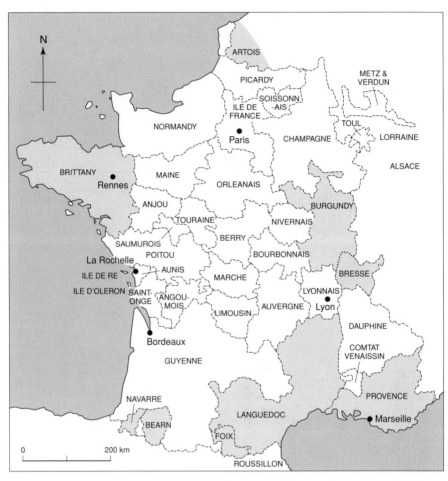

N

ARTOIS

METZ &
VERDUN

PICARDY

SOISSONN
-AIS

ILE DE
FRANCE

TOUL

LORRAINE

NORMANDY

CHAMPAGNE

• Paris

ALSACE

BRITTANY

MAINE

ORLEANAIS

• Rennes

BURGUNDY

ANJOU

TOURAINE

NIVERNAIS

BERRY

SAUMUROIS

POITOU

BOURBONNAIS

La Rochelle

AUNIS

BRESSE

ILE DE RE

MARCHE

ILE D'OLERON

SAINT-
ONGE

LYONNAIS

ANGOU-
MOIS

AUVERGNE

Lyon

LIMOUSIN

DAUPHINE

• Bordeaux

COMTAT
VENAISSIN

GUYENNE

NAVARRE

PROVENCE

BEARN

LANGUEDOC

• Marseille

FOIX

0          200 km

ROUSSILLON

**Map 4** The provinces of France (shaded areas are those with provincial estates in 1661 and after)

**Map 5** England, Wales, Scotland and Ireland, 1642–1651

N

Haarlem
Amsterdam

GRONINGEN

FRIESLAND

DRENTHE

OVERIJSSEL
Deventer
Zutphen

Leiden
The Hague
UTRECHT
Utrecht
GELDERLAND
Arnhem
Nijmegen

Brill
Rotterdam
Dordrecht
Loevenstein
Cleves
Wesel

H
O
L
L
A
N
D

Middelburg
ZEELAND
Breda
Bois le Duc
THE GENERALITY
LANDS

Flushing
Bergen-op-
Zoom
Venloe

Sluys
Ostend
Antwerp
Roermond

Bruges
R. Scheldt
BRABANT
LIEGE
R. Rhine

Dunkirk
FLANDERS
Ghent

Furnes
Oudenaarde
Brussels
Louvain
Maastricht

Ypres
Courtrai
Tirlemont

Warneton
Menin
Ramillies
OF

St Omer
Steinkirk
Ath
Liège

Aire
Lille
Tournai
NAMUR
R. Meuse

Béthune
Mons
Namur
BISHOPRIC

ARTOIS
Douai
Malplaquet
Charleroi

Valenciennes
Mauberge
LUXEMBOURG

Cambrai
HAINAULT

Rocroi
BOUILLON

Luxembourg

0                    50 miles
0          50 km

**Map 6**  The Netherlands in the seventeenth century

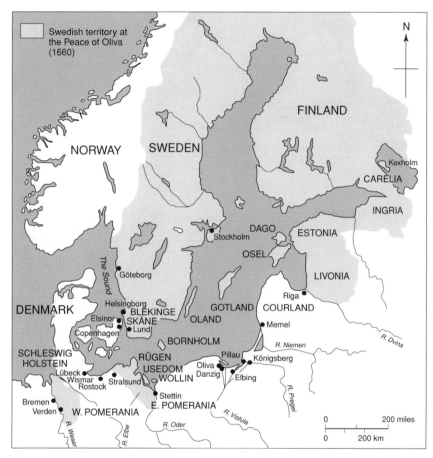

**Map 7**  The Swedish Empire in 1660

**Map 8**  Russia in the late seventeenth century

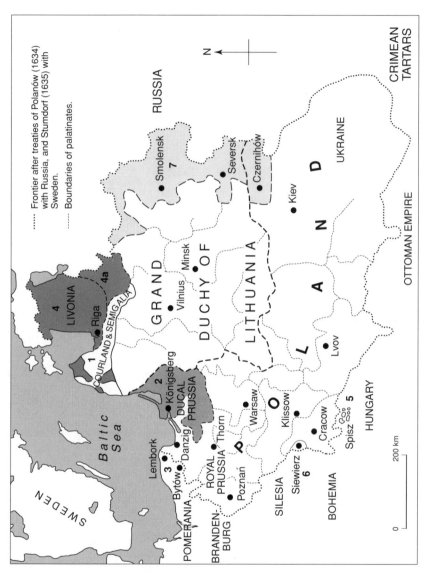

**Map 9** Poland–Lithuania in the mid-1600s (1, Courland and Semigalia: Polish fief, 1561–1775; 2, Ducal Prussia: Polish fief, 1525–1657; 3, Lembork and Bytów: Polish fief, 1637–57; 4, Livonia: Polish fief, 1561–1621; 4a, Polish Livonia: remaining to Poland, 1660–1772; 5, Spisz: 13 towns mortgaged to Poland, 1412–1769; 6, Duchy of Siewierz: possession of bishops of Cracow, 1443–1790; 7, Smolensk, Seversk, Czernihów: ceded to Poland, 1619–67)

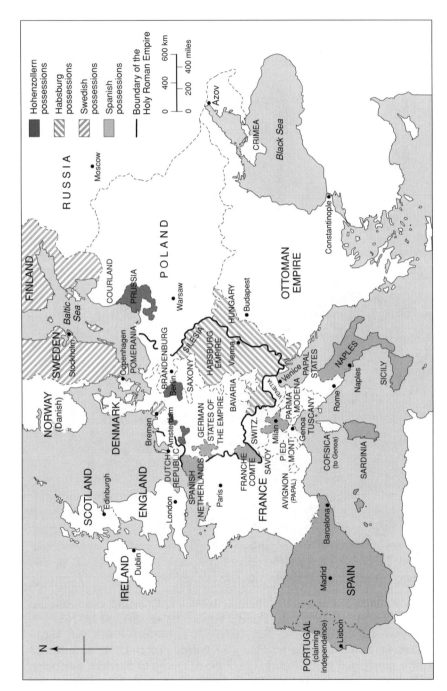

**Map 10** Europe in 1660

# 1

# *The Context of 1600*

---

Historians regard the seventeenth century as one of political division, religious confrontation, social conflict, revolution and international rivalry leading to seemingly interminable wars. Such sombre themes must provide much of the material of the chapters which follow, yet there is a positive corollary: some of the finest minds of the age wrestled with the problem of how to bring order and stability out of insensate strife, and purge Europe of the self-destructive forces which precipitated that continent into sustained crisis. Some of the strategies which they pursued will look strange and unfamiliar to present-day eyes, for they were usually rooted in seventeenth-century realism rather than ahistorical idealism, the achievable rather than the utopian; yet, without adopting a simple, programmatic view that Europe progressed from disorder to order, chaos to harmony, this book will contend that headway towards order was made, and that by 1720 Europe in most respects was in a healthier condition than in 1600.

Pre-industrial Europe was vulnerable to the vicissitudes of nature to an extent inconceivable today, and the unfavourable environment which prevailed exerted a decisive influence on the history of the period. Historians of climate contend that the seventeenth century formed part of the 'little ice age' which affected the whole world from about 1400 to the mid-1750s. Summers frequently were cool and short, with autumn, winter and spring on average being longer, wetter and colder than at present. The relationship between climatic factors and the production of crops and maintenance of livestock, the management of agricultural prices and wages is extremely complex, for in all these spheres Europeans proved adaptable, adjusting their agricultural and commercial practices accordingly. On the other hand, sudden extremes of cold or heat could have a widespread impact by creating a lethal combination of subsistence crisis and disease. Thus, in France, adverse weather conditions coincided with, and helped to cause, harvest failures from 1661 to 1663, from 1691 to 1694 and in 1709; they in turn led to famine which, in the case of the crisis of 1691–4, reduced the population of France by about 10 per cent. Some famines were general or sustained. Much of eastern Europe suffered famine between 1590 and 1602; likewise the entire Mediterranean region was badly hit from 1606 to 1609 and from 1628 to 1631; and serious food shortages verging on famine afflicted the whole continent during 1648–51, 1664–6, 1672–7 and, as in France, the early 1690s and 1709.

For the majority of Europeans – peasants and poorer townspeople – it was their generally meagre diet and unhealthy living conditions which diminished their capacity to resist disease. Most people relied upon local produce, for slow communications meant that perishable foodstuffs could not be transported over long distances. On the other hand, grain, which did not rot quickly, could be carried from, say, Poland to the Mediterranean. The diet of most Europeans was based on cereals – wheat, rye, barley, oats – made into various forms of bread, gruel, porridge or cakes. Depending upon its geographical location, a particular region's diet could be varied by the addition of seasonal vegetables, fruit, fish or dairy produce. Meat was comparatively rare, the most common being pork, but chicken, wildfowl and rabbit were also consumed. Crops had been introduced from the New World, but although they enriched the European diet in the long run, they were not sufficiently widespread in the early seventeenth century to have an appreciable effect. Traditional European diets continued to be rich in starches but low in proteins and vitamins.

The combination of adverse climatic conditions, unpredictable harvests and a limited diet meant that Europeans were, by modern standards, under-nourished and unhealthy. Infant mortality was high, often of the order of 15–25 per cent or even higher in times of famine, and only about half of those born survived long enough to reach the age of marriage. Women were especially vulnerable when giving birth; and since it was normal for married women of childbearing age to produce a child each year, the danger of succumbing to the experience itself, or to a related disease, was high. It was common, therefore, for men to marry more than once as they sought new wives and stepmothers for their children. However, the life expectancy of men too was low, and women frequently were left as widows with several children to support. It has been calculated that even in the eighteenth century, when the climate was beginning to improve and the food supply was expanding, about half of the marriages in rural France lasted less than fifteen years because of the death of the husband or wife; and, if Europe as a whole is taken from the sixteenth to the eighteenth centuries, about 25 per cent of all marriages were remarriages.[1]

The exigencies of nature in the seventeenth century, some of which are illustrated to telling effect in winter scenes depicted by landscape painters of the period, imposed their limitations on everybody. It will be seen in later chapters that warfare had to be seasonal, beginning in spring and ending with the onset of winter; commerce in northern Europe was regularly interrupted by frozen rivers and seas, while in southern Europe, during summer, bubonic plague and other diseases brought Mediterranean ports to a halt as ships suspected of carrying disease were debarred. The industrial and transportation revolutions of the nineteenth century enabled Europeans to overcome many of the limitations imposed by forces of nature; in the seventeenth century, Europeans had to adapt to nature.

## Political Contours

A glance at a political map of Europe at the beginning of the seventeenth century suggests that politically the continent was divided into three broad zones. First, the frontiers of most western European states bore a tolerable resemblance to those of their modern counte parts. Scandinavia, Britain and Ireland, France, Spain and Portugal, even the Spanish Netherlands and the Dutch Republic (or United Provinces) have their modern continuities. By contrast, eastern Europe was very different from its twenty-first century profile. It was encompassed within the Ottoman Empire, an emerging Russia and the kingdom of Poland; but the apparent simplicity of this arrangement belied a more complex reality, for the populations of these multi-linguistic, multi-ethnic and multi-religious entities enjoyed considerable practical, if not theoretical, autonomy. The third zone likewise contrasts with modern configurations: a belt of kingdoms, principalities, duchies, bishoprics and city-states running from the German Baltic coastline, through central Europe and Italy down to Sicily. While some of these territories were reasonably extensive, others were small; some were independent, some were dependencies of larger states, while yet others enjoyed varying degrees of autonomy. Many central European territories formed part of the Holy Roman Empire, a polity which, in spite of the grandiosity of its title, relied heavily on the consent of its member territories.

This rough division along geographical lines is more apparent than real and should not be elevated into a definitive classification. Like the eastern empires, the kingdoms of western Europe showed few signs of effective centralization. Even in France, normally placed by historians among the more centralized states, the king ruled a country which was a collection of disparate provinces, each with its own legal and financial traditions and privileges. Further west, the kingdoms of England, Scotland and Ireland shared the same monarch, but preserved their own parliamentary, legal and monetary systems. The theme of localism was especially characteristic of the Dutch Republic, where the powers of the provincial estates exceeded those of the Estates General. Governments everywhere lacked anything in the nature of a modern civil service. In central government, ministers were appointed by, and responsible to, the head of the state, but had few resources with which to administer the country. Bureaucracies in the present-day sense did not exist; in France, Spain and elsewhere, posts in such spheres as the administration of law or collection of taxation were put up for sale. Those who bought them – office-holders – regarded their posts as private property rather than positions through which to give dispassionate service to a minister or head of state. Powerful ministers tried to place their own followers in key central and provincial administrative positions, but otherwise had to contend with office-holders whose political reliability could not be taken for granted. Indeed, later chapters will show that some of the fiercest political and constitutional contests of the century were generated by conflict between ministers and office-holders.

The states of western Europe also displayed multi-linguistic features akin to those of central and eastern Europe. It was not simply that different languages were spoken within the same kingdom (in Spain, the Catalan and Basque languages flourished; in France, Occitan was commonly spoken in Languedoc, Provençal in Provence and Breton in Brittany); even the predominant language contained dialects which were almost mutually incomprehensible. When Jean Racine travelled from Paris to Uzès in 1661, he encountered confusions which he recounted to his friend, Jean de la Fontaine:

From Lyon onwards I could scarcely make sense of the language of
the region, and could hardly make myself understood in return. This
difficulty increased at Valence where...when I asked a servant for a
chamber pot [*un pot de chambre*], she put a heating stove [*un
réchaud*] under my bed. You can imagine the result, and what misfor-
tune could befall a sleepy fellow who tried to use this stove as a
chamber pot during the night. But it is even worse here [Uzès]. I
swear to you that I need an interpreter as much as a Muscovite would
in Paris.[2]

Among learned sections of society, Latin still served as a lingua franca
in 1600. Scholars frequently corresponded in Latin, much theology,
philosophy and science was published in Latin, and, of course, for
Catholics throughout Europe, Latin was the language of worship.
Change nevertheless was in the air as modern languages advanced at
the expense of Latin. In literature, most poetry, prose and plays were
in vernacular languages by 1600, and even other printed works were
showing the same trend. In Paris, about 30 per cent of books printed
between 1601 and 1605 were in Latin, but by 1700 the figure had
declined to under 10 per cent.[3]

By 1600, Portugal and Spain possessed extensive overseas colonies.
In the seventeenth century, the United Provinces, Britain and France
were to join them. The origins of European expansion to other parts
of the world go back to the fifteenth century when the Portuguese
established a chain of trading bases down the west coast of Africa and
round to Mozambique; they crossed the Indian Ocean and created
depots in Goa from which to conduct commerce with India, in Malacca for the Malay peninsula, and Macao for China. In the sixteenth
and seventeenth centuries, Dutch merchants moved into the Indian
Ocean and East Indies, and built up an extensive commercial network which rivalled that of the Portuguese. The Dutch established
their first eastern trading base in Sumatra in 1595, followed by one
in Mauritius in 1598. Thereafter they extended their activities to
Java, Ceylon (which they conquered between 1638 and 1656), Malacca (taken from the Portuguese in 1640) and the Cape of Good
Hope in 1652. The Dutch also established bases in India, first at
Pulikat near Madras (1609) and later at Hougli near the mouth of
the Ganges.

On behalf of the Spanish crown, the expeditions of Christopher
Columbus and other explorers in the 1490s and early 1500s sought
a westerly sea route to Asia, and inadvertently encountered what
Europeans only gradually recognized to be, as they put it, a New

World. The Spanish, Portuguese, and in due course the English, French and Dutch, established colonies there. As Europeans moved into America, as the New World came to be called, they brought with them political, legal and social systems, languages, educational institutions, and the Catholic and Protestant faiths. Colonial economies developed which required large labour forces, and as the indigenous populations suffered demographic collapse, mainly because of devastation wrought by diseases which Europeans brought, labour was acquired by transporting African slaves to the colonies. By 1600 colonial societies based on slave labour were flourishing in the Americas, and not only transformed the face of that continent, but had a profound impact upon the 'mother countries'.

American colonies gave Europeans access to plentiful supplies of primary materials, including precious metals, timber, and crops such as cane sugar and tobacco, which were grown on plantations. Plants from the New World were introduced into Europe and proved capable of being grown and harvested on a large scale. Two crops – maize and the potato – were to prove of inestimable benefit to Europeans in the long term. Both were highly nutritious and easy to grow, and their steadily increasing importance in the European diet made an outstanding contribution to the battle against food shortages. Ever-increasing Atlantic commerce led to the expansion of the great ports of Europe's western seaboard – Seville, Lisbon, Bordeaux, La Rochelle, Bristol and others – which increasingly turned into commercial 'frontiers' linking the 'old' world to the 'new'. The commercial revolution of the sixteenth and seventeenth centuries, which owed much to the colonies in the Americas, stimulated 'home' industries such as ship-building and the manufacture of navigational instruments, and provided opportunities for Europeans to export finished goods overseas. Of all the commodities coming out of the New World by 1600, however, it was gold and silver which was of supreme political significance. The Spanish colonies in Mexico and Peru produced gold and silver on an immense scale, 20 per cent of which went to the king of Spain. The 'Spanish preponderance' in western Europe, which was to be one of the major themes in the international history of Europe down to 1660, was financed in large measure by New World precious metals.

When we turn to the varieties of government in Europe in 1600, the image of a tripartite division between east, centre and west should be replaced by that of a gigantic crescent, one horn of which was planted in Portugal and Spain and the other in Turkey. The crescent describes an arc through France, Britain and Ireland, Scandinavia, down through Poland and Russia, the Balkans and so to Turkey. Generally speaking, the territory so covered was ruled by monarchs. Yet monarchy itself was far from uniform. Some countries, such as Castile, Sweden, England and Scotland, permitted a queen regnant. France, on the other hand, did not and could be ruled only by a king. In some monarchies, succession was governed by rules of heredity (France, England, Scotland and the kingdoms of Spain and Portugal were of this type), whereas in others it was by election: the Holy Roman Emperor and the kings of Poland, Hungary and Bohemia came into this category.

Most of the territory encompassed by the arms of this imaginary arc was ruled through non-monarchic forms of government, the main exception being southern Italy which, with the island of Sicily, formed a kingdom. A few republics existed: Venice, Switzerland and the self-styled Dutch Republic or United Provinces. The status of this last was still far from decided in 1600. The provinces of which it was composed were in rebellion against Spain, which had not recognized their independence. In 1609, Spain and the United Provinces signed a twelve-year truce, but the question of Dutch independence remained a contentious issue and was to return to the forefront of international affairs when the truce expired in 1621. Germany and much of Italy comprised principalities, duchies, city-states, ecclesiastical territories and a host of other entities intent upon preserving their distinctiveness. In a Europe wherein several of the larger states had predatory ambitions, the survival of smaller territories frequently depended on their ability to attach themselves to a protector.

## State and Society

The theme of variety which has run through the preceding few paragraphs applies with equal force when social structures in Europe are considered. The medieval notion that society is divided into three broad categories – those who safeguard the spiritual well-being of society (the clergy), those who rule and protect society (crown and nobility), and those who provide the material, legal, administrative and other frameworks necessary to communal life (commoners) – still found expression at the institutional level. Thus, the English parliament was composed of the House of Lords, comprising bishops

and nobles, and the House of Commons. In France, provincial
estates and the Estates General were made up of clergy, nobility and
the third estate (commoners). In reality, social structures were more
complex and diverse than this tripartite division would suggest. All
societies were hierarchical, but the nature of stratification varied.
Formal hierarchies existed within the clergy and nobility (an archbishop was superior to a bishop, or a duke to a baron), but hierarchies among commoners were far from clear, as was the location of the
'frontier' between commoner and noble. England was unusual in
that it possessed a land-owning group which was wealthy but not
noble: the gentry.

Many ambiguities arose from the interaction between prestige and
wealth. In predominantly rural regions across Europe, most wealth,
as represented by land, was held by the nobility and the church.
Within towns, cities and ports, and along the great commercial
routes, however, the situation was more complicated. Profits generated by commerce, finance and their associated activities were usually
in the hands of commoners, who often purchased land and even
noble titles (several monarchies, including the French and English,
sold titles in the seventeenth century). Were such upwardly mobile
families genuinely noble, or were they impostors pretending to a
status which they did not deserve? And if the monarch invented and
sold noble titles, was he or she not allowing money to subvert the
'normal' social hierarchy? And what about noble families which lost
all or part of their estates, perhaps in civil or international war, or
because they sold them to pay off debts? Could they retain their
social status, or did economic decline imply a reduction in social
status?

Similar incertitude existed at the other end of society, among those
who made their living on or from the land and are usually designated
'the peasantry'. The notion that there existed such a creature as the
'typical' peasant must be resisted. It is not just that the life of a
peasant in, say, Sweden was different from that of his counterpart in,
say, southern Italy because of climatic factors; peasants lived under
different systems of government, law, land-owning practices (in some
parts of Europe peasants could own or lease land, in others they
could not) and social structure. Again, not all peasants earned their
income exclusively from the land. Those who lived near urban
markets or commercial networks commonly engaged in artisanal production and supplemented their earnings by selling the goods which
they manufactured. Others lived in towns or villages rather than on a

farm, some members of the family working the land while others followed urban pursuits. There were also contrasts in the historical evolution of peasant life in Europe. Such factors as demographic trends within particular regions, the social and economic impact of warfare, patterns of the settlement or resettlement of population, and the great cultural, religious and intellectual changes of the sixteenth and seventeenth centuries, affected peasants in varying degrees and reinforced differences between them. In much of central and eastern Europe serfdom became the norm, tying peasants to the land to an extent that had no equivalent in western Europe. In short, we should stress the diversity of peasant life in Europe and avoid thinking in stereotypes.

Europe possessed many types of social structure. In the economically advanced areas of western Europe, notably those locked into Atlantic or Asian commerce, capitalist forces were at work and social classes as defined by economic criteria were emerging. In Russia, on the other hand, a social structure based on service to the tsar was being forged, as will be seen in later chapters. In the papal states, status was determined by service to the pope. Across large areas of central Europe and parts of Italy, a feudal nobility existed: it exercised legal powers over the lower social orders (noble estates often had their own law courts to hear cases involving tenants), and received labour service from tenants as well as a proportion of the produce of the land which they worked. Moreover, social structures were constantly changing in response to political, social and economic influences, even if slowly. The older idea that social structures in early modern Europe were rigid and immutable needs to be modified, and the reality of social change acknowledged.

## International Relations and War

In the modern world, the term 'international relations' implies formal contacts between states through the medium of sophisticated engines of diplomacy; it also carries connotations of long-standing alliance systems and permanent international organizations devoted to the regulation of the conduct of member states. No such apparatus existed in the Europe of the early modern period, but relations between states were conducted through procedures appropriate to the age. Governments made use of ambassadors and other categories of representatives and envoys, but on a scale which was small by modern standards; in 1715 even France maintained only fifteen ambassadors and about the same number of envoys. Professional diplomats did not exist in the seventeenth century. Ambassadors and other representatives were chosen because of their domestic political contacts, wealth or prestige, rather than because of their diplomatic skills; and when they went abroad they had to find their own residences and meet the costs of the embassy themselves (their governments might reimburse them, but frequently did not). Ambassadors and other envoys fully represented the majesty and honour of their monarch or other head of state, and were extremely sensitive to rebuffs or insults; countries could and did come close to war over real or imagined affronts offered to their representatives.

This raises another feature of international relations in this period: their intensely personal nature. The family interests, rights and claims of European monarchs determined the course of international affairs just as much as commercial, strategic or any other imperatives. This was bound to be the case given that marriages between royal families were arranged for political and diplomatic reasons. In the pages which follow, many instances will occur of marriages whose purpose was to harmonize relations between kingdoms, and even provide a foundation for coordinated action on the international stage. Yet royal marriages almost invariably stored trouble for the future: the partners brought to their marriage a wide range of titles and claims which, in due course, could be the occasion of disputes between their two dynasties. From the vantage point of the twenty-first century it is tempting to assume that seventeenth-century wars fought over, for example, economic resources or the control of commercial routes were 'modern', and that those arising from dynastic conflicts were relics of medieval mentalities. Yet it was precisely the 'succession wars', both great and small, which helped to create the map, certainly of western Europe, as we know it today. However, even contemporary rulers themselves gradually came to accept that the unrestrained pursuit of dynastic claims would condemn them and their territories to permanent warfare. One of the most influential ideas to emerge in international relations was that of 'equivalence': the readiness of a ruler to yield a particular dynastic claim on condition of being compensated by an equivalent concession elsewhere. The peace treaties and other international agreements signed during the course of the century reveal an increasing awareness by governments of the attraction of the principle of equivalence, and many months, even years, of negotiation were devoted to that end.

The great set-pieces of negotiation were the principal peace congresses of the century. Warfare was endemic in Europe, and while some conflicts involved only two or three states, others turned into wider conflagrations which required large congresses to settle general peace. Those congresses – Westphalia, Nijmegen and others – will be discussed in later chapters, but a close study of their organization and conduct would reveal much about the evolving art of negotiation. Indeed, contemporaries themselves began to write about the subject; influential works included *El embajador* (1620) by Juan Antonio de Vera y Zuñiga (a French translation appeared in 1642), *Mémoires touchant les ambassadeurs et les ministres publics* (1677) and *L'Ambassadeur et ses fonctions* (1689), both by Abraham van Wicquefort; an English translation of this last work appeared in 1716. The possibility of regulating relations between states by appealing to a concept of international law was raised by the great Dutch jurist Hugo Grotius; his *De jura belli et pacis* (1625) called for an international system in which the conduct of states would be based on principles of reason rather than, for example, dynastic claims.

The statement has just been made that warfare was endemic in Europe, but what was war? It is not easy to establish a satisfactory definition. If we say that it was the use of force by one state against another in a formal conflict, that would be too restrictive: states frequently resorted to armed force without issuing declarations of war; furthermore, some parts of Europe, especially the Ukraine, existed under the nominal rule of a particular government, which used the army to assert a modicum of control. In the context of this book, therefore, warfare is deemed to be the use of military violence by states, irrespective of context: thus there will be declared and undeclared wars, civil wars, guerrilla wars, wars on land and sea. The changing nature of war in the early modern period has generated debate among historians as to whether a 'military revolution' took place. This is a subject to be discussed at a later juncture (see below, pp. 248–50). For the time being it is sufficient to note that the evolving nature and functions of war will raise such topics as the recruitment and training of armies, the means whereby they were administered and equipped, their leadership and control both from the government and on campaign, conditions of service, and the relationship between their purely military activities and the political and diplomatic purposes which they served.

## The Holy Roman Empire

So far this chapter has introduced its subjects in general terms, but it is time to shift focus and become much more precise. Reference was made earlier to the Holy Roman Empire, an assemblage of some 360 territories under the largely nominal rule of the emperor. Its origins went back many centuries and it was involved in almost all of the great international crises of the seventeenth century. It had no parallel elsewhere in Europe, and certainly has none in the modern world. In view of its importance in early modern European history, however, its constitutional foundations, structure and organization should be understood, for they in turn were to influence the character of imperial policy, and the responses of the empire itself to the challenges of the century.

In the fourteenth century the empire encompassed Germany (with Austria) and regions which were either non-German or where German speakers were a minority: Bohemia, northern Italy, Switzerland, Dauphiné, Burgundy, Franche Comté and the Netherlands. Over the next two centuries some of these peripheral regions were lost, so that by 1600 it consisted, for practical purposes, of Germany, Austria and Bohemia. A product of medieval concepts and forces, the empire nevertheless proved to be remarkably durable; it was dismantled only in 1806 amidst the Napoleonic wars.

Although the Holy Roman Empire predated the fourteenth century, its structure was defined in 1356 when Emperor Charles IV issued the Golden Bull (a document so called because its seal or *bulla* was in gold). At the head of the empire was an elected emperor, chosen by a college of seven electors: there were three prelates (the archbishops of Mainz, Trier and Cologne) and four secular princes (the king of Bohemia, the count palatine of the Rhine, the duke of Saxony and the margrave of Brandenburg). It will be seen in later chapters that in 1623 the Count Palatine Frederick V was deprived of his vote because of his involvement in the Bohemian rebellion of 1618; his vote was transferred to the duke of Bavaria. At the Peace of Westphalia (1648), Frederick V's son, Charles-Louis, recovered the vote and Bavaria was elevated to an electorate, so making a total of eight. In 1692 Hanover acquired a ninth vote. When the imperial throne was vacant, the archbishop of Mainz convened a meeting of the college of electors in Frankfurt to choose a new emperor. If one of the electors was a candidate, he was permitted to vote for himself.

In the Middle Ages, the newly elected emperor had two coronations. He was crowned king of the Germans at Aix-la-Chapelle/ Aachen, where Charlemagne, first of the emperors, was buried; he also went to Rome to be crowned by the pope as king of the Romans. This too maintained a link with Charlemagne, who was crowned there in AD 800. However, in the fifteenth and sixteenth centuries, these traditions were modified. Frederick III was the last emperor to be crowned in Rome (1452); when Charles V, elected in 1519, was crowned by Pope Clement VII in 1529, it was at Bologna, not Rome. Thereafter the ceremony relapsed, and no other papal crowning of the emperor occurred. One reason was that Frederick III had introduced a 'secondary' election which henceforth normally took place during an emperor's lifetime: the electors chose a separate 'king of the Romans', nominated by the emperor himself on the understanding that this person (in Frederick's case, his son Maximilian) later would be Holy Roman Emperor. Thereby the title 'king of the Romans' came to resemble that of prince of Wales in England or dauphin in France by signifying the heir apparent. This practice was one factor enabling the House of Habsburg, to which Frederick III belonged, to monopolize the imperial crown. To counterbalance this hereditary tendency, the electors, from the election of Charles V onwards, required the chosen candidate to agree to certain conditions (known as the *Wahlkapitulation*) before they proclaimed him emperor: he must swear to honour the rights of his subjects, consult his subjects in the traditional manner, and employ only Germans in imperial offices.

## Imperial Government

The emperor enjoyed many of the attributes of a sovereign ruler: he was head of imperial justice, implemented foreign policy, and oversaw the security of the empire. Nevertheless, the Golden Bull provided little institutional apparatus through which to fulfil these duties. Imperial structures did gradually emerge, but the Holy Roman Empire was far from being a unitary state; it remained a collection of about 360 principalities and other territories which enjoyed a high degree of autonomy. The empire functioned through negotiation, collaboration and persuasion rather than through formal instruments of government. Among the institutions which did exist, the most important was the imperial diet (*Reichstag*) which, until 1663, met when and where the emperor convened it; thereafter it sat permanently in the imperial city of Regensburg. It was the principal forum wherein the emperor consulted the rulers of the imperial territories. The diet was composed of three colleges: the electors, the princes (usually about 150 attended), and representatives of the sixty or so free or imperial cities (cities responsible directly to the emperor, not to the local princes). For a matter to become law it required the consent of the emperor and two of the three colleges. Procedures were slow, for the colleges met separately and communicated only in writing.

The fact that the diet was unwieldy should not cause us to underestimate its significance. When it assembled, its members and their followers numbered several thousand, and whichever town hosted the diet was expected to provide hospitality on a lavish scale. The diet brought together the elites of the empire and was essential to the preservation of the imperial spirit. The principal binding forces of the empire were tradition, prestige and personal contact, rather than instruments of government. Meetings of the diet fostered loyalties and sentiments without which the empire could not have survived. In the sixteenth century, however, the religious and political controversies caused by the Protestant Reformation introduced ideological divisions into the diet, whose meetings turned into forums of conflict rather than cooperation. This is one reason why the diet met only six times between 1555 and 1603, and only once between 1608 and 1640.

Once law had been created by the diet, responsibility for enforcement lay chiefly with the rulers of the territories of the empire, who in effect could ignore a law with which they disagreed. To assist the administration of imperial law, much of the empire had been divided into ten regions or 'circles' (*Kreise*) by the early 1500s, each with its own administrator and council.[4] By 1600, some of the circles had become obsolete; part of the circle of Burgundy, for example, had been absorbed by France and the rest by the Dutch Republic. The empire possessed only two law courts. One was the Supreme Court of the Empire (*Reichskammergericht*) which sat at Spire until 1693, when it transferred to Wetzlar; it served as a court of appeal. The other was the Aulic Council (*Reichshofrat*) in Vienna, which generally dealt with cases involving the most important princes. There were other imperial institutions – for example, the Chancery (*Reichshofkanzlei*) in Vienna, which managed the diplomatic relations of the empire – but they were too few to administer its affairs efficiently.

This was not necessarily a source of weakness, since powerful vested interests were served. Although the heads of the territories took pride in belonging to the empire, they placed equal value on their autonomy, and had no desire to see the powers, as against the prestige, of the emperor augmented. This sense of independence was especially characteristic of larger states such as Bavaria, Brunswick, the Palatinate, Saxony and Brandenburg, which conducted domestic and foreign policies on a basis similar to that of any other European state.

It is a remarkable feature of the empire that, apart from a brief hiatus in the eighteenth century, every Holy Roman Emperor from 1452 to 1806 came from the Habsburg dynasty; and from this latter date they ruled the successor Austrian Empire until 1918. Given the unique imperial and European role of the Habsburgs, it is appropriate to cast a brief eye over their origins.

### The House of Habsburg

The Habsburgs emerged in Switzerland in the twelfth century as lords in the Aargau region to the west of Zurich, and gradually extended their influence further afield. By the mid-fifteenth century they had become archdukes of Austria, which henceforth they regarded as their chief patrimonial possession. A simplified family tree will help to make the points which follow.

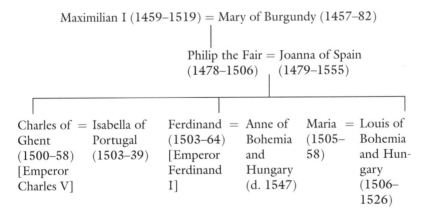

After Austria, the Habsburgs acquired three other major segments of territory: Burgundy (with Franche Comté and Flanders), Spain and its possessions, and the kingdoms of Bohemia and Hungary. The process began with Frederick III's son, Emperor Maximilian I, who in 1477 married Mary, daughter and heiress of the recently deceased Charles the Bold, duke of Burgundy. Through his wife, Maximilian now ruled the Burgundian succession. He came into direct conflict with French interests, for Louis XI of France also claimed Burgundian lands. He and Maximilian fought two wars, but by the Treaty of Arras (1482) agreed on a partition. Louis XI received Burgundy and Artois, while Maximilian retained Flanders and Franche Comté. This episode marks the beginning of a major theme in European international relations: rivalry between the Habsburgs and France.

Two decades later another marriage paved the way to an even greater prize: Spain and its possessions. In 1496 the son of Maximilian and Mary, Philip the Fair, married the Spanish princess Joanna ('the Mad'), youngest daughter of King Ferdinand and Queen Isabella. Joanna was sixth in line to the Spanish throne, and, although she and Philip the Fair had two sons and a daughter, she had no serious expectation that she or her children would rule Spain. After her husband's death in 1506, her behaviour became so eccentric that she was incarcerated in a castle and her succession rights devolved to her children. Meanwhile the unexpected happened: her brothers and cousins, who preceded her children in line of succession, predeceased her father. When Ferdinand died in 1516, his successor was the elder son of Joanna and Philip the Fair, Charles of Ghent. The inheritance into which Charles entered in 1516 comprised Spain, the Spanish Netherlands, Spanish possessions in Italy, and a rapidly expanding empire in the New World. More was to come. Charles had been king of Spain for only three years when his grandfather, Emperor Maximilian I, died. From him Charles inherited Austria, Franche Comté and Flanders. As the Habsburg candidate for the imperial crown he was duly elected in 1519 and took the title Charles V. It was beyond the powers of one man to rule so many territories. In 1521 Charles ceded the regency of Austria to his younger brother Ferdinand, but retained Spain and its possessions, plus the Burgundian inheritance and the imperial crown.[5]

The central European presence of the Habsburgs – now overseen by Ferdinand – was augmented in 1526 when this prince secured the kingdoms of Bohemia and Hungary through marriage. Maximilian I had agreed a compact with Wladislaus II, king of Bohemia and Hungary, whereby Wladislaus's son, Louis, married Maximilian's granddaughter, Maria (1516), and Wladislaus's daughter, Anne, married Maximilian's grandson Ferdinand (1521). Wladislaus died in 1516, and his son Louis was duly elected king of Bohemia and Hungary. Louis died at the battle of Mohács (1526), fought against the Turks, and since he and Maria had no children, the Bohemian diet quickly elected Louis's brother-in-law, Ferdinand, as king of Bohemia.

Hungary proved more problematic. After Mohács, the country in effect was divided into three parts. The largest – central Hungary – was occupied by the Turks. Next was 'Royal Hungary', a narrow band of territory adjoining the eastern border of Austria. This was all that remained outside direct or indirect Turkish control. The final portion was the province of Transylvania which, while not formally occupied by the Turks, was a Turkish dependency. Whereas Ferdinand was elected king of Bohemia with little difficulty, in Hungary he faced a rival, John Zapolya, former governor of Transylvania. The main Hungarian diet elected Ferdinand as king of Hungary (in effect, Royal Hungary), but a rival assembly of nobles in Transylvania chose Zapolya. Several wars followed in which Ferdinand tried to recover those parts of Hungary held by the Turks or Zapolya. The fighting was indecisive, and on Zapolya's death in 1540 the Transylvanian lords elected his son, John Sigismund, in his place. Transylvania retained its semi-autonomous state, acknowledging Turkish suzerainty in defiance of Ferdinand.

Notwithstanding the setbacks in Hungary, the Habsburgs were the wealthiest and politically the most powerful dynasty in Europe by the late 1520s, and herein lies an explanation for their monopoly of imperial elections over the next three centuries. It was an arrangement which satisfied two sets of imperatives. One was Habsburg family honour. The imperial crown carried unrivalled prestige, hence the readiness of the Habsburgs to stop at nothing to retain it. Correspondingly, they possessed the political, financial and military resources to make the Holy Roman Empire a reality as against a fiction. In view of the centrifugal forces and external threats to which the empire was vulnerable, the Habsburgs were the only German family with the capacity to hold it together. The electoral college understood this, and although imperial elections sometimes were contested, the electors never lost sight of this inescapable reality: no Habsburgs, no Holy Roman Empire. Accordingly, one Habsburg followed another as emperor.[6]

## Religious Division in Europe

In the sixteenth century, no force fractured European society with
such profound consequences as the Protestant Reformation. When,
in 1517, Martin Luther publicly protested at what he regarded as
abuses perpetrated by the Catholic church, he triggered a movement
which spread across Europe with astonishing speed. His example
spurred other reformers into action, so that within a few decades the
Lutheran church had been joined by Calvinist and Zwinglian
churches and a number of smaller, radical sects. Calvinism was widely
embraced in France, Scotland and parts of Switzerland and Germany;
in England a complicated religious mosaic emerged whose ambiguities were reflected in the nascent Anglican church, which combined
elements of Catholicism and Protestantism.

So deeply were religious categories of thought embedded in the
political institutions of Europe that the Reformation crisis rapidly
acquired political as well as social implications. Much of Germany
collapsed into socio-political turmoil overlaid by religious zealotry.
After almost four decades of conflict, involving Emperor Charles V,
many of the imperial territories and all classes of society, a comprehensive peace was signed at Augsburg (1555). It rested on the pragmatic acceptance that a multi-confessional Germany was a reality. To
prevent future religious conflict, the Peace of Augsburg incorporated
four major principles. One was that of *cuius regio, eius religio* ('whose
the region, his the religion'): in each state or territory of the Holy
Roman Empire, the religion of the head would be that of his subjects. This principle applied only to Catholicism and Lutheranism; it
was not extended to Calvinism, which as yet had no legal status in
the empire. The second provided that former Catholic church lands
held by Lutheran princes in 1552 should remain so, but no more
lands were to be sequestrated. The third stated that if any Catholic
bishop or prelate became a Lutheran, he should resign his see in
favour of a Catholic. The fourth confirmed that in imperial cities
which had multi-confessional populations, Catholics and Lutherans
would both enjoy freedom of worship.

Whatever the qualities of Augsburg as a settlement, the post-war
conditions which it sought to create had changed by the end of the
century, and the principles which it embodied were undergoing
renewed tension. Part of the explanation is to be found in the evolving
nature of Catholicism. In the second half of the sixteenth century the

Catholic church showed remarkable powers of recovery after the trauma of the Reformation. This movement of Counter-Reformation should be understood as a conjunction of militant anti-Protestantism and vigorous internal reform. The contours of the Counter-Reformation were defined by the General Council of the church which met in the Italian city of Trent (apart from a brief period at Bologna) in three sessions between 1545 and 1563.[7] The council condemned central tenets of Lutheran and Calvinist doctrine and ruled out any prospect of accommodation with Protestantism. It defined Catholic doctrine, took measures to raise the spiritual and educational standards of the priesthood, and imposed a more demanding discipline upon bishops and other members of the ecclesiastical hierarchy. The Council of Trent avoided decisions on two crucial issues, probably because they were highly contentious and risked dividing the council: a definition of the church, and of the exact nature of papal authority. Nevertheless, by the time it disbanded, the Council of Trent had endowed the Catholic church with formidable doctrinal and organizational powers with which to combat Protestantism.

The Counter-Reformation also drew inspiration from a reform movement which, while not independent of the Council of Trent, arose from tangential or even pre-Tridentine sources. Existing religious orders were reinvigorated and new ones founded. Especially significant in a German context was the Society of Jesus, founded by Ignatius Loyola in 1534; the order received papal approval in 1540. Unlike, say, Benedictines or Dominicans, the Jesuits were not a monastic order. They served as missionaries in Europe, Asia and the New World, and established colleges which, in their size, resources and quality of teaching, surpassed many universities. Jesuits were appointed as professors in some of the great universities of the Holy Roman Empire, including Vienna from 1552, Prague from 1556 and Innsbruck from 1561. Jesuit strategy in Germany was master-minded by Peter Kanis ('Canisius'), who was sent by the order to Vienna in 1552. He brought Jesuit professors into the university, founded a Jesuit college in Vienna in 1552, and opened a seminary in 1556. His famous catechism (1555) was adopted widely throughout Catholic Germany, where his organizational and educational talents made an outstanding contribution to the cause of Counter-Reformation.

Although confronted by a more resolute Catholicism, Protestantism also displayed continuing powers of expansion and adaptation. Lutheranism profited from the sympathetic attitude shown towards it by Emperor Maximilian II, whose personal religious commitments were

Lutheran, even though he remained nominally Catholic. In 1568 Maximilian allowed his Austrian noble subjects to convert to Lutheranism if they wished. Lutheranism thereby gained a significant foothold in Austria, and these territorial gains were complemented in 1584 by an important doctrinal settlement. Since 1548, when Emperor Charles V had attempted to reconcile Lutheran and Catholic doctrine through a document known as the Interim of Augsburg, Lutherans had been divided in their attitude to this initiative. Those who followed the distinguished theologian Philipp Melanchthon (the 'Philippists') were favourably disposed towards the project, whereas the 'pure' or 'genuine' Lutherans (in German the *Gnesio-Lutheraner*) were hostile. The two camps remained divided until the 1580s, by which time the Counter-Reformation was making sufficient progress to persuade them that they must bury their differences and reunite. In 1584 they did so by the Formula of Concord, which brought Lutherans together again. On one point, however, all Lutherans were agreed: Calvinism should be resisted as resolutely as Catholicism. This question was especially sensitive in the Palatinate. During the reign of the Elector Palatine Frederick III (1559–1576), the Palatinate was a Calvinist state, even though the Peace of Augsburg denied recognition to Calvinism and a high proportion of the populace was Lutheran. Frederick's son, Louis VI (reigned 1576–1583), reverted to Lutheranism and, in accordance with the principle of *cuius regio, eius religio*, required his subjects to follow suit. At the same time, he oversaw discussions between Calvinist and Lutheran leaders in the hope of securing reconciliation, but without success. After his death, the pendulum swung back: his son and heir Frederick IV (reigned 1583–1610) reimposed Calvinism.

From the early 1560s to 1598, France too was torn asunder by socio-political conflict, the French Wars of Religion. The product of a disastrous combination of a weakened monarchy, aristocratic rivalry, socio-economic malaise, and the impact of dynamic Calvinist missionaries armed with a religious message which had radical social, political and perhaps even economic implications, the civil wars continued almost to the end of the century. They were punctuated by short-lived truces and peace treaties, and were the occasion of some of the worst atrocities of the century. Most notable was the Massacre of St Bartholomew's Day (1572) when there began a massacre of many thousands of Huguenots, as French Calvinists were known.[8] In political and constitutional terms, the most critical moment came in 1589 when Henri III, last member of the Valois dynasty, was assassinated. He had no direct heir, and his successor was a cousin twenty-three times removed, Henri de Navarre, a member of the Bourbon dynasty. However, Henri de Navarre (Henri IV) was a Huguenot. Civil war flared up again and was only moderated when Henri IV adopted two measures: in 1593 he converted to Catholicism, and in 1594 held his coronation. These acts were a public commitment to his Catholic subjects – about 90 per cent of the population – that he had embraced traditional French monarchy. In 1598 he ended religious conflict by issuing the Edict of Nantes, which incorporated Calvinists into the state. The edict listed those parts of the kingdom where they would enjoy rights of worship; it allowed them the liberty to pursue such careers as they wished; it created special tribunals to adjudicate disputes between Catholics and Huguenots; and, as a guarantee of their safety, it allowed the Huguenots to fortify certain towns. The Edict of Nantes was not founded on the principle of religious toleration, nor was it envisaged as a permanent settlement; like the Peace of Augsburg, it acknowledged the reality of a religious minority, and sought to avert further conflict by defining the place of that minority in French society. The edict was an act of the royal will and, by implication, would remain in force only as long as the king desired. In the event it lasted less than a hundred years, being revoked by Louis XIV in 1685. France began the new century in a state of domestic peace after almost forty years of civil war, but formidable tasks of political, economic and social reconstruction awaited the Bourbon regime.

## Religious and Political Tensions in Germany

It is tempting to presume that, in a central Europe wherein a resurgent Catholicism was conducting a campaign of vigorous Counter-Reformation, it was only a matter of time before another conflagration occurred. We should beware of such a simple approach to historical causality, for the territorial rulers in the Holy Roman Empire needed no education in the horrors of religious warfare. From time to time problems arose which threatened the settlement arrived at by the Peace of Augsburg, but German political leaders mainly strove to preserve its essentials. One such crisis occurred in Cologne in 1582. The archbishop, Gebhardt Truchsess, was living openly with a mistress whom he intended marrying. To that end he became a Calvinist, but added to the sense of shock which his announcement caused by proclaiming that he would remain in post. Here was a direct challenge to Augsburg, which had provided that any Catholic prelate who converted to Protestantism must resign in favour of a Catholic. Pope Gregory XIII deposed Truchsess in April 1583 and replaced him with Duke Ernest of Bavaria, bishop of Liège. This latter figure, who, like Truchsess, possessed little sense of religious vocation and was notorious for the debauchery of his life-style, nevertheless belonged to the powerful Wittelsbach family which ruled Bavaria and had the military resources to impose Duke Ernest by force. Accordingly, Bavarian troops, assisted by Spanish regiments, occupied Cologne and oversaw the enthronement of the new archbishop. For several years Gebhardt Truchsess sought to have the decision reversed, but in 1589 accepted defeat and retired to Strasbourg. The principle that a Catholic convert to Protestantism must relinquish his see had been upheld.

Some years later, another principle of Augsburg was reaffirmed, but only through a piece of neat legal legerdemain. It concerned the imperial city of Donauwörth, whose population and municipal council were overwhelmingly Protestant. Urged by monks of the Benedictine monastery of the Holy Cross in the city, Catholics affirmed their presence through public processions to mark the festivals of the Catholic calendar. The processions were a cause of much tension in the city as Protestants objected that they were offensive and triumphalist. In September 1606 a Catholic parade took place, accompanied by elaborate banners and loud music. It provoked extensive anti-Catholic rioting in the town. The affair was reported to Emperor Rudolf II, who referred it to the Aulic Council. The Aulic Council invited Duke Maximilian of Bavaria to suppress the violence and secure from the municipality a guarantee that Catholic worship and processions would continue unhindered. Maximilian moved into Donauwörth but, after several fruitless months of discussions, was unable to secure the necessary promises from the city fathers. The Aulic Council – with the consent of the emperor – revoked Donauwörth's status as an imperial city in 1607 and placed it under Maximilian's authority. Maximilian cancelled Protestant rights of worship, and with the help of teams of Jesuits reimposed Catholicism within the city. Neighbouring Protestant territories – Neuburg, Ansbach and Württemberg – objected that the emperor had broken the spirit, if not the letter, of Augsburg. The imperial response was that, because the status of Donauwörth had been annulled, the principle of Protestant rights of worship had been replaced by that of *cuius regio, eius religio*; Augsburg had not been violated. Protestants also raised a question of imperial law. Donauwörth lay within the circle of Swabia, not of Bavaria; therefore, they argued, Maximilian ought not to have been involved in the city's problems. Their protest availed nothing, and Donauwörth remained in Maximilian's hands.

This episode was the catalyst which led to the formation in 1608 of the Evangelical Union. In that year an imperial diet was called at Regensburg. The emperor sought money and troops to fight the Turks, but recent events in Donauwörth left Protestants in the diet little disposed to cooperate. Catholic members likewise were in no mood to strike a deal with Protestants; indeed, several contended that, as far as they were concerned, the Peace of Augsburg was redundant: it was the decrees of the Council of Trent which now commanded their obedience, not the compromises of Augsburg. The Protestants staged a walk-out, and under the leadership of the Elector of the Palatinate formed the Evangelical Union. It was joined by most, although not all, Protestant territories; Saxony and Brandenburg, for example, remained aloof. The Union sought and acquired the protection of Henri IV of France who, although a Catholic, feared for the future of a part of Germany crucial to French interests. The following year a counter-organization was formed: the Catholic League led by Maximilian of Bavaria under the patronage of Philip III of Spain.

It is tempting to interpret the emergence of the Union and the League as evidence of a drift towards war in Germany. Even here we should exercise caution and remember that these organizations were an attempt to impose a measure of control upon a situation which otherwise might acquire unstoppable momentum. Although they did provide for self-defence, the Union and League were primarily pressure groups seeking to advance their causes through cooperation between their respective members. It is highly significant that they looked outside the empire for protectors. As will be seen in chapter 2, imperial authority at this juncture was dangerously weak, and Rudolf II was unable to provide the resolute leadership which the volatile politico-religious atmosphere required. Neither the French nor the Spanish government approached the affairs of the empire with unalloyed altruism, nor were the Union and League so naïve as to believe that they would. All recognized the dangers in allowing the French and Spanish an opportunity to intervene in the affairs of the Holy Roman Empire; the challenge was to secure sufficient French or Spanish support to realize the aims of the Union or the League, without allowing that support to turn into control.

## The Jülich–Cleves Crisis

Just how difficult it could be to strike this balance was illustrated by
the Jülich–Cleves crisis which broke out in 1609. In that year William,
the Catholic duke of Jülich–Cleves, died without heir. His territories,
which included Mark and Berg, lay in one of the most sensitive parts
of the Rhineland. Apart from bestriding, and therefore controlling,
movement up and down the Rhine, they gave easy access westwards
into the Spanish Netherlands and the Dutch Republic, and eastwards
into Germany. There were two chief claimants to the duchy, but both
were Protestant: Elector John Sigismund of Brandenburg, and Duke
Wolfgang William of Neuburg. Whoever succeeded, Jülich–Cleves
would become a Protestant territory. Unwilling to countenance this
eventuality, the emperor exercised his imperial privilege and proclaimed that he would hold the duchy himself until a Catholic successor was found. Both claimants resisted this course of action. They put
troops into the duchy and agreed to hold it jointly until a tribunal of
Protestant princes had adjudicated their respective claims. Although
they occupied most of the duchy, they failed to secure the fortress of
Jülich. The emperor had instructed Archduke Leopold, bishop of Passau and Strasbourg, to administer the duchy pending the choice of a
Catholic successor. With a small force Leopold entered the fortress,
and for the time being held it on behalf of the emperor.

Non-German interests quickly became involved. Henri IV of
France had followed affairs in Jülich–Cleves for several years, his
principal fear being that, if this strategically crucial territory passed
under the direct control of the Habsburgs, it would add to the
dangers on France's eastern frontier. In 1609 he devoted considerable energies to persuading the newly formed Evangelical Union that
it was essential to preserve Jülich–Cleves as a Protestant territory. He
urged the Union to make preparations for its defence, and promised
extensive military assistance. At the same time his agents contacted
leading members of the Catholic League, including Maximilian of
Bavaria, to point out that a Habsburg victory in Jülich–Cleves would
simply augment imperial and perhaps Spanish power at the expense
of the autonomy of the imperial princes; the Catholic League should
not sacrifice its long-term interest for the short-term gains of Catholicism in Jülich–Cleves. At Rome, French diplomats presented a
similar case to the pope: Catholicism was being exploited by the
Habsburgs to legitimate their pursuit of political power in Germany.

The governments of the Dutch Republic and England were also called upon by Henri IV to help to resist the Habsburgs in Jülich–Cleves.

Early in 1610 Henri IV invited Christian of Anhalt, a leading figure in the Evangelical Union, to Paris, where they planned a campaign to dislodge imperial forces from Jülich. A French army gathered in the east of the country, and James I of England sent a supporting force of 4,000 troops. For its part, the Catholic League had rejected French overtures and, with Spanish help, was mustering forces. War was imminent when there occurred the tragedy of 14 May in Paris: Henri IV was assassinated just a few days before he was to join his army. Although the campaign went ahead, and the mainly Franco-Union armies besieged Jülich (which capitulated on 1 September), the death of Henri removed the one figure who could have held the Protestant side together. His successor in France, Louis XIII, was only eight years old; Louis's mother, Marie de' Medici, became regent of France. Immersed in domestic crisis, she had no desire to be dragged into a European war. All the foreign troops quickly withdrew from Jülich–Cleves, and the Union and League both agreed that force alone could not decide the succession. They too stood down their armies in November 1610, leaving token forces to hold the duchy as before. Here matters remained until 1613 when Wolfgang William of Neuburg seized the initiative by becoming a Catholic and marrying the sister of Maximilian of Bavaria. In the short run, this again created the possibility of war, for the Spanish government sent troops to occupy Cleves as a first step towards imposing Wolfgang William throughout the duchy. But neither the two claimants nor the Evangelical Union and Catholic League desired war; the new emperor, Matthias, who had succeeded Rudolf II in 1612, similarly sought a peaceful resolution of the question. By the Treaty of Xanten (1614), John Sigismund and Wolfgang William agreed to partition the duchy: the former retained Cleves and Mark, and the latter Jülich and Berg.

The outcome was a compromise which demonstrated a willingness to repudiate a winner-take-all mentality. In 1609 the empire had come close to a general war because of French intentions, and could have done so again in 1613 had Spanish plans been realized. In spite of their belligerent stance, the Union and League had worked towards a settlement in Jülich–Cleves which conceded a modest advance of Protestantism in the interests of wider peace. But Germany could not isolate itself from events elsewhere. Within a few years there occurred a crisis in Bohemia which quickly assumed implications for Germany; and out of this complex knot of problems came that European catastrophe, the Thirty Years War. To Bohemia we therefore turn our attention.

# 2

# *Central and Southern Europe, 1600–1635*

Some wars in the seventeenth century were consciously conceived, planned and executed by governments, but the Thirty Years War, which started in Bohemia in 1618, was desired by nobody. Having begun, it acquired a momentum which for almost three decades resisted decisive military resolution or political control. When the war terminated in the Peace of Westphalia (1648), the settlements owed as much to exhaustion as to the negotiating skills of diplomats. Even then the peace was not comprehensive, for France and Spain continued fighting until 1659. In view of its duration and complexity, the war has been integrated by historians into various interpretative schemes. Some have seen it as the last phase of the religious wars of the sixteenth century; others as the climax of a 'crisis' through which Europe was struggling to move from its predominantly 'feudal' to its predominantly 'bourgeois' phase of history. Some have portrayed it as a stage in modern state formation; others as a German civil war which non-German states cynically manipulated, or perhaps a European civil war which foreshadowed the increasingly destructive conflicts of later centuries. In short, scholars have not reached consensus in their expositions of a war whose consequences for European history were to be profound.

For all its complexities, changing nature and at times its apparent lack of purpose, the Thirty Years War did revolve around certain central issues. First there was Bohemia itself. What form would the relationship between the king and his subjects take in future? Would the 'liberties' of Bohemia survive intact, or would they be curtailed by the king? Second, a similar question concerned the Holy Roman

Empire. In future, what would be the relationship between the emperor, the princes and other heads of the territories of the empire? The territories enjoyed a high degree of autonomy. Would they continue to do so, or would the Habsburg emperors subvert that independence and move towards an 'integralist' empire? Third, the war provided an opportunity for Sweden to attempt hegemony throughout the Baltic region. Would Swedish aspirations be realized, or would they be frustrated by Denmark, Poland and other rivals? Fourth, the volatile international context created by war revived the struggle between France and Spain. Since the fifteenth century, the French ruling dynasties – the Valois until 1589 and the Bourbons thereafter – had harboured profound misgivings over the dynastic ambitions of the Habsburgs. It was an axiom of French foreign policy that fundamental French and Habsburg interests (especially those of the Spanish line) were irreconcilable, and that the one could flourish only at the expense of the other. The Thirty Years War pitted Habsburg against Bourbon once more; indirectly at first, but openly after 1635. Fifth, the war posed the question of whether the Dutch Republic had the capacity to preserve its independence from Spain, or whether Spain would achieve *reconquista* and recover its former Dutch provinces. And, finally, running throughout the Thirty Years War (although its importance waxed and waned) was the perennial question of religion. How should Catholics, Lutherans, Calvinists and other Protestant groups, and the various tendencies of which they were all composed (for it is a mistake to assume that the churches were monoliths whose members thought, believed and behaved alike), relate to each other? Must they remain in confrontation, or could they achieve accommodation?

This list of themes is not comprehensive, but it does provide a framework for analysing a chain of conflicts which despoiled much of central Europe. This and the following chapter will be devoted to the war, the divide coming in 1635 when the Peace of Prague might have ended the German conflict. The declaration of war by France upon Spain in that year began a new phase of fighting.

### Background to the Outbreak of War in Bohemia

Bohemia – which included the provinces of Moravia, Silesia, Upper and Lower Lusatia – had the distinction of being the only part of the Holy Roman Empire which was a kingdom, although the nature of

Bohemian monarchy was difficult to define with precision. Like the Holy Roman Emperor and the kings of Poland and Hungary, the king of Bohemia was elected, in his case by the Bohemian diet. Ambiguity attached to the status of the election. The diet contended that the crown was wholly elective, while the Habsburgs, who ruled from 1526, argued that it was hereditary, and that their election was but a form of reception or acceptance by the diet. This divisive question of principle was circumvented by a practice reminiscent of that whereby imperial electors chose a 'king of the Romans' who later became emperor: the king of Bohemia would propose his successor to the diet; the nominee would be elected and then would succeed when the king died. The diet thereby claimed that the electoral principle had been honoured, while the Habsburgs were satisfied that hereditary succession had been preserved.

Bohemia was the backbone of the Holy Roman Empire in that it contributed more in money and troops to the imperial armies than any other territory. In the sixteenth century it appeared well capable of performing this role. With a population of about four million, Bohemia was, by contemporary standards, densely populated. Its economic life displayed 'modern' features. Bohemia was to the forefront of the textiles industry in central Europe; its mines were important producers of silver, iron and tin; its glassware industry was highly profitable; and Bohemian entrepreneurs pioneered fish-farming on a large scale. In the early seventeenth century, however, the economic cycle – as in many parts of Europe – was slowing down, and as it did so economic, religious, political and constitutional tensions were exacerbated. The burden of imperial war had taken its toll, especially in the realm of finance. The heavy taxes and forced loans which towns had borne for many decades were diminishing the profitability of business communities; and as silver poured into Europe from the New World, the Bohemian silver mines at Jachymov and Kutna Hora declined in significance.

The religious configuration of Bohemia was complicated, for even before the Reformation, non-Catholic movements spread throughout the country, notably that of the Hussites in the fourteenth and fifteenth centuries.[1] In the sixteenth century the impact of Lutheranism, and the proliferation of smaller groups such as Calvinists and Bohemian Brethren, reduced Catholicism to a minority faith observed by only about 10 per cent of the population in the early 1600s. The University of Prague was Protestant in ethos, and Protestants dominated the Bohemian diet. The responses of the

Habsburg kings of Bohemia were marked by caution. Maximilian II opted for pragmatic toleration, especially since his personal beliefs were closer to Lutheranism than to Catholicism (although for political reasons he remained a Catholic). His successor, Rudolf II, was a convinced Catholic who encouraged the Counter-Reformation, but even he refrained from attempting to impose Catholicism rigorously throughout Bohemia. It was during his reign that in 1609 the Protestants secured extensive legal concessions in a document known as the 'Letter of Majesty'. Since the crisis of 1618 arose out of a clash over these and other 'rights', the origins of the Letter of Majesty require explanation.

### Rudolf II and the Letter of Majesty

Rudolf II has often been judged harshly by historians. He exhibited symptoms of serious mental instability, being prone to hallucinations and long periods of depression. He never married. This in itself was not necessarily detrimental to Habsburg family interests, since he had brothers and cousins who could succeed him, but he took no steps to arrange for their election to any of the offices to which they aspired: king of the Romans, king of Hungary, king of Bohemia or Holy Roman Emperor. So serious did the situation become that, against his wishes, a family compact was arranged in 1605 whereby his brother Matthias replaced him as head of the dynasty. A feud broke out between Rudolf and Matthias which lasted until the former's death.

Shortly after becoming king of Bohemia in 1576, Rudolf decided to transfer his seat of government from Vienna to Prague. He did so in recognition of the prestige which attached to the Bohemian crown, but also for military reasons, Vienna being dangerously close to the frontier of the Ottoman Empire. Rudolf was installed in Prague by 1583, where he spent much of the rest of his reign as a recluse in the Hradschin castle. With the imperial court now based in the city, Prague entered upon one of the most brilliant periods of its history. The population grew to about 60,000, and the city became a truly multi-confessional, cosmopolitan metropolis. Whatever Rudolf's failings in other spheres, Prague under his rule was a queen of cities. He made his palace a *Kunstkammer*: the depository of a rich and eclectic collection of paintings, sculptures, furniture, jewels, manuscripts, books, scientific instruments and other artefacts. To his court were invited astronomers, philosophers, mystics, writers, musicians and other luminaries. An older historiographical tradition depicted the Rudolfine court and *Kunstkammer* as wasteful self-indulgence, but more recent scholarship has interpreted this side of Rudolf's activities sympathetically: as one of the last, if somewhat exotic, manifestations of Renaissance aesthetics. Before long, however, the principles of cultural cosmopolitanism, bold intellectual inquiry and religious coexistence which the Rudolfine court upheld were lost amidst the clamour of the Thirty Years War.

It was the Turks who set in train the events which resulted in the Letter of Majesty. In 1593, having ended a war against Persia, they began a campaign in Hungary. For several years Rudolf's armies engaged in indecisive warfare against the Turks, and in the course of the fighting committed widespread atrocities against Protestant towns and villages in Hungary and Transylvania. Moreover, when these towns fell under his control, Rudolf confiscated the property of Protestant nobles and restored Protestant churches to Catholic worship. The misconduct of the imperial forces, and the uncompromising religious policy of Rudolf in the Hungarian lands, occasioned popular risings in Transylvania where, in 1604, a convention of nobles chose one of their number, Stephen Bocskay, as their prince. Unable to defeat the Turks, and faced by risings in Hungary, Rudolf had no option but to negotiate. In 1606 he entered into two agreements: by the Convention of Vienna he restored religious freedom to the Protestants of Hungary, and by the Treaty of Zsitvatorok he ceded yet more towns to the Turks.[2]

This dual crisis of war against the Turks and risings in Hungary contributed to the Habsburg family compact of 1605, mentioned above. Matthias, now head of the Austrian branch of the family, took steps to rectify what he regarded as a situation of great danger. In 1608 he persuaded the Hungarian diet to recognize him as king of Hungary in his brother's place; the price was Matthias's confirmation of the liberties of the diet and freedom of worship for Protestants. He secured *de facto* control of Austria by offering similar concessions to its estates and Protestant communities. Only Bohemia remained in Rudolf's hands. In 1608 Matthias led an army towards Prague with the intention of forcing Rudolf to abdicate. On this occasion, however, Matthias failed to persuade the Bohemian diet to support him; most nobles, of whom the majority were Protestant, remained faithful to Rudolf. Unable to defeat his brother, Matthias negotiated a settlement whereby Rudolf formally ceded Hungary and Austria to Matthias, but remained king of Bohemia. Rudolf rewarded his

Protestant Bohemian subjects – but in effect purchased their continuing loyalty – by issuing the Letter of Majesty in 1609. It guaranteed
their freedom of worship and the right to build churches; it conceded
a wide range of rights to the diet, and created a body of commissioners (defensors) to supervise the implementation of the Letter. If anybody triumphed in 1609 it was the Protestant nobility of Bohemia.

The Letter of Majesty is sometimes likened to the Edict of Nantes
(1598) in France, but there are significant differences between the two
settlements. Henri IV conferred the Edict of Nantes from a position
of relative political strength, whereas Rudolf conceded the Letter of
Majesty from one of weakness. Henri IV's constitutional position as
king of France was secure, whereas Rudolf II faced a rival in Matthias.
The French Protestants were a small minority whose future depended
on a favourably disposed king, whereas the Protestants of Bohemia
were a large majority who held Rudolf in their grasp. In 1611 Rudolf
attempted to break the stranglehold of the defensors by encouraging
his cousin Leopold of Austria to invade Bohemia and 'liberate'
Rudolf. The enterprise misfired. Leopold's army was repulsed by
forces of the Bohemian diet. The diet declared that Rudolf had forfeited the loyalty of his subjects; it deposed him and offered the crown
to his brother Matthias, on condition that Matthias confirm the Letter
of Majesty. He agreed, and in May 1611 was crowned king of Bohemia. Rudolf died the following year; in the imperial election which
followed, Matthias was chosen as Holy Roman Emperor.

## The Habsburgs and Central Europe

Central Europe in 1612 presented a political paradox. The Habsburgs
had restored their ascendancy in the person of Matthias, but the splendour of his many titles could not conceal the fact that his powers were
circumscribed by those of the diets or estates, and by the 'rights'
secured by Protestants. His reign was short (he died in 1619), but
enabled a reassessment of strategy by the Austrian Habsburgs. They
attributed the fluctuations in their fortunes to the dynastic quarrels
which had divided the family, the inconclusive wars against the Turks
and rebels in Hungary, and the exploitation of these contingencies by
the various diets and Protestant groups of central Europe. Some in the
Austrian Habsburg camp concluded that they must pursue a two-fold
strategy: to attenuate the rights acquired by diets and Protestants, and
to assist the Catholic church to advance the Counter-Reformation.

Much Austrian Habsburg policy after 1612 conflated secular and religious purposes to the point where it is all but impossible to distinguish between them. The Habsburgs were not alone in so doing. Many governments operated on the premise that political loyalty and religious conformity were interdependent. As a principle it was attractively, if deceptively, simple.

One Habsburg who thought in these terms was Ferdinand of Styria, in Inner Austria, cousin to Emperor Matthias. Born in Graz, he was brought up in the spirit of Counter-Reformation Catholicism. His education by Jesuits and at the Catholic University of Ingolstadt reinforced his predisposition to reduce intricate questions to uncomplicated formulae; the outcome was a young man imbued with a sense of mission to eliminate Protestantism. When he became duke of Styria (Inner Austria) at the age of seventeen (1595), he subjected Protestants to systematic persecution. He expelled their clergy, closed their churches, authorized the mass burning of Protestant books, and obliged Protestants who refused to become Catholic to sell their property, donate 10 per cent of the proceeds to the Catholic church, and leave the country. The measures worked. Within ten years Styria was purged of Protestantism. The effectiveness of the policy confirmed Ferdinand's belief that he had a divine commission, not just in Styria but in the wider European field.

Within Bohemia itself, another source of such thinking was to be found in Catholic ministers of the crown who regarded the Letter of Majesty as a humiliation for king and Catholic church alike. Foremost among them was Zdenko Lobkowicz, grand chancellor of Bohemia from 1599. He belonged to one of the great aristocratic families of Bohemia which, along with the Liechtenstein, Slavata and Martinitz clans, formed a powerful Catholic minority at the court of Rudolf II. Although the chancellorship had not hitherto been the premier public office in Bohemia, under Lobkowicz it came to resemble a central ministry overseeing the internal affairs of the country. Rudolf II allowed this to happen largely through indifference, but his successor Matthias, who moved his court from Prague back to Vienna, left Lobkowicz to administer Bohemia in his name. Lobkowicz strove to undermine the Letter of Majesty, and had numerous clashes with the defensors. The opportunity for a comprehensive assault on its provisions came in 1617 when Ferdinand of Styria was elected presumptive king of Bohemia.

The question of a successor to Matthias had become urgent, for neither he nor his brothers, Maximilian and Albert, had direct heirs.

Philip III of Spain raised the possibility of the reunion of the Spanish and Austrian titles after the death of Matthias, but the Austrian Habsburgs were determined to keep central Europe in their own hands. In 1615 they privately agreed that Ferdinand of Styria would be their candidate to succeed Matthias in Austria, Bohemia, Hungary and the empire. He was their cousin, but more importantly was married with four children through whom the succession into the next generation looked reasonably secure.[3] Philip III of Spain was persuaded to consent to the arrangement in return for promises of land in Italy and Alsace. Matthias and his brothers devoted the next two years to securing Ferdinand's election to the respective crowns. The tortuous discussions whereby they persuaded the Bohemian diet to 'elect' or 'accept' Ferdinand (the nature of the exercise remained imprecise) in 1617, and the Hungarian diet to do so in 1618, need not detain us. Nevertheless, given that in both assemblies there was a Protestant majority, their choice of an avowed Catholic zealot does require explanation. The first point is that in each case the election was conditional upon Ferdinand's promise to safeguard the rights of his subjects, including the Letter of Majesty. Ferdinand provided the necessary assurances (although his Jesuit confidants quietly informed him that he was not bound by commitments to heretics) and was given the benefit of the doubt by the diets. After all, Bohemia and Hungary were not Styria, and it could not be presumed that in these large and diverse kingdoms he would simply replicate the religious policy which he had pursued in the smaller, more heterogeneous, Styria. The second point arises out of the 'elective' nature of the two crowns. If Ferdinand did not adhere to his promises, but behaved as a 'tyrant', the diets reserved the right to depose him and choose a different king; it was by just such a process that Matthias had re-placed Rudolf II as king of Hungary in 1608 and king of Bohemia in 1611. Thirdly, the two diets did not constitute solid voting blocs. Both contained factions gathered around powerful aristocrats defending family or regional interests. The Habsburgs, who had their own cabals in the diets, understood how these bodies operated, and were adept in the necessary manipulative techniques.

## The Crisis of 1618–1619

After going to Prague for the election of Ferdinand, Matthias returned to Vienna to begin preparations for the Hungarian election.

He left the government of Bohemia in the hands of a council of ten regents, seven of whom were Catholic. In practice the council was dominated by Vilém Slavata, Zdenko Lobkowicz and Jaroslav Martinitz. In the name of Matthias, but with the assent of Ferdinand, they implemented a vigorous anti-Protestant policy, the most contentious aspect of which was the closure of Protestant churches in the face of objections from the defensors. The latter called an assembly of Protestant nobles to Prague in 1618 to draw up formal representations to be sent to Matthias in Vienna. Matthias rejected their remonstrances and ordered the assembly to disband. On 23 May 1618, leaders of the Protestant nobles confronted two of the regents, Slavata and Martinitz, at the Hradschin castle in Prague to demand that the regents observe the Letter of Majesty. The ill-tempered meeting ended in deadlock. The nobles seized the regents and flung them with their secretary, Fabricius, from a window into a ditch some fifty feet below. All three survived what was a consciously symbolic act, for it was by such a 'defenestration' that Hussite risings had begun in 1419. By this calculated and well-publicized gesture, the Protestant nobles signalled open resistance to Matthias and Ferdinand. The nobles nominated a provisional government headed by thirty-six directors. A few moderates hoped that the breach with Matthias and Ferdinand could be healed, but the chances of reconciliation were rendered even less likely by the fact that one week before these events in Prague, Ferdinand had been elected king of Hungary. With the Hungarian crown secured, he was little disposed to compromise over Bohemia.

The Bohemian diet set about imposing military control throughout the country, and completed the task by early 1619. Matthias was still formally king, but his death on 20 March 1619 transformed the political context. It removed any pretext that the diet was acting to preserve the Letter of Majesty in the face of 'illegal' conduct by the regents, for Ferdinand now claimed to be king and approved what the regents had done. Furthermore, he was the Habsburg candidate for the imperial crown, and by virtue of being king of Bohemia possessed an electoral vote. The armies of the diet invaded Austria in an attempt to force Ferdinand (still in Vienna) to confirm the Letter of Majesty. In June they besieged Vienna, but in the absence of significant help from outside had to withdraw. In July 1619 the Protestant nobles convened a special General Diet in Prague to review the 'constitution' of Bohemia. The diet affirmed the electoral nature of the crown, designated war, finance and the appointment of ministers as spheres in which royal decisions required the consent of the diet, and proclaimed the Letter of Majesty a 'fundamental law'. The assembly defined Bohemia as a confederation of the provinces of the kingdom of St Wenceslas: Bohemia, Moravia, Silesia, Upper and Lower Lusatia; the confederation entered into an alliance with the Protestant-dominated Estates of Upper Austria. On 19 August 1619 the General Diet took the decisive step: it decreed that the new constitutional arrangements replaced the old, and that the election of Ferdinand in 1617 therefore was null and void. The diet instituted a search for a successor to Matthias.

By this time the imperial electors or their representatives had gathered in Frankfurt to choose the next Holy Roman Emperor.[4] Ferdinand came as king of Bohemia, but a delegation arrived from the Bohemian diet protesting that he had no authority to vote since he was not their king. What attitude should the other electors take? The three Catholic archbishops sided with Ferdinand. Two of the three Protestant secular electors – the Lutheran John George of Saxony and the Calvinist John Sigismund of Brandenburg – also backed him, although their decision was based on pragmatism as much as principle. John George knew that his own name had been raised in the Bohemian diet as a possible king, but he had sufficient grasp of political realities to appreciate that under no circumstances would the Habsburgs allow either the imperial or the Bohemian crown to elude them. He rejected the overtures of the diet and recognized Ferdinand's claim to be an elector. The elector of Brandenburg's interpretation of the situation was similar, and he too sanctioned Ferdinand's imperial vote. Frederick V, elector of the Palatinate, and a Calvinist, threatened to break ranks, but was dissuaded by the others. On 28 August 1619 Ferdinand was elected unanimously as Holy Roman Emperor.

The reason for Frederick V's hesitation was that, on 26 August, the Bohemian diet agreed to offer him the crown of Bohemia. He looked suitable on several counts. He was a senior prince of the empire, and as a Protestant could be trusted to respect the Letter of Majesty; if he accepted the crown, he would be confirming its elective nature. Frederick was a man of status on the international stage. Since 1609 he had been head of the Evangelical Union, and his marriage in 1613 to Princess Elizabeth, daughter of James I of England, attached him to one of the leading Protestant monarchies. Frederick weighed the offer carefully, for if he accepted, it would be on terms laid down by the diet. On the other hand, here was a chance to wear one of the most prestigious crowns in Europe, and who knew what the future might hold? Even the imperial crown might come into his possession. If Bohemia could be locked into the Protestant camp and its electoral vote cast in the Protestant cause (forming a majority in the electoral college with Saxony, the Palatinate and Brandenburg), then the religious and political complexion of the Holy Roman Empire might be transformed.

Frederick recognized the risks in accepting the Bohemian crown, for Ferdinand II would attempt to recover it by force. Moreover, Frederick had just voted for Ferdinand in the imperial election, thereby acknowledging him as king of Bohemia; if Frederick now replaced Ferdinand in Bohemia, his legal position *vis-à-vis* Ferdinand the emperor would be equivocal in the extreme. Ferdinand would have grounds for proclaiming him a usurper and charging him with treason. Much therefore depended on whether Frederick could defeat Ferdinand militarily and force him to surrender Bohemia in a legally binding treaty. Some German princes, including the elector of Saxony, warned Frederick that victory was impossible and that he should desist from becoming embroiled in Bohemian affairs. Others, among whom Christian of Anhalt was conspicuous, assured Frederick that he could defeat Ferdinand. Christian promised that if war broke out, the Evangelical Union would provide troops and money; he also reminded Frederick that assistance might be forthcoming from Protestant states such as England and the Dutch Republic. Other circumstances favoured Frederick. By now, Ferdinand II was facing a crisis in Hungary akin to that in Bohemia. In the autumn of 1619, Bethlen Gabor, prince of Transylvania, invaded Royal Hungary with the aim of replacing the beleaguered Ferdinand on the throne. Like the Bohemians earlier in the year, he laid siege to Vienna (October 1619), although within a few weeks he too had to withdraw when his neighbour to the north, King Sigismund of Poland, took this opportunity to raid Transylvania. Nevertheless, Ferdinand's position in Hungary looked perilous in the autumn of 1619. If Frederick and Bethlen Gabor could coordinate their campaigns, there seemed every possibility that Ferdinand would lose both crowns. After pondering these factors, Frederick V decided to accept the Bohemian crown. He announced his decision on 28 September; with his wife and entourage he travelled to Prague, where he was crowned on 4 November 1619.

## The Defeat of Frederick and the Restoration of
## Ferdinand II in Bohemia

Frederick's euphoria did not last, for Ferdinand II's position proved to be less precarious than it appeared. He received promises of help from Philip III of Spain, who undertook to occupy the Lower Palatinate. Louis XIII of France offered assistance, although before long he curtailed his contribution when he realized the adverse implications for France of a Habsburg victory in Bohemia. Significantly, Ferdinand received backing from the elector of Saxony. John George feared that the elector of the Palatinate risked plunging Germany into a disastrous war; better to crush this adventurer, restore Ferdinand and mediate a *rapprochement* between Ferdinand and the Bohemian diet. There was an element of self-interest in John George's stance: he coveted the Lusatias and was promised them by Ferdinand in the event of the defeat of Frederick. The Catholic League under the leadership of Maximilian of Bavaria offered troops to Ferdinand. Maximilian aimed to replace Frederick V in the Palatinate (thereby acquiring its imperial vote), and then turn the Palatinate into a Catholic territory. He undertook to invade the Upper Palatinate and Upper Austria, which was allied to Bohemia. While Ferdinand's prospects were improving, those of Frederick were worsening. He failed to collaborate with Bethlen Gabor; James I of England refused to be drawn into a venture which he considered foolhardy; and although the Evangelical Union did raise troops, by the Treaty of Ulm in July 1620 it was persuaded by the French to remain neutral.

Against this evolving background, Frederick spent the first few months of his reign preparing for war. To pay for it, he was obliged to impose punitive fiscal measures on his new subjects: extra taxes, higher existing levies, and more forced loans from the towns. These measures provoked revolts which spread in 1620 when Ferdinand's forces invaded Bohemia and further destabilized the country. Although Frederick's armies were supplemented by troops from Hungary, the Dutch Republic and mercenaries recruited by the German professional soldier Count Ernest von Mansfeld, they could not drive back the imperial forces. After a summer of destructive campaigns which further aggravated social unrest, the two armies fought their final battle on 8 November 1620 at the White Mountain, not far from Prague. The imperial army routed that of Frederick, and proceeded to occupy and sack Prague. Frederick and his family fled, eventually settling in the Dutch Republic; he spent the rest of his life vainly attempting to recover the Palatinate and Bohemia. Meanwhile, Ferdinand completed the occupation of Bohemia and Moravia, and the elector of Saxony occupied the Lusatias and Silesia.

Ferdinand did not remain long in Bohemia, for emergencies in Hungary and Austria commanded his attention, but he instituted a programme of 'restoration' which he placed in the hands of a Moravian aristocrat, Karl von Liechtenstein. The policy had three main strands. The first affected land. On 21 June 1621 twenty-seven leaders of the rebellion were publicly executed in Prague and their estates seized by the government. The expropriation of land was taken further. A Commission of Confiscation was established to investigate the conduct of nobles – Catholic as well as Protestant – during Frederick's brief 'reign'. It checked on thousands of suspects, drew up lists of their properties, and imposed fines or confiscations in proportion to the degree of their collaboration with Frederick. The concept of collaboration was interpreted broadly, extending to the payment of taxes or submission of petitions to Frederick. The process was slow, but over the next ten years or so, as religious conformity was imposed throughout Bohemia, the scope of the commission's inquiry expanded to include those who refused to become Catholic. By the early 1630s over half of the estates of Bohemia had changed hands (about 500 out of some 930 domains); they were taken by the government and either distributed to its most trustworthy supporters such as Lobkowicz, Slavata and Martinitz, or sold to pay off government debt. Most of the new land-owners were Bohemian Catholics, but a significant proportion were foreigners: Germans, Spanish, French, Italians, Scots, Irish and others purchased estates. The implications of this 'revolution' in the composition of the land-owners of Bohemia were considerable. Politically it meant that, whereas in the past the land-owning nobles had displayed a spirit of independence which had undermined Habsburg authority, the new men were beneficiaries of Habsburg victory and, for the time being at least, were pro-Habsburg in their political affiliations. Socially, the confiscations hit the lesser nobles or knights particularly hard. Many were ruined as they lost their property. On the other hand, their estates often were bought by wealthy nobles whose domains expanded.

The transfers of land assisted the second strand of Ferdinand's policy, namely the progress of the Counter-Reformation in Bohemia. Although an ardent Catholic, Ferdinand understood that he must tread more circumspectly than in Styria many years before; a crude application of the mailed fist might simply incite further uprisings. Furthermore, he had promised the elector of Saxony that the Protestants of the Lusatias and Silesia would be treated more leniently than those in Bohemia and Moravia. Working through von Liechtenstein, he introduced a series of laws between 1621 and 1627, relying upon the new land-owners – all of whom were Catholic – to help to oversee their application. The laws authorized the closure of Protestant churches and imposed heavy financial sanctions on Protestants who refused to convert. The Jesuits and other religious orders were invited to supervise mass conversions, aided and abetted by the billeting of troops on Protestants. Jesuit colleges were established in major towns, the Jesuits were placed in charge of the censorship of books, and the University of Prague (whose rector was among those executed in June 1621) was turned into a Catholic institution. In 1627 the Letter of Majesty was revoked, and members of the nobility who had not yet converted were given six months to sell their property and leave the country. Commoners as well as nobles chose exile: by 1623, some 12,000 Protestants had left Prague and its environs; by 1628 about 150,000 – just under 4 per cent of the population – had emigrated from Bohemia.[5] Many *émigrés*, especially nobles, joined the mercenary armies which fought in the Thirty Years War. Whatever hopes they entertained of a return to Bohemia were never realized, for the Treaty of Westphalia (1648) imposed permanent banishment. Of the majority of Protestants who remained in Bohemia, most followed the dispirited nobility and municipal councils into the Catholic church. By the early 1630s, Bohemia and Moravia, which only ten years before had been almost 90 per cent Protestant, were restored to the Catholic fold.

The third strand was constitutional. In view of recent history it was inevitable that a victorious Ferdinand would exploit the opportunity to reform the diet. He was sufficiently a man of his times to repudiate any notion of abolishing that body. He did not question its right to exist, since it was one of the principal channels through which the king communicated with the 'nation' (which in practice meant the nobility); his aim was to redefine its composition and functions. The principal change which he imposed upon its structure was the addition of an ecclesiastical estate through which the Catholic church was afforded a direct role in the political life of the kingdom. The diet could no longer initiate laws (now a royal prerogative), all ministerial and other senior appointments were made directly by the king without reference to the diet, and, most important of all, the crown in 1627 was declared the hereditary possession of the Habsburgs: the elective principle would be restored only if the male and female lines of the family ran out. The Chancery of Bohemia was moved from Prague to Vienna, from where Bohemia henceforth was governed. Whereas the constitutional provisions of 1619 had turned the monarchy into an instrument of the diet, those of 1627 transformed the diet into an instrument of triumphant Habsburg monarchy.

### The Bohemian Rising in Retrospect

Before we turn to the wider ramifications of the collapse of the Bohemian rising, a few reflections on its nature are appropriate. The political and constitutional struggles of the 1610s and 1620s had been conducted chiefly at the level of the social and political elites, as the nobles, great land-owners and municipalities of Bohemia struggled against the Habsburgs and their supporters. To this extent, the Bohemian struggle was not 'popular', even if its outcome affected all ranks of society. Ferdinand understood that the constitutional struggle would be determined by relatively few, for by seizing and redistributing noble land and 'reforming' the diet, he broke all serious resistance to his rule and asserted the primacy of government from Vienna. On the other hand, in their defence of Protestantism, the older noble elites could call upon popular consent. The abrogation of rights listed in the Letter of Majesty (which Ferdinand publicly and ostentatiously sundered in two by personally slashing it with his dagger) touched almost everybody. Apart from a few favoured regions in the Lusatias and Silesia where Protestantism was allowed to survive, Catholicism was imposed throughout the whole of Bohemia. The question of how genuine the mass proselytizations were is a matter for speculation, for neither Ferdinand nor the religious orders to which he entrusted the task were so naïve as to suppose that a century of Protestantism could be eliminated at a stroke. The crucial point was conformity. Converts must learn their catechism, attend mass and observe Catholic festivals; in short, they must behave as Catholics whatever their innermost thoughts. In the fullness of time, so the expectation went, they, their children and grandchildren, would turn into genuine Catholics.

One other respect in which the generality of the population suffered was that of finance, for Ferdinand authorized a *de facto* devaluation of currency. He was deeply in debt and needed 6 million gulden to meet his immediate commitments. He resorted to currency manipulation. A group of merchants, financiers and nobles approached him with an offer to pay this sum in return for the exclusive right to mint coinage for Bohemia. The leading members of this consortium included Prince von Liechtenstein, Hans de Witte, a merchant from Antwerp, Jacob Bassewi, a Jewish merchant from Verona who had settled in Prague, and Albrecht von Wallenstein, a Moravian nobleman who later was a prominent military commander. They signed a contract with Ferdinand in 1622 by which existing currency was called in and replaced by new coins containing less than half the former silver content. The introduction of a debased coinage into an economy suffering recession allowed the consortium to make large fortunes, but created a severe problem of inflation for everybody else.

Although the Bohemian crisis had its special features, variations upon its main themes appeared elsewhere in Europe during the course of the century; there are, for example, interesting comparisons to be made between the policies of the Habsburgs towards Bohemia and those of the Stuarts and the Commonwealth towards Ireland. By interpreting the crisis in seventeenth-century terms, we resist the temptation to which many nineteenth-century Czech scholars were vulnerable, namely to see '1618' as a forerunner of the nationalist struggles of their own day. Many later Czech nationalists interpreted '1618' as a courageous struggle of Czechs against the German Habsburgs. The transfer of land in the 1620s allegedly created German elites at the expense of Czech. The diffusion of German values supposedly was accelerated when the crown in 1627 conferred upon the German language the same legal standing as Czech. Nineteenth-century Czech nationalists contended that the Habsburg subjection of Bohemia included a cultural as well as political purpose: to 'Germanize' Bohemia at the expense of Czech national identity. To modern scholars this indictment looks anachronistic. Czech aristocratic families included aristocratic supporters and opponents of the Habsburgs; native Bohemians were prominent among those who acquired land in the 1620s; and since the principal languages spoken by Bohemian aristocrats at the royal court in Prague were Italian, French and Spanish (not Czech, which they regarded as the tongue of commoners), the promotion of German did not imply the elimination of Czech. One realm in which it is plausible to speak of a cultural programme is that of the imposition of Catholicism, but of course this was rooted in religion not ethnicity. Tridentine Catholicism was surrounded by, and expressed itself through, an elaborate programme of music, architecture, painting and literature, not to mention educational institutions, but there was nothing specifically 'anti-Czech' in the cultural weapons wielded by the Counter-Reformation.

## The Settlement in the Palatinate

Ferdinand's victory in Bohemia caused alarm but not action among Protestant princes of the empire. Most shared the opinion of the elector of Saxony that the Bohemian diet had behaved irresponsibly and that Frederick V had conducted himself with the utmost folly. The Evangelical Union had disbanded in May 1621, thereby abandoning Bohemia and the Palatinate to their fate. Most Protestant princes hoped that Ferdinand would content himself with chastising Bohemia and the Palatinate, while respecting the religious and political configuration of the rest of the empire.

The question of the Palatinate remained to be settled. Between 1620 and 1622, the armies of Maximilian of Bavaria and the king of Spain had conquered the Palatinate on behalf of Ferdinand II, and expected to be rewarded. There was also the question of what to do with Frederick V. On this point Ferdinand acted with caution, for he recognized that in deciding the fate of Frederick he must be seen to be treating this senior prince of the empire with consideration. In January 1623 he called to Regensburg a *Deputationstag* – a meeting between Ferdinand, the electors (although the electors of Brandenburg and Saxony did not attend; the latter sent representatives) and other princes – to decide Frederick's punishment. Ferdinand was anxious that any judgment could be shown to have received the consent of at least some princes, especially since Frederick was being 'tried' in his absence. Most delegates argued that, although Frederick deserved retribution, he should not be deprived of his entire patrimony. Spanish diplomats also counselled moderation. They feared that if Ferdinand imposed excessively harsh terms on Frederick, James I of England might be forced to intervene on behalf of his son-in-law. The Spanish at this particular juncture sought good relations with England, and resisted any course of action which might incite James I to take action. The decisions of the *Deputationstag* attempted a balance between punishment and mercy. Frederick was deprived of the Palatinate, but without prejudice to the rights of his son Charles-Louis. Pending the succession of this prince, the administration of the Upper Palatinate was conferred on Maximilian of Bavaria; this allowed him to collect taxes which he could offset against his war debts. Maximilian also assumed the title of elector of the Palatinate.[6] The administration of the Lower Palatinate (also with powers of taxation) was shared between Bohemia and Spain. Ferdinand considered these decisions equitable. Frederick V had played a dangerous game and lost, but his penalty respected the succession of his son. The duke of Bavaria and king of Spain had received generous financial compensation.

## The Habsburgs in Hungary and Austria after 1620

Although Bohemia dominated, it could not monopolize Ferdinand II's concerns. His two other great central European possessions, Hungary and Austria, also demanded his attention. In Royal Hungary, the diet and Protestants continued to enjoy numerous 'liberties' for reasons which had much to do with geopolitics. Given his existing problems in Bohemia and imminent difficulties in Germany, Ferdinand II could hope to do little more than hold the line in Hungary; any ambition to impose Catholicism throughout Royal Hungary, or still less to expel the Turks from central Europe, had to be held in abeyance. For its part, the Turkish government too was in no position to exploit Ferdinand's problems by tightening its hold in Hungary. When Sultan Ahmed I died in 1617, his eldest son and eventual successor Osman II was confronted by court intrigue and military revolt. Osman was assassinated in 1622, and although his brother Murad IV, whose reign lasted until 1639, proved a vigorous and effective ruler, his chief preoccupations were to the east. From 1623 to 1639 he was involved in several wars with the Persians which forced him to refrain from provocative acts towards the Habsburgs. Royal Hungary therefore was spared both Turkish expansionism and Habsburg political and religious 'reform'. Hungary was a land in which powerful and wealthy aristocrats possessed extensive estates. The great families, which included such names as Rákóczy, Bathory and Esterhazy, were native Magyars. Hungary experienced nothing like the confiscations of land which took place in Bohemia; and given relative Habsburg and Ottoman political paralysis, the magnates continued to control both the political life of the provinces and the diet.

The Bohemian crisis of 1618 created an opportunity for Bethlen Gabor, prince of Transylvania, to exploit the situation in Hungary. Transylvania technically was a vassalage of Ottoman Hungary, but in practice enjoyed a high degree of autonomy. Bethlen Gabor regarded himself as protector of the rights of Protestants in Royal Hungary, and it was this assertion which justified his intervention there. He was a devout Calvinist (he composed hymns and claimed to have read the Bible from beginning to end twenty-five times) who first came to prominence as an adviser to Prince Stephen Bocskay. He continued as a counsellor to Bocskay's successor, Gabriel Bathory, but after a dispute with this prince, took refuge with the Turks. In 1613 he led an army against Bathory, but when Bathory was murdered later in the year, both the Turks and the Transylvanian diet recognized Bethlen Gabor as prince of Transylvania. Like Ferdinand II and Frederick V of the Palatinate, Bethlen felt himself to be the preordained instrument of a divine plan which involved his own political glory. During his more prophetic musings, Frederick V had seen himself as the first Protestant Holy Roman Emperor. Bethlen felt an analogous mission to replace Ferdinand as king of Hungary, after which he would drive the Turks from the rest of the country and rule a united Protestant kingdom.

Bethlen Gabor interpreted the Bohemian crisis of 1618 as a heaven-sent opportunity to strike at the Habsburgs in Hungary. Admittedly, the Hungarian diet had just elected Ferdinand as king, but in the autumn of 1619 Bethlen invaded Austria in an attempt to drive Ferdinand from the Hungarian throne. Although he had to withdraw from the siege of Vienna, he did occupy parts of Silesia and northern Royal Hungary. His best chances of success lay in collaboration with Frederick V, but we have already seen that, although Bethlen sent troops to assist the 'Winter King', they made no serious attempt to coordinate their campaigns. In August 1620 the estates of Northern Hungary elected Bethlen as king of Hungary in place of Ferdinand, but as news from Bohemia arrived it became increasingly clear that Frederick's enterprise – upon which Bethlen's chances also rested – would not succeed. After the defeat of Frederick at White Mountain and the Habsburg repression of Bohemia, Bethlen decided that he too must seek peace before Ferdinand mustered resources for a campaign in Hungary. On 31 December 1621 Bethlen and Ferdinand signed the Peace of Nikolsberg by which the former relinquished the title king of Hungary in return for territory in Silesia, and Ferdinand confirmed the rights of Protestants in Hungary as granted by the Convention of Vienna (1606). Bethlen Gabor took up arms against Ferdinand again in 1623 and 1626 as an ally of German Protestant states fighting the emperor; but although he managed to safeguard the terms of the Convention of Vienna, he never secured the Hungarian crown.

In Upper Austria, whose estates had lent aid to the Bohemians in 1619, the outlook for Protestants was decidedly inauspicious. Between 1619 and 1620, Maximilian of Bavaria conquered Upper Austria on behalf of Ferdinand II. The Bavarian troops were ill disciplined and committed widespread violence and pillage. Once Maximilian had subdued Upper Austria, Ferdinand allowed him to govern it and collect taxes. Maximilian departed for the invasion of the Upper Palatinate, and left Upper Austria in the hands of Count Adam von Herbertstorff, a former Lutheran who had converted to Catholicism. Maximilian's primary interest in Upper Austria was financial: his aim was to collect taxes with as little trouble as possible, which implied leaving the Protestants with their rights of worship, at least for the time being. Ferdinand, on the other hand, placed the restoration of Catholicism at the top of his list of priorities. He authorized an influx of Italian priests from Rome to supervise the conversion of Protestants. In 1624 all Protestant pastors were expelled from Upper Austria, and in the following year the Protestants were given until Easter 1626 to convert, otherwise they must emigrate. The hostility generated by this combination of financial levies and religious coercion erupted in the great peasant uprising of 1626. Brutalities were committed on all sides, and it was only when the Bavarians left Upper Austria in 1628 that a more stable situation was restored.

## The Habsburgs in Italy

The consequences of the collapse of the Bohemian rising were not limited to central Europe; they were felt in Italy also, the link between the two regions being provided by Spain. Italy contained a variety of political systems – duchies, republics, kingdoms and the theocratic states of the papacy – but since the late fifteenth century the Spanish Habsburgs had acquired extensive territories until, by the early 1600s, they ruled Milan (through a governor), Naples, Sicily and Sardinia (through viceroys). The importance to the kings of Spain of their Italian possessions is indicated by the fact that in 1600 the population of Spain was about 8,235,000, and that of Spanish Italy some 6,020,000 or 73 per cent of that of Spain. In other words, the Italian lands greatly augmented the taxable resources of the king of Spain.[7] As the Thirty Years War progressed and Spain became heavily involved in the conflict, Philip III and Philip IV imposed increasing fiscal demands upon their Italian subjects. The kingdom of Naples illustrates the point. In 1616, the Spanish crown drew 835,000 ducats from Naples. The amounts went up to 3,920,000 ducats in 1621, 6,800,000 in 1626, and 50,000,000 by 1646.[8] The fiscal burden of war imposed considerable strains upon the social fabric of Spanish Italy, and was to trigger the rebellions which occurred in Sicily and Naples in 1647.

Milan shared the financial burden of Spain's involvement in the Thirty Years War, but was also affected directly by the fighting because of its geographical position. Milan's strategic importance derived from the fact that it commanded most of the passages through the Alps. Three were especially significant to the Spanish army, since they provided land routes to the Spanish Netherlands and Austria. One went west from Milan through the Duchy of Savoy and thence to Franche Comté and on to the Netherlands; a second went north alongside Lake Como into Switzerland, then to Lake Constance and across to the Rhine, from where the Netherlands were easily accessible; the third turned east at the top of Lake Como and went through the Valtelline into Austria. It was this last which became the focus of a struggle in the 1620s.

The population of the Valtelline was predominately Catholic, but was ruled by Protestant lords united in 'the Grey League' (the 'Grisons'). In the late 1500s and early 1600s several Catholic risings had been followed by fierce repression. Another rebellion occurred in 1620, but this time the Spanish decided to intervene. They were committed to helping Ferdinand II in central Europe, and the seizure of the Valtelline would guarantee the passage of their troops into Austria and beyond. Another factor in Spanish thinking was the imminence of war against the Dutch Republic. After several decades of Dutch revolt in the second half of the sixteenth century, the Spanish and their former provinces (Spain did not recognize 'the United Provinces' as an independent state) had signed a twelve-year truce in 1609. It would expire in 1621, and in anticipation that conflict might possibly be renewed, the Spanish aimed to secure as many routes as they could between their military bases in northern Italy and the Netherlands. In 1620 Spanish forces entered the Valtelline, expelled the Grison lords and set up a provisional government under Spanish protection. This action created widespread consternation. The Republic of Venice, which bordered on Milan, felt directly threatened: might not the Spanish be tempted to tighten their hold on northern Italy by finding a pretext to annex part of the republic? Other neighbouring states – Savoy and Mantua – had similar fears. Further afield, the German Protestant princes and the governments of the Dutch Republic and France saw the Spanish seizure of the Valtelline as yet another stage in the spinning of an extensive Habsburg web which threatened to envelope central and western Europe.

The only country with the resources to restore the Valtelline to the Grisons was France, and it was to the French that the Venetians and others looked. French interest in northern Italy went back at least to the fifteenth century, when kings of France had attempted either to annex territory or turn the region into a dependency. However, it was the Spanish, not the French, who triumphed in Italy, and the domestic crises arising out of the French Wars of Religion in the second half of the sixteenth century forced the French government to suspend its Italian ambitions. When civil war ended in the late 1590s, Henri IV signalled a renewed French interest in northern Italy by arranging an Italian marriage: in 1600 he married Marie de' Medici, daughter of the grand duke of Tuscany. When the Spanish occupied the Valtelline in 1620, the French government therefore responded quickly to the appeal from Venice and other states. The chief difficulty was that the French themselves were again faced with urgent domestic problems: a rising of Protestants had occurred in the west, and a power struggle was taking place within the government. The French could not risk a military assault on the Valtelline, and instead opened negotiations with the Spanish. The Spanish government proved to be surprisingly amenable to compromise: by the Treaty of Madrid (April 1621) they agreed to restore the Valtelline to its pre-1620 condition. They did so because their government too was in a state of uncertainty. Philip III had died on 31 March 1621, and the distribution of power among the ministers serving the sixteen-year-old Philip IV was not yet clear. Moreover, in his dying days Philip III had urged that, in view of a possible Spanish war against the Dutch, the French must not be alienated over the Valtelline; they might then be drawn into an alliance with the 'United Provinces'. The new pope, Gregory XV, also used his influence to secure Spanish flexibility over the Valtelline. Elected on 9 February 1621, Gregory XV was utterly devoted to the Counter-Reformation. He gave strong backing to Ferdinand II in central Europe, and was equally resolute that the two other great Catholic powers – France and Spain – should be at peace with each other. Gregory's ambition was to create a pan-Catholic alliance whose political and military resources, if placed at the disposal of the Counter-Reformation, would make this movement irresistible. Given the prospect of a re-Catholicized Europe, a Franco-Spanish dispute over the Valtelline was a side-show which must not be allowed to thwart the greater Catholic programme.

The Treaty of Madrid proved to be short-lived. The Spanish governor of Milan, Gómez Suarez de Figueroa, duke of Feria, acted on his own initiative by frustrating the efforts of the international commission appointed to oversee the implementation of the treaty. When the Grisons attempted to reoccupy the Valtelline as the treaty provided, Feria expelled them. They and the Venetians appealed again to the French, but in view of their domestic problems the French could do nothing. By the Treaty of Milan (January 1622), the embittered Grisons surrendered to the Spanish their claims to the Valtelline. The Spanish followed this triumph with a master-stroke: they transferred their military bases in the Valtelline to the pope, while reserving right of passage for their troops. If the French or Venetians attempted to restore the Protestant Grisons by force, they would be in the embarrassing position of doing so by driving out the head of the Catholic church. In 1623, France, Venice and Savoy formed a league whose aim was to revive the terms of the Treaty of Madrid. At the same time, French diplomats went to Switzerland to persuade the cantons to support the restoration of the Grisons through negotiation. No declaration of war was made on Spain, for none of the members of the league dared risk the consequences of defeat (Venice and Savoy in particular feared that the Spanish would annex part of their territory). Over the next three years, however, troops of the league fought a sporadic campaign in the Valtelline, seeking to disrupt the movement of Spanish forces heading for Germany.

For the time being the situation in the Valtelline remained fluid, but both the French and Spanish governments accepted that a definitive solution could not be achieved given the unpredictable international context of the mid-1620s. They held secret talks from which Venice and Savoy were excluded (when the Venetian government taxed the French ambassador with the rumour that talks were being held, he indignantly denied that the king of France would negotiate behind the backs of fellow members of the league) and reached agreement by the Treaty of Monzón (1626). The authority of the Grisons was restored in the Valtelline subject to the Catholics retaining a series of rights, and the Spanish agreed to dismantle their fortresses. This latter provision left the Valtelline open to Spanish intervention in the future, since the Valtelline now lacked serious defences.

## The Spread of War in Germany and the Intervention of Denmark, 1624

In response to Austrian and Spanish triumphs in central and southern Europe, the Dutch Republic, France and England formed a defensive alliance in 1624 to provide mutual assistance. The Dutch in particular were obsessed with the Spanish threat, for after the expiry of the truce of 1609 they and the Spanish had opened war again in 1621. Into the rapidly evolving situation there now stepped Christian IV of Denmark for reasons which mixed a genuine concern for Protestantism and the liberties of the imperial territories with territorial, ecclesiastical and commercial calculation. Christian ruled a kingdom which was among the most extensive of any governed by a European monarch. Apart from Denmark itself, his lands included Norway, Greenland and Iceland. Christian IV was a man of excess and paradox, the scale of his consumption of food and alcohol being matched only by that of his womanizing and by the intensity of his religious faith. His interest in Germany owed much to his affiliation to the empire: the southernmost province of Denmark, Holstein, lay within the Holy Roman Empire and formed part of the Lower Saxon circle; as duke of Holstein (but not as king of Denmark) Christian was a prince of the empire. He also had blood ties with Germany. His father, Frederick II, had been half-German, and his mother, Princess Sophie of Mecklenburg, was fully German. Christian himself married Princess Anne of Brandenburg. At his court German was spoken in preference to Danish, and the sons of Danish noblemen commonly studied at German Protestant universities. He could not but observe the advance of the Catholic League, the Austrian Habsburgs and the Counter-Reformation in Germany with trepidation, and he shared the assessment of other Protestant princes that it was only a matter of time before Lower Saxony too was confronted by this formidable alliance of forces.

Commercial factors also weighed with Christian. Denmark controlled the maritime passages between the Baltic and North Sea via the narrow belts and sounds which threaded their way around the islands between mainland Denmark and Norway. The principal sound between the two seas was guarded by the fortresses of Elsinor on the Danish side and Helsingborg on the Norwegian; every ship passing through the sound paid a duty to the king of Denmark. This lucrative source of income afforded him an independence in foreign affairs which other monarchs, especially those who relied upon grants from 'parliamentary' bodies, envied. Christian sought further territorial and commercial expansion in north-west Germany around the mouths of the Elbe with its port of Hamburg, and the Weser with Bremerhaven and Bremen. Were he to annex these river mouths, he would monopolize customs dues in north-west Germany. Then there were his ecclesiastical ambitions. His son Frederick exercised the administration of the bishopric of Verden, to which Christian wished to add the bishoprics of Minden and Osnabrück. His ecclesiastical influence then would parallel his commercial interests in north-west Germany.

The timing of his intervention in the war was forced on him by the Dutch, English and French governments. Already in 1620 the Dutch had raised with Christian the possibility of an alliance of Protestant states. Christian had given a positive if guarded response, thinking that he might use an alliance to further his commercial and ecclesiastical plans. Nothing immediately came of the idea, but by 1624 fear of the Habsburgs was such that the alliance of the Dutch, English and French was signed and in 1625 was reinforced by an Anglo-French dynastic marriage: Charles, prince of Wales, married Henriette-Marie of France, sister of Louis XIII. The sense of urgency was all the greater as Frederick V of the Palatinate had set up base in the Netherlands and, with Dutch money, had two armies in the field: one was under the command of Mansfeld and occupied East Friesland; the other was led by Duke Christian of Brunswick. Brunswick headed towards Bohemia in 1623. The plan was to liberate Bohemia by a pincer movement. Brunswick would attack from the west, while Bethlen Gabor (with whom contact had been established) did so from the east. The project was a disaster. An army of the Catholic League under the command of Jan Tserklaes, count of Tilly, advanced towards the Dutch border and on 6 August 1623 caught Brunswick's forces at Stadtlohn. The imperial victory was as complete as White Mountain (1620). When he received the news, Bethlen

Gabor made peace again with Ferdinand II. It was against this depressing background that in 1624 an emissary went from England to Denmark on behalf of the Anglo-Dutch-French alliance. Christian IV was offered a financial subsidy if he would invade Germany and restore Frederick V to the Palatinate and Bohemia. He was also informed that if he declined, a similar overture would be made to the king of Sweden, Christian's main rival in the Baltic. Christian felt that he had no option but to accept. He raised an army and negotiated terms of engagement with other princes of the Lower Saxon circle, who elected him their head. In the spring of 1625 he entered Germany.

The imperial army was now commanded by one of the most enigmatic figures of the Thirty Years War, Count Albrecht von Wallenstein, a member of the syndicate which issued coinage in Bohemia in 1622. After the victory at Stadtlohn, Ferdinand II decided that the war in effect was won and that he could disband his army in Germany. But he was warned by Maximilian of Bavaria that, if he did so, Protestant princes would seek external support to attempt a restoration of Frederick V. Ferdinand must keep his army up to strength. A second source of pressure was the Spanish government, which urged Ferdinand to join them in their war against the Dutch Republic. Ferdinand was loath to be dragged into a conflict in which he had no direct interest, but if he maintained an army to intimidate German princes, he would both be spending much-needed money and would have difficulty in resisting Spanish demands. He was rescued from his dilemma by Wallenstein, who offered to raise a private army and place it at Ferdinand's disposal. Wallenstein would meet the cost himself, the emperor repaying him later at interest. This arrangement would allow Ferdinand to disband his existing forces in northern Germany and inform the Spanish that he could not assist them against the Dutch Republic. Ferdinand accepted Wallenstein's offer.

Who was Wallenstein?[9] He was born into a Moravian noble family of divided religious loyalties. Both his parents were Protestant, his mother belonging to the prominent Smiricka family. After his father's death, Albrecht was brought up by a Catholic uncle who entrusted his education to the Jesuits. They instilled in him a love of learning and high culture, and in due course he was to become a noted collector of paintings and other *objets d'art*. His sister married the Protestant grandee Karl von Zierotin who, in spite of his religion, was pro-Habsburg in politics and did much to advance the young

Wallenstein's career. Wallenstein's two marriages considerably augmented his wealth and influence. His first in 1608 was to a widow,
Lucretia von Landek, who died in 1614 leaving him a large fortune.
His second, in 1623, was to Isabella von Harach, whose father was
an adviser to Ferdinand II; one of her brothers, Ernst Adalbert,
became archbishop of Prague.

During the Bohemian crisis of 1618 Wallenstein was part of the
Catholic minority which remained loyal to Ferdinand. After White
Mountain, when confiscated land came on to the market, Wallenstein
set his sights on the vacated Duchy of Friedland in northern Bohemia, whose former Protestant owner had left the country. Wallenstein
bought the estate in 1622, and over the next eighteenth months
acquired yet more land. He created a domain of over 1,000 square
miles. In return for gifts of money to the emperor, he was rewarded
with titles: 'count of the Empire' in 1622 and 'duke of Friedland' in
1623. He ran his estates as a semi-autonomous province, and proved
to be a gifted administrator. Not least among his achievements was
his rejuvenation of the economy: he imported cloth weavers, silk
workers, arms manufacturers and other artisans from Germany and
Italy, who turned his duchy into an island of prosperity. After
following the emperor's fortunes in Germany, and sensing an opportunity for further land and wealth, he made his offer of an army to
Ferdinand II.

## The Conflict Renewed to 1629

In 1625 there were four principal armies operating in northern Germany. On the 'Catholic' side were those of Wallenstein in the personal service of Ferdinand II, and of Tilly under the authority of the
Catholic League (still led by the duke of Bavaria). The 'Protestant'
cause was represented by the armies of the king of Denmark and of
Mansfeld. In the short run, neither side coordinated its efforts, a
failure which was especially damaging to Wallenstein and Tilly, who
potentially had the resources to overwhelm Christian IV. Meanwhile,
Christian's position was weakening. James I of England died in
1625, and his successor Charles I failed to persuade parliament to
provide the necessary funds for a German campaign. In 1626 the
French government faced a Protestant rising in the west of the country, and effectively withdrew from the alliance. Christian could expect
little from these quarters, and when Wallenstein defeated Mansfeld at

Dessau on 26 April 1626 Christian and Mansfeld had to work out a new plan.

Mansfeld retreated to Silesia, where Bethlen Gabor now had territory ceded to him by Ferdinand II at the Peace of Nikolsberg (1621). Mansfeld tried to persuade Bethlen Gabor to join him in an attack on Bohemia from the east, while Christian IV invaded Bohemia from the west. Bethlen agreed, partly because he was offered subsidies from the Dutch, but also because he was alarmed at the progress of the Counter-Reformation in Royal Hungary. At Nikolsberg, Ferdinand had guaranteed the rights of Protestants in Hungary, but those rights were being eroded by Cardinal Peter Pazmany, archbishop of Esztergom, an energetic agent of Counter-Reformation. Bethlen planned to approach Bohemia through Royal Hungary, where he would restore the rights of the hard-pressed Protestants. The plan was put into effect, but failed. Christian IV moved south with his army, but was defeated by Tilly at the battle of Lutter (26 August 1626). Meanwhile, Wallenstein set off in pursuit of Mansfeld. Anticipating the line of attack upon Bohemia to be taken by Mansfeld and Bethlen, he placed himself just north of Budapest to await their approach. However, Mansfeld died and Bethlen was reluctant to go on alone. On 28 December 1626 he signed an armistice with Wallenstein. From this point onwards, the Protestant position in northern Germany went into sharp decline. Throughout 1627 and 1628 Christian IV, now fighting alone, could do nothing to stop the advance of imperial and League forces which occupied Mecklenburg, Pomerania and other northern territory. Wallenstein invaded Denmark itself, and in October 1627 the remnants of the Danish army surrendered.

Wallenstein now proposed to Ferdinand II to extend Austrian Habsburg territories from central Europe to the Baltic. In 1628 Wallenstein occupied Mecklenburg, whose two dukes Ferdinand deposed for having given assistance to Christian IV. Wallenstein was granted the administration of their duchies. This shocked Catholic as well as Protestant princes. When Frederick V of the Palatinate was defeated, the emperor discussed his position with a *Deputationstag* before proceeding to judgement; now Ferdinand unseated the dukes unilaterally and gave Mecklenburg, including the title of duke, to an upstart Moravian nobleman. To many princes, Ferdinand's conduct resembled that of an 'absolute monarch', not an emperor bound by the conventions of empire. To the east of Mecklenburg lay Stralsund. Wallenstein calculated that if he could capture this great port, adding it to Rostock and Wismar in Mecklenburg, he would be a major figure in Baltic commerce. He laid siege to Stralsund in July 1628, but the city received assistance from Denmark and Sweden which forced Wallenstein to retreat. Nevertheless, it was everywhere assumed that this withdrawal was only temporary, and that Wallenstein would return.

## The Edict of Restitution and the Treaty of Lübeck, 1629

Ferdinand controlled much of northern Germany, and inferred that here was a unique and divinely ordained opportunity to right a deplorable wrong: the extension of Protestantism since the Peace of Augsburg of 1555. He decided upon a measure which a more prescient statesman might have avoided: on 6 March 1629 he issued the Edict of Restitution. He did not do so lightly. He had consulted leading prelates such as the archbishop of Mainz, various political advisers, theologians and his Jesuit confessor William Lamormaini. He did not, however, seek the advice of the imperial diet, where Protestants undoubtedly would have put up resistance. After long reflection accompanied by many hours of prayer, he decided that God had revealed the way ahead: restitution. By the edict, Ferdinand ordered all Catholic lands in Germany which had turned Protestant since the Treaty of Passau (1552) to be restored to Catholicism;[10] this reversed the status of two archbishoprics (Bremen and Magdeburg), twelve bishoprics (including Verden and Halberstadt) and over fifty monasteries and convents, as well as numerous towns and villages.

Ferdinand knew that the edict would be controversial. Quite apart from its strictly religious provisions, the fact that it had been promulgated without his consulting the imperial diet heightened the suspicion of critics such as the electors of Brandenburg and Saxony that the edict was further evidence that the emperor combined 'integralist' ambition with aggressive Catholicism. In his defence Ferdinand could reply that he was doing no more than enforce the agreement of 1555, which had suffered numerous infringements by Protestants in the intervening period. As Holy Roman Emperor he was responsible for executing the will of the diet; until and unless the Peace of Augsburg was superseded, he was obliged to implement its provisions. To this his opponents responded that Augsburg had never been intended as an inflexible settlement, incapable of adaptation to new circumstances; the Germany of the late 1620s was not that of the 1550s, and an attempt to turn back the clock in this way could end only in disaster. Again, Ferdinand could justify the edict on the pragmatic ground that the victorious imperial armies already had reimposed Catholicism in territories which they occupied; the edict simply acknowledged in law what had already happened in practice. Such arguments were of little avail in answering critics to whom the Edict of Restitution was but a device with which the Ferdinand who had crushed Protestantism in Styria and Bohemia, confiscated more than half of the landed estates of Bohemia, and driven thousands of his subjects into exile, was preparing Protestant Germany for similar treatment. Whatever the reality of Ferdinand's motives, in the taut atmosphere of the late 1620s the Edict of Restitution was bound to excite such fears. Ferdinand nevertheless regarded it as a triumph; he had crowned imperial military conquest with Catholic restoration. Hindsight was to show that it was a blunder. A conciliatory emperor, thinking in terms of political peace and social stability, would have shunned such an edict. Instead of terminating the war that began in 1618 it inspired a new phase of conflict, and one in which the imperial cause came close to collapse.

Wallenstein had played no part in the formulation of the Edict of Restitution, whose provisions he deplored, but he was closely involved in the second major decision of 1629: peace with Denmark. From Vienna, Ferdinand observed in Christian IV a vanquished enemy upon whom crushing terms could be imposed. He considered depriving Christian of much of Jutland and imposing a heavy indemnity, after which a Commission of Confiscation modelled on that in Bohemia would punish Protestants who had 'collaborated' with Christian. Wallenstein dismissed such thinking as dangerous fantasy. He implored Ferdinand to treat Christian leniently; if an emperor who had just issued the Edict of Restitution insisted on humiliating the king of Denmark and imposing a Commission of Confiscation on the German princes, he would create a pan-Protestant alliance against himself. With some reluctance Ferdinand conceded the force of the argument. Wallenstein negotiated with Christian's representatives, and concluded the Treaty of Lübeck on 22 May 1629. Christian retained Jutland, and was excused from an indemnity; in return he relinquished his claims to German bishoprics and promised to remain neutral in any future war involving the emperor. At Lübeck, the placatory principles advocated by Wallenstein triumphed over the more bellicose instincts of Ferdinand II.

## The Dismissal of Wallenstein

Ferdinand had lavished his largesse on Wallenstein, but by 1630 he detected unmistakable signs of insubordination in his general. The emperor's vexation was exacerbated by complaints at the conduct of Wallenstein's army, which numbered over 120,000. It was responsible for widespread destruction and atrocities in which distinctions were rarely made between Catholics and Protestants. Leading Catholic princes such as the archbishops of Mainz and Cologne, and the duke of Bavaria, demanded that Ferdinand order Wallenstein to decrease the size of his army, which was in danger of running out of control. If no remedial action were taken, they would raise armies of self-defence against the imperial force, and would refuse to elect Ferdinand II's son, the Archduke Ferdinand, as king of the Romans.

Such admonitions worried Ferdinand. His son had been elected king of Hungary in 1625, and the emperor was anxious that he be elected king of the Romans as soon as possible. In June 1630, Ferdinand called a meeting of electors at Regensburg to discuss this and other matters. Because of the Edict of Restitution, the electors of Saxony and Brandenburg boycotted the assembly, but Maximilian of Bavaria attended as elector of the Palatinate. Even the Catholic electors refused to countenance the election of the archduke until something was done about Wallenstein and his army. Partly to placate the electors, but also because of his own misgivings with regard to Wallenstein, Ferdinand dismissed the general in August 1630. Wallenstein's army was reduced to 40,000 and placed under the command of Tilly. Ferdinand hoped that these decisions would open the way to the election of the archduke, and silence critics who alleged that the emperor had monarchic intentions towards the empire. Since Tilly's army operated under the authority of the Catholic League, Ferdinand no longer had an imperial army in Germany; how then could he be suspected of 'imperial monarchy'? Even so, the electors harboured doubts. They disbanded without a decision on the archduke, who was not elected king of the Romans until 1636.

## Italy and the Mantuan Succession Question

In addition to Wallenstein's army and the election of the king of the Romans, the meeting at Regensburg discussed the Mantuan succession. Its importance is explained by geography, for the Duchy of Mantua comprised two main parts: Mantua itself on the south-eastern border of Milan (whose geopolitical significance to the Spanish Habsburgs was discussed earlier), and Monferrat with the great fortress of Casale on the western frontier. It was vital to Spanish interests in northern Italy that the duke of Mantua be pro-Spanish; the Gonzaga family, which ruled Mantua, had no illusions about the facts of international life, and took care not to antagonize the Spanish Habsburgs. When, however, the duke of Mantua died in 1627 without a direct heir, the chief claimant to the duchy was French: Henri de Gonzague, duc de Nevers. The attraction to the French of such a prize is self-evident, as was the resolve of the Spanish that strenuous efforts be made to forestall such an outcome.

Mantua was unusual in that it was one of the few Italian territories to come under the authority of the Holy Roman Emperor. The Spanish government persuaded Ferdinand II to hold Mantua himself until a Spanish claimant could be found and installed as duke. Meanwhile, a Spanish army laid siege to Casale to prevent it falling into the hands of the French. The Spanish position was supported by the duke of Savoy (resentful at what he regarded as his betrayal by the French at the Treaty of Monzón); he put forward a claim to the western part of the duchy of Mantua. French armies twice came to break the siege of Casale, and in the process captured the Savoyard fortress of Pignerol. When the assembly of electors gathered at Regensburg, French representatives attended to press the French claim to Mantua. They found a ready response among the Germans at the conference: already they were being critical of Wallenstein and were holding up the election of the archduke. Ferdinand II had no desire to increase his difficulties with the electoral representatives by digging in his heels over Mantua, especially as events in northern Germany took a turn for the worse (as is about to be seen). Accordingly, he gave way on the Mantuan question: by the Treaty of Cherasco (1631) he recognized the duc de Nevers as duke of Mantua. France retained the fortress of Pignerol.

### The Intervention of Sweden

Among the factors which had convinced Wallenstein that peace with Christian IV must be signed in 1629 were signs that the king of Sweden, Gustavus II Adolphus, was preparing to come to the assistance of the Protestants. Gustavus had sent aid to Stralsund during the siege of 1628, and there were other indications of his intentions. Since the beginning of his reign in 1611, Gustavus had fought highly profitable wars: by the Treaty of Stolbova in 1617 he acquired the provinces of Carelia and Ingria from Russia, but more recently by the truce of Altmark (1629) with Poland, secured Livonia and the ports of Elbing, Pillau, Memel and a share of the customs dues of Danzig. He commanded an excellent army that was supported by a fine fleet. The truce of Altmark released Gustavus from international entanglements; his army was still on a war footing; and as a devout Lutheran he felt called to assist German Protestants. Gustavus was equally concerned for the security of Sweden. He had followed events in Germany closely, and perceived in the military and political advance of the Habsburgs a potential threat to Swedish commerce and territory.

He was in contact with several Protestant princes, but they were reluctant formally to invite him into Germany. The reason was legal. Princes of the Holy Roman Empire were debarred from signing alliances with external governments to fight against other imperial territories. If they did, they could be charged with treason. Christian IV's accords with princes in the Lower Saxon circle did not contravene this rule since he was a prince of the empire. The king of Sweden, however, had no standing in the empire. If he crossed into Germany at the behest of Protestant princes, his presence would leave them in an equivocal legal position. For his part, Gustavus was anxious to be seen as a liberator, not an invader. Before landing his forces at Peenemünde near Stralsund in July 1630, he therefore sent a message to several foreign governments explaining that his aim was to rescue Protestants from the Catholic yoke; and, to legitimate his position, he imposed an alliance upon Bogislaw XIV, duke of Pomerania, in whose territory Peenemünde and Stralsund lay. The duke immediately wrote to Ferdinand II apologizing and claiming that he had no option but to comply with Gustavus's demand. Bogislaw also insisted upon a clause in the treaty stating that:

> this union is not directed against the majesty of the Emperor or the Empire, but is rather designed to maintain the constitution of the Empire in its ancient state of liberty and tranquillity, and to protect the religious and secular settlements against the ravages of the disturbers of the public peace, and thereby not only to leave intact the relationship which binds us, Bogislaw... to His Imperial Roman Majesty...

but also to preserve our lawful duty and obligations to the same....[11]

Over the next few months Gustavus brought into his alliance system other princes whose territories bordered on one another, and resembled an enormous dagger plunging into the heart of Germany: Pomerania, Mecklenburg, Hesse-Kassel and Brunswick-Wolfenbüttel. To change the metaphor, Gustavus thereby created a passage through which to launch his assault upon the emperor.

To this bold strategic thinking Gustavus added financial calculation. Sweden was a poor country with a population of just over two million; it could not be expected to meet the cost of war alone, especially when Gustavus felt it necessary to expand his army by recruiting mercenaries. His 'native' Swedish troops (who included Lapps and Finns) constituted the core of his army, but it grew from 42,100 in 1630 to almost 150,000 in 1632.[12] To pay for the army, Gustavus exacted large financial donations from the princes in the form of customs dues, a share in their taxation, or direct gifts. His outstanding diplomatic and financial triumph was the alliance which he signed with the French government by the Treaty of Bärwalde in January 1631. French policy towards the German conflict will be discussed in due course, but it was governed by French apprehension over Habsburg expansion. Louis XIII's chief minister, Cardinal Richelieu, had kept France out of the German war, although he had striven in other ways to confront the Habsburgs. By the Treaty of Bärwalde, however, he entered into a full alliance with Gustavus. This was a controversial step, for powerful Catholic groups at the French court were scandalized that France would finance a heretic to fight the Catholic Holy Roman Emperor. The treaty provided Gustavus with French subsidies for at least five years; in return he promised that members of the Catholic League would not be attacked, and that in towns or regions where Catholicism was the majority faith, Protestantism would not be imposed. Bärwalde was the product of shrewd political thinking by both parties. By defining the Catholic League as neutrals, it served Richelieu's purpose of separating the League from Ferdinand, and reduced the number of enemies whom Gustavus would have to fight. Gustavus's promise not to molest Catholics helped Richelieu to answer critics who accused him of aiding and abetting a Protestant king; and Gustavus had the enormous financial resources of France at his disposal.

## From Swedish Advance to the Death of Gustavus Adolphus

The reversal of military, religious and political fortunes which took place in Germany within eighteen months of the Swedish landing was extraordinary. Led by one of the finest commanders of the age, the Swedish army rapidly conquered much of northern and central Germany. Whether Gustavus could have held to his promise not to molest members of the Catholic League is open to question, but he felt absolved from his commitment when news arrived of the worst atrocity of the entire war: the sack of Magdeburg by Tilly's army in May 1631. The city, one of the largest and most prosperous in Germany (its population was about 20,000), lay on the Elbe. Tilly, whose troops were underpaid and undisciplined, laid siege to the city. On 10 May they breached its defences. Over the next few days they committed destruction, looting and violence on a scale which caused international outrage. 'Magdeburg' became a symbol, or rather several symbols: to Protestants it represented the barbarity of their Catholic enemies; to civilians it stood for the pitiless cruelty to which they were subjected by vicious and depraved soldiers; to nineteenth-century German nationalists it epitomized the sufferings of their country during the Thirty Years War.

Magdeburg had more immediate consequences. The electors of Brandenburg and Saxony, who so far had stood aloof from Gustavus Adolphus, signed alliances with him. As the two leading Protestant princes in Germany, their association greatly enhanced his cause. Gustavus pursued Tilly and caught him at Breitenfeld near Leipzig, where they fought on 17–18 September 1631. Gustavus inflicted a heavy defeat on his enemy. Hereafter the 'Catholic' cause collapsed as comprehensively as did that of Protestantism after White Mountain. Many Catholics feared and many Protestants hoped (especially Bohemian *émigrés*) that Gustavus now would occupy Bohemia, reimpose Frederick V and restore land which the Commission of Confiscation had sequestered. He did not. Reckoning that his army needed to recuperate, he moved west and spent the winter at Mainz after having taken Frankfurt, Mannheim and Heidelberg. Meanwhile, the elector of Saxony invaded Bohemia and occupied Prague with little resistance.

In the spring of 1632 a new season of campaigns began with more victories by the Swedes and their allies. Gustavus fought Tilly again at Rain near the Danube. It was Tilly's last battle: his army was defeated once more, and he received wounds from which he died. In contravention of the Treaty of Bärwalde, Gustavus led his troops into Bavaria, whose duke was head of the Catholic League. Much of the duchy was ravaged by the Swedish army, and on 17 May 1632 Gustavus, accompanied by Frederick V, made a triumphal entry into Munich. Gustavus and his allies enjoyed control of almost the whole of Germany, but this in itself posed the question of what to do next. The chief aims of his entry into Germany – the salvation of Protestantism and the security of Sweden – had been achieved, but Gustavus had not anticipated so much success so quickly. Should he press on to Vienna or concentrate on restoring Frederick V in the Palatinate and Bohemia? Should he think more radically and consider a partition of the Holy Roman Empire? The fact was that Gustavus had no grand design; he was discovering that it was more difficult to extricate himself from Germany than it had been to enter. His victories were alarming even his Protestant allies. He continued to impose crippling fiscal demands on them, and they knew that when peace was eventually settled, he would extract a territorial price at their expense. The French government too was uneasy. It had supported him to prevent Habsburg hegemony in Germany, but Swedish hegemony would be just as objectionable.

Ferdinand II, faced with the prospect of the collapse of the Habsburg position in Germany, heeded the advice of Maximilian of Bavaria and agreed to recall Wallenstein. Since his dismissal, Wallenstein had resided on his estates, concentrating on securing them against the bands of troops that roamed the countryside. Working through intermediaries, he was in contact with such diverse figures as the king of Denmark, the elector of Saxony and Gustavus Adolphus himself, offering his services in return for unspecified rewards (although it is possible that he aspired to become king of Bohemia). In April 1632 he was invited by Ferdinand II to raise a new army. Wallenstein struck a hard bargain. He must be supreme commander of the imperial forces, he would recruit and organize a multi-confessional army himself, the emperor would meet the costs of war, and in any peace settlement Wallenstein would receive more land and titles. Once his army was mustered, Wallenstein moved quickly. He drove the Saxons out of Bohemia, then headed for Nuremberg to repel a Swedish force. As the Swedes headed north to Saxony to meet the main army of Gustavus Adolphus, Wallenstein followed, intending to spend the winter there. Gustavus had no intention of affording Wallenstein several months in which to build up his army; on 16 November 1632 he attacked Wallenstein at Lützen, near Leipzig. The battle, much of which was fought in a fog, was one of the bloodiest of the war, both sides suffering heavy casualties. Wallenstein was defeated and retreated to Bohemia, but Gustavus was killed, having become isolated from his troops in the confusion.

## Lützen to the Peace of Prague, 1635

News of the death of the one man capable of holding the Protestant side together spread quickly. There were, naturally, important consequences for Sweden itself, for Gustavus left an infant daughter, Christina, to succeed him; but it was the ramifications in Germany which were of primary concern to the parties involved in the war. Both sides had to rethink their position, for neither had the resources to achieve conclusive victory. Moreover, each had cause to be disillusioned with its 'saviour'. German Protestant princes resented the 'imperium' imposed upon them by Sweden, and Ferdinand's patience with Wallenstein was exhausted. Through his agents, the emperor knew that Wallenstein was secretly in touch with Protestant princes and the French and Swedish governments. Ferdinand's mistrust was heightened in 1633 when Wallenstein blatantly refrained from attacking vulnerable Swedish regiments, now deprived of Gustavus's leadership. The emperor quietly let it be known that, since Wallenstein could no longer be trusted, Ferdinand would not object if the general were assassinated. The deed was carried out by army officers on 25 February 1634. Immediately, the emperor placed his son Ferdinand in charge of the imperial army; never again would he allow an independent military entrepreneur to command.

Many German princes were reassessing their situation. Swedish policy now was administered by the chancellor of Sweden, Axel Oxenstierna, who travelled to Germany to bolster the alliance. Gustavus had been considering the formation of a league of German princes under Swedish direction. Oxenstierna took this as the basis of a meeting between himself and several princes at Heilbronn. He persuaded them to form such a league (the treaty was drawn up 13 April 1633), but failed to secure the membership of Brandenburg and Saxony; indeed, the only princes to show genuine enthusiasm were those from the south and south-west who were in the frontline of any imperial counter-attack. By the spring of 1633, most north-German princes, including the electors of Brandenburg and Saxony, saw Sweden as part of their problem rather than its solution. They were paying exorbitant amounts of money to Sweden, but the Swedish armies were just as destructive as those of the enemy; and if peace were restored to Germany, Sweden undoubtedly would demand territory on the Baltic coast to add to its acquisitions of 1629. John George of Saxony argued that, if Ferdinand II would rescind the Edict of Restitution and recognize the fact of military stalemate, the Protestant territories were prepared to discuss peace.

The course of the war in 1634 reinforced John George's stance. The imperial army, joined by 15,000 Spanish troops, headed for Regensburg where the main Swedish army was based. The Swedes retreated, but Ferdinand fought and defeated them at Nördlingen on 5 September. Without Gustavus, the Swedes were not the invincible force of old. John George exploited the dismay at the imperial victory, mixed with relief that the Swedish burden now might be eased, felt by many Protestant princes when they heard about Nördlingen. He contacted the emperor and suggested negotiations. Before responding, Ferdinand assessed not just the political, but the moral and theological arguments for and against peace; after all, he had fought since 1618 to restore the ascendancy of Catholicism, and felt bound to abide by the Edict of Restitution. He instructed a commission of theologians to investigate the question; he also sought the views of his confessor and leading prelates; and he invited his political advisers to express their frank opinions. The balance of their advice was that peace could be signed without offence to his standing as a Catholic emperor. There also pressed on his mind the matter of his son being elected king of the Romans; the longer the war continued, the more the election would be delayed. He authorized discussions with representatives of the elector of Saxony. The negotiators met in November 1634 and formulated preliminary terms which were turned into the Peace of Prague (30 May 1635) signed by Ferdinand II and John George.

By the treaty, the elector of Saxony annexed the Lusatias, which he had held since 1620, and the emperor confirmed Protestant rights in Silesia. The most sensitive clauses concerned religion. The emperor agreed to suspend (not abrogate) the Edict of Restitution; the year 1552 would no longer be the year which defined the religious settlement of Germany, but which year should replace it? After much bargaining the choice fell on 1627. From the Protestant point of view this was better than 1552, but worse than 1618 when war began: between 1618 and 1627, the archbishopric of Bremen and five bishoprics had passed to the Catholic church. To the emperor, 1627 was worse than 1552 but preferable to 1618. The year 1627 was an acceptable compromise. In anticipation of disputes arising from this agreement, a period of forty years was set aside for them to be resolved. Calvinism still was denied legal recognition, and Calvinists were excluded from the peace.

The terms were publicized, and Lutheran princes were invited to subscribe. Most did so, including the elector of Brandenburg. Emperor and princes now regarded the revival of the spirit and institutions of a multi-confessional empire as a major priority. Whatever Catholic integralist ambitions Ferdinand II had entertained, they were now at an end. The Swedish government played no part in the Peace of Prague and was not invited to add its signature. Sweden was abandoned by several, although not all, of its German clients, and remained at war with the emperor. Germany faced an immense task of material, economic, constitutional and spiritual reconstruction, but the Peace of Prague had created a solid substructure.

# 3

# *Central and Southern Europe, 1635–1648*

---

Although Sweden made no formal contribution to the Peace of Prague (1635), Ferdinand II had grounds for hoping that this kingdom too might be ready for peace. He was informed of divisions between Oxenstierna (still in Germany trying to hold the League of Heilbronn together) and the Swedish senate or Riksråd. Senators were disillusioned by a war which was imposing severe strains on the economy, the treasury and the government of their country. Pressure upon Sweden came from another quarter. In February 1634, the most recent war between Poland and Russia had ended in a truce; now that Polish armies were free of entanglements in the east, the Polish government might be disposed to attempt to recapture the ports which it had ceded to Sweden by the truce of Altmark (1629). In such an eventuality, Sweden might have to seek the best terms in Germany that it could, and divert its armies to the Polish front.

Ferdinand's aspirations were thwarted by France. French foreign policy will be discussed later, but one of its commanding imperatives was the need to weaken the power of Spain. French and Spanish interests clashed most frequently in Italy, the north-eastern frontier of France, and France's northern frontier with the Spanish Netherlands. We have already observed how France formed a league with Venice and Savoy in 1623 and an alliance with England and the Dutch Republic in 1624, aiming to undermine the Spanish military presence in northern Italy and the Lower Palatinate. The Treaty of Bärwalde (1631), which was still the basis of Franco-Swedish relations, was also motivated on the French side by anti-Spanish concerns. Internal affairs of the Holy Roman Empire were not of primary concern to the French except in so far as they affected the wider context in which French policy had to operate. Richelieu feared that if the emperor secured peace in Germany, Ferdinand might then place his armies at the disposal of the Spanish. This suspicion was given substance when, in the summer of 1635, the French besieged Louvain: they were forced to withdraw when a large force of imperial troops was sent by Ferdinand to relieve the city. Richelieu concluded that he must keep the emperor occupied in Germany by instigating a new phase of warfare. This meant rejuvenating the vacillating Swedes. Richelieu met Oxenstierna and convinced him that the Treaty of Bärwalde was the best safeguard of their mutual interests; Richelieu also guaranteed more subsidies for Sweden's armies. He orchestrated a further diplomatic coup: in May 1635 French diplomats prevailed upon the Polish government to confirm the truce of Altmark. Sweden's Baltic ports were safe from Polish attack. Meanwhile, Richelieu had been making military preparations for entry into the war, and on 19 May 1635 Louis XIII declared war on Spain. Thereafter French armies fought alongside those of their allies, so complicating further the affairs of Germany.

### From the Death of Ferdinand II to Preparations for Peace

In the autumn of 1636, Ferdinand II called an assembly of electors (or their representatives) and other princes to Regensburg. His health was in decline and he was anxious that the imperial succession be settled on his son Ferdinand by having him elected king of the Romans. For their part, the electors wanted to raise the question of a general amnesty for princes who had not signed the Peace of Prague (in imperial parlance, *nobis nondum reconciliati*, that is, those not reconciled to us); this, they argued, would help to detach such princes from their Swedish 'protector' and would make a significant contribution to the restoration of political harmony in the empire. The subject was postponed when the emperor fell gravely ill. The electors moved quickly to confer the title 'king of the Romans' on his son, but only on condition that the archduke abide by the *Wahlkapitulation* or promise to respect the traditions and liberties of the empire (which implied that the future Ferdinand III renounced any integralist intentions). Ferdinand II died on 15 February 1637; the archduke succeeded him as Ferdinand III.

The accession of the new emperor coincided with a marked change in the atmosphere surrounding imperial and international relations. Although the fighting in Germany continued down to 1648, it confirmed the view that an exclusively military resolution of the problems of Europe could not be achieved. By the late 1630s, the outlines of a potential general settlement were emerging. The Swedish government had decided on its major priorities: the annexation of all or part of Pomerania (with the port of Stettin), the mouth of the Oder, and the port of Wismar in Mecklenburg. If Sweden succeeded, its political as well as commercial power in the Baltic and Germany would be enhanced, for these territories lay within the empire and would confer upon Queen Christina of Sweden the right of representation on imperial bodies, including the diet. The Swedish government was thinking in such ambitious terms because of an improvement in its military position. While the meeting between Ferdinand II and the electors was taking place at Regensburg, a Swedish army marched from the Polish frontier across Brandenburg towards Magdeburg. It encountered a joint Saxon and imperial army at Wittstock, and on 4 October 1636 overwhelmed the enemy in battle. The imperial defeat disconcerted those princes who had abandoned Sweden and accepted the Peace of Prague. Had they made a mistake? Could they rely upon the emperor to defend them? On the diplomatic front, the Swedish government renewed its alliance with France in March 1638, but with redefined war aims: the allies would fight specifically against Ferdinand III. The imperial princes would not be molested; the Franco-Swedish campaigns would be directed exclusively against the Habsburg patrimonial lands of Bohemia and Austria.

Ferdinand III wanted to maintain the impetus towards general peace in Europe. In 1640 he called to Regensburg the first imperial diet since 1613. He intended developing an initiative taken the year before by the archbishop of Mainz who, acting as arch-chancellor of the empire, had met the other electors to discuss a strategy for peace in Europe. It was their ideas which shaped much of the thinking of the diet of 1640. The main proposal was for an international peace congress, subject to two conditions: all the princes and other heads of imperial territories must have right of attendance and negotiation (there must be no question of the emperor acting on their behalf), and non-German governments, notably those of Sweden, France, the Dutch Republic and Spain, must be full participants. The first of these provisos reflected the strong sense of autonomy of the princes, and affirmed that Ferdinand did not possess 'monarchic' authority. The second was a frank recognition that without the direct contribution of other major states, no lasting peace would be achieved. The proposed presence of Sweden also met the wishes of princes such as the duke of Hesse-Kassel who had not signed the Peace of Prague, and feared that without Swedish protection they would be vulnerable to retribution by Ferdinand.

These principles were adopted by the diet, which sent a message to Queen Christina of Sweden proposing an international congress and inviting her to nominate its location. The Swedish government discussed the idea and, after consulting its French ally, replied positively, suggesting that a conference take place in the Westphalian circle of the empire, and that it meet in two cities: Münster (where representatives of the emperor, Catholic princes of the empire and other Catholic states would gather) and Osnabrück (where imperial representatives and those of Protestant princes and states would assemble). The diet accepted the plan, and over the next few years the arrangements were put in place.

The planning of the congress, which opened unostentatiously in 1643, does not concern us; but as its complex structure was being put in place, war continued as the emperor, Swedes, French, Dutch and Spanish sought the most favourable military positions from which to negotiate. External contingencies continued to affect the struggle. Sweden's main military stronghold remained Pomerania from where its armies launched a series of offensives against Bohemia between 1642 and 1645. Although they briefly occupied various Bohemian towns, the Swedes lacked the resources to conquer the whole country. Their prospects of doing so diminished further when, in 1643, they found themselves at war with Denmark. This war was short (it ended with the Treaty of Brömsebro, 1645), but it did force the Swedes temporarily to divert forces from Bohemia. Ferdinand III also had to turn his attention from Germany. The Counter-Reformation in Royal Hungary was still being pursued, and tensions between Catholics and Protestants ran high. The prince of Transylvania – George Rákóczy, successor to Bethlen Gabor – offered military assistance to the Protestants. He signed an alliance with Sweden and dispatched troops to Hungary in support of the Protestant uprising of 1643. Ferdinand could not suppress the rebellion, and by the Treaty of Linz (1645) had to confirm Protestant rights. The other major army in Germany was that of the French. Its chief strategy was twofold: protect French interests in Alsace and Lorraine, and occupy as much of southern Germany as possible, thereby exposing Austria itself to invasion. The campaigns of the early 1640s showed the French and Swedish contention that they had no hostile intent towards the imperial princes to be a fiction: much of the fighting took place in Bavaria and Württemberg, which were devastated by the Franco-Swedish and imperial forces.

## The Peace of Westphalia, 1648

By 1643 preparations for the peace congress were sufficiently advanced for diplomats to begin their work in Münster and Osnabrück, but it was not until 1645 that the major delegations arrived and negotiations fully got under way. This was the largest international congress ever attempted in Europe, and there were no self-evident precedents to which delegates could turn for guidance. The nearest examples were meetings of the imperial diet and general councils of the Catholic church, the most recent of which was the Council of Trent. The congress of Westphalia drew on both of these sources: the delegations from the Holy Roman Empire brought valuable organizational experience, while the papal nuncio and future Pope Alexander VII, Cardinal Fabio Chigi, who was one of the official mediators in Münster, acted as a major conduit through whom the advice of Rome was channelled. Although most of the Catholic delegates went to Münster and the Protestants to Osnabrück, the confessional division was not followed to the letter. To Münster, in addition to Chigi and a second mediator from Venice, went delegations from the emperor, France, Spain and the German Catholic princes, but also from the Dutch Republic; since the Republic and Spain were at war, it made sense for them to negotiate face to face. In Osnabrück, where the king of Denmark acted as mediator, there were commissions from Sweden and the Protestant German princes, but also from the emperor and France. Ferdinand III was adamant that the internal problems of the Holy Roman Empire should be discussed exclusively by his own representatives and those of the German princes; foreign states would not participate. In effect there should be two overlapping conferences: an imperial assembly to decide the future of the empire, and the international conference in which all delegations would share.

The negotiations took more than four years to complete, but on 24 October 1648, peace terms were signed simultaneously in Münster and Osnabrück, the two texts comprising the Peace of Westphalia. The congress lasted so long partly because of the number and complexity of the problems to be discussed, but also because of the practice of negotiation itself. Government ministers or heads of state did not attend, but received reports from their delegations and then replied with further instructions; delay therefore was built into the system. Questions of protocol could hold up negotiations. In an age when ritual and conventions of precedence assumed immense significance, the task of soothing the sensibilities of thousands of status-conscious diplomats was inordinately difficult. Procedural disputes easily caused delay. The discussions in Münster, for example, were held up for several weeks in 1645 because of an argument over Cardinal Chigi's chair: should it be at ground level or on a dais? Again, because the congress was not accompanied by an armistice, war continued and the delegations in Westphalia accelerated or slowed down progress in accordance with its fortunes.

What were the main provisions of the final peace? Some concerned the Holy Roman Empire. The question of religion was resolved on the basis that the empire would remain multi-confessional. There were three main strands to the religious settlement. First, the emperor issued a general armistice to all princes, and formally repealed the Edict of Restitution; but he persuaded the princes to agree that ecclesiastical lands would be restored to the position of 1624, not 1627 as in the Peace of Prague. This required territorial concessions from the Protestants. Second, although the religion of each imperial territory would continue to be decided by its head (thus preserving one element of the principle of *cuius regio, eius religio* as established by the Peace of Augsburg in 1555), those subjects who were of a different religion would not be deprived of 'civil rights'. This particular agreement was less an expression of a spirit of religious toleration than a pragmatic acceptance that a price had to be paid in the interests of social stability. Religious conflict had cost Germany dear; it was time to subordinate absolute but divisive religious principle to the expediency of coexistence. Third, Calvinism was granted recognition and status on the same basis as Lutheranism; no longer regarded as pariahs by Catholics and Lutherans alike, Calvinists shared the benefits of the Peace of Westphalia. The religious settlement proved to be remarkably enduring. Although it would be an exaggeration to state that religious harmony descended on Germany in 1648, the peace did conclude that long phase of history, going back to the lifetime of Martin Luther, wherein the political and constitutional topography of the empire was largely fashioned by issues of religion. It would be misleading to interpret the religious clauses in terms of 'victory' or 'defeat' for Catholicism or Protestantism; rather they were a vindication of the ideal of empire, as emperor and princes placed its preservation above a life-or-death struggle between contending faiths. In retrospect we might also say that the religious clauses preserved the imperial crown for the Habsburgs. Ferdinand III's willingness to acknowledge a multi-confessional empire obviated any serious possibility of a Protestant contender at the next imperial election. By accommodating himself to the religious facts of life, Ferdinand secured Habsburg tenure of the imperial office.

The religious settlement of the empire had constitutional and territorial implications, although their discussion was deferred until the next meeting of the imperial diet which convened in Regensburg in 1653. However, Westphalia did confirm the existing legal and administrative institutions of the empire, but on the basis that access to them was open to all qualified people, irrespective of their religious belief. One important imperial body was nevertheless modified at Westphalia: the college of electors. It was agreed that Prince Charles-Louis, son of Frederick V of the Palatinate, be restored to the Lower Palatinate (the Upper Palatinate remained with the duke of Bavaria), and that he recover the title of 'elector'. The duke of Bavaria also was promoted to 'elector', so that the college of electors now had eight members. The right of imperial princes to sign alliances with foreign states was recognized, on condition that such alliances be not directed against other imperial princes. Experience was to show that this provision could easily be circumvented, as German princes increasingly conducted foreign policy as independent agents. Indeed, over the next fifty years some of the larger territories – Bavaria, Saxony, but above all Brandenburg – were to exploit their autonomy to become virtually separate states of middling importance in European affairs. The Peace of Westphalia did not *create* the autonomy of the princes, which had already been a feature of the Peace of Prague: it provided a powerful stimulus to an existing dynamic. The peace confirmed the empire as an entity whose distinctiveness lay, not in locating sovereignty precisely in a given person or institution (a question which obsessed French jurists, political thinkers and leaders), but in the opposite: in leaving the subject of 'sovereignty' within the empire somewhat ill defined.

In view of the pressures to which it had been subjected, the Holy Roman Empire emerged remarkably well from '1648'. The war had

demonstrated not the irrelevance of the empire but the need to redefine its character and institutions. When the imperial diet met in
1653, it turned to the question of institutional reform. Most important was the conversion of the diet, from 1663 onwards, into a body
permanently in session; it remained so until the dissolution of the
empire in 1806. Thereby it provided a certain counter-balance
to the increasing autonomy of the larger states of the empire. Again,
the empire remained not just a multi-confessional entity, but one
which comprised different types of territory: in 1648 there were 8
electorates, 69 ecclesiastical principalities, 96 secular principalities,
and 61 free or imperial cities. The Habsburgs, now that they had
broad agreement on the structures of the empire and had abandoned
any integralist notions, were able to turn their attention to their
patrimonial lands: Austria, Bohemia and Hungary. This last kingdom
in particular had suffered relative neglect; now the Habsburgs were
in a position to give it the attention it deserved.

As regards its international settlements, the Peace of Westphalia
conferred considerable gains upon Sweden. The Swedish negotiators,
headed by Johan Oxenstierna, son of the chancellor, succeeded in
acquiring West Pomerania including Stettin, the mouth of the Oder,
and the bishoprics of Bremen and Verden (once objects of desire for
Christian IV of Denmark). Sweden thus controlled vast stretches of
the Baltic coastline and many of its principal ports; and the possession of West Pomerania brought with it the right of Swedish attendance at the imperial diet. Sweden's ally France also acquired territory
at the expense of the empire. Richelieu and his successor as chief
minister, Mazarin, had aimed to make the north-eastern frontier of
France as secure as possible; accordingly at Westphalia the French
diplomats secured the annexation of the bishoprics of Metz, Toul
and Verdun, parts of Alsace on the left bank of the Rhine, and the
two fortresses at Breisach and Philippsburg. From 1648 onwards, the
French displayed a permanent interest in securing the remainder of
Alsace, and finally did so in 1681. Unlike the settlement with
Sweden, the French acquisitions expressly denied them a presence on
imperial bodies. This is one more example of how political considerations were now outweighing confessional commitments: Ferdinand
III agreed to the Protestant monarch of Sweden being represented in
imperial assemblies, but refused to countenance the presence of the
Catholic king of France. One other agreement which affected the
empire concerned Brandenburg. The elector, Frederick William, had
claims upon Pomerania, and at one stage hoped to obtain the whole

duchy. However, the Swedes annexed the more prosperous west, leaving him with the much poorer East Pomerania; he was compensated with the important ecclesiastical sees of Minden, Magdeburg, Kammin and Halberstadt. Other agreements at Westphalia should be noted at this juncture. Spain and the Dutch Republic signed a peace which included the recognition of the latter by the former, and the formal withdrawal of the Dutch Republic from the Holy Roman Empire (this latter provision simply recognized a *de facto* situation). Switzerland, which had been neutral during the war, also ended its membership of the Holy Roman Empire. One major conflict remained unresolved: that between France and Spain.

More generally, in view of the number and complexity of the problems facing them, it is difficult to see how the negotiators in Osnabrück and Münster could have produced a more satisfactory peace. Recent assessments emphasize how hard it is to discern a new ideological direction to the negotiations, although this is not to say that the peace lacked foundations in principle. The mid-seventeenth century was a period of intellectual turmoil, when much traditional thought about the nature of society, the state, and relations between states, was being challenged. If the delegates who met at Westphalia exhibited little sense of an over-arching ideology to guide their deliberations, this is scarcely surprising since so many socio-political ideas embedded in the past were being loosened if not fully uprooted. The negotiators at Westphalia sought peace, not through one or more systems of abstract thought about the future of Europe, but through the restoration of legal principles which, they believed, had been undermined by thirty years of warfare. The princes of the empire insisted that they were striving to restore traditional imperial institutions and relations which had been overturned in the past three decades. Ferdinand III argued that he was working for the harmony of the empire by forsaking the Counter-Reformation imperatives which had guided his father. Even those states such as Sweden and France which annexed territory in 1648 were reluctant to do so on the basis of right of conquest; instead they advanced claims based in law, however tenuous those claims might be. If there was anything novel in the thinking of diplomats at Westphalia, it lay in their hope that the peace would be universal by including every state then at war; but this was an aspiration rather than a new principle of international relations, and it was frustrated by the failure of the Spanish and French to come to terms in 1648. The Peace of Westphalia is not remembered for any great supporting ideology, but this may

have been its strength. Protestant and Catholic, monarchist and republican, imperialist and autonomist, all felt able to subscribe to its
terms. Admittedly it was denounced by the pope on the ground that
it was too generous towards Protestants, but his protestations went
unheeded; and the two powers still at war were both Catholic:
France and Spain.

The Peace of Westphalia modified the political map of Europe, and
to a war-torn Germany it brought respite; but it also taught practical
lessons on how (or how not) to conduct an international peace congress. Future congresses were held in one, not two, locations; and,
within the city hosting a conference, rules of diplomatic precedence
were suspended: if the ambassador of one state entered a room
before that of another, no insult was implied. Both of these measures
speeded up future congresses. Again, the Peace of Westphalia was not
reinforced by an alliance system to preserve its terms. New wars soon
broke out again, and although they cannot be attributed directly to
the 1648 settlement, it is notable that after the Peace of Utrecht
(1713) – which in many ways superseded Westphalia – a post-settle-
ment alliance system was created to guarantee its integrity.

### Socio-economic Consequences of the War in Germany

Among the principal losers in the Thirty Years War were the Protestant expatriates driven from Bohemia after the battle of White Mountain. Ferdinand III refused to countenance the restoration of their
land, and the very principle of autonomy which Westphalia had entrenched debarred Protestant princes from intervening on behalf of
their co-religionists.

The inhabitants of land and property devastated by the war are
also to be counted among the unfortunates of this period. On this
subject, it is prudent to avoid simple, unqualified judgements. It is
extremely difficult to establish reliable population statistics for a
period in which contemporaries kept figures of births, marriages and
deaths only spasmodically, and when central Europe in particular
contained a large 'floating' population of soldiers, refugees, beggars
and migrants. Such information as we possess nevertheless indicates
that the population of Germany declined from about 16 million to
10 million during the course of the war. Within that global figure
there were considerable variations. The regions which suffered most
were Pomerania and Mecklenburg on the Baltic coast, and the Lower

Palatinate and Württemberg to the south, all of which lost between 60 and 80 per cent of their populations. Brandenburg, Bavaria, Franconia and Alsace lost about half, whereas Saxony, Bohemia, Silesia and the southern parts of Westphalia lost between 15 and 45 per cent. Some parts of Germany escaped relatively lightly, their decline of population being under 15 per cent: north-west Germany, Austria, and the forests and mountains of Thuringia, Bohemia and the Black Forest. On the whole, depopulation affected the countryside more than the towns.

Disease rather than direct military action was the killer, although there was a close relationship between the two. This was the last great European war to rely heavily on mercenaries. Young men from many parts of Europe, often (although not necessarily) from poor backgrounds or refugees from religious or political unrest, signed up with the private armies which were employed by governments. The military life was hard and dangerous. To the hazards of battle were added those of disease, difficulties in securing food, uncertainty of payment, and the physical wear and tear of months on campaign. The experience could be tough and brutalizing. Soldiers frequently resorted to the pillaging of villages and farms through which they passed. In the civilian mind, they were equated with mindless violence, and soldiers who strayed from the main body of their company were in danger of being seized and tortured by vengeful peasants. The picaresque novel by Hans Jacob von Grimmelshausen, *Simplicius simplicissimus* (1669), contains harrowing descriptions of the suffering which could befall the unfortunate victims of marauding soldiers; and even allowing for the exercise of literary licence by the author, the accounts make grim reading. Worse than the direct physical damage which soldiers perpetrated was the longer-term dysfunction which they inflicted on local economies. By living off the land, they consumed or carried away large quantities of grain and other food supplies, leaving peasants short of food and seed to sow for the next harvest; soldiers also took horses, cattle and other livestock upon which peasant economies depended. Even when relations between soldiers and civilians were relatively good (for example, after occupying Munich in 1632, Gustavus Adolphus organized a series of tournaments, wrestling matches and other sporting fixtures to encourage his troops to fraternize with townspeople), the presence of tens of thousands of extra mouths soon exhausted local food supplies; and a 'friendly' army was just as liable to disseminate infectious diseases as one that was overtly hostile. The result was an under-nourished German population whose natural resistance to the epidemics that accompanied warfare was weak. Hence the statistics quoted above.

On the economic front, it can be difficult to distinguish between the extent to which the Thirty Years War caused change as against accelerating trends which were already in progress. In some respects, war stimulated economic growth. The demand for munitions, weapons, gunpowder, shot, horses, wagons, ships, barges, and all the other accoutrements of an army, created a continuous demand which in turn stimulated manufactures in Germany, Italy, Flanders and elsewhere. Likewise, agriculture in those areas which experienced relatively little fighting profited at the expense of those which suffered, and Polish grain producers enjoyed healthy exports to Germany, meeting demands which domestic producers were unable to match.

One casualty of the war was the Hanseatic League, but its demise was accelerated rather than caused by the Thirty Years War. This commercial union of north-German cities had controlled much Baltic commerce in the fifteenth and sixteenth centuries. At its height in the 1500s it comprised eighty-five members, but it was already in decline by the turn of the century. By the early 1600s it was facing competition from Dutch, English, Swedish and other shipping, and the war further diminished its activities, especially when Sweden annexed several Baltic ports. The size of the league decreased until only six members remained in 1669. Yet as with agriculture, so with commerce: decline in one region provided opportunities elsewhere. Bremen and Hamburg, for example, were both little affected by the war, and their go-ahead merchants were not slow to exploit the difficulties of their Baltic rivals. Hamburg, for instance, flourished between 1618 and 1648. Its population rose from about 40,000 to 60,000, for not only did its own commerce prosper, but businessmen came from elsewhere in Germany and the Netherlands and invested their money in existing or new enterprises. Germany, even in its most disadvantaged areas, also showed a capacity for revival during and after the war. Towns like Ulm, Dresden, Leipzig and even Magdeburg were rebuilt, this last being almost fully restored by 1680. Peasants who had been forced to abandon their villages because of warfare, not infrequently returned after 1648 to restore their communities, bringing the land under cultivation once more, and resurrecting their rural industries. Immigrants from other parts of Europe were invited by princes of the empire to resettle their depopulated lands; and, as late as the 1680s, agents of Protestant princes were based in Frankfurt offering land and tax concessions to French Protestant refugees. The socio-economic prospects for Germany by the late 1640s therefore were not uniformly adverse, but this judgement does not invalidate the more general observation that, in the short run, the outlook gave little cause for optimism.

### Effects of War upon Italy: Risings in Sicily and Naples

The ramifications of the Thirty Years War extended beyond Germany, and among the regions which had to contend with its implications was Italy. It was stated earlier that, although northern Italy was exposed to military campaigns in the 1620s, the chief consequences of the Thirty Years War for Spanish Italy lay in the realm of finance. The incessant and mounting fiscal demands of the crown of Spain exacerbated Italian socio-political problems. In Sicily and Naples, fiscal pressure led to insurrection in 1647. The interpretation of these risings presents numerous problems, for although it is possible to present 1647 simply as a violent reaction to decades of financial exploitation, a more sophisticated explanation is required once the risings are investigated in some detail. For example, in Sicily most agitators never wavered from proclaiming their loyalty to Philip IV of Spain, whereas in Naples the king of Spain was deposed and an independent republic under French protection declared. Again, even though the Sicilian movement remained loyal to the king of Spain, it, like that in Naples, produced demands of a political and constitutional nature; this too suggests that there was more to insurrection than straightforward anti-fiscal protest. The historian must also analyse the sociology of rebellion: who were the rebels; who led them; how united were they; what form did their insurrectional conduct take? There are also those sections of society which resisted the risings and threw in their lot with the government: which groups fall into this category, and why did they adopt a pro-government stance? Both risings collapsed, but how complete was their failure? Did the viceroys simply reimpose the *status quo ante*, or did they offer concessions? And how do the risings relate to the movement of Italian history in the seventeenth century? Do they, indeed, belong to Italian history in anything but a geographical sense, and should they be located instead in the evolution of the Spanish state? Such complex questions cannot be answered comprehensively within the limits of the present exercise, but lines of inquiry can be sketched indicating, at the very least, some possible approaches to answers.

The Sicilian rising began on 20 May 1647 with demonstrations in Palermo against duties which the viceroy, the Marquis de Los Velos, had imposed on basic foodstuffs: flour, wine, oil and cheese. These impositions were but the latest in a series of 'special contributions' (*arrendamenti*) which had been introduced since the outbreak of the Thirty Years War. Sicily was regarded by the Spanish crown as one of its wealthier possessions. Grain from Sicily was exported to Spain itself and to northern Italy; the Spanish army in Italy acquired much of its grain from Sicily, but at prices which the government fixed. Sicilian producers regularly complained that prices were too low and profits inadequate. In 1646 the grain harvest was poor: bread prices rose steeply in Sicily as grain continued to be exported. The new duties in 1647 therefore turned potential into actual social protest and violence. The rebels demanded either the reduction or, better still, the abolition of these and other levies.

There was a political dimension to the rising. Sicily possessed one of the oldest parliaments in Europe; seated in Palermo it was composed of three chambers or orders: the nobility (*militare*), clergy (*ecclesiastico*) and the communes (*demaniale*). There was also a senate run by powerful noble dynasties. In practice the parliament too was dominated by the nobility, and by guaranteeing their fiscal privileges and judicial rights, the Spanish viceroys worked with them to ensure the passage of legislation empowering the collection of the *arrendamenti*, which fell on both the rural and urban populations. In short, a form of alliance existed between the viceroy and Sicilian nobility: the crown safeguarded the social and economic position of the nobility which, in return, assisted the crown in its fiscal programme. To their demands on *arrendamenti*, the insurrectionists of 1647 added others calling for the restoration of the liberties of Sicily (especially the rights of the communes), the rehabilitation of the power of the *demaniale* in the parliament, and a reduction in the authority of the senate. However, such entreaties were always accompanied by the slogan, 'long live the king of Spain'. The rising therefore called for the restoration of a pre-war Sicily in which the accumulated powers of the nobility would be reduced, but it would be a Sicily ruled by the king of Spain. Although the Sicilian rising began in Palermo, it quickly spread to other parts of the island, and developed into a movement which attracted peasants, townspeople and artisans. In other words, it evolved into a populist as well as legitimist movement. The peasant communities too were inspired by a combination of economic and constitutional forces, although in their case the latter usually took the form of calling for a diminution of the legal powers which noble land-owners exercised over them.

Leadership of the rising came mainly from artisans based in the cities and towns. For a time the rising in 1647 was led by a goldsmith from Palermo, Giuseppe Alessio, who succeeded in imposing a certain unity on the movement. Under his direction, the 'rebels' laid plans for the 'reform' of the parliament and of several municipal administrations; it was he who organized demands for the reduction of the *arrendamenti*. However, after he was killed in the repression which occurred later in the year, the rising was increasingly vulnerable to factionalism. It was confronted by formidable opposition. Fearful of the consequences of disorder, most nobles and clergy supported the viceroy, even though he fled from Palermo within a few days of the outbreak of the first riots. Throughout the summer of 1647, nobles combined to organize military resistance to the 'rebels', and the viceroy sowed further division in the towns by abolishing the senate and agreeing to changes in the administration of selected municipalities.

In November a new viceroy arrived: an Italian, Cardinal Gian Giacomo Trivulzio. A member of a great Milanese family, he spent much of his career in the service of the Spanish as envoy, ambassador, governor or viceroy. New waves of violence occurred in Palermo, Catania and Agrigento. Trivulzio adopted a policy of coercion combined with concession. He revoked some taxes and negotiated with rebel leaders, but continued to support the nobility in suppressing the rising by force. He established control over Palermo, and by early 1648 had most of the island under his subjection. He tracked down and tried leading subversives, and to that end made extensive use of the Inquisition. Indeed, in the second half of the century the Inquisition was to be the principal tool of repression on the island. Meanwhile, Trivulzio restored the senate and confirmed the primacy of the nobility in the parliament. In this regard the rising achieved little. On the other hand, the viceroy and his immediate successors did ease the fiscal burden which peasants and townspeople had to bear, and Sicily remained relatively stable until the early 1670s when risings again broke out, this time at Messina.

News of the events in Sicily reached the mainland and helped to ignite a rising in Naples and its region, which had its own viceroy. The city was one of the largest in Europe: with a population of over

300,000, it was larger than London and twice as large as Rome. As the residence of the viceroy, it served many of the functions of a capital city, being a centre of government and of the administration of law; it was an important ecclesiastical and commercial centre, and had a large university. It was a city which attracted large numbers of poor people and beggars from the surrounding countryside, especially in times of food shortages; and, like all early modern cities, it lacked anything approximating to a modern police force. The hinterland was among the poorest parts of Italy. Much of it was divided into noble and ecclesiastical estates, the nobility exercising feudal powers over their peasants to a degree matched in few parts of Europe. However, only a small proportion of feudal estates were farmed directly by noble families (many of which resided in Naples); it was often intermediaries who managed estates and were the worst oppressors of tenants or share-croppers. When the rising began in Naples, it soon spread to the countryside and assumed the character of a peasant war against the feudal nobility and its agents.

The short-term causes of the rising were similar to those in Sicily: the imposition by the viceroy of taxes on food after three decades of financial exploitation by the Spanish government. On 7 July, a Sunday and the feast of the Virgin Mary, there occurred a dispute in the main market between fruit vendors coming into Naples from the countryside, and city customs officials who tried to collect a new tax on fruit. A large crowd gathered and the atmosphere turned ugly. The officials beat a retreat, but the demonstrators marched on the custom house and burnt it to the ground. The leader of the crowd was a young fisherman, Tommaso Aniello, who by a contraction of his name came to be known as 'Masaniello' (the first Masaniello was a Neapolitan folk hero who had led a rising in 1547). After the devastation visited on the custom house, he led the crowd, now numbering many thousands, on a march to the viceregal palace. The viceroy, the duke of Arcos, took refuge in a Spanish fortress just beyond the city. Arcos's authority collapsed, and for several days Masaniello was master of Naples. He behaved as if he were governor, administering justice, organizing a militia, and supervising the seizure of the property of financiers to whom the viceroy had farmed taxes.

The character of Masaniello fascinated writers, poets and musicians of later generations; the nineteenth century in particular turned him into a prototype of the Italian romantic hero.[1] But he is notoriously difficult to understand. There is general agreement that this twenty-five-year-old fisherman had a charismatic personality and a natural ability to captivate large crowds by the power of his oratory. On the other hand, his state of mind has puzzled later observers, for there is much evidence (and not all of it from his enemies) that in the short period between 7 July and his assassination on 16 July, he turned from being a populist liberator into a demagogue who, almost on a whim, would have critics executed. Did power go to his head and turn the saint into a sinner, or was he, from the outset, a vicious and arrogant upstart briefly propelled into the spotlight by circumstance? Other problems relate to his thoughts on political and constitutional reform. How and where could a young fisherman come to acquire the sophisticated ideas which he urged upon his followers? It is known that one of his closest associates was a lawyer, Giulio Genoino. It is possible that it was Genoino who orchestrated events, incited the crowd to violence on 7 July, and drew up demands for the restoration of Neapolitan liberties, but that in view of his age (he was eighty in 1647) used the energetic Masaniello as his mouthpiece. Whatever the truth, Masaniello controlled the city of Naples for ten crucial days, during which the urban rioters asserted their fiscal and political demands: reduction of taxes, especially on food; the ending of legal and financial privileges which nobles had acquired since the sixteenth century; and the restoration of the city's privileges as they had existed at the time of King Charles I of Spain (the Emperor Charles V). At this juncture, the rising in Naples, like that in Sicily, still acknowledged the authority of the king of Spain.

Meanwhile, at the behest of the beleaguered viceroy, the arch-bishop of Naples, Cardinal Filomarino, had been using his influence to restore order. He authorized religious processions to remind the populace of their duty of obedience, and acted as a mediator between Masaniello and the viceroy. They met, and on 13 July signed a convention by which many taxes were abolished and a general pardon granted to the rioters. By now, however, Masaniello's conduct had turned eccentric: in addition to his demagoguery he was claiming divine sanction for his rule and the protection of the Virgin Mary. He laid claim to the latter having survived an attempt on his life, but on 16 July he was the subject of a second, and this time successful, assault by a gang of assassins. The details of the plot which led to his death remain obscure, but suspicion has fallen on the viceroy. Masaniello was buried next day after lavish funeral ceremonies attended by tens of thousands of people. With his death, which was followed by the exile of Genoino on 4 September 1647, the character of the revolt changed: it turned explicitly anti-Spanish and, as it spread throughout the countryside, anti-noble.

In Naples a new leadership emerged in the persons of Gennaro Annese, an armourer, and Marco Antonio Brancaccio, a member of the Knights of Malta. The former took charge of the political programme of the rising and the latter its military organization. Under Annese's guidance, a radical constitutional programme was developed as he turned for advice to Neapolitan lawyers. On 23 October 1647, the king of Spain was deposed and an independent republic declared. Emissaries went to Rome to meet the French duke Henri de Guise,[2] who was in the city arranging the annulment of his marriage. They invited him to become head of the republic. The French chief minister, Cardinal Mazarin, perceived the offer as an opportunity to strike at Spain and consented to the plan, albeit with reservations. Guise arrived in Naples with a few ships and troops, and in a ceremony held on 24 December was proclaimed 'duke of the Republic of Naples'. However, the Spanish still held fortresses near Naples, and Guise's failure to capture them exemplified the precarious position of the republic. Little further aid was forthcoming from France. Germany and the Rhineland remained the principal theatre of war between France and Spain, the hard-pressed French government was close to bankruptcy, and it was facing mounting domestic opposition which, in the spring of 1648, burst into the Fronde rebellion. The French government was in no condition to divert a large force to Naples, and when a Spanish fleet arrived in April 1648, it recaptured the city with relative ease. Guise was taken prisoner. He had alienated Annese and his advisers by associating with some of the most conservative noble factions; the suspicion had grown in Annese's circle that Guise was thinking of himself not as duke (with all the limitations that the word implied) but as future king of Naples. When the Spanish entered the city, the disillusioned Neapolitans made no effort to save Guise from the humiliation of arrest. The new viceroy, Inigo Velez de Guerarra, count of Oñate, negotiated conciliatory terms with Annese: a general amnesty was extended to rebels who submitted to the authority of Philip IV. Fighting continued in the countryside between peasants and noblemen. Many of the mercenary armies which had fought in the Thirty Years War were being disbanded, and young men returning from the war were available for hire. Nobles enlisted them, and now that Spanish authority in the city was restored, it was simply a matter of time before the rural rebellion was crushed. By the end of the year most peasants had surrendered. In the summer and autumn of 1647, when the urban rebels were in the ascendant, they had made no serious effort to assist the peasants; the mental and social demarcations between town and country were such that neither Masaniello nor Annese acknowledged any pressing need to create an urban–rural alliance. This lack of coordination proved fatal to the cause of rebellion.

### Consequences of the Southern Italian Risings

By contrast with the disunity in the rebel movements, the viceroys and nobility in Sicily and Naples provided mutual support; this combination was crucial to their victory. Spanish rule was entrenched anew in Naples and Sicily, and remained so into the eighteenth century. The Spanish held Sicily until the Treaty of Utrecht (1713), when the island was conferred upon Victor Amedeo II of Savoy with the title of king. In 1718 he returned it to Spain, which in 1720 surrendered it to Austria. It remained a subject of dispute until 1738 when a more lasting settlement was reached: Don Carlos, son of Philip V of Spain, became king of the independent and united kingdom of Naples and Sicily. Spain renounced all of its claims, although the new kingdom remained within the Spanish orbit of influence. Another outcome of 1647 was that feudal nobility was also confirmed in Sicily and Naples. It continued to dominate the countryside until the era of the French Revolution and Napoleon, and in some respects did so well into the nineteenth century. In the seventeenth and eighteenth centuries, most nobles protected their judicial and feudal rights resolutely, the Sicilian and Neapolitan peasantry remaining among the poorest in Europe. As late as the 1780s, the Spanish viceroy in Sicily was lamenting that the nobles continued to oppress the peasantry, retarding economic growth and preventing enlightened agricultural reform. The divisions between town and countryside, which had so damaged the rebellions, were repeated in suspicions between town and town. Italian 'patriotism' in the seventeenth century was intensely localized, people's loyalty to their town or village outstripping other allegiances. Urban rivalries were especially marked in Sicily, where Palermo, Messina, Catania and other towns were riven by mutual jealousies. Their antagonisms played into the hands of the Spanish viceroys, who exploited them to decisive effect.

Turning to the leaders of the rebellions and the ideas which they held, artisans and lawyers were prominent in the urban risings. Masaniello was a memorable but transient figure. Annese was much more representative of urban leadership, as were the lawyers to whom he turned for political and constitutional advice. The Neapolitan rising was richer in political thought than the Sicilian; figures such as Vincenzo d'Andre, Luigi del Ferro and Carlo Bonnavita, as well as Giulio Genoino and Gennaro Annese, developed radical proposals on social structure, economic rehabilitation and systems of government. Many lawyers, artisans and businessmen looked to the decentralized, commercially based Dutch Republic, especially the wealthy province of Holland, as a model for Naples. They admired Dutch political liberty; they contrasted their own feudal nobility with that of the United Provinces, where peasants were not overburdened with fiscal and manual obligations; and they envied the commercially based wealth of this small country which had both won its independence from Spain and created a vibrant economy. Many of these and other ideas were propagated through hastily printed pamphlets. One of the most influential was entitled *Dall'anticamera di plutone*. Presented as a discussion between Masaniello, the duke of Ossuna and the duke of Alba, it discussed various forms of government, assessing their advantages and drawbacks. It opted for rule by an enlightened prince from a wealthy and powerful dynasty; he would possess the resources to protect the state from external aggression, but would be expected to rule subject to the advice and consent of 'the nation'. Such debates might appear somewhat utopian given the realities of international relations in 1648, for the inability of the French to send adequate military protection cast an air of inevitability over the Spanish reconquest of Naples. But the rebellion of 1647 did demonstrate that radical rethinking of state and society was not a preserve of, say, England and France at this time; it was taking place in southern Italy.

## 1647 and 'Italian Decline'

The history of Italy in the seventeenth century has commonly been depicted in terms which stress decline. Italy, so the argument goes, was the most dynamic region of Europe from the late fourteenth to the early sixteenth century. The economies of its great city-states and republics (Venice, Milan, Genoa, Florence) were among the most advanced; the cultural achievements of Italy, be they in the literary, visual, architectural or musical arts, were nothing short of revolutionary and created new standards which the rest of Europe sought to equal; and the more sophisticated Italian states practised what were recognizably modern politics. In short, the Italy of the Renaissance reformulated concepts of civilization, and adopted civilizing processes which, as they were imitated elsewhere, transformed Europe. Yet for all its dazzling cultural and economic attainments, Renaissance Italy proved incapable of preventing much of the peninsula from falling under Spanish rule. Obsessed by particularist interests, the states of Italy failed to combine against Spanish incursions. In the seventeenth century, even those parts of the peninsula which were not ruled by Spain had to be wary of Spanish intentions. Venice, Genoa, the papacy and other states had to pursue devious foreign policies, only flouting Spain when assured of external support, usually from France.

In the economic sphere, so the argument for decline continues, the most prosperous regions suffered either relatively (by comparison with those parts of western Europe which developed Atlantic commerce) or absolutely, as in the case of Venice, whose overseas trade and possessions contracted in the face of Turkish expansionism. The economic prospects of Italy were rendered even less promising by the impact of epidemics, the greatest disaster occurring in 1630 when disease swept through the peninsula. The effects were worst in cosmopolitan northern Italy: between 1630 and 1650, the states or provinces of Milan lost about 340,000 inhabitants, those of Venice about 420,000, Monferrat and Piedmont about 100,000 each, and Genoa about 90,000. In northern Italy as a whole, there was a decline of just over 20 per cent in the population between 1630 and 1650. Southern Italy escaped more lightly with an average decline of just over 10 per cent between 1630 and 1650.[3]

Other parties to the supposed decline of Italy were the Catholic church and the nobility. During the Renaissance, the church had inspired bold philosophical, theological, artistic and scientific speculation and creativity. After the Council of Trent, however, it allegedly retreated into a baneful intellectual orthodoxy. It insisted on the faithful complying with its philosophical as well as doctrinal teaching, and in its censorship of books and use of the Inquisition possessed formidable instruments of coercion. Confronted by Spanish political omnipotence and the church's stringent supervision of belief and thought, the nobility of Italy evaded its 'historic duty'. Instead of organizing resistance to these two mighty obstacles to the modernization of Italy, the nobility took refuge in an obtuse feudalism. Whereas the United Provinces, Sweden, Britain and France responded to the challenges of the seventeenth century by laying the foundations of modern science, capitalist economies and modern state institutions, Italy languished, its deplorable condition being epitomized by two episodes: the condemnation by the Roman Inquisition in 1633 of Galileo, and the failure of the Sicilian and Neapolitan rebellions of 1647.

Such an interpretation has the attraction of clarity and coherence, but how persuasive is it? There is no question that Italy faced considerable economic difficulties which were accentuated by demographic decline; but, as earlier comments on Germany confirm, these were not especially Italian problems. Indeed, in the first half of the seventeenth century it is difficult to find any part of Europe which was not subjected to economic and demographic crises. The 'decline thesis' looks more convincing in the matter of Spanish rule, but even here we should not jump to premature conclusions. The political presence of Spain in Italy was immense and its character conservative. The Spanish crown never attempted a governmental revolution. The Spanish system, if it may be so called, rested on a 'contract': the king of Spain preserved the rights and privileges of the socio-political elites in Italy; they in return accepted him as legitimate ruler. The kings of Spain made no serious attempt to replace indigenous political and legal institutions with Spanish, and displayed nothing approximating to a mission in Italy. In this regard, Spanish rule may be contrasted with English rule in Ireland. Whereas the latter involved the introduction of English and Scottish settlers, the displacement of native Irish, the adoption of English language, law and administration, and the imposition of Protestantism upon a Catholic country, Spanish dominion in Italy was preservative. Even after victory over the Sicilian and Neapolitan rebels, the Spanish crown carried on as before.

This is not to say that Spanish rule necessarily impeded Italian political and economic development along modernizing lines. The accusation that it did so rests on the assumption that the normal pattern of political evolution in the seventeenth century was towards sovereign states equipped with reformed organs of government and administration, and with economies based on early forms of capitalism; that if Italy had been free of Spanish rule, it too would have evolved into modern states (perhaps even into a united state) with modern economies. The charge also presupposes that the nobility in Italy ought to have developed reformist, forward-looking attitudes, and is to be censured for not having done so. Such claims rest upon a programmatic view of history; they assume that because some parts of Europe moved broadly towards centralization and capitalism, the history of the rest of the continent becomes a question of how far it followed suit. To this it can be objected that there is no reason why this criterion should be adopted as the measure of polities in Italy or anywhere else; that the many varieties of society which existed in early modern Europe developed in terms of their own dynamic and evolution, and that it is tendentious to select one pattern of development and make it the measure of all things. If this objection is admitted, the written history of Italy in the seventeenth century becomes less one of 'missed opportunities' than one in which the singularity of Italy is stressed, and the contingencies which shaped it analysed. Moreover, it cannot be presumed that even if Italy had not been subjected to Spanish predominance, it would have followed a path of modernization. All that we can say is that the history of Italy would have been different; we cannot construct some counter-factual alternative to which Italy inevitably would have conformed. Even the calls by Annese and others for Naples to become like the Dutch Republic were a response to a particular crisis, not an indication of an alternative history which Naples necessarily would have experienced.

## The Catholic Church and Scientific Thought

Reference was made earlier to the supposed stifling of scientific thought in Italy by the Catholic church, the trial of Galileo in 1633 often being taken as an exemplar. The question can be clouded by terminology. Whereas we now allude to 'science' and 'scientists', the seventeenth century referred to 'natural philosophy' and 'natural philosophers'. Bodies of thought now regarded as independent scientific disciplines, such as physics, were considered branches of philosophy. The study of natural philosophy therefore attracted not only scientists – to use this term – but philosophers and theologians, including ecclesiastical authorities charged with upholding doctrinal orthodoxy. A key question was: how far was it possible to expand knowledge of the natural world and the universe without calling into question theological and philosophical orthodoxy? This problem was urgent in Italy precisely because that region stood at the forefront of scientific research. Foreign scholars flocked to Italian universities; the University of Padua in particular attracted students and teachers from abroad, including such scientific notabilities as Vesalius from the Spanish Netherlands, Copernicus from Poland and Harvey from

England. A roll-call of the better-known Italian scientists in the late sixteenth and seventeenth centuries would include Galileo, Torricelli, Borelli, Cesalpino, Fabrizio, Malpighi, Viviani and many others; and when, in 1668, the French government sought an internationally renowned astronomer to supervise the completion of the Paris Observatory and advise on astronomical research in the French Academy of Sciences, the choice fell on an Italian, Gian-Domenico Cassini. Many leading scientists in Italy were members of religious orders, the Jesuits in particular producing much fine science; and the patronage which popes, prelates and dukes extended to the arts was conferred also upon natural philosophy.

Italians were prominent in two aspects of seventeenth-century scientific activity which could be construed as responses to the problem of religious and philosophical orthodoxy. One was the rise of experimentation at the expense of pure speculation. Many natural philosophers argued that, by stressing the primacy of experimentation, or by making scientific hypotheses and theories dependent upon evidence derived from repeatable experiments, knowledge could be advanced without provoking disputes over religion and philosophy. Thus, in the 1580s when Galileo studied the problem of the acceleration of falling bodies, he devised his famous experiment of rolling balls down an inclined plane and measuring their rate of acceleration with the aid of a water gauge. He repeated the experiment hundreds of times before announcing his law of acceleration. It was based upon an experiment which anybody could repeat, and upon measurements and calculations which any competent student of mechanics could verify. Experience was to show that even experimentation was not always value-free, and that it was not possible invariably to divorce empirical knowledge from philosophical or theological debate; but experimental or empirical learning, which was the foundation of much scientific research in the seventeenth century, was pioneered in Italy as much as elsewhere.

The second feature was the emergence of scientific societies which could provide resources and, if necessary, guide members away from philosophically dangerous subjects. Italians were the first to establish recognizably modern scientific societies. Some were short-lived, but two made lasting contributions to organized scientific inquiry. In 1603 there was founded in Rome the Accademia dei Lincei, which remained active until 1630. Its members, who included Galileo, usually numbered about thirty; they conducted experimental research (Galileo made a microscope for the use of the society) and published scientific books. In 1657, in Florence, the Accademia del Cimento was founded by Grand Duke Ferdinand II and his brother Leopold de' Medici. The brothers were enthusiastic scientists. They possessed a well-equipped laboratory and a fine collection of instruments and natural specimens in botany, biology, zoology and geology. As early as 1651 Ferdinand was inviting scientists to conduct experiments in the laboratory; in 1657 his brother Leopold organized them into a formal society. Its most renowned members were Vincenzo Viviani and Alfonso Borelli. The Royal Society in London (founded 1660) and the Academy of Sciences in Paris (founded 1666) were both inspired by the examples of their Italian forerunners, and regarded them as allies in the great enterprise of advancing knowledge of the natural world.

Italy remained a generator of important scientific research, and yet it was there that Galileo was tried by the Roman Inquisition. Was that episode symptomatic of a deepening gulf between the Catholic church and new scientific learning, or was it an exception whose very notoriety proves the opposite?

## The Galileo Affair

Galileo Galilei was acknowledged in his lifetime as one of Europe's great natural philosophers. He was educated in his birthplace of Pisa, and while a student and young teacher at the University of Pisa, displayed exceptional talent in the mathematical sciences. He found the intellectual ethos of Pisa, dominated as it was by Aristotelian philosophy, increasingly uncongenial, and in 1591 moved to Florence where the Medicis became his patrons. In 1592 he was appointed professor of mathematics at the University of Padua, where he remained until 1610; thereafter he lived on Medici patronage and devoted himself to research and writing.

His interests included astronomy. Two chief models of the universe were available to astronomers. One was that of Aristotle as modified by Ptolemy in the second century AD. It depicted the universe as a finite sphere, inside of which were concentric spheres carrying the stars, planets and moon around the spherical and static earth at the centre. The celestial bodies, whose velocity was constant, described epicyclical orbits. This model dominated astronomical thought for centuries, and in the Middle Ages was incorporated into Christian theology. An alternative was proposed by the Polish astronomer Nicolas Copernicus in his *De revolutionibus orbium coelestium* (1543). Copernicus retained a spherical universe with inner concentric spheres, but placed the sun at the centre, with the earth among the planets. He attributed a three-fold motion to the earth: a circular orbit around the sun, a daily rotation of the earth on its axis, and a slow gyration of the axis itself. Ambiguity surrounded the status of Copernicus's ideas. If they were simply working hypotheses which provided a simpler account of the apparent motions of celestial bodies than did Aristotle and Ptolemy, they were philosophically and theologically neutral. If, on the other hand, they claimed to describe reality, then little short of a philosophical and theological revolution was implied. Copernicus died shortly after the publication of the *De revolutionibus*, but those who knew him agreed that he was convinced of the facts of terrestrial motion and of a heliocentric universe. In that case, questions concerning the interpretation of scripture were posed. Aristotelian cosmology had been so closely woven into scriptural exegesis that to undermine the authority of the one was thought to challenge that of the other.

By the turn of the century, however, observational evidence was casting increasing doubt over the Aristotelian system, and this was a process to which Galileo himself made a notable contribution. In 1609 he transformed the practice of astronomy, which hitherto was conducted with the naked eye, by making his own version of the recently invented optical instrument, the telescope. The observations which he then conducted astonished him. He saw ten times more stars than were known, moons around Jupiter, mountains on the moon, sun spots and much more. He announced his findings in 1610 in a short pamphlet, *Siderius nuncius* (*The Heavenly Messenger*). The evidence which he presented, and which could be verified by others who acquired a telescope, corroborated the Copernican rather than the Aristotelian model; indeed, it contradicted the latter on many points. Even so, it would have been premature to crown Copernicus as the new authority, for in 1609 the German astronomer Johannes Kepler announced two new laws of planetary motion which challenged both Aristotle and Copernicus: the orbits of planets are ellipses, not circles; and planets do not maintain a constant velocity, but accelerate as they approach the sun and decelerate as they move away.

Galileo nevertheless had become a convinced Copernican by 1610 when he was recalled to Florence by his patron, the grand duke of Tuscany. In 1611 he visited Rome, where he was received with marks of distinction by other astronomers and by Pope Paul V himself. After returning again to Florence, he began to attract adverse comment, especially from Dominicans worried about the impact of his ideas on their teachings based on Aristotle and Aquinas. In 1613 he published a dissertation on sunspots which expanded material in the *Siderius nuncius*, it not only advocated the virtues of the Copernican system, but could be read as claiming that the structure of the universe is as Copernicus described it, and that terrestrial motion is fact, not hypothesis. Two years later he composed a lengthy letter for Christina, grand duchess dowager of Tuscany, on the apparent contradictions between natural phenomena as they are sometimes represented in the Bible, and as they were understood by 'modern' natural philosophers, a notable case in point being the episode in Joshua 10: 12–13 wherein Joshua commands the sun and moon to stand still. In the letter, Galileo contended that the Bible is a source of authority on faith and morals, but not on natural phenomena; that its references to the latter sometimes alter conventional perceptions in order to drive home lessons in faith and morals; and that scientists and theologians should not be alarmed if empirical observations are at odds with literal readings of its texts. The nature and purposes of God, Galileo contended, are revealed in two 'books', scripture and creation. It was for theologians to interpret the first and scientists the second.

Copies of the letter circulated and, like Galileo's work on sunspots, came to the attention of the Roman Inquisition. Aware of concern in Rome, Galileo voluntarily went there in December 1615 to explain his ideas. He discussed them with a commission of eleven consultants who reported to the Inquisition on 24 February 1616. In their opinion Copernicanism was absurd in philosophy and heretical in theology. The Inquisition studied the report but, recognizing the complexity of the issues which it raised, reacted with caution. It gave Galileo a private warning to cease advocating Copernicanism, and the *De revolutionibus* was placed on the Index of forbidden books. Plans nevertheless were laid for a new edition with 'corrections' to any passage which might imply the reality of the earth's motion. Such an edition came out in 1620; the Inquisition had no objection to Copernicanism as hypothesis.

Galileo returned to his scientific research, and for several years observed the restriction placed upon him. From 1623 onwards, however, he detected a change in the intellectual atmosphere of Rome which, he believed, would allow him to return to the subject of Copernicanism. In that year Paul V's successor, Gregory XV, died; in his place was elected Maffeo Barberini, who took the title Urban VIII. The Barberinis were a powerful Roman dynasty, and Urban was known to be an admirer of Galileo; he allowed the scientist to dedicate to him a book on comets, *The Assayer* (1623), which was published under the auspices of the Accademia dei Lincei. Encouraged by its reception, Galileo went back to Rome in 1624. He met leading church officials and had six audiences with the pope, to whom he explained his understanding of Copernicanism. Galileo returned to Florence persuaded that Urban did not regard Copernicanism as heretical, and that he, Galileo, was no longer bound by the prohibition of 1616. He began to compose a work on the movement of tides and intended turning it into a comprehensive analysis of the issues raised by the Aristotle/Copernicus debate. He also aimed to address the reading public, not just natural philosophers. In 1630 he went to Rome with a draft of the text. It was cleared by the censors, subject to certain modifications. Urban VIII let it be known that Galileo must present all sides of the argument to the best of his ability, and he must observe the convention of discussing the earth's motion only as hypothesis. After many delays the book was completed and printed in Florence in 1632 as a *Dialogue on the Two Chief Systems of the World*.

The *Dialogue* takes the form of discussions between three characters: Simplicio (an Aristotelian), Salviati (a Copernican who represents Galileo's views) and Sagredo, a disinterested adjudicator. It does not disguise Galileo's preference for the Copernican system, and complaints soon reached Rome about its lack of balance. The Aristotelian system, claimed critics, is shown to be almost indefensible, and the book comes close to asserting the earth's motion as fact. Urban himself read the *Dialogue* and felt slighted on two counts: he saw the character of Simplicio as a disrespectful caricature of himself, and felt that Galileo had not upheld the Aristotelian case with anything like the refinement that it deserved. Urban VIII was hard-pressed politically at this stage. Spanish diplomats were protesting at what they considered his pro-French policies, and, at a consistory of cardinals in March 1632, Urban and the Spanish Cardinal Borgia publicly quarrelled over the pope's alleged French sympathies. Under pressure on the political front, Urban could not afford any suggestion that in matters of faith he was failing to uphold orthodox belief. Galileo also had alienated several powerful Jesuits (who earlier had been among his supporters) by failing to acknowledge his indebtedness to their work. They included Orazio Grassi, who was probably one of those who first encouraged the Inquisition to investigate the *Dialogue*.

The pope denounced the censors who had authorized the book, and agreed that Galileo should be ordered to Rome to be tried by the Inquisition. Galileo arrived in 1633, and his interrogation began on 12 April. It lasted until 21 June, the Inquisition's decision being conveyed the next day. He was found 'vehemently suspected of heresy' on two counts: that he contended that the earth moves, and that he believed that one can defend a thesis contrary to the Bible. He was condemned to a public recantation of his views and to indefinite imprisonment. The latter was commuted by Urban VIII, at the request of the grand duke of Tuscany, to house arrest in Galileo's villa near Florence.

The affair was not a simple case of obscurantist church versus enlightened scientist. It was Galileo the polemicist, not Galileo the scientist, who was tried in 1633. His scientific work was not called into question by the Inquisition, and when he returned to Florence after the trial, he wrote what is probably his finest scientific text: *Dialogue on the Two New Sciences* (1638), in which he returned to subjects which interested him as a young man, especially the phenomenon of motion. The affair revolved around questions of theology and philosophy. What standing does theology have in relation to science; is science a branch of philosophy or can it attain independence of method and subject matter; what conclusions may legitimately be drawn from empirical evidence in the sciences; how far are problems in science, philosophy and theology conditioned by their socio-political context; and who has ultimate authority to adjudicate disputes between science and religion? Such questions exercised some of the finest minds of the age, and the Roman ecclesiastical authorities were far from being officiously dogmatic in trying to pin down Galileo on these matters. Ecclesiastical and political struggles near to the pope influenced the outcome of the episode. Galileo seems to have assumed that because Urban VIII seemed favourably disposed towards Copernicanism, he, Galileo, could write a *Dialogue* which reached bold conclusions; but the pope was not a free agent, and Galileo paid the price.

### Italian Baroque

If there were any spheres in which Italy continued to command universal admiration, they were in painting, sculpture and architecture. Italian styles proliferated, Italian artists found commissions all over

Europe, and foreign artists came to Italy to study. The term often used to designate the stylistic features which predominated in the visual and plastic arts in Italy – and which spread elsewhere in Europe and into the colonies – is 'baroque', a word deriving from the Portuguese 'berrueco' and Spanish 'barroco', meaning a distorted pearl. The word was first used by jewellers in the sixteenth century, but soon acquired general stylistic application. Baroque is difficult to define, but it does signify a distortion of the rules of classicism which had governed the visual arts since the Renaissance; a subordination of classical principles of harmony, order, proportion and restraint, to grandeur, exuberance, ornamentation and majesty. Baroque architecture, painting and sculpture sought to excite strong responses in the viewer – awe, indignation, exhilaration – and did so by introducing dramatic innovations: in architecture, curved walls, large domes, irregular ground plans, lavish decoration; in painting, the creation of theatrical effects through powerful contrasts between light and shade, the depiction of human figures in dramatic poses, and the use of deep, vibrant colours; in sculpture, the representation of subjects in twisted, contorted postures. Baroque was flexible and adaptable. It was employed extensively by the Catholic church, but also by secular rulers whose notions of urban and palatial architecture were revolutionized by baroque ideals.

Within Italy, Rome played a unique role in developing and propagating baroque, and in this regard the pontificate of Sixtus V, from 1585 to 1590, is of central importance. In the few years of his reign he began the transformation of what was still a medieval city into a great baroque creation. Some of his predecessors had made piecemeal additions to Rome, but Sixtus conceived a master plan which was inspired by a mixture of ecclesiastical, political and social motives. He aimed to design a city in which the main churches and shrines would be linked by roads enabling pilgrims to move easily from one to another; wide avenues, large squares and imposing buildings would signify *Roma triumphans* politically as well as spiritually; and the provision of fountains, washing houses and water supplies would make it a commodious city in which to live. Sixtus quickly completed a major axis running from the north-west to the south-east of the city (the Strada Felice) with the Piazza and church of Santa Maria Maggiore half-way along; at either end were squares with large buildings and obelisks. Minor axes branched off, horizontally or diagonally, again making imaginative use of squares, obelisks and fine buildings. Water was brought into the city by aqueducts, and by

1589 was servicing the twenty-seven public fountains in the city. Sixtus's successors, notably Urban VIII, Innocent X and Alexander VII, whose pontificates covered the period from 1623 to 1667, continued to beautify Rome; they too required it to fulfil three broad purposes: it must be worthy of the head of the post-Tridentine Catholic church, it must proclaim the princely splendour of the pope,

**Figure 1**   The Triton Fountain, Rome, by Bernini

**Figure 2**   San Carlo alle Quatro Fontane, Rome

and it must be the outstanding example of modern urban planning in Europe.

Many of the characteristic features of baroque style may be observed in the work of the three greatest names in Roman art and architecture of the period: Pietro da Cortona, Giovanni Bernini and

Francesco Borromini. Cortona, an artist who turned to architecture, painted frescos in the Barberini palace in Rome and designed the façades of Santa Maria in Via Lata and of SS Luca e Martina in the Forum. Bernini first made his mark in Rome as a sculptor. Some of his public statues remain among the supreme baroque creations: the Triton fountain in Rome, St Longinus in St Peter's, the 'Ecstasy of St Teresa' in S. Maria della Vittoria, and the sepulchres of popes Urban VIII and Alexander VII. Bernini also master-minded much of the internal and external development of St Peter's, including the famous elliptical colonnade which circumscribes the open space in front of the basilica. Borromini (who learnt his trade as a stonemason working at St Peter's) in some respects was the most adventurous of the three. He introduced a daring elaboration to the curved wall: an undulating wall giving the impression of elasticity. He employed it first for the Oratory of San Filippo Neri, but most famously on the façade of the church of San Carlo alle Quatro Fontane in Rome. His other most notable building was the church of Sant'Ivo, which he built for the University of Rome; its lantern is topped by a flamboyantly baroque spiral in place of the usual cupola cap.

Baroque styles were employed extensively by the Catholic church, not only in Italy, but in central Europe, France, Spain and Portugal, and in their respective overseas colonies. Whilst it would be an exaggeration to present ecclesiastical baroque simply as the artistic wing of the Counter-Reformation, there is no question that the new styles served the purposes of Tridentine Catholicism. Responding to the emphasis which Trent had placed on the centrality of the eucharist in worship, new churches were designed to allow congregations an easy view of, and access to, the altar where mass was celebrated. Churches were also built with close attention to the acoustics: congregations must be able to see preachers easily and hear sermons clearly. Trent's call to the faithful to venerate saints, especially the Virgin Mary, and to seek their intercession between worshipper and God, found reflection in the paintings and statues of saints which proliferated in churches. Ecclesiastical baroque proclaimed the doctrine and dogma of the Catholic church with confidence and ostentation; it sought to instruct as well as impress; it appealed to the mind and the emotions; and it conveyed to worshippers a sense of belonging to the church triumphant.

A comprehensive study of baroque would trace the influence of Italian styles, architects and painters throughout much of southern and central Europe, France and European colonies in the Americas.

# 4

# *Western Europe, 1600–1665: Spain and France*

## SPAIN, 1600–1665

The most imposing of the powers of western Europe was Spain. Historians follow contemporaries in referring to Philip III, who ruled from 1598 to 1621, as 'king of Spain', but this was a term of convenience, for strictly speaking there was no such title. Philip inherited three crowns: those of Castile (with Granada and Léon), Navarre and Aragon (which included Catalonia, Valencia and the Balearic Islands). Spain was a composite kingdom, each part of which had its own assembly (*Cortes*) and other political, administrative and legal institutions. In this sense Philip III and his immediate successors resembled James and Charles Stuart who ruled the kingdoms of England, Scotland and Ireland. In addition to the three Spanish crowns, Philip III inherited those of Naples and Portugal. The latter had been ruled from Spain since 1580. It had a population of just over one million, but, of course, possessed colonies in Brazil and commercial bases in Asia. To these kingdoms should be added the Spanish New World (with some 10 million subjects), Italy (about 6 million), Flanders (about 2 million)[1] and the Franche Comté with under half a million.

Every king since Charles I of Spain (the Emperor Charles V) regarded Castile as the core of the Spanish empire. It covered over half of the area of Spain, and its population of some 6,600,000 in the early 1590s was just over three-quarters of that of the three kingdoms combined (Aragon had about 1,500,000, and Navarre about 350,000).[2] Castile contributed more to the crown in taxes than any other part of Spain, and the New World territories were its dependencies. The centrality of Castile was confirmed in 1561 when Philip II made Madrid his capital, a status which no city hitherto had enjoyed. By the end of the sixteenth century, however, there were unmistakable signs of socio-economic malaise. Agriculture was failing to meet the demands of this large population, and in the mid-1590s a run of bad harvests led to famine in Castile, followed by the great plague of 1599–1602 which killed about 10 per cent of the population. The epidemic was worst in the countryside, and further reduced the food-producing sector. Meanwhile, the pressure of war forced the government drastically to increase taxes, thereby driving the economy into deeper recession. By the early 1600s, the kingdom of Castile could not continue to sustain the burden which Charles I and Philip II had placed upon it; the impoverishment of Castile was one of the factors which decided Philip III to accept the truce with the United Provinces in 1609.

One sphere in which the kings of Spain deemed their reigns to have been successful was that of religion. Their subjects remained Catholic, crown and church having collaborated to exterminate nascent Protestantism. Spain and Portugal were thus preserved from the politico-religious crises which affected France and much of central and northern Europe in the sixteenth century. However, Spain did contain about 300,000 Moriscos: people of Moorish descent whose forebears had converted from Islam to Catholicism in the aftermath of the fall of Granada in 1492. Commonly suspected of being Catholic in name only, they were the object of popular resentment which varied in intensity according to political and economic circumstance. At the beginning of the seventeenth century, when the war against the United Provinces looked incapable of resolution and economic recession was hitting hard, anti-Morisco paranoia grew. Moreover, the government of Philip III strongly suspected that Henri IV of France was secretly fomenting rebellion among the Moriscos. Playing upon popular hostility towards this minority, Philip III in 1609 ordered their expulsion from Spain. It is thought that about 275,000 Moriscos were driven out of the country, most going to North Africa. This was a measure which earned Philip III much praise from the church, and enhanced his popularity among his subjects; it also sweetened the bitter pill of the humiliation of the truce signed with Dutch 'rebels' that same year.

Given the composite nature of the Spanish crown and the extent of Spanish possessions elsewhere, a pattern of central government had evolved which attempted to coordinate the interests of the various territories. It was based on a number of councils, three of which were central to government: the Council of State (usually with about eighteen members, all chosen by the king), the Treasury (*Hacienda*), and the Council of Castile. There were royal regional councils for Aragon, Portugal, Flanders, Italy and the Indies (these were separate from the various *Cortes*), a Council of War, and councils of relatively minor importance, such as the Inquisition and Royal Forests. The councils could be excruciatingly unhurried in their procedures and were a by-word for delay. When circumstances required more speedy action, the king would create special councils (*juntas*) to by-pass the regular processes.

Philip II had governed personally, devoting many hours of each day to administrative tasks. Philip III showed no such disposition, relying instead on 'favourites' (*validos*) who carried out government in his name. The most notable was Francisco de Sandoval y Rojas, duke of Lerma, who throughout most of Philip III's reign exercised both political power and patronage on an extraordinary scale. He devoted his energies as much to personal enrichment and the advancement of his family and friends as to the demands of government. In domestic affairs, he made extensive use of *juntas* at the expense of the advisory councils, and preferred to deal directly with the various *Cortes*. Lerma was disgraced in 1618 and replaced by his son, the duke of Uceda, but a pattern had been established.

When a new king succeeded in 1621, Philip IV, aged sixteen, he too relied upon a favoured minister: at first Don Baltasar de Zúñiga, and after Zúñiga's death, his nephew Gaspar de Guzmán, count of Olivares and duke of San Lúcar la Mayor. The Count-Duke Olivares[3] remained *valido* until his disgrace in 1643. Philip IV was confronted by formidable fiscal problems. The kings of Spain did have enormous financial resources, for in addition to the taxable potential of their subjects and the 20 per cent tax on all precious metals imported from the New World, the great financial houses of Germany and Italy had offices in Madrid which negotiated the extension of loans and credit to the Spanish government. On the other hand, because Spanish commitments were proportional to the geographical spread of their possessions, costs consistently outstripped revenue, especially when the Castilian economy went into decline in the late sixteenth century.

Of all the demands upon royal finance, the two most burdensome were the interest on public debt and the financing of war. Accumulated debt sometimes forced the crown to resort to bankruptcy.

Philip II had recourse to this measure in 1557, 1575 and 1596, while Philip III did so in 1607, and Philip IV in 1627 and 1647. At the turn of the century, accumulated debt was almost seven times higher than annual revenue: in 1598 revenue stood at about 10 million ducats and debt at 68 million.[4] Meanwhile, warfare continued. It is true that the Peace of Vervins which Philip II signed with Henri IV of France a few months before Philip's death, eased some of the pressure, but the war against seven of Spain's former provinces in the Netherlands lasted until the truce of 1609. Between 1598 and 1609, that war cost Philip III's government another 37.5 million ducats, to which should be added 4.5 million in interest.[5] This incessant outpouring of money forced Philip III into the bankruptcy of 1607; and although the 1609 truce provided respite, the Thirty Years War once again faced Philip IV with familiar fiscal problems. The parlous financial condition of the Spanish crown also owed something to structural deficiencies: no machinery existed whereby a coordinated fiscal system could be imposed throughout the kingdoms. Philip IV, like his predecessors, was compelled to work through the individual and cumbersome fiscal procedures of Castile, Aragon, Navarre, and elsewhere.

### Philip IV, the Count-Duke Olivares and Reform

In 1619 Philip III appointed Zúñiga, his former ambassador to the Holy Roman Emperor, as head of his son and heir's household. Having an eye to his own family's future prospects, Zúñiga brought into the royal entourage his nephew, Olivares. After the death of Philip III and the succession of Philip IV, the new king chose Zúñiga as his *valido*, and when the minister died in 1622, the king replaced him with the nephew. Eighteen years older than the king, Olivares had grown up in the world of politics and diplomacy. He was born in Rome, where his father was Spanish ambassador to the papacy, and after having spent part of his youth in Italy, he returned to Spain to study at the University of Salamanca before entering the young Prince Philip's household. Unlike Lerma, who exhibited little by way of a sustained political philosophy or strategy, Olivares brought a first-class mind to government. His political thought and practice were influenced by his family background, but also by his extensive reading on public affairs. He was deeply impressed by two works: *De constantia* [*On Constancy*] (1584) by the Flemish philosopher Justus

Lipsius, and *Ragio di stato* [*Reason of State*] (1589) by the Italian Giovanni Botero. The first of these, which discussed statesmanship, advocated constancy or stoicism. Lipsius commended the virtues of diligence, unremitting hard work, perseverance, single-mindedness and unflagging vigilance. The statesman who develops these properties, argued Lipsius, will triumph over every adversity. Botero compared the resources and performance of the Spanish monarchy with those of other European kingdoms, laying particular stress on the importance of the size of the population, the king's finances, and the condition of agriculture and industry. Botero maintained that in all these spheres Spain was performing poorly. His *Reason of State* sounded both a warning and a call for reform, especially the development of an energetic maritime policy. In spite of the geographical dispersion of the king of Spain's possessions, too little attention, contended Botero, had been paid to the question of linking them by well-controlled sea routes. The king's far-flung empire was vulnerable to attack by his enemies. Until the sea routes were secured, the king's resources would remain potential rather than actual. The maritime theme in Botero was rendered all the more poignant by the fact that his book appeared one year after the disaster of the Armada. Olivares was also aware of the work of pamphleteers (*arbitristas*) writing in the early 1600s. They too protested against the failures of the Spanish monarchy, and campaigned for political, financial and economic reform. One of the best known, Jerónimo de Cevallos, dedicated to Olivares his *Arte real para el buen gobierno de los reyes y príncipes* [*Royal Art of Good Government by Kings and Princes*] (1623). In this text, of which Olivares possessed a personal copy, the author called for a new, simple taxation system, and for the creation of a national bank which would reduce governmental debt.

Olivares became chief minister at a time when change was in the air. In 1619 the Council of Castile had issued a formal call for reform, and shortly before his death, Zúñiga had formed a Great Council of Reform (*Junta Grande de Reformación*), whose meetings had been attended by the king. Olivares had already worked out a broad strategy of sweeping reform. He aimed to reorganize taxation, simplify judicial procedures, stimulate economic activity and expand the fleet. He was resolved to impose higher levels of uniformity upon Spain. He ascribed the crown's failure fully to exploit its financial, economic and military resources to the fact that it had made no serious attempt to turn Spain into a political reality. In Olivares's view, Philip IV must demand of his subjects a far higher degree of political, military and financial uniformity than existed hitherto. He explained his ideas to the king in a document known as the Great Memorial, which he presented to Philip on Christmas day 1624. Olivares advocated economic regeneration, the repopulation of Castile, changes in government, justice and administration (especially finance), the rehabilitation of royal prestige and power, a diversion of some of the wealth of the Catholic church into secular purposes, and the diminution of the particularism of the territories which composed the kingdom.

Olivares stressed this last point. A composite kingdom like Spain could not hope to organize its fiscal and military potential effectively without political, judicial and administrative uniformity. In a famous passage, Olivares wrote:

> The most important piece of business...is for Your Majesty to make yourself King of Spain...Your Majesty should not be content with being King of Portugal, Aragon, and Valencia, and Count of Barcelona, but should work and secretly scheme to reduce these kingdoms of which Spain is composed to the style and laws of Castile...And if Your Majesty achieves this, you will be the most powerful prince in the world....[6]

In short, the process of uniformity would be synonymous with Castilianization. By this, Olivares meant that there should be fostered among all of the king's subjects, irrespective of their social status or the region in which they lived, the same degree of obedience and devotion towards the king which Castilians displayed. Moreover, all of the king's subjects should acquire duties and rights towards each other and the king, such as those which Castilians possessed. Olivares's desire to extend the legal, financial and political structures of Castile throughout the whole of Spain was less an expression of an ambition to centralize government for reasons of efficiency than to create a sense of unity, harmony and loyalty to the king of Spain.

Such a strategy could easily be misunderstood and could provoke resistance from the non-Castilian regions. Olivares accepted that, if he were to succeed in his purpose, he would need the active support of the king. Accordingly, he encouraged Philip IV not to neglect government as his father had done, but to familiarize himself with its complexities, attend meetings of the Council of State, and involve himself in the administration of his kingdoms. Philip responded positively, and by the late 1620s was taking a close interest in government. The chief body through which Olivares worked with the king was an inner council normally composed of the king, the *valido*, three secretaries of state, and the king's confessor. Such bodies had been created in the past; this one met regularly to discuss and decide policy. Once decided, policy was carried out sometimes by the advisory councils, but often by *juntas* answerable directly to Olivares: in 1622, for example, he created a *junta* for trade and in 1625 one for population and mines. Olivares also insisted that, if 'Castilianization' were to succeed, Philip IV must modify the nature of the monarchy. He counselled Philip IV to act less as the king of Castile writ large, and more as the 'king of Spain'. Philip should visit his non-Castilian lands, and appoint to his immediate entourage subjects from Aragon, Portugal, Italy and Flanders. By so doing, Philip IV would both alleviate opposition to centralization and stimulate loyalty to the 'Spanish crown'.

In November 1625, Olivares presented to the Council of State a proposal which, he hoped, would lay the foundations of Spanish unity: the Union of Arms, which bore some resemblance to the Swedish system of military levies. Olivares proposed that, in addition to the existing armies of the king, there should be formed a reserve of 140,000 troops. They would be raised throughout Philip IV's European possessions (although the scheme eventually would be extended to the colonies) according to a formula based on size of population; this reserve would be used exclusively to defend any part of the Spanish monarchy which might be attacked, and in the fullness of time would help both to create and to symbolize the essential unity of the lands which comprised the kingdom of Spain.[7]

Early in 1626 the king personally attended assemblies of the *Cortes* of Aragon, Catalonia and Valencia to discuss the Union of Arms. Considerable resistance to the plan was expressed in all the *Cortes*. The Union allegedly would contravene privileges (for example, by Aragonese law, its soldiers could be used only to defend Aragon itself; what if Philip IV wanted the Union to defend, say, Milan?); the cost of training and maintaining the Union would add to the already hard-pressed finances of the kingdoms; fears were expressed that the Union was the thin end of a wedge whose function was to prise out and eventually dislodge local laws and privileges in favour of Castilian law. Conscious of this last threat, the regional assemblies used the presence of the king to demand redress of grievances. The Aragonese, Castilian and Valencian *Cortes* obstructed the immediate formation of the Union, but at a price: recognizing that they could not send the king away empty-handed, they agreed to raise financial subsidies to help Philip IV fight the war in Germany. The immediate outcome of the meetings of the *Cortes*, therefore, was the assumption by the non-Castilian kingdoms of a higher proportion of the funding of warfare than in the past. Later in the year Olivares publicly announced the creation of the Union, although it was several years before it was fully operational.

In 1628 Olivares reformed the currency. There existed no single Spanish currency, different coins being minted throughout the Iberian peninsula. However, in the second half of the sixteenth century there had grown the practice, authorized by the crown, of issuing coins made mostly of copper (*vellón*). Unlike gold and silver coins, *vellón* was cheap and easy to produce, and the mints did so on an enormous scale. In Castile between 1621 and 1626 alone, there were minted *vellón* coins to the value of 20 million ducats. The growth in the volume of *vellón* at a time of economic depression, especially in Castile, led to rampant inflation which caused concern not only to Olivares and the Council of State, but to the *Cortes* of Castile. Already in 1627 Olivares had been forced into another suspension of payment on state debt, although the bankruptcy of that year was aimed in particular at Genoese bankers who had loaned money to the government at exorbitant rates, and who were extremely unpopular in Castile; 1627 was an expression of Spanish hostility towards foreign financiers rather than an admission of governmental insolvency. After consultations with the *Cortes*, Olivares in 1628 revalued *vellón* by 50 per cent. In the short run, people with large holdings of *vellón* found their value reduced by half, but the *Cortes* consented to this device as necessary to the re-establishment of sound money.

## Spain at War

Olivares's approach to the domestic affairs of Spain was governed by the exigencies of war. In the early 1620s there were two major interlocking conflicts with which Olivares had to contend: the Thirty Years War in which the Austrian Habsburgs looked to their Spanish cousins for assistance, and Spain's renewed hostilities with the United Provinces in 1621. To these was to be added in 1635 the third great challenge of war against France. The Bohemian rising of 1618 resulted in a decade of Austrian Habsburg expansion, aided and

abetted by the Spanish whose motives were partly rooted in family
solidarity, but also in geopolitical calculation: they needed to preserve
land communications between their military bases in Milan and those
in Flanders; thus they occupied that part of the Lower Palatinate
which dominated the Rhine near its conjunction with the Main.
Within a few years, when war had broken out again against the
Dutch, Olivares came to regard this as an acquisition of major importance.

As 1621 came ever closer, the question of whether to renew the
twelve-year truce with the Dutch became ever more pressing for
Philip III. Some of the strongest pleas in favour of its prolongation
came from the Spanish governor in Flanders, the Archduke Albert,
and the general commanding Spanish forces there, Spínola (who had
led the occupation of the Lower Palatinate). The governor argued
that the economy of Flanders would be ruined if it found itself once
more in the frontline of war against the Dutch, while Spínola warned
that, from a military viewpoint, the chances of conquering the republic were minimal: the Dutch had an excellent fleet and a fine army
(which they could afford to expand by hiring mercenaries). Spain, so
this argument went, should confirm the truce and await more advantageous circumstances before resuming war. The Council of Finance
likewise urged that the truce be extended: royal finances were such
that another long war against the Dutch would be disastrous. The
contrary argument insisted that the truce had been a humiliation for
Spain, and that Spanish honour must be satisfied by another war. To
this were added economic reasons: the Dutch were expanding their
empire at the expense chiefly of Portuguese possessions in the Americas, the Indian Ocean and the East Indies. If further Dutch expansion were to be frustrated, war must be undertaken in 1621.

Equivocation was ended by Spanish occupation of the Lower Palatinate and the emergence of an energetic team around the new king,
Philip IV. The decision was taken to exploit the favourable circumstances of the early 1620s and reopen war against the United Provinces. Dutch subjects and ships were expelled from Philip IV's
territories, and Spínola led an army of invasion towards the republic.
The Spanish were able to keep their forces in Flanders well up to
strength, thanks to their success in the Valtelline, which kept the
supply route between Milan and Flanders open, but the progress of
war was slow and involved lengthy sieges of well-fortified towns. The
capture of Breda in 1625 was trumpeted by the Spanish as a triumph
(celebrated by Velázquez in his famous painting of the surrender of

the city), but it was of limited strategic consequence. To counterbalance Spanish success in Europe, the Dutch occupied Bahia from 1624 to 1625, and in 1630 seized Pernambuco. The Dutch had also been active on the diplomatic front, signing defensive treaties with Denmark (1621), Barbary coast princes (1622), Brandenburg (1623), and France and England (1624). Conscious that one of the most effective ways of combating the Dutch was to deprive them of their commerce, in 1626 Olivares discussed with the Polish government a plan to drive the Dutch from the Baltic. Sigismund III of Poland proposed joint military campaigns with the objectives of expelling the Swedes from Germany, making Sigismund king of Sweden (he had a dynastic claim to the crown), and excluding Dutch ships from the Baltic. The prospects looked promising as Wallenstein defeated the Danes and advanced towards the Baltic coast. However, the plan was abandoned. Olivares was nervous about committing a large fleet with soldiers to the enterprise, and in 1629, Poland signed the truce of Altmark with Sweden.

The failure of the Baltic plan was symptomatic of a more general reversal of Spanish fortunes. In 1631, by the Treaty of Cherasco, the Mantuan succession was settled in favour of the French candidate, while in France itself a political challenge to the authority of Cardinal Richelieu, chief minister of Louis XIII, was crushed personally by the king. Now secure in his position, Richelieu was to bring to French foreign policy a coherence and consistency which hitherto had been lacking, and he regarded the breaking of the Spanish preponderance in western Europe as a major priority. In Germany, the intervention of Sweden signalled a dramatic collapse in the Habsburg position, and even the Spanish war against the United Provinces turned in favour of the latter: in 1632 the Dutch captured several important towns including Venloo and Maastricht. In Germany, informal contacts between the belligerents were taking place after the deaths of several leading military commanders – Tilly, Wallenstein and Gustavus Adolphus – and in the wake of the Swedish defeat at Nördlingen; these approaches led to the Peace of Prague (1635). Meanwhile, the Spanish and Dutch were also talking informally about peace. The Dutch war had proved Spínola right, for Spain could not reconquer the northern Netherlands. However, at this juncture, Richelieu, as was stated earlier, regarded a general European settlement as inimical to French interests; he forestalled a general peace by his declaration of war against Spain (1635) and the Holy Roman Emperor (1636).

## War between Spain and France, 1635

The French declaration was received with despondency in Madrid, especially as Richelieu signalled his aggressive intentions towards northern Italy by signing alliances with Savoy and Parma. France had a much larger population than Spain, and although the French government faced financial problems, they were not as serious as those confronting Spain after fourteen years of warfare. On the other hand, Spain could anticipate help from the emperor, and Olivares secured from Charles I of England a benevolent neutrality. Charles agreed that Spanish ships would have the use of English ports.

In its early phases the war went well for Spain. Perhaps this was unsurprising: the Spanish armies had been fighting for many years and were far more experienced than the French. The first French attacks against Flanders failed, allowing the Spanish to invade France from the north in 1636. When they reached Corbie to the east of Amiens, panic gripped Paris, for the route to the capital now lay open. The Spanish were halted only after desperate French resistance. Nevertheless, 1636 was a black year for France: rebellion broke out in the south-west (the rising of the 'Croquants'), to be followed in 1639 by that of the 'Nu-pieds' of Normandy. These risings greatly embarrassed the French government, forcing it to withdraw troops from the war front. Likewise, the French cause in Italy faltered. In 1637 Olivares authorized the seizure once more of the Valtelline, while the death of Charles, duke of Mantua on 21 September, followed by that of Victor Amedeo I, duke of Savoy on 7 October, removed Richelieu's principal allies in northern Italy. So badly had the war gone from the French point of view that in 1637 Richelieu proposed a truce. Olivares spurned the offer. He calculated that it was a confession of weakness by the French, and that, if he pressed on with war, he might achieve victory.

By the end of the decade Olivares knew that he had made a mistake in rejecting a truce, for the war against the Dutch Republic took a turn for the worse. The Dutch recaptured Breda in 1637, while in 1639 and 1640 the most serious maritime disasters since 1588 hit the Spanish. In 1639 Olivares amassed an armada of over seventy ships with, in addition to their crews, 9,000 soldiers. Placed under the command of Don Antonio de Oquendo, its mission was to supply the forces in the Netherlands and advance the cause of controlling the North Sea. If Spain could do so, it could secure communications with Flanders and incapacitate much of the commerce upon which the Dutch depended. A Dutch fleet, under the command of Maarten Harpetszoon Tromp, encountered Oquendo off the English coast. The first engagements were indecisive, and the Spanish took temporary refuge near Dover. Tromp used the pause to reinforce his own fleet, and on 21 October 1639 attacked. At the battle of the Downs, just off the coast of Kent, he inflicted heavy defeat on the Spanish. The second catastrophe occurred in Brazil. The Dutch had been occupying Pernambuco since 1630; in 1639 Olivares sent another fleet of Spanish and Portuguese ships to expel them. This campaign also failed, and it was not until 1654 that the Portuguese recaptured Pernambuco. Even the land war produced bad news: in December 1638 the fortress at Breisach, so important to the movement of Spanish troops along the Rhine, fell to allies of the French.

The disasters in the North Sea and Brazil implied that Olivares now might have to think in terms of a compromise peace with the United Provinces, rather than victory. This possibility was heightened when, in 1640, two great rebellions broke out: those of Catalonia and Portugal. They were by no means the first uprisings against the fiscal burden of war (revolts had taken place in the province of Biscay between 1631 and 1634), but they were on a scale sufficient to force Olivares and Philip IV to question how much longer they could sustain the wars against the Dutch and the French.

## The Revolt of Catalonia

Catalonia was known for its distinctiveness from Castile. Its *Cortes*, dominated by the nobility, was obsessed with the protection of the province's rights (*'fors'* in Catalan); and when Philip IV attended the *Cortes* in 1626 to discuss the Union of Arms, that assembly left him in no doubt as to its opposition to Castilianization. Olivares had little patience with the *Cortes* of Catalonia, regarding the appeal to *fors* as little more than a pretext whereby Catalans evaded their duty to the king. Catalans did not serve in the Spanish army, nor did they contribute taxes directly to the crown. In 1639 the French occupied Spanish Roussillon, and Castilian troops were sent to defend the rest of Catalonia. Olivares insisted that they be billeted at the expense of Catalans themselves, and that the province make direct financial contributions to the defence of their province. There was much popular resistance to this policy, and numerous clashes between soldiers and

Having escaped the worst excesses of the Thirty Years War, Italy provided a cultural leadership to which churches, kings, princes and aristocrats elsewhere looked for inspiration. And it was not only Catholic Europe which responded. England, the Dutch Republic and other Protestant states and territories continued to regard Italy as the arbiter of artistic values; in these countries, too, Italianate styles and principles governed much architecture, painting, sculpture and town planning. Catholicism and culture, which came together in baroque, were the two great spheres in which Italy made its most distinctive contributions to the history of Europe in the seventeenth century. Other parts of the continent might surpass the states of Italy in economic vitality or military strength, while Protestant Europe regarded the Catholic church with varying degrees of hostility; but in an age which afforded the highest respect to religion and high culture, Italy remained spiritually and culturally, if not geographically, at the centre.

civilian bands occurred. By June 1640 protests were taking place in Barcelona against this 'violation' of rights, and quickly got out of hand. Magistrates who had professed support for royal policy were assaulted; most shocking was the killing of the viceroy, the count of Santa Coloma, himself a Catalan. A tenuous calm was restored, but when news arrived in December of the Portuguese revolt, violence broke out in Barcelona on an even larger scale. People from the countryside poured into the city, where divisions developed between magistrates and lawyers who sympathized with the crown's military and financial plight, and nobles, urban and rural masses, who resisted the crown. The British ambassador to Madrid reported that 'in Barcelona there is serious dissension between the magistrates and other officers of justice, who hope to reach an agreement with the king, and the people who do not...I am beginning to think that this foolishness by the people...will throw the principality into the arms of the French.'[8]

That indeed is what happened. In 1641, noble leaders of the insurgents met French agents to discuss military aid. Louis XIII offered assistance on condition that Catalonia accept his formal protection and recognize him as count of Barcelona. The rebels agreed, and French troops speedily occupied key strong-points in Catalonia, including Barcelona. When Philip IV personally headed an army into Catalonia in 1642, he was repulsed by joint Catalan–French forces and retreated to Madrid, a disillusioned man. He blamed this and other disasters on Olivares, whom he dismissed in 1643. Philip was afraid that the Catalan and Portuguese risings might encourage independence movements elsewhere in Spain. Later in the 1640s there were aristocratic plots in Aragon and Andalucia, aiming at varying degrees of separatism. That they came to nothing could not disguise the centrifugal pressures under which the kingdom of Spain strained.

The accord between Catalonia and France extended into the reign of Louis XIV, while Philip IV's military engagements elsewhere in Europe, to which were added the risings in Sicily, Naples and Portugal, prevented him from concentrating his resources on Catalonia. By the late 1640s, however, the outlook for Philip was improving. The Peace of Westphalia released Spain from the war against the United Provinces, while in 1648 the French government found itself having to cope with the 'Fronde' risings which were to last until 1653. The French crown now faced the kind of socio-political turbulence that confronted Philip IV, and was forced to withdraw many of its troops from Catalonia. Those who remained were under-fed, under-supplied and mutinous. In 1651, Philip IV's armies once again entered Catalonia, placing Barcelona under siege. More French troops were diverted from Italy, but they found their comrades in such a demoralized state that many officers judged that an orderly retreat was the only option. The French attempt to relieve Barcelona failed, and on 13 October 1652 the city surrendered to the royal forces. After negotiations between Catalan notables and representatives of Philip IV, the king in February 1653 confirmed the *fors* of Catalonia, but retained the right to occupy Catalan fortresses and impose control over several municipal authorities.

Philip IV's treatment of Catalonia in 1653 was remarkably indulgent given that for thirteen years it had repudiated his authority and fought against him with the help of a foreign army. His leniency was an act of political sagacity. Although he had long since dispensed with the services of Olivares, he remembered his former *valido's* advice to act as king of Spain. Philip recognized that this rising had been no radical movement, either in its constitutional or social demands. The defining question of the rising had been: who would best guarantee the *fors* of Catalonia? For a time the rebel leaders had placed their hopes in the king of France, but the retreat of the French in 1652 had removed them from the equation. Philip IV's objective now was to restore relations between himself and his Catalan subjects, to convince them that he, and nobody else, embodied the surest defence of their rights. The generous terms upon which Philip IV settled the Catalonian rising therefore arose out his notions of Spanish monarchy, as well as from the pragmatic need to alleviate the internal strains upon Spain. Conciliation was the order of the day in 1653. Philip abstained from the punitive treatment that Ferdinand II had meted out in Bohemia in the 1620s, or Cromwell imposed upon Ireland in the 1650s. Philip's foresight was vindicated by future events. The Catalan rising was not repeated, even though tensions between crown and *Cortes* did recur; both sides refrained from actions which might provoke another '1640'.

## Portugal

The other great rising in 1640 was that of Portugal. Unlike Catalonia, which had been part of the kingdom of Spain since 1469, Portugal had been ruled by kings of Spain for only sixty years. In 1578, King Sebastian of Portugal disappeared on campaign in Morocco.

His body was never found. He left no direct heir and, after a succession crisis, the crown passed to his cousin, Philip II of Spain, in 1580. There developed in Portugal a cult of Sebastianism: a belief that Sebastian had not died, but had either gone into hiding or was being held secretly in a Moroccan or Spanish prison; one day he would return. Philip II ruled Portugal through a viceroy, and prudently ensured that the machinery of government and administration remained in Portuguese hands. When the *Cortes* met in 1581, he formally acknowledged and guaranteed Portuguese rights. In most respects the two kingdoms remained independent, although there was a certain amount of *de facto* collaboration. Much Portuguese international commerce was conducted through the medium of Spanish coinage, while Spanish goods were often carried overseas in Portuguese ships. In the Americas, the Portuguese and Spanish cooperated in their efforts to resist the inroads of the Dutch and English.

Some Portuguese intellectuals lamented that their country was vulnerable to a creeping 'Castilianization'. Two leading writers – Frei Luis de Sousa and Francisco Rodrigues Lobo – advocated cultural resistance by devoting their literature to the praise of the Portuguese language, the beauty of the countryside and the glories of Portuguese cultural achievements. Many Portuguese aristocrats resented the loss of the royal court at Lisbon (especially since they were debarred from holding royal household offices in Madrid, and were excluded from Castilian patronage), and questioned whether an absentee king could be trusted indefinitely to observe the liberties of Portugal. They also feared that Portugal's association with Spain could involve their country in wars in which Portuguese interests were not at stake. The armada of 1588 had included Portuguese ships which shared in the disaster of that campaign, and the attacks which the Dutch made upon Portugal's Asian and American possessions were attributed by many Portuguese to the fact that their king was Spanish.

Warfare was the main driving force behind the growth of anti-Spanish feeling. Philip III and Lerma conspired to shift more of the financial burden on to Portugal. In 1600 a commission of Castilians was sent to Portugal to manage the finances of the kingdom, with the aim of diverting money into the Spanish war effort, and a series of forced loans was imposed upon the mercantile communities. Anti-Spanish sentiment increasingly expressed itself through Sebastianism, which acquired millenarian, prophetic and mystical characteristics.

Popularized versions of Sebastianism spread, announcing the imminent return of a redeemer-king who would liberate Portugal from foreign rule. Various 'false Sebastians' emerged – most were arrested and executed – but by about 1620 Sebastianism was finding a political focus in John, duke of Braganza. John was a descendant of Catherine of Braganza, a cousin of King Sebastian. His supporters looked to him, not Philip III, as the legitimate king of Portugal. John for his part discouraged such speculation; he was by nature cautious, and had no wish to provoke Philip III. In an attempt to appease Portuguese opinion, Philip III made a formal visit to the country in 1619, but as the wars of the 1620s and 1630s forced Olivares, in the name of Philip IV, to impose yet more financial demands, John of Braganza found it difficult to dissociate himself from Sebastianism.

Olivares did make concessions in an effort to ease Portuguese grievances. Between 1622 and 1633 he dispensed with a viceroy and operated through Portuguese-born regents; he also assigned commissioners to investigate financial abuses among the Portuguese themselves, in an attempt to prove that protests should not be aimed exclusively at the crown. Such palliative measures availed little. On several occasions in the 1620s, Olivares imposed forced loans upon the city of Lisbon, and when, in 1628, he extended the loans to the whole country, there were riots in several towns. Even so, Olivares devised other means of extracting money from Portugal. In 1631 the wealthiest merchants were obliged to pay a special 'contribution' to the crown, and office-holders, when they assumed their functions, had to pay a tax equal to half of their annual salary; in 1631 he created a state monopoly on the sale of salt. In 1633, Olivares ended the system of regents and reverted to that of viceroys. The following year he appointed Marguerite of Savoy, the dowager-duchess of Mantua and granddaughter of Philip II. She was in office when rebellion occurred in 1640. The office of viceroy was difficult to fulfil, for whereas Olivares considered Marguerite an agent of royal policy, she felt bound to represent Portuguese grievances to the king and to mitigate the financial pressure which Olivares was exerting. By the 1630s another problem had arisen: the Union of Arms. To his financial demands, Olivares was adding his insistence that Portugal be incorporated fully into the Union. This provoked widespread resistance, for Portuguese, like Italians, Aragonese and Catalans, could not understand why they should be expected to fight the wars of the king of Castile. Risings against these provisions broke out in the Algarve in 1637. Castilian troops were dispatched; meanwhile,

French agents were in Portugal, urging Sebastianists to foment general revolt.

John of Braganza still resisted leadership of a general anti-Spanish movement, but found himself swept along by events. Olivares attempted to weaken Sebastianism by what he regarded as a masterstroke: in 1639 he appointed John as military governor of Portugal, and ordered him to recruit soldiers to fight in northern Europe and Catalonia. Olivares calculated that John would now be compromised in the eyes of Sebastianists who, deprived of their figurehead, would lose coherence. Olivares's plan failed. After procrastinating for several months, John of Braganza decided to throw in his lot with aristocratic Sebastianists and other malcontents. On 1 December 1640 a group of nobles seized the viceregal palace in Lisbon and placed the viceroy under arrest. They proclaimed John to be King John IV, and he made a formal entry into Lisbon a few days later. The Portuguese *Cortes* recognized him as king, as did the colonies shortly afterwards. The rebellion added to the many crises facing Philip IV and Olivares, notably war against the Dutch and French, and the rising in Catalonia. The *coup* of December 1640 had been executed by a minority of nobles with popular acquiescence. A few nobles remained loyal to Philip IV, but most approved of the 'restoration' of John IV. Among office-holders and bureaucrats there was a large majority in favour of John, but the mercantile communities were less sure, for many had property or business interests in Spain and feared for their security. The clergy were divided. Most of the lower clergy and the Jesuits supported John, but the senior hierarchy and other religious orders were much more hesitant; the Portuguese Inquisition was pro-Spanish. Such diverse reactions confronted John IV with a formidable double challenge: at one and the same time he had to reconcile powerful interest groups to his accession, and organize his kingdom's defence against Spanish attack. Failure in either sphere could have disastrous consequences for the other.

John secured external help. In 1641 he entered into an alliance with France and an *entente* with the Dutch Republic, and in 1642 he signed an alliance with England. The agreement with the United Provinces did not mean the end of Dutch attempts to capture Portuguese possessions overseas, for in 1641 they occupied Angola. Although the Portuguese recovered Angola in 1648 and Pernambuco in 1654, they suffered permanent losses in the Indian Ocean. The Dutch took Malacca in 1641, part of Ceylon in 1644 and the remainder of the island by 1656; the Portuguese were also driven from

Arabia and the Persian gulf. In the sixteenth century, the Portuguese empire extended throughout the Atlantic and Indian oceans as far as the East Indies; by the second half of the seventeenth, it was a predominantly Atlantic empire.

Meanwhile, John had to fight the 'war of restoration' against Spain. Within a few days of his accession he created a council of war and a council to oversee the construction of fortifications near the frontier, which lacked serious defences. Fortunately for him, Spain's best soldiers were in Germany, Flanders and Catalonia, and he was helped by a rising against Philip IV in Andalucia in 1641. Portuguese soldiers deserted the Spanish army and returned home; John also hired mercenaries from the Netherlands, England and Germany. Because of his other commitments, Philip IV could never devote enough forces to the invasion of Portugal. Throughout the 1640s and 1650s the fighting was spasmodic; when John died in 1656, his young successor, Alfonso VI, continued the war. The greatest danger to Portugal came after the Peace of the Pyrenees (1659) between Spain and France, for Philip IV now could concentrate upon Portugal. In 1660 he sent three armies to invade Portugal from the north, east and south. However, Louis XIV had dispatched one of his finest generals, Schomberg, to coordinate Portuguese resistance. Portuguese victories at Ameixial (1663) and Villaviciosa (1665) effectively nullified the Spanish military threat, and when Philip IV died in September 1665, leaving a potential succession crisis, the Spanish government decided on negotiations with the Portuguese. Peace was signed at Lisbon in February 1668 by which Spain recognized Portuguese independence.

## Peace between Spain and the United Provinces, 1648

While Philip IV, Olivares and his successor Luis de Haro were attempting to crush the risings in Catalonia and Portugal, they had to contend with the continuing wars against the Dutch Republic and France. Although there were disagreements within the Spanish Council of State as to whether peace with France or the United Provinces was the more urgent, there were no objections when it became clear that the latter was much more ready than the former to reach accommodation. Ironically, one of the factors in the growing Dutch readiness to sign peace with Spain was French military successes against the Spanish in the mid-1640s. The first was the great victory at the battle of Rocroi (1643), followed by the capture of Thionville (which left the route to Luxembourg open), Gravelines, Courtrai, Mardyck, Furnes and – of immense significance to the maritime war – Dunkirk in 1646. The Dutch viewed French successes with concern, for they had no desire to see a powerful Spain in Flanders simply replaced by a powerful France; they preferred a situation in which neither kingdom enjoyed hegemony. For his part, Philip IV accepted by 1646 that the danger from France was such that he must end the war against the Dutch, even at the cost of abandoning hitherto sacred principles. Direct negotiations took place – to the consternation of the French, who urged their Dutch allies not to make a separate peace with Spain – which resulted in the Treaty of Münster (1648). Spain yielded on almost every key issue. It formally recognized the United Provinces as an independent republic, it abandoned its demand that Dutch Catholics suffer no religious or civil discrimination, and it recognized the Dutch occupation of Portuguese colonies in the Americas. When the Peace of Westphalia was signed, these terms became the Dutch–Spanish section of the general settlement.

The 1648 peace marked a recognition by Philip IV that Spain must adjust its aspirations to international realities. For almost eighty years it had attempted to reconquer its former Dutch provinces, at great human, financial and political cost. By 1648, when Catalonia, Portugal and parts of Italy were in open revolt, it was evident to Philip IV that a radical reassessment of Spain's international commitments was required. The very fact that Spanish delegations attended the negotiations in Westphalia was an admission that Spain now must integrate itself into whatever configuration of international relations might emerge; Spain could no longer aspire to shape western Europe in accordance with its own interests and those of the Catholic church. In a changing Europe, France increasingly presented the major challenge to Spain, as was signified by the absence of a Spanish–French treaty at Westphalia. To Philip IV the great challenge now was to pursue war against France, while at the same time dealing with rebellion at home.

## War between Spain and France to 1659

By the end of 1648, Louis XIV's government found itself in a situation analogous to that of Philip IV. The outbreak of the Frondes, which for almost five years consigned much of the country to civil war, brought the monarchy almost to its knees and seriously hampered the French war effort; not the least problem was that two of France's finest commanders, the duc de Condé and the vicomte de Turenne, deserted to the Spanish. Domestic crisis in France played into the hands of the Spanish who, in 1652, enjoyed three outstanding victories: they retook Dunkirk and Barcelona, and overran the fortress of Casale in northern Italy. However, the war was complicated by the intervention of a third party which, for many years, had avoided direct involvement in European wars: England. Under Charles I, English foreign policy generally had been pro-Spanish: first, because Charles still hoped to see the son of Frederick V of the Palatinate restored to the electorship, a measure that would require the consent of Philip IV who still administered part of the Lower Palatinate; second, because Charles hoped to persuade Philip IV to allow English ships to trade with Spanish and Portuguese America. In spite of the blandishments of Charles I, Philip IV refused to yield on either of these two points.

By the early 1650s, however, the political situation in England had been transformed: the country now existed as a Commonwealth headed by Oliver Cromwell. Cromwell, for whom the question of commerce was uppermost, decided on direct action. At the end of 1654 he sent a fleet to occupy the Spanish island of Hispaniola (modern Haiti and the Dominican Republic), and although it failed to do so, it did take Jamaica in 1655. Cromwell also had his eye on Dunkirk, but its capture from the Spanish would be extremely difficult, and the English dared not attempt it alone. In October 1655 he signed a treaty with the French, and declared war upon Spain. Philip IV was faced by an alliance whose combined naval forces were superior to his own. In 1656 and 1657, the English intercepted and captured the annual Spanish treasure fleets transporting gold and silver from the Americas. Meanwhile, Turenne returned to France and was pardoned by Louis XIV. He was placed in command of a joint Anglo-French force whose aim was to capture Dunkirk. At the battle of the Dunes (14 June 1658), Turenne defeated the Spanish; a few days later Dunkirk surrendered and was transferred by the French to English control. The loss of Dunkirk by the Spanish was followed by other disasters as the French advanced into Flanders, occupying Gravelines, Oudenaarde, Menin and Ypres.

In 1656 secret talks had taken place between Luis de Haro and a French representative, Hugues de Lionne. The broad terms of a possible agreement had been resolved, but there was a major obstacle. Mazarin, chief minister in France, proposed that Louis XIV should marry Philip IV's eldest child, Maria Teresa. Philip IV refused. He had three children: Maria Teresa, Charles and Margaret. Charles would succeed him, but was a weak child who was not expected to survive into adulthood. Castilian succession law permitted a queen regnant. If Charles died before or shortly after his father, the succession would pass to Maria Teresa; and if she were married to Louis XIV and had children, the kingdom of Spain in the next generation would be ruled by a French prince; hence Philip IV's refusal to countenance the marriage. By late 1658, however, the military situation had become so bad that Philip felt that he could no longer resist French demands. After further negotiations, the Peace of the Pyrenees was signed on 7 November 1659. The French acquired Roussillon, Artois and a number of towns in Flanders, Hainault and Luxembourg; they also promised to cease assisting the Portuguese rebellion and to pardon the duc de Condé. The marriage between Louis XIV and Maria Teresa went ahead, but in an attempt to forestall her possible succession as queen of Spain, Philip IV insisted that, before the marriage, she renounce her claim to the crown. Maria Teresa did so; she and Louis XIV married in June 1660.

The Peace of the Pyrenees completed what Westphalia had begun: the adjustment by Spain to the 'new' Europe. Having conceded Dutch independence in 1648, Spain now recognized France as at least its equal in western European affairs. The French acquisitions in Roussillon and Flanders rendered Spain and the Spanish Netherlands more vulnerable in any future Franco-Spanish war, and within a few years Philip IV's apprehensions about his daughter's marriage were to be vindicated when Louis XIV claimed further territory in Flanders on his wife's behalf. Spain's adverse position with regard to France worsened when, in 1661, Louis XIV's brother Philippe d'Orléans married an English princess, Henrietta Maria, the sister of the restored Charles II; in 1662 Charles II sold Dunkirk to the French. Increasingly, Spanish foreign policy in western Europe was to take on a defensive character, as it sought to avert further French expansion.

## The Spanish 'Balance Sheet', 1665

Philip IV's reign conventionally has been equated with the 'decline of Spain'. There are senses in which such an all-embracing phrase can be justified. By 1665, when Philip IV died, the United Provinces had already acquired their definitive independence, and Portugal was on the verge of doing so. The treaties of Westphalia and the Pyrenees had redefined Spain's position in its relation to other European states. The Spanish crown lived permanently on the verge of bankruptcy during a half-century when the imports of precious metals from the Americas were declining.[9] By the mid-1660s, France had emerged as Spain's principal rival in Europe, for this emerging giant, which possessed demographic and economic resources far greater than those of Spain, looked poised to supplant Spain as the predominant power of western Europe. The fact that during the reign of Philip IV's son, Charles II, there was a permanent question mark over Charles's succession, with the French Bourbons pressing their claim, symbolized the relative weakness of Spain *vis-à-vis* France.

Such evidence might indicate straightforward decline, but recent scholarship proposes a more nuanced interpretation. First, as regards Spain itself, it is true that the crown was faced by insurgency in Catalonia and Portugal (to which can be added other risings in the peninsula and in Italy), but almost every other government in Europe was faced with similar difficulties within its territories. In due course, reference will be made to the 'general crisis' in Europe, a thesis which justified itself in part by the universality of uprisings and civil war in Europe in the first half of the seventeenth century (see below, p. 248). Set within this context, Spain was not declining relative to other states; it was experiencing a general phenomenon which also affected its neighbour and rival France. Indeed, one might go even further and suggest that by excluding Protestantism, the Spanish Habsburgs saved Spain, Portugal and their Italian possessions from the religious conflict which so embittered socio-political relations in Britain, Ireland, France and Germany. As regards finance, the Spanish crown in the second half of the century was to adopt reforms which rendered taxation and other fiscal devices less socially disruptive than in the past. This too was a European phenomenon. The incidence and seriousness of rebellion throughout Europe declined after 1660. This is not to say that a blessed state of fiscal stability and social harmony was achieved, but the financial reforms which the Spanish government later pursued contributed to a marked decrease in social unrest. In the international sphere, Spain remained one of the major powers. In 1665 it still retained most of its possessions in the Americas, while, within Europe, most of Flanders remained in Spanish hands as a potential threat to the northern frontier of

France. The Spanish–Austrian Habsburg axis remained one of the determining facts of international relations (which was one reason why the Bourbons were so anxious to acquire the Spanish crown), while Spanish armies and fleets were still among the elite of Europe. In short, the phrase 'decline of Spain' should be interpreted with caution and moderation; it does not imply that, by 1665, Spain was of little consequence in European affairs.

## FRANCE, 1610–1661

It is tempting to presume that there was an inevitability to France's replacing Spain as the major power in western Europe, but modern historians are little disposed to argue in such terms. They stress the role of contingency in their accounts of changes in the relative positions of Spain and France. It is true that France enjoyed certain advantages. Its population of 16–17 million in 1618 surpassed that of Spain, while French monarchy was unitary, not composite, and the kingdom was geographically compact. On the other hand, France was still recovering from the legacies of some thirty-five years of Wars of Religion, and unlike Spain it was a multi-confessional kingdom in which a Calvinist (Huguenot) minority comprised 6–7 per cent of the population. The Huguenots were concentrated in certain areas, chiefly in an arc running from Poitou through Languedoc into Provence. The Edict of Nantes (1598) afforded them legal recognition, but the potential for religious conflict remained. Even the succession to the French crown looked uncertain. Henri III in 1589 and Henri IV in 1610 were both assassinated. Louis XIII and his advisers invested much energy in propagating respect for the person of the king. Moreover, although Louis XIII and his wife, the Spanish princess Anne of Austria, married in 1615, it was not until 1638 that the future Louis XIV was born; during most of the reign of Louis XIII, it looked as if the crown would pass to his brother, Gaston d'Orléans.

France shared the socio-economic distress that affected much of Europe in the first half of the century. It experienced food shortages, epidemics and rebellion; and even though the Thirty Years War and the Spanish–Dutch war had implications for France, it was not until 1635 that Louis XIII dared intervene openly, fearing that war would fatally reopen wounds in French society. Louis XIII, the young Louis XIV and their ministers engaged upon a massive task of reconstruc-

tion, involving the restoration of royal authority, the creation of political and social stability, measures to enhance economic prosperity, and
the securing of French interests in a turbulent Europe. The demands
of these imperatives were not easily reconciled, and the crown frequently had to adjust its priorities in the light of circumstance.

### The Domestic Situation in 1618

Until Louis XIII reached his majority (his thirteenth birthday) on 2
October 1614, his mother, Marie de' Medici, governed as regent.
She had to struggle against the ambitions of princes of the blood and
great aristocrats. Chief among them was Henri II, duc de Condé.
The Condé family were of Bourbon stock, and had there been no
Henri de Bourbon to succeed to the throne in 1589, the duc de
Condé considered that he would have been king.[10] This near miss
left Condé with an abiding sense that he deserved honours little
inferior to those attaching to monarchy. His audacious conduct, and
that of his son Louis, the 'Grand Condé', caused consternation in
royal circles. Condé was but an extreme example of a more general
disposition among the aristocracy. The duc de Guise, the duc d'Epernon, the duc de Rohan, the duc de Bouillon and others had large
estates, served as provincial governors and commanded private
armies. On several occasions they defied the regent and took up arms
to wrest more land and privileges from her.

Marie responded by exploiting her greatest asset, the young king.
She negotiated a prestigious double wedding: in 1615, Louis XIII
married Philip III's daughter Anne of Austria (who renounced her
claim to the throne of Spain), while Louis's sister Elisabeth married
the future Philip IV of Spain. These marriages were important diplomatically, but they also served Bourbon dynastic interests: the fact
that the Habsburgs agreed to the matches confirmed that the Bourbons belonged among the elite of royal families, and deflated the
pretence by Condé and other aristocrats that their status approxi-
mated to that of monarchy. In 1614, Marie de' Medici took the king
on a tour of the Loire, the heartland of aristocratic opposition.
Splendid royal entries were made into Orléans, Tours and other
towns, until the royal retinue reached Angers and Nantes, where the
king presided over an assembly of the Estates of Brittany. This triumphant expedition was followed by two more affirmations of royal
majesty. On 2 October 1614, Louis XIII's majority was proclaimed

in the ceremony of the *lit de justice*, held at the *parlement* of Paris.[11] There, in the presence of the king and the magistrates of the *parlement*, the regent formally 'handed over' the kingdom to her son on his thirteenth birthday. Aristocratic or other rebels could no longer resort to the pretence that they were resisting an 'unjust' regent. On 20 October the coronation took place at Rheims cathedral. This, the most solemn as well as the most magnificent, expression of royal sovereignty was attended by princes of the blood and aristocrats, who formally submitted themselves to him. One other major assembly gathered in 1614: an Estates General which, in a negative sense, demonstrated the appeal of strong monarchy. It met in response to demands from aristocrats who hoped to impose limitations on Louis's freedom of action. This elected body of clergy, nobility and commoners (the Third Estate) met in Paris on 27 October, but by the time it dispersed in February 1615 it had achieved little, having been riven by disputes. Here was palpable evidence that the aristocracy had little to offer France politically.

Relations between Louis and his mother declined, a particular source of tension being the influence on her of Italians who enjoyed her patronage. She was especially close to Concino Concini and his wife Leonora Galigaï, a childhood friend of Marie. As regent, Marie lavished pensions and honours upon them. Concini was admitted to the royal council and was appointed governor of fortifications in Picardy; he received the title of marquis d'Ancre, and in 1613 was appointed Marshal of France. He built up a team of 'clients' whom he placed in influential positions; they included Claude Mangot in foreign affairs, Claude Barbin in finance, and Armand-Jean du Plessis de Richelieu, bishop of Luçon, also in foreign affairs. Concini and his wife were hated by other factions at court. In 1617 Louis XIII authorized the assassination of Concini, which occurred on 24 April; a few weeks later Concini's wife was executed. The *parlement* of Paris pronounced the killing an act of royal justice against a traitor. In the aftermath of Concini's death, his clients were exiled from Paris (including Richelieu, who was sent to Avignon), and Marie de' Medici was ordered by Louis to retire to Blois.

## Huguenot Rebellion in the 1620s

Although the Edict of Nantes had conferred legal recognition upon the Huguenots and authorized them to fortify some two hundred 'places of security', they displayed a defensive mentality which became even more pronounced after the assassination of Henri IV. The regency seemed disposed towards a 'Catholic' policy in which the Huguenots anticipated renewed persecution: in 1610, Marie de' Medici guaranteed the Edict of Nantes, but confirmed the 'places of security' for only five years, while the Spanish marriages of 1615 suggested that the Bourbons might be joining the Habsburgs in a programme of aggressive Counter-Reformation. After Louis XIII's majority, Huguenot anxieties were increased by the incorporation of Béarn into France in 1620. This province was part of the kingdom of Navarre, not France, and as such formed part of the patrimonial lands of the Bourbons. It was a Protestant territory, but in 1599 Henri IV authorized Catholic worship. For reasons mainly to do with the succession, Louis XIII decided to integrate Béarn into France. Béarn succession law permitted a female to rule, whereas that of France did not. Louis XIII wanted to prevent a situation whereby a future king of France might be deprived of Béarn by an accident of birth. As a preparatory step, in 1617 he restored to the Catholic church in Béarn its property and rights. The sovereign council of Béarn, composed of Huguenots, refused to register the proclamation, but its protest was rendered pointless when in 1620 Louis joined the province to France. The immediate background to this move was another aristocratic revolt. In 1619 Marie de' Medici escaped from Blois to Angoulême, where she joined rebels led by the duc d'Epernon. A brief reconciliation between Marie and Louis was brokered by Cardinal Richelieu (now rehabilitating himself after his disgrace in 1617), but in 1620 their relations broke down again. The queen mother now backed aristocratic rebels in Normandy and Anjou. Louis raised an army and crushed his opponents. He decided to proceed to Béarn, which quickly fell into his hands; he entered Pau in October 1620. He proclaimed the union of Béarn and France, replacing the sovereign council of Béarn with a French-style *parlement* in which only Catholics could sit.

In response to these developments, a Huguenot assembly gathered at La Rochelle in December 1620. Encouraged by the duc de Rohan and his brother Soubise, it announced in May 1621 the creation of a *de facto* state within the state: taxes would be raised from Huguenots and an army created. James I of England was invited to be protector of the Huguenots. Such a radical stance alienated some Huguenot aristocrats, including Bouillon and Lesdiguières; the latter converted to Catholicism. In the spring of 1621, Louis XIII, now back in Paris, gathered his troops and marched west to suppress the Huguenots. They proved a tougher proposition than the aristocrats a year before. Although many Huguenot towns surrendered, he failed to capture Montauban and La Rochelle. The rising spread to Saintonge and Languedoc, and was joined by the city of Montpellier. In 1622, Louis renewed his campaign. He headed for Poitou, avoiding Huguenot strongholds and concentrating on relieving Catholic towns or occupying small Huguenot centres. It was during this phase that there occurred the worst atrocity of the campaign, the massacre of the inhabitants of Négrepelisse on 10 June 1622. Louis besieged Montpellier, whose defences were organized by the duc de Rohan. By this stage, other problems at home and abroad were demanding Louis's presence in Paris. In October 1622 he agreed terms with the Huguenots in Montpellier, which the Huguenot assembly at La Rochelle also accepted: the Edict of Nantes was confirmed, but the Huguenots would dismantle eighty places of security and revoke their 'constitution' of 1621. In the long term the rising of 1621–2 damaged the Huguenot cause by heightening Catholic fears that Huguenots could not be trusted, and by scandalizing many Huguenot nobles who were horrified by the spectacle of their co-religionists taking up arms against the king. Huguenot nobles drifted back into the Catholic church; by the late 1630s, leadership of the Huguenots had largely passed from the nobility to urban oligarchies.

The peace of 1622 proved transitory. The Huguenots of La Rochelle and the duc de Soubise were displeased with the Peace of Montpellier. To the municipal authorities of La Rochelle, their disputes with the crown involved more than religion. The port was one of the most prosperous in France; it enjoyed many fiscal privileges and a high degree of autonomy. The defeat of the Huguenots would, they feared, be used as an excuse by the crown to diminish the privileges and autonomy of La Rochelle. When, in 1624, Soubise called upon Huguenots to rise again, he found a ready response in La Rochelle. He calculated that this was a propitious time to move against the government, for it was embroiled in the Valtelline crisis and would, he hoped, be reluctant to divert troops to the west of France. However, the implications of the Valtelline crisis were counterbalanced by better relations between France and the Protestant states of England and the Dutch Republic. In 1624 the three states formed an alliance, which was reinforced in 1625 by marriage between the French princess Henriette-Marie and Charles, prince of Wales. Neither the English nor the Dutch government wished to see

Louis XIII caught up in a lengthy campaign against the Huguenots. The Dutch sent ships to assist a royal fleet in an attack on La Rochelle, and the English ambassador to France urged the Huguenots to end their rebellion. A French royal naval expedition, assisted by the Dutch, defeated the fleet of La Rochelle in September 1625, forcing Soubise to flee to England. Huguenot representatives petitioned the king for peace, which was accorded in February 1626: the Peace of Montpellier was confirmed, but the defences of La Rochelle were to be reduced and its war fleet decommissioned.

The third Huguenot rebellion of the decade, that of 1627, was forced upon La Rochelle by extraneous factors. Richelieu was now a minister of Louis XIII, having been admitted into the royal council in 1624, and it was his plan to expand French maritime activity which occasioned the events of 1627. In 1626 he took the title of *grand maître de la navigation et du commerce*, and announced a strategy to create commercial companies and expand the war fleet. The city fathers of La Rochelle objected to a scheme which involved the expansion of rival ports, and the English and Dutch governments feared the strengthening of the French fleet. The English government decided on a pre-emptive strike, and found a pretext in the Huguenots. Responding to an appeal from the duc de Soubise, still in exile in England, Charles I sent eighty ships and 10,000 men in June 1627 officially to force the king of France to fulfil his 'obligations' to his Huguenot subjects; in reality, Charles aimed to strike a blow at Richelieu's maritime plans. The English force arrived on 10 July and disembarked on the Ile de Ré, just off the coast from La Rochelle. Two forts on the island, which were manned by French troops, were besieged. Within La Rochelle itself there was consternation. The city authorities had not invited the English, and were reluctant to bring upon themselves the wrath of the king. Matters were taken out of their hands by the dowager duchesse de Rohan, the mother of Soubise and Rohan. She fomented popular agitation among the Huguenots of La Rochelle who, in September 1627, threw in their lot with the English. By now a royal army, headed by Louis XIII and Richelieu, had arrived. Siege was laid to the city.

The siege lasted a year and imposed desperate hardship on all sides. The English failed to capture the French forts, and withdrew in November 1627. Richelieu ordered the construction of dike and breakwater systems to shut off La Rochelle from the sea. This immense project took several months, during which the siege continued. It became the talk of Europe, with military commanders from elsewhere, such as Spínola, travelling to La Rochelle to observe progress and offer advice to Louis and Richelieu. Twice in 1628 English fleets reappeared, but failed to penetrate the royal defences. Disease and famine took a heavy toll of the city, whose population fell from 28,000 to 6,000. By the autumn of 1628 the starving defenders could hold out no longer and surrendered on 28 October. Louis and Richelieu entered the city on 1 November. The king was magnanimous towards the surviving inhabitants: he exiled some leaders of the rebellion, but otherwise granted a general amnesty. The Huguenots retained their right to worship, but Catholicism was reintroduced into the city. In his treatment of the municipal institutions, Louis was more severe: he ordered the complete destruction of the fortifications and the abolition of the city's privileges. The insurrection was not completely over. Soubise's brother, Rohan, had raised rebellion in Languedoc, but the fall of La Rochelle knocked the heart out of the southern movement. When, in the spring of 1629, a royal force massacred the inhabitants of Privas, other Huguenot towns quickly surrendered. Louis XIII was in Alès near Nîmes, and it was there on 28 June 1629 that, following the advice of Richelieu, he issued the 'peace' or 'grace' of Alès: Huguenots kept their right to worship, but lost their military privileges.

The fall of La Rochelle and the Peace of Alès redefined relations between crown and Huguenots, whose defeat was so complete that never again did they rebel as a group. Thereafter they hoped that the crown would accept them as loyal subjects who could be left to enjoy their rights of worship. The fall of La Rochelle augmented the political prestige of the king and Richelieu, enabling them to crush powerful factions at court as effectively as they had the Huguenots. Foreign governments admired Louis's victory at La Rochelle, but recognized that his freedom of action in the international sphere would now be enhanced; indeed, within a short time Richelieu had signed the Treaty of Bärwalde with Sweden. The victory at La Rochelle strengthened the bonds between the king and Richelieu. The Peace of Alès was criticized by ultra-Catholic groups, who accused Richelieu of having dissuaded Louis from seizing this opportunity to eliminate heresy. Richelieu's answer was that internal peace was more important than religious conformity; the time was not right for both. Louis protected his minister, and developed with him a relationship which, while not without its tensions, endured until the cardinal's death in 1642.

## Richelieu and Louis XIII

Richelieu came from a well-to-do, noble family, and his career was assisted by powerful patrons. His family belonged to the old military nobility of Poitou, where they possessed the domain of Richelieu. His father, François du Plessis, distinguished himself in royal service during the Wars of Religion, and became a personal friend both of Henri III, who appointed him Grand Prévôt de France, and of Henri IV. François married Suzanne de la Porte from a wealthy Parisian legal and noble family. The fortunes of François's family suffered a set-back when he died in 1590, for most of his money was sunk in investments. Herein lay the origins of the later story that Armand-Jean du Plessis, Cardinal Richelieu, was born into poverty. He was not; and he belonged to a family which, through its royal connections, was favourably placed to advance the careers of Armand-Jean and his siblings. His eldest brother, Henri, served at the court of Henri IV and became an officer in the army. Armand-Jean trained for the priesthood. The family estate lay within the diocese of Luçon; his brother Henri and other members of the family used their influence with Henri IV to have Armand-Jean nominated to the bishopric in 1605 when aged only twenty. He was installed in 1607.

After the death of Henri IV, Richelieu began to appear at the royal court and preached before the royal family. He impressed Concini and Marie de' Medici with his erudition. When the Estates General met in 1614, Richelieu attended as a representative of the clergy of Poitou; once again, the skill with which he conducted himself commended itself to Marie de' Medici. In 1616 she and Concini brought him into the secretariat of foreign affairs. Because of his association with the queen mother and her favourite, Richelieu was exiled to the papal territory of Avignon after the assassination of Concini. It was only in March 1619 that he was allowed to leave, when the king ordered him to go to Marie and seek a resolution to the differences between Louis and his mother. Marie's admiration for Richelieu grew apace, and it was mainly through her patronage that in 1622 he was made a cardinal. This honour raised his political profile at a time when the young king was surrounded by cabals. From 1617 to his death in 1621, the duc de Luynes was principal minister; then the Brûlart faction took over until they were disgraced in 1624. In that year, Marie de' Medici persuaded her son to bring Richelieu into the royal council. Richelieu dared not take his new position for granted, especially as he was a protégé of the queen mother. He gradually distanced himself from Marie de' Medici and the ultra-Catholic or *dévot* policy with which she was associated. Richelieu regarded the view that Louis XIII should suppress Protestantism at home and join the Habsburgs in a grand strategy of Counter-Reformation as misconceived and dangerous. He preferred the *bon Français* strategy of Henri IV: respect for the religious clauses of the Edict of Nantes, and alliances with anti-Habsburg states, even if they were Protestant.

Richelieu forged a close relationship with the king which enabled the cardinal to survive the crises with which his career was studded. Although he held certain political principles with consistency, Richelieu was pragmatic in their execution. He was accused by his enemies of adopting amoral Machiavellian precepts of *raison d'état*. He certainly belonged to a generation which considered *raison d'état* a legitimate theoretical foundation of policy, but this is not to say that his policies lacked a basis in morality. He was well versed in recent French political treatises such as Jean Bodin's *Six livres de la république* (1576), which provided a stout defence of absolute monarchy. Richelieu was also influenced by the 'mechanical philosophy' which found expression in the thought of his contemporary, René Descartes. In science, this philosophy depicted the structure and nature of material bodies as determined by the interaction of tiny particles. Richelieu thought of internal and international order in such terms. He developed a concept of equilibrium which, in international relations, could be secured by balancing the Habsburg bloc with leagues of smaller states or territories under French protection. Medium or small territories, which individually counted for little, could find strength in unity under French leadership, just as combinations of particles of matter could affect larger objects. There was also a religious dimension to his search for equilibrium. Throughout his career, Richelieu sought to relate his policies to the moral teaching of the church. It was precisely in a harmonious, balanced Europe, contended Richelieu, that the Catholic church would progress towards the conversion of Protestants. In the alliances and accords which Richelieu signed with Protestant states, he insisted upon clauses according rights of worship to Catholics; thereby, he anticipated, the Catholic church would have a foundation from which to launch conversion.

Within France, equilibrium could be achieved only by a powerful monarch. The relationship which Richelieu developed with Louis XIII, sixteen years his junior, was one of mutual respect. Louis had a hesitant, retiring character, and given Richelieu's immensely imposing personality, the impression grew that the minister commanded the king. In fact, Louis, for all his diffidence, was quietly resolute and capable of knowing his own mind. Richelieu invariably deferred to him. All major decisions were taken by the king. Richelieu had his critics inside and outside the royal council, and had to contend with plots against himself. In November 1630, encouraged by victory over the Huguenots, Louis XIII purged the royal council of *dévot* elements who had been urging that Richelieu be disgraced. Marie de' Medici went permanently into exile, and *dévot* ministers such as Marillac were dismissed. After this episode, the 'Day of Dupes', Richelieu's position was secure. He brought his own 'creatures' into government. They included Abel Servien in the war department, Claude Bouthillier in finance, while in foreign affairs Richelieu made extensive use of the Capuchin friar, François le Clerc du Tremblay, better known as Père Joseph. After Père Joseph's death Richelieu employed the Italian Giulio Mazzarini, who changed his name to Jules Mazarin. Richelieu also selected writers to compose treatises explaining the rationale behind his policies. The works of some of these authors acquired enduring fame. They included *De la souveraineté du roi* (1632) by Cardin le Bret, and the *Panégyrique à Monseigneur le Cardinal de Richelieu* (1629) and *Le ministre d'état, avec le véritable usage de la politique moderne* (1631), both by Jean de Silhon.

## International Challenges and War

When Richelieu entered the royal council, the government was embroiled in the Valtelline crisis, followed in 1627 by that of the Mantuan succession. Richelieu was involved in both of these issues. If the Treaty of Monzón (1626) left much to be desired from the French point of view, the Treaty of Cherasco (1631), by which the French claimant succeeded to the Mantuan duchy and France retained the fortress of Pignerol, was a success. Richelieu prided himself on his knowledge of Italian affairs, but was less confident regarding Germany; for guidance on this latter region he relied on Père Joseph, who had a deep understanding of the politics of the empire. When the imperial electors met in Regensburg in 1630 to discuss the election of the king of the Romans, Père Joseph attended as an observer and was instrumental in persuading them to demand the dismissal of Wallenstein, while refraining from electing a king of the Romans.

One region about which Richelieu was extremely sensitive for geo-political reasons was Lorraine. This independent duchy between France and the Rhineland had linguistic and cultural links with France, and its three bishops of Metz, Toul and Verdun were French nominees. The dukes of Lorraine normally avoided antagonizing both Spain and France, but Charles IV, who succeeded as duke in 1624, made no secret of his Habsburg and Counter-Reformation sympathies. In the late 1620s, Richelieu feared that Charles might admit Spanish or imperial troops into Lorraine. In 1631 the cardinal was faced by an alternative possibility: that France's ally Gustavus Adolphus might occupy Lorraine. If Gustavus did so, he would doubtless use the occasion to wrest more subsidies from France. All of these prospects – the Spanish, imperial or Swedish investment of Lorraine – alarmed Richelieu, who sought to cajole Charles IV into allowing French troops into certain strong-points as a guarantee of security. Charles refused. Unwilling to delay, Louis XIII marched into Lorraine in December 1631. In 1632 he imposed the Treaty of Liverdun upon Charles, forcing him to cede control of several cross-ings over the river Meuse.

Relations between France and Lorraine declined further over the affair of Gaston d'Orléans, heir to the French throne. Gaston detested Richelieu and espoused the Catholic policy of the *dévots*. Gaston was an inveterate intriguer. During French negotiations with Charles IV of Lorraine in 1631, he travelled to Nancy and, without consulting Louis XIII, secretly married the duke's sister, Marguerite, in January 1632. It was several months before Louis XIII and Riche-lieu heard the news. They were furious, for the marriage of a prince of the blood required the consent of the king. Gaston's action was an affront and, given Louis XIII's childless state, potentially made a member of the house of Lorraine queen of France. Louis XIII appealed to the pope to have the marriage annulled on the ground that Gaston had been forced into the match. The argument was manifestly spurious and Rome refused. Louis XIII moved to punish Charles IV and solve the problem of Lorraine. He invaded again in 1633. Gaston fled to the Spanish Netherlands, and Charles IV was forced to abdicate (he joined the imperial army). As in Béarn a few years earlier, a *parlement* was created in Metz. Lorraine was annexed by Louis XIII in practice if not legally.

By this time France was moving towards intervention in Germany and the Netherlands. So far it had remained officially neutral, while providing financial support to its allies and securing the passages or 'gates' to northern Italy and Germany. However, if peace were signed within the Holy Roman Empire, France would be exposed to Habsburg aggression. Louis XIII ordered Richelieu to prepare for war. Richelieu made the necessary diplomatic arrangements. In addition to the alliance with Sweden, he had signed a secret treaty with the duke of Bavaria in 1631; Bavaria, he hoped, would lead a league of German Catholic princes under French protection. In 1635, Richelieu persuaded Sweden to renew the Treaty of Bärwalde and Poland the Treaty of Altmark. He signed agreements with the United Provinces, various Italian princes, and several towns in Alsace. He also expanded the army. In peace time it stood at about 10,000 men, but the suppression of the rebellions of the 1620s forced numbers up to 39,000 (the siege of La Rochelle alone required about 28,000). In 1634, Richelieu made plans to increase the army to 150,000, and although he never reached this figure, he was able to put between 75,000 and 90,000 troops into battle by the late 1630s.[12] He had also built up the navy. His aim was to expand the Atlantic fleet to forty-five ships of the line. Shipyards capable of building the ships were constructed or extended at ports such as Brest, Saint Malo and Bordeaux. Dieppe, Le Havre, Honfleur and other ports were equipped to build smaller vessels. By 1635, thirty-five ships of the line were in service; Richelieu further expanded the fleet by purchasing ships from the Dutch. He did not neglect the Mediterranean fleet, based upon the galley. The number of galleys rose from twelve in 1631 to twenty-one in 1635, and twenty-five by 1642.

The episode which led to war occurred in the winter of 1634–5. A French garrison in Trier was expelled by a Spanish force, and the archbishop of Trier took refuge in France. Louis XIII and his advisers decided that this 'outrage' merited a declaration of war; it was delivered to Philip IV on 19 May 1635. As was observed earlier (see above, p. 110), the war began inauspiciously for the French. In conjunction with the Dutch, they attacked the Spanish Netherlands, but came up against superior defences; and, as Richelieu had feared, the Peace of Prague released the emperor from military engagement in Germany, allowing him to send troops to assist the Spanish. In 1636 the Spanish invaded northern France and the emperor declared war. Although Corbie was relieved in November 1636, the situation remained so grim that Richelieu in 1637 sought an armistice, which Olivares rejected. By the end of the decade Richelieu was facing another crisis: rebellion at home.

## Popular Insurrection

War forced Richelieu to raise revenue and borrow on a scale which triggered widespread insurrection. Total governmental expenditure went up from about 41 million livres in 1630, to 65 million in 1633 and 100 million in 1636; then there was a slight decline to 88 million in 1639 and 89 million in 1642, the year of Richelieu's death, by which time warfare was accounting for about 72 per cent of expenditure.[13] To meet these costs, Richelieu resorted to borrowing, often at extortionate rates of up to 30 per cent. In addition, he raised levels of taxation. The principal direct tax was the *taille*, which in southern France was usually paid on land (*taille réelle*), and in northern France on the estimated wealth of the tax-payer (*taille personnelle*). Some sections of society – notably, although not exclusively, the church and the nobility – were exempted from most *taille*, which fell mainly on the peasantry. Richelieu drove up the *taille*. In 1632 it constituted 40 per cent of revenue, but by 1639 came to 54 per cent; this pattern continued until, in 1648, it reached 62 per cent of revenue.[14] In 1638 a new subsistence tax was introduced to maintain troops during the winter months when campaigning was suspended. Indirect taxes were augmented. Many were contracted out to 'tax farmers' who advanced money to the government, and then collected the revenue themselves. Two such taxes were *gabelle* on salt, and *aides* mainly on drink. The levels at which they were paid rose (the price of salt was doubled in 1634), while in various parts of the country new local charges were imposed on food and drink.

The government also exploited the sale of offices (*vente d'offices*). When new posts were created in, say, law courts, they were sold by the government. This practice went back to the fourteenth century, but had been formalized in 1522 when a government bureau, the *Recette des parties casuelles*, was created to oversee the process. Under the pressure of war, the government created and sold more offices, whether or not they were needed for 'professional' reasons. The cost of offices had been going up: for example, whereas the office of a *conseiller* in the *parlement* of Paris cost 60,000 livres in 1616, it was up to 120,000 livres by 1635; the office of *président à mortier* in the *parlement* of Rouen rose from 120,000 livres in 1623 to 186,000 livres in 1632 and continued on its upward track.[15] Not only did the government derive income from the sale of offices, it collected what was, in effect, an annual tax. Since 1604, office-holders (*officiers*) had been allowed to pay an annual sum (*paulette*), which permitted them to nominate their successors to the posts. Thereby, offices became a form of private property which families bequeathed from one generation to the next. From the government's point of view, the greater the number of *officiers*, the higher the *paulette*. Richelieu also resorted to a device known as *augmentation de gages*. Every office carried a 'salary' (*gages*), which was a certain percentage of its value. From time to time the government announced an increase in this 'salary', but in order to maintain the ratio between salary and value of offices, it required the *officiers* to lay out more capital; in short, an *augmentation de gages* was a thinly disguised form of borrowing.

The torrent of fiscal devices to which Richelieu subjected France unleashed widespread violence, for by the 1630s most of France was suffering economic recession. Risings took place in town and country. Between 1631 and 1636 there were anti-fiscal revolts in Paris, Lyon, Marseille, Bordeaux, Rennes and several smaller towns in Provence; in 1635 there were rural uprisings in the south-west. Most of these revolts were scattered and uncoordinated, but two occurred on a scale which forced the government to suppress them by diverting troops from the war front: those of the Croquants in 1636, and the Nu-pieds in 1639. The rising of the Croquants[16] began in 1636 around Angoulême and spread along the Garonne. It first manifested itself in town and country fairs where crowds gathered and protested against the taxes and other charges which the government was imposing. Manifestos bearing the slogan, '*Vive le roi sans gabelle*' or '*Vive le roi sans taille*', were sent to the king. There were attacks on tax-collectors, and in 1637 the revolt spread to Périgord, where it was given military organization by a local nobleman, La Mothe la Forest. The Croquant army seized Bergerac and other towns. La Mothe sent an appeal to Louis XIII to reduce taxes. Richelieu normally left the suppression of uprisings to local authorities, but this one was so general that he had to divert troops from the Spanish frontier. The royal army defeated the Croquants at La Sauvetat on 1 June 1637. Violence continued a little longer, but most Croquant leaders were captured and either imprisoned or sent to the galleys; about ten were executed. Richelieu granted an amnesty to rank-and-file Croquants on condition that they paid the *taille* in full.

The background to the rising of the Nu-pieds in Normandy in 1639 resembled that of the Croquants. Normandy was a wealthy province with a varied agriculture and industry, including salt, metal-lurgical and leather products; its ports, especially Rouen, were to the forefront of French maritime commerce. However, the economic life of Normandy in the 1620s and 1630s was hit by natural disasters and recession, and plague ravaged the population. Anti-fiscal riots had occurred at Caen in 1630 and 1631. The principal area through which taxes were collected in France was a *généralité*. Normandy contained two *généralités*, Rouen and Caen, but in 1636 a third was created, Alençon, by merging parts of the first two. The government sold the new offices, but increased the *taille* to be paid by Rouen and Caen. In December 1636 another forced loan was imposed upon Normandy, and in 1638 a new law court, a *Cour des Aides*, was created at Caen with ninety-three offices for sale. For several years Richelieu had been sending special commissioners, *intendants*, into the provinces to oversee the imposition and collection of taxes. By 1639, the *intendants* in Normandy were reporting widespread obstruction by urban and rural communities.

Alienation from the government had reached such a pitch that it was a rumour of a new tax, not an actual tax, which triggered the rising of 1639. The Cotentin peninsula was one of the main salt-producing regions of France; because of the corrosive effect of salt on shoes, the labourers worked bare-foot – *nu-pied*. This area was exempted from *gabelle*, but in 1639 a story spread that the tax was to be introduced (although the government had decided against doing so). When, on 16 July 1639, there arrived in Avranches a legal officer from Coutances, word spread that he carried a royal edict imposing *gabelle*. A crowd gathered, and the officer, whose business had nothing to do with the salt tax, was beaten to death. From this incident sprang the revolt which spread throughout Normandy, and involved almost every section of society. In the west it was predominantly rural in character, but in the east several large towns, including Caen and Rouen, were affected. Around Avranches, Nu-pied activists killed tax-collectors. In Caen and Rouen, gangs under the command of a populist leader, Jean Nu-pieds, assaulted and killed royal fiscal agents. The municipal authorities did little to restrain the rising, which was joined by nobles and even priests. In November 1639 royal forces occupied Caen and Avranches, and scattered the Nu-pied army. Richelieu, scandalized by the want of courage in the authorities, sent the chancellor, Pierre Séguier, to decide their punishment. Having ordered the execution of some rebel leaders and the consignment of others to the galleys, Séguier suspended the *parlement* of

Philippe. The birth of Louis, after so many years of the parents' childless marriage, was celebrated with public festivities. The possibility that Gaston d'Orléans would become king diminished. Gaston and other princes of the blood had never reconciled themselves to Richelieu's position, and had been implicated in several conspiracies against him. In 1641, for example, Louis de Bourbon, comte de Soissons, attempted to overthrow the cardinal by force. The king sent an army against Soissons, and, although it was defeated, Soissons was killed and his victorious but leaderless force dispersed. In 1642, the cardinal was again the object of intrigue, this time involving Henri d'Effiat, marquis de Cinq-Mars. Introduced into the royal court by Richelieu, Cinq-Mars became the favourite of Louis XIII, who developed a passion for this elegant and ambitious young man. Cinq-Mars made extravagant demands: a place in the royal council and a prestigious marriage. Richelieu obstructed Cinq-Mars, who attempted to take vengeance. He plotted with Gaston d'Orléans to have Richelieu assassinated, and foolishly signed a secret treaty with Olivares, who promised to send money and troops. Richelieu secured a copy of the treaty and presented it to the king. Cinq-Mars was arrested and executed.

By this stage, the health of both the king and his principal minister, neither of whom was physically robust, was breaking under the strain of government and war. In the summer of 1642 Richelieu's health collapsed and he died on 4 December. Louis XIII died a few months later, on 14 May 1643. News of the death of Richelieu was a cause of rejoicing in many sections of French society. This iron-willed minister was widely detested, especially by the generality of the nobility and *officiers*. The immense efforts which he had put into cultural activities (he was a bounteous patron of scholars, writers and artists, and founded the Académie Française in 1635) could not compensate for his reputation as an autocrat who had ridden roughshod over the normal procedures of law and taxation, usurped the powers of magistrates and financial *officiers*, suppressed noble and popular resistance, and bequeathed France a war to which no end was in sight. He remains a figure of controversy. The contending elements in his make-up – ideologue or pragmatist, self-seeker or disinterested servant of the king, man of steely self-control or sentimentalist – contribute to the abiding fascination which he exerts. What is beyond dispute is that he was one of the outstanding architects of the France of the seventeenth century. The principles which underlay his policies continued to guide the young Louis XIV and his ministers for at least twenty years after the cardinal's death; and it is possible to argue that those principles were never entirely abandoned by the Bourbons. Richelieu died an extremely wealthy man. He accumulated land and benefices, built a large palace in Paris close to the Louvre (he bequeathed it to the crown), and left a fortune of some 20 million livres.

## The Advent of Mazarin

During Richelieu's final days, the king made several visits to him. In their conversations, Richelieu recommended that Louis make further use of Mazarin, a naturalized Italian. Who, then, was Jules Mazarin who had so impressed Richelieu? His rise in French government was meteoric. This Roman-born papal diplomat first went to France in 1630 when the pope was attempting to mediate a settlement of the Mantuan succession. Mazarin had dealings with Richelieu, who was greatly impressed by his diplomatic acumen. His second visit was in 1634, this time as papal nuncio. Mazarin returned to Rome in 1636, where he served as an unofficial French agent seeking to limit the influence of the Habsburgs. As a reward, Louis XIII granted him letters of naturalization in 1639, and in 1640 Richelieu invited him back to France to enter his personal service and that of the crown. Mazarin agreed. To strengthen Mazarin's hand, Louis XIII had him made a cardinal in 1641 (although he was not ordained as a priest). Mazarin proved an immediate success. The quality of his work confirmed Richelieu's expectations, and his personal charm made a favourable impression at the royal court. When the future Louis XIV was baptized, Mazarin had the honour of being a godfather. When the question arose of a principal minister to succeed Richelieu, Mazarin had the attraction of belonging to no faction. The association between Louis XIII and Mazarin was brief, for within five months the king was dead. There followed a sequence of events which recalled the aftermath of the assassination of Henri IV. Louis XIV was a minor, and his mother, Anne of Austria, was recognized as regent at a *lit de justice* on 18 May 1643. She was assisted by a council of regency, with Mazarin as principal minister. Mazarin remained utterly devoted to Anne of Austria (there were rumours that they secretly married in 1643 or 1644), and she in turn protected him, just as her husband had defended Richelieu.

## The Years of Regency to the Frondes

Mazarin's status was called into question as early as the summer of 1643 when aristocrats led by François de Vendôme, duc de Beaufort, sought to revive the *dévot* programme and dismantle Richelieu's governmental team. As a first step they urged Anne of Austria to dismiss Mazarin. With the support of Gaston d'Orléans and the duc de Condé, the regent broke up the so-called *cabale des importants*. Beaufort was imprisoned and other conspirators were exiled to the provinces. Later in the year, Anne of Austria and Louis XIV moved their residence to Richelieu's former palace, the Palais Royal. Mazarin bought and expanded an adjoining property, his proximity to the regent being a potent political symbol.

Although his political style was different from that of Richelieu – he relied on guile and intrigue rather than on direct confrontation – he preserved Richelieu's strategy: war against Spain, supported by the necessary fiscal devices. In May 1643 excellent news arrived: Louis II, duc de Condé, had defeated the Spanish at Rocroi. This was followed by the extension of French control along the Moselle, and in 1644 the seizure of several key towns and fortresses on the Rhine: Philippsburg, Mainz, Spire and Worms. Other successes followed. In 1645 Mazarin mediated the Peace of Brömsebro between Sweden and Denmark, thereby alleviating pressure on France's ally, Sweden. He secured the marriage of a French princess, Marie de Gonzague-Nevers (daughter of Charles de Gonzague, duke of Mantua), to the king of Poland, Wladislaus IV; Marie later married Wladislaus's successor, John Casimir in 1649. Again in 1645, Mazarin persuaded George Rákóczy, prince of Transylvania to accept French subsidies in return for military support for the Swedish army. Mazarin's successes in Scandinavia, Poland and Transylvania threatened Austria from the north at a time when the French position in Germany also was improving. But then Mazarin, normally so sure in his grasp of international relations, lost his touch. He sacrificed his advantage in Germany by diverting forces to Flanders and Italy on campaigns which achieved little, and he alienated his Dutch allies by secretly proposing to Philip IV that France would deliver Catalonia into his hands if Philip would exchange it for the Spanish Netherlands. Philip IV revealed the plan to the Dutch, who felt betrayed by Mazarin. They had no qualms about opening their own peace negotiations with Spain, and in January 1648 a Dutch–Spanish treaty was signed;

it was confirmed by the Peace of Westphalia. When the Frondes broke out, Mazarin's critics cited such 'bungling', and his failure to secure a Franco-Spanish peace at Westphalia, as evidence of his un-suitability to be principal minister.

At home, Mazarin continued the endless rounds of borrowing, taxing, sale of offices and financial legerdemain which Richelieu had practised. In matters of finance he relied on Michel Particelli, seigneur d'Hémery, *contrôleur général des finances* from 1643, then *surintendant des finances* in 1647. In 1643 the anticipated revenue for 1644, 1645 and 1646 had already been spent. Particelli's aim at first was to reduce the burden of *taille* (and with it the incidence of rebellion) by finding means of taxing the wealthier sections of soci-ety. They included the city of Paris, which enjoyed immunity from *taille*. Richelieu had always avoided antagonizing Paris; he could cope with provincial rebellion, but had regarded rebellion by Paris as something to be avoided at all costs. Mazarin and Particelli aban-doned Richelieu's caution. In 1644 and 1646 they attempted to impose charges and forced loans upon Paris, but were resisted by the *parlement* and had to abandon the attempt. Even more drastic was the decision in 1645 to farm the *taille*. Indirect duties were often farmed out to financiers, but not the *taille*. Financial desperation was driving the government into increasingly irregular practices.

In 1648 Mazarin provoked the *parlement* of Paris into open resist-ance. The issue at stake was the renewal of the *paulette*. The rate at which *officiers* paid was revised every nine years, and the most recent cycle had ended in December 1647. Mazarin announced the renewal of the *paulette* on 30 April 1648, but on condition that four years' salary (*gages*) attaching to the offices in three of the sovereign courts (the *Grand Conseil*, the *Cour des Aides* and the *Chambre des Comp-tes*) be withheld; the *parlement* of Paris was not affected. This trans-parent attempt to buy off the *parlement* failed. On 13 May 1648 the four sovereign courts, including the *parlement*, issued a declaration of union, and agreed to elect deputies who would meet in the Cham-bre Saint Louis in the *parlement* to draw up a plan of action.

## The Chambre Saint Louis and the Spread of the Frondes

Anne of Austria and Mazarin reacted to the meeting in the Chambre Saint Louis with alarm. If the sovereign courts united, the political consequences could be incalculable. The regent ordered the deputies to disband. They refused and drafted twenty-seven demands which included the suppression of the *intendants*, a ban on the creation of new offices, the ending of extraordinary judicial procedures, and no new taxes without the consent of the sovereign courts. This was a conservative programme aiming to restore what the magistrates considered to be traditional procedures which Richelieu and Mazarin had undermined. The *parlement* of Paris backed up the articles with supplementary demands: the cancellation of contracts between the crown and tax farmers, and a reduction of the *taille* by a quarter. The government was in no position to resist, and made concessions. Particelli was dismissed, the *intendants* were recalled (except those on the frontiers), the *taille* was reduced by 12 per cent, and the *paulette* was renewed on terms favourable to *officiers*.

The *parlement* nevertheless continued its resistance, and the Council of Regency decided to arrest the 'trouble-makers', among whom Pierre Broussel was prominent. The opportunity came at a *Te Deum* celebrated in Notre Dame, on 26 August, to give thanks for another victory by Condé, at Lens. As Broussel and others were leaving the cathedral, they were seized by Anne of Austria's bodyguard. News of the arrest spread and provoked mass demonstrations. Broussel was a highly respected figure in Paris. He lived simply in a modest residence, and was popularly viewed as an incorruptible public servant whose probity contrasted with the grasping of tax farmers, courtiers and ministers of the crown. Over the next two days, barricades appeared throughout the city, and the violence came close to running out of control. On 28 August the regent ordered the release of Broussel and his colleagues, and relative calm returned. During the demonstrations the most common weapon used by the rioters was the 'fronde' (sling); the word became the sobriquet of the entire rising. There also appeared 'Mazarinades': pamphlets attacking the principal minister. Thousands were printed over the next few years, subjecting him to a torrent of abuse and malediction.

The *parlement* continued to debate its relations with the crown, but divisions began to appear in its ranks. Not all *parlementaires* were happy with the claims being made by the more radical magistrates, and some were sympathetic to the royal cause. Aware of discord in the *parlement*, Mazarin refrained from provocative action and awaited the return of the duc de Condé from the war. Condé was back by the end of the year. On the night of 5 January 1649, Mazarin and the royal family slipped out of Paris and went to Saint Germain. At the instruction of the regent, Condé blockaded the capital. Several princes and aristocrats, including Conti, Beaufort and Bouillon, proclaimed their solidarity with the *parlement*, as did Jean-François-Paul de Gondi, coadjutor to the archbishop of Paris and later Cardinal de Retz. Nevertheless, many municipal leaders, as well as *parlementaires*, feared the consequences of a long siege. Negotiations between the regency and the *parlement* took place, and peace was signed at Rueil, on 1 April 1649. The regent agreed to respect most of the demands of the Chambre Saint Louis, and the *parlement* ended its opposition. The 'Fronde of the *parlement*' was over for the time being.

### The Fronde of the Princes and the Union of the Frondes

The peace of Rueil did not end the Frondes. In January 1649, Gondi, acting as coordinator of aristocratic opposition to the regency, persuaded Conti, Beaufort and others to take an oath of unity. Gondi was infuriated when the *parlement* signed peace; in his opinion it had missed a prime opportunity to destroy Mazarin and force the queen mother to accept its programme. Meanwhile Condé, the hero of Rocroi and Lens, was behaving with cocksure arrogance and posing as the saviour of the crown. His sister, the duchesse de Longueville, engineered his reconciliation with the rest of his family, and persuaded him to support their attempt to accomplish what the *parlement* had failed to do: overthrow Mazarin and dictate terms to the regent. Mazarin attempted to neutralize Condé. Aware that Gondi had influence with the Parisian masses, Mazarin promised to secure him a cardinal's hat if he would keep Paris quiescent in the event of a royal *coup* against the princes. On 18 January 1650 Mazarin had Condé, his brother Conti and brother-in-law Longueville, arrested. Paris remained quiet, but there did break out rebellion in the provinces where the princes were governors or had estates: Normandy, Burgundy and Bordeaux. Mazarin gathered a royal army and, with Louis XIV at his side, moved against Bordeaux, which capitulated in October. By the end of the year, other forces of the princes had been defeated and Mazarin seemed to be in control of the kingdom.

Within a few weeks, however, he was forced to flee, thanks mainly to Gondi. Mazarin had made no move to have Gondi made a cardinal, and, feeling betrayed, Gondi persuaded Gaston d'Orléans, Gaston's daughter the duchesse de Montpensier, other aristocrats and *parlementaires* to unite against Mazarin. In February 1651 Gaston formally broke with Mazarin, who fled to Germany where he was protected by the archbishop of Cologne. Condé and the others were released from prison and returned in triumph to Paris. The Fronde of the princes had spread to lesser nobles, and in February 1651 there had taken place an assembly of notables which called for a meeting of the Estates General to review the issues behind the present crisis: the nature and limits of monarchy, the role of ministers, the functions of the sovereign courts and other legal bodies, relations between the crown and provincial assemblies, procedures for assessing and raising taxation and for borrowing money, and the methods whereby the kingdom was administered. Had an Estates General met, the institutional structures of the French state might have been changed, but events dictated otherwise. Now that Mazarin was in exile, the unity of the Frondeurs disintegrated. Gaston d'Orléans alienated *parlementaires* by letting it be known that an Estates General should enhance the powers of the princes and limit those of the *parlements*. Condé offended other aristocrats by his arrogance (he forbade his brother Conti from marrying the daughter of the duchesse de Chevreuse), and he quarrelled with Gondi over questions of precedence. By the autumn of 1651 there were deep divisions between and within the Frondeur camps.

The political context changed on 7 September 1651, Louis XIV's thirteenth birthday. On this day, solemnized at a ceremony in the *parlement* of Paris, the regency ended and Louis's majority was proclaimed. There could now be no pretence by Frondeurs that they were resisting an ill-advised regent and the principal minister. Anne of Austria, still in contact with Mazarin, urged her son to detach Gondi from other Frondeurs by requesting the pope to make him a cardinal. Louis XIV did so, and Gondi was nominated in February 1652 (he took the title of a family estate, Cardinal de Retz). By now the final and most destructive phase of the Fronde had begun, with rebellion by the duc de Condé. Condé had exchanged his governorship of Burgundy for that of Guyenne, and it was there that he assembled an army in September 1651 to march on Paris; he intended occupying the capital, and marshalling princes and aristocrats behind him.

At first he received little help from other Frondeurs, but when, in December 1651, Mazarin returned to France, the Frondeurs rediscovered their unity and rebellion spread; the chevalier de Rohan, for example, raised Anjou in support of the Fronde. A royal force commanded by Turenne suppressed the rising in Anjou. Condé was put under so much pressure that in April 1652 he fled to the Spanish Netherlands. The Spanish equipped him with troops, and he invaded France from the north. At the same time, Charles IV of Lorraine, also in Spanish pay, moved in from the north-east. The Paris basin became a war zone, widespread devastation being perpetrated by royalist and Frondeur armies alike. In July 1652, after being beaten by Turenne, Condé and his army took refuge in Paris and imposed a reign of terror. Mazarin knew that his best tactic was to let the hostility of Parisians towards Condé grow. In August 1652, many *parlementaires*, who were appalled at the conduct of Condé, left Paris; the *parlement* was now split. Deputations of leading Parisians went to the king at Compiègne, begging him to return to the capital. Louis and his mother agreed, on condition that Broussel resign from the *parlement*; Broussel did so. Aware that the end was near, Condé fled again to the Spanish Netherlands, and the duke of Lorraine withdrew from France. On 21 October 1652, Louis XIV made a triumphant return to Paris. Condé was stripped of his dignities, Cardinal de Retz was imprisoned, and Mazarin returned in February 1653. Gradually the provincial risings subsided, the last to do so being Bordeaux.

## The Character of the Frondes

The Frondes have been depicted as everything from a dress rehearsal for 1789 to anarchy devoid of historical significance. Neither of these extremes attracts much support among modern historians, but the Frondes do present considerable problems of interpretation. Historians set them within various contexts: the general crisis of the seventeenth century, the rise of absolute monarchy in France, an attempted revolution on the model of that in contemporary England, aristocratic feuding, or a rising of the people against an exploitative state. Each of these schemes has something to commend it, but none has won definitive approval. In part this is because much work remains to be done on topics such as the socio-economic context of the Frondes (especially in the provinces), and the multitude of socio-political grievances and ideas as indicated, for example, in the Mazarinades. Even so, some concluding statements are possible. The Frondeurs did have genuinely felt grievances. There was no denying that the Bourbon regime had been bringing to bear enormous financial and centralizing pressure upon its subjects; it had been by-passing regular financial and legal procedures, and had been calling into question many rights of intermediate bodies such as the *parlements*. The twenty-seven articles of the Chambre Saint Louis were not wild, ill-considered demands; they were an expression of the coordinated thought of experienced magistrates and judges concerned for the future of the kingdom. Had the sovereign courts limited their programme to the pursuit of reform, they might have made progress, but they allowed the question of Mazarin to cloud the issue. By making the political survival of Mazarin a matter of principle, they forced the regency to fight them on all fronts.

Behind the posturing and intriguing of princes and aristocrats, there were also genuine concerns. They too felt that Louis XIII with Richelieu, and now Anne of Austria with Mazarin, denied them their rightful influence upon government. Princes of the blood and aristocrats enjoyed their share of provincial governorships and high commands in the army, but felt excluded from political influence at the centre. Their conduct was complicated by what might be termed values of aristocratic honour: the notion that the social elites were not constrained by the moral and political standards applicable to commoners, but owed allegiance to precepts of honour. The point finds illustration in Condé. Brought up in a family which felt that it had missed the crown by a hair's breadth in 1589, he felt free to indulge in actions which would have been inadmissible in persons of lower rank. He saw no contradiction between commanding French forces against the Spanish in 1648, subduing Paris on behalf of the regent in 1649, then transferring his support to the Frondeurs, raising rebellion and accepting help from Spain. Such conduct by lesser mortals would have brought down the full retribution of the state. Condé, and others of his ilk, regarded it as justified by their code of aristocratic honour.

At certain stages the Frondes resembled a civil war, but never threatened to become as serious as the Wars of Religion or the contemporary crisis in England. Whereas earlier civil conflicts in France often contained a religious element, the Frondes did not. The Huguenots remained loyal to the crown between 1648 and 1653, being no longer willing to risk their religious 'rights' by resisting the king. The 'Puritan ideology' which confronted the crown in England had no equivalent in the Frondes. Again, the *parlement* of Paris and other sovereign courts never created a 'parliamentary cause', as in England. There were too many divisions between and within the sovereign courts for such a constitutionally portentous development. Weak and vulnerable though the regency often was, it represented a royal authority whose legitimacy nobody challenged; the great question was what kind of monarchy France should have, not whether it should have a monarchy at all. Many parts of France were untouched by the Frondes, although areas that were affected suffered heavily: not only the Paris basin, but parts of the Loire, Anjou, Champagne, Poitou, Guyenne and Provence. Ultimately, the divisions between Frondeurs reduced them to a disparate collection of factions incapable of sustaining a united opposition to the regency. The Frondes undoubtedly presented the regime with a crisis, but it was one which lacked the capacity either to turn into '1789' or into the England of the 1640s and 1650s.

## The Post-Fronde Years to the Death of Mazarin

The end of the Frondes brought only relative peace to the kingdom, for war against Spain still had to be fought and the royal treasury was all but empty. The *parlement* of Paris still harboured ambitions to influence policy. In April 1655 it made plans to discuss financial edicts which it had already registered; on 13 April Louis XIV entered the *parlement* and instructed the assembly to limit itself to the registration of edicts, and to desist from debating them. This is the occasion on which he is reputed to have stated: *'l'état c'est moi.'* Louis was receiving tuition in government from Mazarin, who had come to the conclusion that, after his own death, the king should rule personally. Louis attended meetings of ministers and learned the techniques required to govern a large kingdom. When Mazarin died in 1661 and Louis announced his intention to rule personally, the king was not reacting against his former principal minister, he was fulfilling Mazarin's wish.

There were still rumblings of rebellion. In 1658, ex-Frondeur nobles in Normandy were troublesome, and along the Loire an anti-fiscal peasant uprising occurred. In the south, the provincial estates of Languedoc and Provence demanded reductions in taxation, and in 1658 and 1659 there was serious violence in Marseille and Aix. The war against Spain at last was turning in France's favour, and relations had improved with England (an alliance was signed in 1657), and with German princes (in 1658 France joined the League of the Rhine which aimed to limit the influence of the new emperor, Leopold I).

Rouen for a year, dismissed some members permanently, and withdrew the fiscal and legal privileges of the city. Other towns, including Avranches and Caen, received similar treatment.

The government coped with the revolts of the 1630s because they remained localized and poorly coordinated. They were a price which Richelieu was willing to pay in the interest of pursuing war against Spain, but they spelt a danger which the regime could not ignore indefinitely. Risings had united peasants, townspeople, rural and municipal elites against crown fiscal policy. The crown was in danger of being associated with exploitation and disunity. Popular and elite hostility was directed mainly at Richelieu rather than Louis XIII, but the regime could not assume that such a distinction would invariably be made. The reluctance of financial and legal *officiers* to take a stand against rebels and even, on occasion, their readiness to assist them, was particularly disturbing. The grievances of *officiers* were many, but the intrusion of *intendants* was a major cause of animosity. *Intendants* could, and did, override the authority of local *officiers*. The *parlements* expressed their objections to the crown, calling upon Louis XIII to respect the normal legal and financial procedures, but to little avail. Richelieu continued to employ *intendants*, not for ideological reasons, but under the pressure of war. War, not political philosophy, was the determining factor.

## The Last Years of Richelieu and Louis XIII

While domestic tensions and rebellion continued to reverberate, the war against Spain ground on indecisively. In 1635, Richelieu had engaged a mercenary commander, Prince Bernard of Saxe-Weimar, to raise an army and fight in Germany. Bernard achieved a striking success in December 1638 when he captured the fortress at Breisach, which commanded a stretch of the Rhine crucial to Spanish communications between Milan, the Netherlands and central Germany. The news brought relief to Richelieu, for a few weeks earlier the French had suffered a humiliating defeat against a smaller Spanish force at Fuenterrabía on the Franco-Spanish border. In 1639, the French military position fluctuated, but was helped in 1640 by the risings in Catalonia and Portugal which weakened the Spanish war effort.

At home, events of major dynastic importance occurred: in 1638 the future Louis XIV was born, followed in 1640 by his brother

Spain was facing enormous internal difficulties, and agreed to the negotiations which culminated in the Peace of the Pyrenees. Louis travelled south in 1660 to meet his bride, Maria Teresa, and escort her to Paris. Mazarin accompanied the king, but fell ill. He recovered a little in the summer, but as the year wore on he declined. He died on 9 March 1661.

Mazarin had modelled himself on Richelieu. He built up teams of 'clients' through whom he transmitted his ministerial authority; some, such as Fouquet and Colbert, were to be employed by Louis XIV in ministerial positions. Like Richelieu, he was a patron of scholarship and the arts; and, like Richelieu, he amassed a huge fortune, of about 35 million livres. In his will Richelieu had provided for the construction of a magnificent chapel at the Sorbonne. Mazarin bequeathed money for a new college at the University of Paris. The Collège des Quatre Nations, as it was known, was built facing the Louvre on the opposite bank of the Seine, another architectural symbol of the special relationship between this remarkable Italian and the king of France.

# 5

# *Western Europe, 1603–1660: Britain and the United Provinces*

---

## BRITAIN AND IRELAND, 1603–1660

England, Wales, Scotland and the United Provinces were bulwarks of Protestantism, but this statement requires qualification. There were different and contending tendencies among the Calvinists of the United Provinces, and the religious commitments of the English and Welsh were extremely diverse. Scotland was predominantly Presbyterian, with a large Catholic minority concentrated in the north. Ireland was overwhelmingly Catholic, the established Anglican church – the Church of Ireland – commanding the allegiance only of an English-speaking minority. The movement of Scots Presbyterians into Ireland added further complications. In an age which assumed that socio-political stability was conditional upon religious conformity, the composite kingdom of England (with the principality of Wales), Scotland and Ireland looked a recipe for disaster.

In 1603, James VI of Scotland became James I of England and Ireland at the age of thirty-seven. He and his son Charles I faced problems akin to those of the Habsburgs in Spain. Like Castile in the Iberian peninsula, England was the most populous of the kingdoms. In 1600 it numbered about 4 million, Wales about 380,000, Scotland under a million and Ireland about 1.4 million. By 1700 the figures were 5 million for England, 1 million for Scotland, 400,000 for Wales and 2 million for Ireland. England thus accounted for some 60 per cent of the population of the three kingdoms. Should these kingdoms, with their differences of language, legal and judicial customs and religious affiliation, be treated as separate entities, or should moves be made towards the kind of uniformity which Olivares desired for Spain? James I was attracted by this latter course. In the first year of his reign he proclaimed that England and Scotland were to be known as 'Britain', and combined their flags into a Union flag. For all his efforts, he never succeeded in persuading his English and Scottish subjects that they were one people. His tentative moves towards a single legal code for the two countries, and his suggestion that England and Scotland might adopt a common monetary system, elicited little positive response in either country. For the time being 'Britain' remained an idea rather than a reality.

## Social and Economic Change in England

James inherited an English kingdom in which the social elites were increasingly defensive over their status. Some noble families died out altogether (21 of the 63 peers of the realm in 1558 had no direct descendant in the House of Lords in 1641).[1] They were replaced by others ascending the social scale. Old land-owning families sold estates to convert their wealth into money or pay off debts. Between 1601 and 1640, about one-third of the manors of England changed hands by sale. One group which profited was the gentry, a stratum between the nobility and commoners. In the sixteenth century, gentry families had purchased former church property, and further increased their possessions by buying noble land. They also acquired royal property. Elizabeth had sold about half of the royal domain to pay for warfare, and James I continued to dispose of land. The gentry played a prominent role in local and national life: they supplied a high proportion of the justices of the peace and members of the House of Commons. The crown's financial problems exacerbated tensions among the elites of English society. James I created and sold titles and invented the rank of baronet, which was also sold. The effect was to ennoble commoners on an unprecedented scale. Between 1603 and 1628, the number of English peers almost doubled to 126; between 1603 and 1641 the Irish peers quadrupled from 25 to 100, and in the same period almost 3,300 knighthoods were created and sold in England.[2] Old noble families were offended; the king, who in their opinion ought to uphold tradition and social distinction, was undermining both.

In the economic sphere, England was experiencing a commercial revolution. In the sixteenth century England's principal export was woollen cloth. Until the 1580s, most went to European markets from London via Antwerp, but Antwerp's standing as an international entrepôt declined as it suffered the effects of the Dutch revolt against Spain. English merchants had to find new outlets, and were helped by the production in East Anglia of 'New Draperies': worsted-type cloths which had a wider appeal than the rougher woollen products of the past. Diversification did encounter the difficulty of England's war against Spain from 1587, which cut off the markets of Spain and its dependencies from English merchants. One of James I's first acts was to sign peace with Spain in 1604, a measure received with approbation by English exporters. In the early 1600s, Bristol and ports on the south and east coasts were trading their woollen goods in the Baltic as well as the North Sea; merchants from London were exploiting markets in Spain, Portugal and the Mediterranean as far as Constantinople. The pattern of English trade in the Atlantic and Asia was also changing, although the economic consequences were not significant until the second half of the century. English colonies grew in North America from 1607, and in the West Indies from the 1620s; in 1600 the East India Company was founded with the aim of developing Asian commerce. Commerce with the Americas remained at a low level until the 1660s, but Asian trade did better, pepper being imported into England in quantities sufficient to permit re-export to the Mediterranean. Even so, exports continued to be dominated by cloth, which in 1660 still constituted 80 per cent of the total. Although the first half of the century was a period of economic decline in most parts of Europe, English merchants displayed enterprise and ingenuity. This was to benefit Charles I who, between 1629 and 1640, ruled without calling parliament and therefore needed the contribution which customs dues made to his income.

## Ireland under James I

Along with England, James inherited Ireland, which had been a kingdom since only 1541; before that it was a 'lordship'. Ireland had a parliament which since 1494 had been subject to Poynings's law (so named after Sir Edward Poynings, lord deputy of Ireland, 1494–5): it met only with the king's permission, and its legislation required the consent of the king and his privy council in England. At the beginning of the reign of James I, the 'Nine Years War' or 'Tyrone's rebellion' had just ended. This rising of Gaelic lords led by Hugh O'Neill, earl of Tyrone, had received Spanish aid, and for a time had all but eliminated English authority in Ireland. However, the military position was reversed, and in 1603 O'Neill and his supporters surrendered, leaving James in control of the whole country. In 1607, O'Neill, with Rory O'Donnell, earl of Tyrconnell, and Cúconnacht Maguire, lord of Fermanagh, fled from Ireland. This 'flight of the earls' deprived Gaelic Ireland of its principal leaders. James's predecessors had exerted direct control only over Dublin and an area around it known as 'the Pale'. Their rule over the rest of the country depended on the compliance of Gaelic and 'Anglo-Irish' lords; if, as the Nine Years War showed, Gaelic lords turned against the crown and obtained foreign assistance, English authority was in grave danger. James exploited the flight of the earls by extending a policy pursued by the Tudors: plantation. This involved bringing English settlers into strategically important areas, 'planting' them on land taken from native Irish, and introducing English agriculture, language, law and Protestantism. Thereby, it was hoped, the English presence in Ireland would be augmented, the security of Ireland enhanced, and the native Irish 'anglicized'. The Church of Ireland would undertake the task of converting the native Irish. A plantation had taken place in Munster in the 1560s. It was dispersed during the Nine Years War, but was re-established thereafter. By 1611, about 14,000 English settlers were living in Munster, and about 22,000 by 1641.

In 1609 James I authorized another plantation, this time in Ulster, the backbone of Gaelic Ireland. James and his advisers calculated that if Ulster could be 'anglicized', it was only a matter of time before the rest of the country followed suit. English and Scottish 'undertakers' contracted to bring in settlers. The region between Derry on the Foyle and Coleraine on the Bann was granted to a group of London companies incorporated into the Irish Society. The Society developed the two ports (renaming Derry by adding the prefix 'London'), and undertook to bring in settlers. The Ulster plantation proved to be less successful than the government intended. The number of immigrants was disappointing, and many native Irish remained. By 1641, there were about 15,000 English and Scots in Ulster, many of the latter being Presbyterian. Ulster developed a mixture of Catholics, Anglicans and Presbyterians which was unique in the three kingdoms. Other plantations took place; some, as in County Down, were private enterprises by Scotsmen, while others, as in Leitrim and Longford, were supervised by the crown.

## James I, the English Parliament and Foreign Policy

Relations between James I and the English parliament fluctuated for reasons similar to those which affected monarchs and assemblies else-where: conflicting claims over prerogatives and rights. The Stuart kings considered that they ruled personally, while at the same time respecting the liberties of their subjects. Parliament perceived itself as the upholder of those liberties. Discord arose over the limits of royal authority, and it was usually finance which triggered disputes. Eliza-beth had left royal finances in a parlous state. Necessity forced James and Charles to attempt to extend the boundary of their fiscal powers, while parliament resisted in the name of the rights of the king's subjects. Although he held a divine right theory of monarchy, James I had the good sense to avoid unnecessarily 'despotic' acts; thus, he refrained from imprisoning people without trial. The growth in the size of parliament also forced James to handle it with care. Lords and Commons both expanded, the latter from 467 members in 1601 to 507 in 1640. During James's reign, four parliaments met: the first from 1604 to 1610, the second for a few weeks in 1614 (the Addled Parliament, so called because it passed no legislation), the third from 1621 to 1622, and the fourth in 1624. The Gunpowder Plot (1605) created a wave of sympathy for James, and he made a practice of attending the opening of each session of parliament; but he found himself falling foul of the Commons over financial levies. It is indica-tive of relations between James and parliament that, apart from the Addled Parliament, James ruled between 1610 and 1621 without calling the assembly. The irregularity with which parliament assem-bled did not offend any contemporary 'constitutional' principles. Parliament was but one source of advice to the king, who also con-sulted ministers, nobles, prelates and indeed anybody whom he wished. The English parliament was like the diets or estates of con-tinental Europe: it was called as and when the king desired.

Early in his reign, and without consulting parliament, he imposed additional customs duties on a wide range of goods. Since the four-teenth century, English monarchs had imposed duties only with the consent of parliament, although Mary and Elizabeth occasionally departed from this tradition. James claimed that he was simply following their precedent. In 1606 a merchant, John Bate, refused to pay duties and was taken to court by the crown. Although the decision went in favour of the king, parliament took the view that the case was won on a technicality, and that the principle of no duties without consent remained intact. The parliamentary debates of 1610 focused on this subject. When James's chief minister, Robert Cecil, earl of Salisbury, had it explained to the Commons that royal revenues were insufficient, and that it was necessary for the king to impose duties as he saw fit, the Commons responded with a Petition of Grievances calling for the abolition of duties to which they had not agreed. Between 1611 and 1621, when no parliament other than that of 1614 met, James raised money chiefly by selling titles and monopolies, and by raising customs duties. When they assembled again in 1621, the Commons protested against these 'extraordinary' measures with such vehemence that James sacrificed his chancellor, Francis Bacon, who was impeached.

In foreign affairs, James inherited a war against Spain when he ascended the English throne. After signing peace in 1604, he set about constructing a foreign policy appropriate to the newly created 'Britain'. Scottish and English policies were harmonized, and James conceived of Britain as a mediating force between the Catholic and Protestant states of continental Europe. He sought to advance this objective by the marriages which he planned for his children. In 1613 his daughter Elizabeth married the Protestant, Frederick, elector of the Palatinate (later to be 'king of Bohemia'), and for his son Charles, James sought a Spanish marriage. The latter was not secured, for it was to the house of Bourbon that the Spanish turned for spouses, not the Stuarts. This did not deter James from pursuing good relations with Spain, convinced that this served both Britain's interest and that of peace in Europe.

In parliament, most of whose members found it difficult to abandon the assumption that Spain was England's permanent enemy, James's pro-Spanish policy was a cause of disquiet. When the Bohemian rising of 1618, which led to the elector of the Palatinate becoming 'king of Bohemia', was followed by the disaster at White Mountain, Protestants in England were loud in their denunciations of a 'Habsburg plot'. When parliament met in 1621, members demanded military intervention to restore Frederick to Bohemia, but they were willing to vote only a small sum to that end. James remained convinced that it was wiser to cultivate relations with Spain and attempt to restore Frederick by negotiation. In 1623, the prince of

Wales, accompanied by the duke of Buckingham, travelled allegedly incognito to Spain (they took the names of Smith and Brown) to arrange a Spanish marriage. They returned to England empty-handed. James accepted that his pro-Spanish policy had failed, and that the Habsburgs would have to be fought. In 1624 he agreed to a marriage between the prince of Wales and a French princess, Henriette-Marie, and signed with the Dutch Republic an alliance which the French joined later in the year. In 1625 a British expedition was sent to restore Frederick to the Palatinate. It proved an embarrassing failure.

## Charles I, Europe and the English Parliament

James I died on 27 March 1625. His twenty-five-year-old son Charles I lay under the spell of his father's favourite, George Villiers, who had been knighted in 1616 and thereafter was promoted rapidly by James I. Villiers was made earl of Buckingham in 1617, marquis in 1618, and duke in 1623. This last title provoked hostility among other peers, for the rank of duke was normally reserved for the royal family. James handed powers of patronage to Buckingham, and heeded his advice on matters of high politics. Charles too revered the favourite, who persuaded him to undertake the ill-fated journey to Madrid in 1623. In spite of its failure, Charles did not hold Buckingham responsible. It was Buckingham who negotiated the marriage of Charles to Henriette-Marie. Charles married the French princess by proxy on 1 May 1625. She arrived in England in June. Parliament was unsettled by the marriage, for Henriette-Marie was Catholic. Charles had assured parliament that anti-Catholic legislation would remain in force, but he had also informed Louis XIII that concessions would be granted to Catholics. This was one of many occasions when Charles made contradictory promises to different parties. When Henriette-Marie arrived, she brought over four hundred attendants including about thirty priests, for the marriage settlement allowed for a Catholic establishment at the royal court. Their presence in London and Henriette-Marie's thoughtless behaviour (she openly paraded her Catholic belief) caused resentment not only in parliament, but within the wider populace. A year later, in response to public pressure, Charles ordered most of his queen's attendants and priests back to France.

At his first parliament in 1625, he sought money to finance the Danish invasion of Germany. The Commons refused, several members subjecting Buckingham to fierce criticism. In order to protect the duke, Charles dissolved parliament. He and his favourite attempted to cultivate a more compliant mood among parliamentarians by resolute strokes of foreign policy. In October 1625, Charles signed the Treaty of Southampton with the Dutch Republic, and declared war on Spain. A fleet was assembled to attack Cádiz. Buckingham was involved in organizing the expedition, which again proved a fiasco. It was placed under the command of Sir Edward Cecil, an admiral who had never been to sea. Although he landed troops near Cádiz, they made little progress and had to be taken on board again. Supplies ran out and the fleet returned to England in ignominy. Desperately short of money, Charles called another parliament in February 1626. In the aftermath of Cádiz, the Commons recognized that a serious financial effort was required, but refused to vote funds so long as Buckingham was close to the king. Charles imprisoned some of Buckingham's severest critics, but parliament still insisted that any grants of money must be preceded by the duke's removal. Charles dissolved parliament in June 1626.

Still short of funds, Charles remained embroiled in European affairs. In spite of his marriage to Henriette-Marie, he felt obligations to the Huguenots. Moreover, Richelieu was developing a maritime strategy whose implications for England were adverse (see above, p. 133). In June 1627, Buckingham commanded the fleet which sailed to 'assist' the Huguenots of La Rochelle. This episode too was a disaster. The English force failed to capture forts on the Ile de Ré, and returned home in November 1627. Two further expeditions in 1628 proved equally futile. To pay for these enterprises, Charles had levied duties, tonnage and poundage, without parliamentary approval,[3] and attempted to impose a forced loan upon the country. The Lord Chief Justice, who challenged the legality of the loan, was dismissed, and several knights who refused to pay were imprisoned. Charles called his third parliament in March 1628. It went on the offensive by drawing up a Petition of Right demanding no taxation without parliamentary approval, no arbitrary arrest, and no compulsory billeting of troops. Charles reluctantly consented and the Commons voted him subsidies, although they were insufficient to meet his foreign policy requirements. More calls were made for the dismissal of Buckingham, and once again Charles prorogued parliament to protect his favourite. It was to no avail, for on 23 August 1628 Buckingham was assassinated. Charles was devastated, but there was no denying that the death of Buckingham removed one of the most disruptive elements in the relationship between Charles and parliament. Even so, cooperation proved difficult. The king called parliament again in January 1629, but the abiding problem of customs duties kept him at loggerheads with the Commons. A rancorous session ended when Charles dissolved parliament in March. He did not call it again until 1640. Shortage of money forced him to reduce expenditure on foreign affairs. He signed peace with France in 1629 and Spain in 1630.

## The Question of Religion

By the early 1630s, the question of religion had become as pressing as that of finance. The Tudors had preserved England from the religious wars which affected much of continental Europe, and Elizabeth had reached a religious settlement in which the Anglican church encompassed several theological 'schools'. James I dreamed that the stabilizing role in international relations which he envisaged for Britain would be paralleled in the ecclesiastical sphere: if a degree of liturgical and theological conformity could be created within and between the Reformed Church of Scotland and the Church of England, this might inspire churches on the continent to follow suit. Religion, so long a cause of socio-political conflict, could become a force for stability across Europe. The Church of England was poorer in material terms than in pre-Reformation days, for much of its property had been sequestered in the aftermath of the Reformation. There was a shortage of clergy, and Catholic priests were entering the country and, with some success, attempting to reconvert members of the gentry and nobility.

James I took a personal interest in theology; indeed, in 1604 he organized a conference at Hampton Court, where theologians ranging across a broad Protestant spectrum debated their positions. It was as a result of this conference that James approved a new translation into English of the Bible. Two versions of the Bible currently were used: the 'Bishops' Bible', read in most church services, and the 'Geneva Bible', which was popular among the laity. A team of fifty-four scholars began work in 1606 and completed the task in 1611, when the first edition was printed. A second edition with over 400 changes appeared in 1614. It took about forty years for this Authorized Version to supplant others in popular use; but in a country where the reading of the Bible became part of the daily routine of the life of literate families, the triumph of this standard text was to be of profound significance, both to the religious and literary history of England.

In liturgy and theology, James favoured a 'middle way' or 'broad church' capable of holding together the Protestants of Britain and Ireland. A strong element of Calvinism had emerged within the Anglican church. It did not necessarily challenge the authority of bishops, many of whom were themselves attracted by Calvinist theology, but it included a minority of 'godly people' or Puritans who regarded themselves as members of the community of the elect whom God had predestined to salvation. James refrained from favouring any particular section within the church, and made ecclesiastical appointments in the interest of the middle way. In 1604 he appointed as archbishop of Canterbury Richard Bancroft, who was no lover of Calvinism, but as his successor in 1611 James selected the Calvinist George Abbott. In Scotland, James chose bishops who would follow the middle way; they included Alexander Forbes and his namesake Patrick Forbes, each of whom served as bishop of Aberdeen. It was far from easy to extend Anglican practices to Scotland. Although a general assembly of the church held in Glasgow in 1610 restored the episcopacy, Presbyterians were opposed to the move. In 1617 James visited his homeland and insisted that the Church of Scotland adopt Five Articles dealing with religious practice.[4] Although an ecclesiastical assembly at Perth accepted them in 1618 and the Scottish parliament in 1621, the articles were deeply resented and widely ignored. Recognizing the potential political danger in insisting on their application, James quietly let them fall into abeyance. In England, most bishops under James I were conscientious administrators if not spiritual giants, and they generally sought to make the 'broad church' work. The prelacy contained fine scholars such as Lancelot Andrews, bishop of Winchester, and Joseph Hall, bishop of Norwich. The number of men entering holy orders also increased; so did their intellectual calibre as the church moved towards a clergy of university graduates. Whereas in 1580 only 23 per cent of the clergy in the diocese of Worcester were graduates, the figure rose to 52 per cent in 1620 and 84 per cent in 1640; by this latter date, the figure for the diocese of Oxford was 96 per cent.[5]

Under Charles I the ecumenical aims of James I were replaced by a provocative drive towards religious uniformity; and as the political atmosphere in England turned increasingly confrontational, religion once again became a source of socio-political division. The 'broad church' of James I had maintained equilibrium between, on one side, those who stressed the eucharist in worship, the location of the altar at the east end of the choir, and its isolation by a rail at which communicants had to kneel, and on the other, 'godly Calvinists', including Puritans, for whom worship focused on the reading and preaching of the word. The latter denounced 'ritualism' as 'Romish idolatry'. This view was shared by Calvinists of the Church of Scotland. They and their English colleagues were alarmed by the favours which Charles bestowed upon 'Romish' clergy, who benefited from most of the promotions to the English prelacy between 1625 and 1641. The choice of William Laud as archbishop of Canterbury conformed to this pattern.

Laud, who was forthright in his high church convictions, was advanced rapidly by Buckingham and Charles. He served as bishop of St David's (1621) before going on to Bath and Wells (1626), London (1628) and Canterbury (1633). In all of these posts Laud was an energetic reformer who aspired to purge worship of its 'Calvinist' elements. His concerns were not just liturgical. Convinced that the mission of the church had been compromised by its loss of property, and that a materially poor clergy was vulnerable to pressure by secular patrons, he used his influence to enforce the payment of tithes by the laity, and pressed wealthy laymen to make generous bequests to the church. He also insisted that the clergy adhere to the Thirty-nine Articles.[6] This was a cause of much tension, for some of the articles raised Calvinist objections, especially those dealing with the creeds, predestination, and the authority of the church. Laud's approach to the Sabbath caused further offence among 'godly people'. Christian churches traditionally adapted Jewish practice by treating Saturday as the Sabbath, with its prohibitions on labour. Sunday, the first day of the week, was 'the Lord's Day' when worship and recreational pursuits took place. Many preachers of a Calvinist persuasion (including Scottish Presbyterians) transferred the Sabbath to Sunday, which they devoted exclusively to worship. Laud denounced Sabbatarianism, insisting that Sunday could also be a day of diversion. In this and other controversies he was supported by the king. Indeed, Charles and Laud operated a mutually supportive pact: the king backed Laud's ecclesiastical policy, and the archbishop used his authority to ensure that the clergy preached regularly on the theme of obedience to the king.

Although Laud had no formal standing in Ireland and Scotland, he exercised influence via the king or, in the case of Ireland, through Charles's Lord Deputy from 1632, Thomas Wentworth. The Church of Ireland in the early seventeenth century became increasingly

Puritan and 'British' in ethos. Most bishops were English, and most clergy were English or Scottish Puritans. In James Ussher, the Church of Ireland had a native-born primate of the greatest intellectual distinction, his studies of biblical chronology earning him an international reputation. As archbishop of Armagh since 1625, he sought to defend the church against the interventions of Laud. He was only partly successful, for in 1634, at Laud's recommendation, Wentworth appointed John Bramhall, an Englishman of high church convictions, as bishop of Derry. When a synod met in Dublin that year, Bramhall was instrumental in forcing through its acceptance of the Thirty-nine Articles (hitherto the Church of Ireland had its own articles of faith). Thereafter Ussher was steadily sidelined as Bramhall, with the support of Laud and Wentworth, worked to bring the Church of Ireland into conformity with that of England.

In Scotland, Laud had no direct authority; moreover, the Scottish prelacy was composed of Scotsmen, there being nothing equivalent to the imposition of Englishmen in the Irish sees. Laud operated through the king, whom he had accompanied to Edinburgh when Charles was crowned in 1633. Through Charles, he sought to extend Anglican practices into Scotland, and in 1636 plans were announced to introduce a modified version of the Prayer Book. Scottish bishops prepared drafts of the text, to which Laud responded with 'fraternal advice' bringing it as close as possible to the English version. Presbyterians were shocked at what they regarded as a slide towards Arminianism and 'English' forms of worship. When the new Prayer Book was first used, in St Giles's Cathedral in Edinburgh in 1637, there was a riot which sparked off a chain of supportive protest. An assembly of Scottish nobles and clergy petitioned the king to abandon the Prayer Book; by the end of the year, committees ('Tables') were formed to coordinate further opposition. Resistance was led not only by leading members of the clergy such as Alexander Henderson and Robert Baillie, but by noblemen such as the marquis of Montrose and the earl of Argyll. In 1638, opponents of the king's reforms launched the National Covenant in an attempt to draw the nation together. In November 1638 a general assembly of the Scottish church met in Glasgow. It rescinded the ecclesiastical legislation of James and Charles, and disowned bishops and clergy who had conformed to the Prayer Book. Whereas James VI and I, when faced with Scottish resistance to his religious proposals, prudently had let them lapse, Charles denounced the Covenanters as rebels and gathered a small army in England. After a fruitless campaign, he signed a truce with the Covenanters at Berwick in June 1639. He planned another invasion, and recalled Wentworth from Ireland to assist him. Wentworth and Laud gave Charles the same advice: he needed a much larger army, and that meant recalling parliament to vote the necessary funds.

## The Religious Situation in Ireland, 1629

Over 90 per cent of the population of Ireland were Roman Catholic, and although anti-Catholic legislation existed, it was enforced by the English authorities in Dublin only spasmodically. It was generally limited to requiring Catholic officers, including members of parliament, to take an oath of loyalty to the crown and attend Anglican worship at least once a year ('occasional conformity'). Catholic priests conducted private and even public worship to the extent that in 1629 the government forbade the public celebration of mass. Catholics included a wealthy and powerful minority who regarded themselves as English, not Irish: some 2,000 families of 'Old English' whose forebears had gone to Ireland before the Reformation. Traditionally they upheld the interest of the crown, but remained Catholic. The Old English attempted to prove their loyalty to the crown when England went to war with Spain in 1625 by offering to undertake the defence of Ireland should the Spanish invade. In 1628, a commission of Old English went to England and secured concessions ('Graces') from Charles I: the king guaranteed the security of their land and removed some of their more onerous religious restrictions. Since neither the English nor the Irish parliament registered the Graces, they remained conditional on the royal will.

The *modus vivendi* whereby the authorities turned a blind eye to most Catholic worship, and Catholics refrained from 'provocative' displays of faith, was threatened from three sources. First, young men training for the Catholic priesthood studied in Irish Colleges in Paris, Salamanca, Louvain and elsewhere, and returned to Ireland imbued with the Counter-Reformation spirit. They chided their fellow countrymen for having compromised with Protestant heresy, and urged Catholics not to take an oath of loyalty to the king or practise occasional conformity. To the government, Catholicism was becoming assertive and therefore dangerous; hence the law of 1629 forbidding the public celebration of mass. Second, most Scottish immigrants into Ulster were Presbyterian. They contrasted the government's lack of enthusiasm for persecuting Catholics with the vigour with which it sought to impose Laudianism. To Presbyterians, the government was oppressing Protestants while conniving at the 'idolatry' of Catholics. Third, the stability of Ireland was undermined by the arrival of Wentworth as Lord Deputy. His principal task was to ease Charles I's position by securing greater financial contributions from Ireland; but he also threw his weight behind the Laudian pro-gramme for the Church of Ireland. This tough-minded administrator secured grants from the Irish parliament in 1632, but refused to guarantee the security of Old English land as promised in the Graces. The reason for his reticence became clear when he confiscated Old English land in Connacht with a view to another plantation. Char-les's promise had been broken. Wentworth also imposed stiff fines on the London companies which had failed to bring sufficient settlers to Ulster. The Lord Deputy did increase revenue, but at a cost: he alienated the social and political elites of Ireland and alarmed those of England, who feared that, when he returned, he would attempt similar measures there.

## The Recall of Parliament in England, 1640

The English parliament had not met since 1629. Charles's adversaries later dubbed this period 'the eleven years' tyranny', although it should be recalled that his father too had dispensed with the assem-bly for many years. The principal reason for Charles refusing to call elections was his knowledge that parliament would attach unaccept-able conditions to subsidies. After the dispersal of the 1629 parlia-ment, Charles continued to rely on customs duties and royal lands as his main source of income, although he employed other devices such as the sale of monopolies and the Star Chamber and other law courts to extract heavy fines. In 1634 Charles revived Ship Money, a prop-erty tax to help pay for the fleet. It was imposed first upon London, but in 1635 was extended to the rest of the country. In 1637, John Hampden, a Buckinghamshire gentleman, challenged its legality by refusing to pay. He was tried before the Court of Exchequer and lost, but only narrowly: seven judges found against him, but five in his favour. Like the Bate case in 1606, this was a pyrrhic victory for the king: it did not materially improve income from Ship Money, but provided more evidence to his critics that he was tending towards 'absolute monarchy'. Even so, it would be a mistake to suppose that

England was heading for civil war. It was Charles's mishandling of the Scottish rising of 1639 which turned English discontent into a constitutional crisis. His responsibility for the genesis of the civil war was considerable. His subjects had a profound respect for monarchy. Even his fiercest critics distinguished between the office and the man, and denunciations of Charles did not necessarily imply rejection of monarchy. Through his blunders, Charles succeeded in identifying his own fate with that of his office.

Following the advice of Wentworth (now the earl of Strafford) and Laud, he called parliament which met on 13 April 1640. This 'Short Parliament' lasted only until 5 May for, as Charles feared, it demanded concessions which he was unwilling to give. In the Commons, John Pym and others called for the impeachment of the king's advisers, and Charles's request for subsidies to raise an army was refused. He dissolved the assembly and raised another army from his own resources. He was encouraged by the fact that Strafford had called the Irish parliament, which agreed to provide Charles with soldiers, but he opened his second campaign against the Scots before Irish help was organized. Thereby he deprived himself of badly needed troops, while fuelling the suspicions of English parliamentarians that he might eventually deploy his army, enlarged by Irish units, against them. The second Scottish campaign turned out worse than the first. A Scottish army defeated the English at Newburn and occupied Northumberland and Durham, forcing the king to accept humiliating terms by the Treaty of Ripon (October 1640): he must recompense the Scottish army and recall the English parliament. Charles assembled nobles at York to seek their assistance, but they too urged him to recall parliament. Given his military and financial plight, he had no option but to agree.

When parliament met in November 1640, the beleaguered king was at its mercy. Under the leadership of John Pym, the Commons proceeded to impeach and then subject to bills of attainder Wentworth and Laud (the former was executed in 1641, the latter in 1645); they abolished the Star Chamber and other prerogative courts, and confirmed that customs and 'extraordinary' dues must be raised only with parliamentary consent. These were conservative measures, but the Commons did enact a radical provision: the king could no longer dissolve the parliament of 1640 without its agreement, and in future a parliament must meet at least every three years. This did not necessarily mean that parliament would sit permanently (although the body which met in November 1640 lasted until 1653, hence its sobriquet 'the Long Parliament'), but the act placed parliament alongside the king at the centre of the constitution. Divisions now emerged in the Commons. A large minority felt that they had gone far enough and should assist Charles against the Scots; the majority did not trust the king, claiming that if he had an army, he would employ it against parliament, dismantle the new legislation, and impose 'absolute monarchy'. This parliament is significant at another level. It showed that in the eleven years during which the country was deprived of a national forum, popular grievances had accumulated. Parliament was showered with petitions from London and elsewhere on the abolition of Laudian changes in the church, constitutional change, economic reform and a host of other causes. The political atmosphere was tense; and it was rendered even more so in 1641 when news arrived that an insurrection had begun in Ireland.

## Ireland and 1641

To many in Ireland, the recent acquisition of greater powers by the English parliament had implications for themselves. The Irish parliament had helped the English body to prepare charges against Strafford by sending a deputation, including Old English members, to give an account of his 'crimes' in Ireland. Charles attempted to divide the Old English from the others by offering to enact the Graces, but Strafford fell and Charles no longer felt bound to honour the offer. The actions of the English parliament showed that constitutional change was in the air, but to the groups in Ireland which had united in opposition to Strafford, the English parliament was appearing potentially more hostile than the king. On the other hand, the conflict between crown and English parliament provided an opportunity to modify the situation in Ireland. Many Irish parliamentarians favoured the restoration of their legislative autonomy. Gaelic lords and Old English land-owners desired a halt to land confiscations. The Catholic hierarchy sought a reduction of anti-Catholic laws. Inspired by the success of the Covenanters, a plan was laid in 1641, mainly by Ulster Gaelic lords including Sir Phelim O'Neill, his brother Turlough, and Lord Connor Maguire, to seize Dublin castle, impose military control throughout the country, and wrest concessions from a weakened Charles I. Although the plot was discovered, it went ahead in Ulster in October 1641. The Ulster lords mustered their forces, while at the same time a popular Catholic insurrection led to the massacre of over 4,000 'English' Protestant settlers. In principle, Scottish immigrants were to be spared, but amidst the violence this was a distinction that was often ignored. In their turn, settlers turned on native Irish where the latter were in a minority. Ulster became a war zone reminiscent of some of the more violent parts of Germany, as refugees sought the security of towns or fled to England. The army of the lords headed south and was joined by the Old English of the Pale. The rising spread, and in June 1642, military leaders and members of the Catholic hierarchy formed a Confederation in Kilkenny. Nevertheless, they proclaimed that they were not rebels against the king, to whom they remained loyal.

## Steps to Civil War in England

Frustrated by his relations with the English parliament, Charles sought to ameliorate his position by two measures. First, he agreed to the marriage between his ten-year-old daughter Mary and a Dutch prince, William of Orange, son of the Stadtholder Frederick Henry. Politically this was an astute move, for William was a Calvinist. Charles expected that the marriage would appeal to his Presbyterian critics; moreover, Frederick Henry promised him arms and money. Secondly, in the autumn of 1641, Charles travelled to Scotland hoping to heal the breach with the Scots and, as English parliamentarians feared, gather an army with which to restore his 'prerogatives' in England. He failed, for neither the Scottish parliament nor the Presbyterian church authorities desired to become embroiled in English affairs. Charles further alienated Scottish opinion by an ill-judged attempt to have the earl of Argyll and duke of Hamilton, two of his main opponents, arrested. Charles returned to England where, in December 1641, parliament presented Charles with the Grand Remonstrance, a comprehensive attack on royal policy. However, the Remonstrance passed the Commons by only eleven votes, and Charles felt that he could risk tough measures. On 3 January 1642, he ordered the arrest of Pym and four associates in the Commons, and Viscount Mandeville (later the earl of Manchester) in the Lords. The next day, the king shocked members of parliament by entering the chamber to execute the arrest personally, only to find that the accused had fled. A few days later, Charles and his queen left London (in March, Henriette-Marie sailed for France). Charles set up his base in York. He had lost control of London.

The question of who should command the army remained. The king insisted that it was his right to do so, but parliament continued to suspect that he would employ an army to crush opposition at home. It set about raising its own forces. In March 1642, it passed the Militia Ordinance (an ordinance did not require royal assent) by which it proceeded to muster forces in its own name. On 1 June it issued the Nineteen Propositions: the king must agree to the Militia Ordinance and disband his own forces, the Church of England must be reformed, the education and marriages of the royal children and all governmental appointments would be overseen by parliament. Charles rejected the Propositions. On 6 June, parliament responded: it drew a distinction between the office of kingship and the person in whom it was vested. Charles, it proclaimed, was failing to fulfil his duty as king. Parliament therefore must exercise royal powers on his behalf. Relations between crown and parliament had broken down. War followed.

## Civil War to 1648

Loyalties in England and Scotland during the civil war were rarely simple. Most English nobles were royalist, although some, including the earls of Essex and Warwick, backed parliament. Similarly in Scotland, the nobility was divided. The English gentry split, some siding with the king, others, of whom Oliver Cromwell was one, supporting parliament. 'Godly' people generally favoured parliament, but there was also a great deal of neutralism within the country; the notion that the mass of the population felt obliged to adopt fixed, enthusiastic positions is mistaken. Most of the fighting in the war took place from 1642 to 1647, and in 1648. At first there were no decisive battles, although after Edgehill (23 October 1642) Charles did get close to London; he withdrew in the face of a hostile force. Unable to take London, he based himself in Oxford. Parliament enjoyed certain advantages: its army in 1642 was larger than that of the king (some 20,000 as against a few thousand royalist troops), it had command of the navy and controlled the material and human resources of London. However, it lacked skilled commanders, and the quality of its soldiers was poor. It was only when the New Model Army, based on the Swedish army, was forged between 1644 and 1645, that its potential superiority was realized.

Parliament strengthened its hand by forming an alliance with the Scots. In September 1643 it entered into league with the Covenanters, whose price included the demand that England adopt their Presbyterian pattern of worship; this was an ironical reversal of Laud's attempts to impose Anglican worship in Scotland just a few years before. The Scots Covenanters sent an army whose first test came at the battle of Marston Moor near York on 2 July 1644. Royalist troops led by the king's nephew, Prince Rupert,[7] had driven back a parliamentarian force besieging York, but at Marston Moor Rupert was heavily defeated. This battle, in which English troops commanded by Cromwell were joined by their Scottish allies, inflicted a blow on the royalist cause in northern England from which it never recovered. Prince Rupert escaped to Scotland where, with the marquis of Montrose, he began to gather another army made up mainly of the Gordon, Ogilvie, MacDonald and other clans, plus levies from Ireland.

The New Model Army, commanded by Cromwell, contained a core of Independents, so called because they rejected the right either of state or national church to determine patterns of worship. These religious radicals advocated independent congregations which would decide their own rules of worship. As the war progressed, Independents came to see themselves less as instruments of parliament than of God; for them, the war became a conflict whose aim was to 'liberate' England from religious conformity, and allow the spirit of God free reign among the people. The degree of control which parliament exercised over its army was a sensitive matter by the end of the decade. In the short run, the New Model Army proved to be superior to the royalist forces, and when they met again at Naseby, on 14 June 1645, Charles's army was crushed. Prince Rupert advised Charles to seek peace, but the king approached the Irish Confederates, offering toleration for Catholicism if they would assist him. In Scotland, the army of Montrose and Rupert was defeated by the Covenanters at Philiphaugh near Selkirk on 13 September 1645.

During the war, a new ecclesiastical arrangement for England was created by the so-called Westminster Assembly: a gathering of clergy, plus some members of the Houses of Lords and Commons, and Scottish theologians, who met at Westminster from 1643 to 1648. It produced four principal texts: the Westminster Confession of Faith based on Calvinist theology, two catechisms (a 'great' and a 'small') which upheld the sanctity of the Sabbath, and a Discipline which suppressed the episcopacy, the Prayer Book, clerical dress, ornaments and music in church. Parliament confirmed these decisions with some modifications, and in effect turned England into a Presbyterian country. Criticism of the Westminster provisions came from several quarters. Independents objected that one form of compulsion, Laudianism, had been replaced by another, and Anglicans resented the imposition of Presbyterianism. The question of religion, far from having been resolved, had been given a new twist as the Scottish form of worship was imposed on England.

The war aim of parliament was to preserve the monarchy, but on parliament's terms. After Naseby and Philiphaugh, the king abandoned Oxford and, in April 1646, gave himself up to the Scottish army at Newark. The Scots moved to Newcastle, where, in July, Charles was presented by parliament with the 'Newcastle Propositions'. He must accept the decisions of the Westminster Assembly, relinquish control of the army, and cancel his offer to the Irish Confederates. For the time being Charles temporized, but in January 1647, parliament paid off the Scottish army, which returned home leaving Charles in the hands of parliament. He still attempted to play off his enemies, and was encouraged by the fact that relations between the army and parliament were strained. Army pay was in arrears, and no indemnity was forthcoming from parliament. As officers and men alike felt that parliament held them in low esteem, the army was becoming increasingly politicized. A General Council of Army was formed, which drew up 'Heads of the Proposals': a set of demands which it presented to parliament in June and to the king in July 1647. The proposals called for religious toleration for all Protestants, the dissolution of parliament, its replacement by regular assemblies elected by a reformed franchise, and a council of state to run foreign affairs. In an attempt to force parliament to comply, the army occupied London; meanwhile Charles, observing the divisions among his opponents, continued to foment discord. He gave no formal response either to the Newcastle Propositions or the Heads of the Proposals, but negotiated secretly with Scottish commissioners, calling on them to raise another army on his behalf. In December Charles moved to the Isle of Wight, where he was still held by parliament. He managed to sign a deal with the Scots who, in 1648, invaded England; a number of royalist risings broke out.

## Revolution in England

Although many members of the Commons still favoured agreement with the king, most army leaders, including Cromwell, had concluded that he must be deposed. This revolutionary decision was driven in part by religious sentiment: many army officers had come to see Charles in Old Testament terms, as 'a man of blood' who, by his outrageous conduct, had fallen under the judgement of God, and therefore must be brought to justice. The royalist risings were suppressed, and Cromwell defeated the Scots at Preston in August 1648. In November, the General Council of Army demanded that Charles, now in their custody, be tried. On 6 December, troops under the command of Colonel Thomas Pride entered the Commons and expelled over one hundred members suspected of still approving negotiations with the king. The House of Commons was reduced from a nominal membership of 507 to a radical group, nicknamed 'the Rump', of approximately 200. On 1 January 1649, the Rump agreed that Charles should be brought to trial. The question was, by whom and by what authority? The Rump appropriated the right to make laws without reference to Lords or king, and on 6 January created a 'high court of justice' before which Charles was arraigned. His trial began on 10 January. He refused to answer charges on the ground that the 'court' had no authority. Legally he was on strong ground, but tactically it might have been wiser to have drawn out the trial as long as possible. There was widespread resentment at the proceedings, for most people rejected the 'man of blood' epithet which the army had attached to the king; in the eyes of the majority of his subjects, Charles remained a 'sacred' figure whose person should not be violated by his subjects. A long trial might have provoked a reaction in the king's favour, possibly leading to its abandonment. Charles's silence allowed the court to proceed with haste. On 26 January he was pronounced guilty of treason, and he was executed on 30 January 1649. Parliament abolished the monarchy, the House of Lords and the Anglican church; it turned England into a Commonwealth run by a council of state appointed by parliament.

Could Charles's death have been avoided? Probably, if he had pursued other actions or had other conditions prevailed. If Charles had been more 'Machiavellian', it is conceivable that he could have survived by limiting the issues between himself and parliament to matters of emphasis rather than of principle, means rather than ends. Elizabeth I and James I had quarrelled with parliament, but never allowed disputes to turn into questions of ultimate constitutional authority. Unlike his two immediate predecessors, however, Charles was not given to compromise, and it is significant that his advisers Laud and Wentworth likewise thought in 'thorough' terms. Charles held views on royal prerogative from which he refused to budge, even temporarily in the interests of their longer-term preservation. He stuck to his constitutional principles, intriguing with all and sundry, making and breaking promises and alienating even those who wanted to avoid a total rupture in relations. Even so, he might have survived had it not been for his characteristically unbending stance on religion. James I had placed great hopes in a 'middle way' to which the majority of his subjects could subscribe. Charles espoused Laudianism, and thereby estranged a high proportion of British and Irish society. Whilst it would be a gross exaggeration to claim that thousands of Charles's subjects would have preferred martyrdom to Laudianism, religion was a subject which raised high passions and drove people to violent resistance. Charles ignored the lessons of the recent history of continental Europe, and allowed 'wars of religion' to break out in the three kingdoms. Parliament too shared responsibility for the collapse of monarchy. Between 1625 and 1629 it called for an aggressive 'Protestant' foreign policy, whilst refusing to furnish Charles with adequate finances. After its recall in 1640, most members were monarchists who still sought a 'right' relationship between themselves and their sovereign. By late 1648, however, they no longer controlled the army, and Pride's purge left parliament in the hands of a minority willing to do the army's bidding. It is inconceivable that a full House of Commons would have authorized the events of January 1649. The factions which conceived and carried out the trial of the king succeeded because war had undermined the authority of the institutions which normally held the political nation together. Far from resolving the national crisis, the execution of Charles guaranteed its continuation. The king of England was dead, but he had a nineteen-year-old son; and what of Ireland and Scotland, neither of which had repudiated Charles I? What were the implications for these kingdoms of January 1649?

### War in Ireland

The Confederation of Kilkenny controlled most of the country, but failed to capture Dublin. The Confederation ran its affairs through an elected general assembly, with executive authority vested in a supreme council. Its army was organized on a provincial basis. Confederates took an oath of loyalty to the association, but also to Charles I, for their aim was to protect royal prerogatives against the English parliament, as well as to secure an alleviation of anti-Catholic legislation and a reversal of seizures of land. The Confederates viewed the English parliament as their principal antagonist, and denied that it had any authority in Ireland. Charles I, on the other hand, was their legitimate king; the Confederates were fighting to preserve the kingdom of Ireland, but on their terms. It proved inordinately difficult to maintain unity. Provincial and noble rivalries emerged, and disputes occurred as to whether religious or territorial aims should have priority. These and other problems nullified the attempt by Charles I's lord lieutenant, James Butler, marquess of Ormonde, to sign a peace with the Confederates in 1646. Meanwhile, they sought assistance from the papacy (which sent Giovanni Rinuccini, archbishop of Fermo, to advise them) and other Catholic governments, but to little effect. When Charles I was executed, Confederate Ireland found itself deprived of the source through which its aims might be achieved. It faced a hostile English parliament and army inspired by anti-Catholic zeal and a desire to avenge '1641'.

The English parliament placed Oliver Cromwell in command of an army of 20,000, with instructions to reconquer Ireland. His campaign, which lasted from August 1649 to May 1650, aimed to subject Catholics to more rigorous persecution, fortify Protestantism, secure Ireland against foreign powers, eradicate the possibility of another Irish rising and augment the English presence by extensive transfers of land. Cromwell's New Model soldiers were battle hardened and driven by a desire to avenge '1641'. The campaign began successfully, with Confederate strong-points falling at Drogheda and Wexford. On both occasions, massacres of the defending garrisons took place. On the other hand, at Clonmel, on 17 May 1650, Cromwell fell into a trap, his army suffering its heaviest losses of the civil war. Nevertheless, Ireland was subdued, and over the next few years over half of the land was confiscated and redistributed. Over one hundred Confederate land-owners were executed, exiled or transported, and many more lost their property. Whereas earlier plantations had brought in civilian settlers, the Cromwellian settlement mostly rewarded his soldiers. The scale of the exercise resembled that which had taken place in Bohemia in the 1630s. Redistribution took place against a background of physical devastation and depopulation caused by war, disease and hunger. Whereas the population of Ireland was probably about 2.1 million in 1641, it fell by about 500,000 in the 1640s, and was still only about 1.7 million in the early 1670s.

## The Conquest of Scotland

After Philiphaugh (1645), Covenanters subjected royalists to harsh repression, but when word arrived that the Scottish army in England had handed Charles I to parliament in return for pay, accusations of 'Judas money' were heard within parliament and church. Those who contended that Charles should not have been surrendered included the duke of Hamilton. It was members of his faction who in 1647 negotiated with Charles I and 'engaged' to raise the army which invaded England and was defeated at Preston. The Scottish parliament contained a majority of Engagers, but was purged by Covenanters much as the English parliament had been by Pride. The Scottish 'rump' passed the Act of Clauses depriving Engagers of civil and military offices. Nevertheless, even the Covenanters were not regicides. They urged the court which was trying Charles not to impose the death penalty. When they heard of Charles's fate, they were in a quandary. On 5 February 1650, the Scottish parliament stepped in and acknowledged Charles I's son as Charles II. In June the young king travelled to Scotland from the continent, signed the Covenant and was crowned in January 1651.

The English parliament interpreted this as hostile intent, for Charles undoubtedly would attempt to gain the English throne. Cromwell, back from Ireland, was instructed to invade Scotland and drive out Charles. Cromwell crossed the border in July 1650, but failed to take Edinburgh on his first attempt. He retreated to Dunbar where, on 3 September, he was attacked by a Scottish force. In one of the most decisive battles of the war he defeated the Scots, took Edinburgh and subdued most of the lowlands. However, during the winter of 1650–1 Charles II gathered an army, and in the summer of 1651 by-passed Cromwell and entered England. Full of confidence, he expected English royalists to flock to him. Cromwell, who had captured Stirling and Perth, headed south. On 3 September 1651, he overwhelmed Charles II at Worcester. The king fled to France. The authority of the English parliament was imposed throughout Britain as well as Ireland. General George Monck completed the conquest of Scotland, where the estates of royalist leaders were confiscated and the General Assembly of the church was dissolved. Constitutional union was achieved by admitting Scottish members to the English parliament, free trade between the two countries was instituted, and Scotland was placed under the administration of a Council of Nine appointed from London. James I's 'Britain' was a reality, but at the cost of civil war and conquest.

### England under the Commonwealth and Protectorate

The civil war created a context in which religious and intellectual ferment flourished in England. Religious and social movements spread or emerged, proclaiming a variety of social as well as religious programmes. Groups such as the Quakers and Muggletonians emerged, in addition to the earlier Baptists and Independents. The sects stressed personal salvation, but disagreed as to whether its foundation was predestination, justification or grace. Almost all believed that the Second Coming was imminent, although again they differed as to whether it would be accompanied by the end of the world and the Final Judgement, or whether these apocalyptic episodes would unfold sequentially. On the other hand, the Fifth Monarchy men drew upon the biblical Book of Daniel to contend that a fifth kingdom – following those of Assyria, Persia, Alexandrine Greece and Rome – was about to be instituted by God, and would last for a thousand years. Among the radical social movements were the Diggers, who demanded the abolition of private property and championed the right of 'the people' to work common land. The Levellers demanded a written constitution and an expansion of the parliamentary franchise. They supplied some of the more extreme elements in the army, and in both 1647 and 1649, Leveller-inspired mutinies had to be put down. In addition to sects, the civil war generated thousands of pamphlets and tracts similar to the Mazarinades in France; they testified to an eruption of new social, political and economic thought now that traditional political and religious institutions were collapsing.[8]

Against this background, the Commonwealth had to govern Britain and Ireland. Tensions between the army and the Rump Parliament remained. Some army officers were demanding a new type of representative assembly to replace the existing parliament, while parliamentarians were critical of the high financial cost of the army. A crisis was provoked in April 1653 when leaders of the Rump attempted to perpetuate the parliament and dismiss Cromwell as commander-in-chief of the army. On 20 April, Cromwell, accompanied by soldiers, entered parliament and drove out the Rump. The Long Parliament was finished. Over the next few years, Cromwell attempted various constitutional experiments. In May 1653, an assembly was nominated by army officers and some church leaders to replace parliament, but it proved too radical and was dismissed in December.[9] Cromwell now authorized an 'Instrument of Government' in which he held the title Lord Protector, assisted by a council of state and a parliament which would be elected every three years. It would comprise only one House of 460 members: 400 for England and Wales, and thirty each for Ireland and Scotland. Under the Protectorate, parliament proved less submissive than Cromwell hoped. It criticized his powers, objected to his practice of governing through ordinances which did not require prior parliamentary consent, and protested that it had not agreed to the Instrument. In 1654, parliament attempted to reduce Cromwell's control over the army and public finance. Angered at this 'incursion' into his prerogatives, he dismissed parliament again in January 1655.

He replaced it with military rule. In July 1655, England and Wales were divided into eleven districts, each of which was administered by a Major-General. The principle of military rule was provocative in itself, but the army now found itself responsible for imposing unpopular policies, especially taxation and laws on religion and public morality. Opposition also came from the legal institutions of the country. Judges and juries refused to be the tools of the army, and in numerous cases against royalists they found in favour of the accused. To most people in England and Wales, the rule of the Major-Generals was infinitely more tyrannical than anything perpetrated by Charles I. Cromwell recognized the untenability of the system, and reluctantly accepted that if the Instrument of Government were to survive, another parliament would have to be called. Without its approval, the Instrument would collapse.

The parliament which met in September 1656 proved to be politically astute. It sought to detach Cromwell from the army and bind him to itself, first by proposing that the protectorship be hereditary and then by offering him the crown (by the Humble Petition and Advice of May 1657). Although Cromwell refused the crown, he did compromise: he would name his successor as Lord Protector, and a second House would be restored to parliament. In practice it proved extremely difficult to introduce these arrangements. The second session of the 1656 parliament met briefly in January 1658, but Cromwell died on 3 September 1658 before a workable system could be put in place. His son Richard succeeded him as Lord Protector, but Richard lacked the personality of his father or a base in the army, and was caught in a web of intrigue involving army leaders and would-be parliamentarians. It was again a military man who imposed a settlement. General Monck, commander of the army in Scotland, had been observing the stalemate in England with frustration. He marched on London and in January 1660 reconstituted the Long Parliament, including members who had been purged by Pride. Monck had contacted Charles II in the Netherlands. There followed a carefully orchestrated sequence of events: parliament dissolved itself; on 4 April, Charles issued a conciliatory declaration; a new parliament was elected and on 25 April invited Charles to return as king of England. He arrived at the end of May. Amidst widespread jubilation, monarchy was restored with astonishing ease.

## The Commonwealth and Europe

The civil war and revolution in Britain were observed by continental governments with mixed feelings, for many faced their own socio-political unrest in the 1640s, even though none led to a 'January 1649'. The execution of Charles I created widespread revulsion. The assassination of a monarch by a deranged individual was one thing, but for a 'constitutional' assembly, however exceptional its composition, to have voted to execute the king was offensive to contemporary political values. When the tsar, Alexis, heard the news, he expelled English merchants from Russia. In an attempt to reassure foreign states, the Council of State, which ran foreign affairs until 1653, issued the Commonwealth Declaration in April 1649, promising to honour all existing international obligations; and it soon became evident that the new regime in London behaved in international affairs, and was treated by most other governments, much as before. Political ideology had little effect on the conduct of international relations; Catholic states did not ostracize the Commonwealth, nor did fraternal relations with the Dutch Republic follow automatically.

France took an interest in English affairs, not least because Henriette-Marie was queen of England. In the mid-1640s there were occasional rumours of French intervention in support of Charles I, but there was little substance to them. Mazarin was preoccupied with the Congress of Westphalia and the war against Spain. The failure to end that war in 1648, and the outbreak of the Frondes, precluded any possibility of French military assistance for Charles I. However, unlike the government of Spain, which recognized the republican regime in England as early as 1650, the French refused to receive an ambassador from the Commonwealth and instead recognized Charles II as king. They also allowed Prince Rupert to launch attacks on English shipping from their ports. Based in the Mediterranean, Rupert used English royalist ships supported by French vessels to harry English merchant ships *en route* to the Levant. Seventeen merchantmen were sunk between 1649 and 1650, causing London trading companies to complain to the government. In response, English warships attacked French ships in the Channel, the North Sea, and as far away as the Caribbean. The two countries engaged in a *de facto* maritime war in the early 1650s. Commercial factors further soured relations. In 1648, France had placed an embargo on all imports of woollen and silk products. This hit English exports hard, and led to reprisals in 1650 when the English placed a similar ban on imports from France.

Between 1648 and 1653, France was crippled by the Frondes. Now it was the turn of Mazarin to fear English intervention; he also suspected that Puritan elements might urge the Huguenots to rise again. In 1651, English agents were in touch with de Retz in Paris, and the duc de Condé sent representatives to London in 1651 and 1652 to secure military aid. By 1652, however, the Council of State was seeking better relations with France. The object of English ambition was Dunkirk, which was held by the French but threatened by the Spanish. French and British representatives discussed the possibility of a joint defence of the port, after which it might be transferred to England. The talks came to nought, for Dunkirk fell to the Spanish and remained in contention for several more years. Meanwhile the Frondes continued, and although they collapsed in Paris in 1652, they continued in Bordeaux until 1653. Two English agents were operating there, Edward Sexby and his associate Arundel, who came from the radical wing of English politics. They brought to France the 'Agreement of the People' (1649), a document stating Leveller demands. Frondeur leaders in Bordeaux adopted a modified version of the text, calling for the government of France by an elected assembly, an end to religious persecution, trial by jury, the restoration of peasant rights, and other demands which mixed French 'native' grievances and English Leveller concerns. The collapse of the Fronde in Bordeaux rendered the demands otiose, but they constituted a transitory attempt to integrate English radical politics into a French rebellion.

After the Frondes, Anglo-French relations entered a short period of uncertainty. Cromwell suspected that Mazarin now might help Charles II, who was residing in France, to recover the throne by force, and such fears were enhanced by the continuing attacks on English ships by 'royalist' vessels sailing from French ports. However, Mazarin's chief priority remained the war against Spain, and he took steps to win over Cromwell. In 1654 he paid Charles II and most of his court to leave France for Cologne, and in the autumn of 1655 signed the Treaty of Westminster with Cromwell: the trade war and embargoes between the two countries ceased, the attacks on English ships would end, and neither government would harbour domestic enemies of the other (which in effect meant that Charles II would not be allowed back into France). The treaty was turned into an alliance in 1657, and together the French and English undertook the successful campaigns against the Spanish in the West Indies and Dunkirk (which passed into English possession) as described above (p. 119). Interest of state took precedence over religious or ideological divisions in determining the course of Anglo-French relations in the 1650s.

The same may be said about Anglo-Dutch relations. The Dutch Republic and England appeared to have much in common as both were Protestant states and each regarded Spain as its main enemy. Nevertheless, for several decades the English and Dutch had been at odds over commercial matters. English merchants took exception to the monopoly over the carrying trade of the North and Baltic seas which the Dutch had established, a situation made worse from the English point of view when, in 1651, the Dutch signed a treaty with Denmark strengthening their position in the Baltic. For many years English fishermen had complained that Dutch ships 'poached' fish in 'English' waters. In the East Indies, the Dutch resisted attempts by English merchants to trade; violent clashes occurred in 1618 and 1623 resulting in English deaths and their expulsion from the Moluccas and Java. Once the Peace of Westphalia was signed, the Dutch moved quickly to raise their trading presence in the Mediterranean, and did so at the expense of much English shipping. Dutch ships also conducted commerce with Ireland and English colonies in North America and the West Indies.

The Council of State decided that a more aggressive approach to the Dutch must be taken. In 1651 the Rump Parliament passed the Navigation Act, by which goods carried to Britain, Ireland or the colonies must be transported in British or colonial ships. The Dutch understood this for what it was: a direct assault upon their carrying trade. They entered into negotiations with the Rump, which made an astonishing constitutional proposal that Commonwealth England and the Dutch Republic should unite. The intention of the Council of State was far from clear. Was it thinking of a single state, or perhaps some kind of federation? What kinds of joint institutions or authorities would be set up? And was this a plan about which the Council had thought at length, or was it an idea which had only just emerged? The Dutch rejected the proposal, but sought the repeal of the Navigation Act. Meanwhile, they were in dispute with the French government, which also resented their maritime power. French warships were stopping and seizing the cargoes of Dutch ships. The Dutch government gathered a large war fleet to protect their shipping. In the spring of 1652, an English fleet under the command of Admiral Robert Blake encountered the Dutch. Fighting took place, and it was in the aftermath of this incident that England declared war on the Dutch Republic. Economic factors were the deciding motivation.

The war was fought entirely at sea, but spread across much of the globe. Both sides enjoyed victories, but in broad terms the English had the better of the fighting in the North Sea and Channel where they concentrated their forces, while the Dutch continued to exclude the English from the Baltic and Mediterranean, and proved stronger in the East Indies. The war proved costly, especially to the Dutch, who suffered heavy losses of trade. During the war, English privateers and warships seized well over 1,000 Dutch ships, losing about 250 in the process. Ironically, successes in war threatened to encourage royalism in Britain. After the defeat of the Dutch fleet at Portland Bill in 1653, Charles II, in exile in France, offered his services to the Dutch government. Cromwell was alarmed at the prospect of a Dutch fleet possibly commanded by Charles II; would English sailors, among whom royalist sentiments remained, fight, or was there a threat of desertions? By the autumn of 1653, both governments wanted to end a war which was economically harmful. In 1654 the Peace of Westminster was signed. The Navigation Act remained in force and the Dutch agreed that henceforth their ships would dip the flag when they encountered British ships in the North Sea.

If there was one country towards which Cromwell, as head of state after 1654, allowed his Protestantism rather than political calculation to determine his attitude, it was Spain. One can understand why he thought of Spain as a hostile state, yet there were sufficient anomalies in recent history to give pause for thought. Both James I and Charles I had pursued better relations with Spain, and in the 1650s, when Philip IV was struggling to recover from internal revolt while conducting war against France, he raised the question of an alliance with Commonwealth England on more than one occasion. Spain had recognized the Commonwealth quickly, and among Cromwell's advisers, there were some, such as Major-General John Lambert, who favoured a more pro-Spanish policy. If Spain could be persuaded to offer access by British merchants to its trade and that of its empire, this would counterbalance the embargoes which the French had imposed. To Lambert, there was no self-evident advantage to Britain of a pro-French as against a pro-Spanish policy. It was religion which decided Cromwell. In his mind, Spain represented Counter-Reformation Catholicism at its most extreme. Spain could not be trusted to refrain from encouraging British and especially Irish Catholics to rise up again. A weakened Spain might express pro-British sentiments now, but if it emerged triumphant from the war against France, it would resume the anti-British and anti-Protestant policies of earlier decades. Accordingly, Cromwell rejected Spanish advances and cooperated with the French to break Spanish Habsburg power in western Europe. The next two or three decades were to show that the pro-Spanish lobby had been far-sighted. By the 1670s it was to be France which threatened hegemony, the British, Dutch, Spanish and others having to combine to resist the armies of Louis XIV. Cromwell's support for France helped to create the giant which, before too long, menaced western Europe as Spain had done earlier.

## A Verdict on the Civil War and Revolution

The origins, course and consequences of the English civil war and revolution have generated an immense volume of historical literature. Rather like the Frondes in France, the rebellions in Spain and Italy, and the Thirty Years War, the civil war has been analysed from various, even contending, viewpoints. Fundamental economic change, social change leading to class conflict, and struggles over British state formation, have all been invoked as 'profound causes'; more recently, historians have displayed renewed interest in three principal fields of research. One is the religious forces at work throughout Britain and Ireland which were undermining the hopes of James I that his three kingdoms might, in a limited sense, become one. In so far as the civil war may be seen as the failure of the Jacobean 'programme', that failure seemed to corroborate contemporary assumptions concerning the inherent weakness of a multi-faith polity. The Tudors saved England from religious war, but James I and Charles I operated in a more challenging context: they ruled three kingdoms, not two, and espoused a more interventionist policy towards Ireland than the Tudors. Moreover, the Thirty Years War had evoked a Protestant crusading spirit in England which could not be ignored. Religion was not a secondary phenomenon simply signifying other factors at work in British society; it was a force which has to be analysed and understood in its own terms.

Second, historians are now very conscious of the extent to which the civil war in England was part of a wider crisis concerning the relationship between the three kingdoms. It is now impossible to study the history of any one of England, Scotland or Ireland between 1603 and 1660 in isolation from the others. The relationships of the three parliaments with their king and between themselves, the connections between the nobility of the kingdoms, the movement of English and Scots into Ireland, the effects of rebellion in one kingdom upon another, the popular as well as elite reactions to those rebellions, and the attempts of Charles I to employ the military resources of one kingdom in another, bound the three kingdoms together in ways which James I had not envisaged but which in a perverse way did make 'Britain and Ireland' a reality. The 'Commonwealth of England, Scotland and Ireland' was the outcome.

Third, the local effects of civil wars throughout the three kingdoms have attracted much attention from historians. For all that the wars were episodes in 'national' history, they had a profound impact at the regional and local level. Just as the military aspects of the Thirty Years War had differing social and economic effects in the regions of Germany, so did the civil war in Britain and Ireland. In this regard, the reactions of London throughout the civil war were crucial to its course and outcome. By the beginning of the seventeenth century, London had acquired an imposing political, economic and cultural importance. Whilst it is too much to claim that whoever controlled London held England, the reverse proposition was true: whoever did not control London could not hold England.

Civil war occurred in Britain and Ireland, but was there a revolution? Much depends on definition. If revolution is understood to be a compound of fundamental political, economic, social and cultural change achieved over a short period of time through the use of force, then the answer must be that by the mid-1650s all the member countries of the Commonwealth had experienced revolution in varying degrees. Politically a republican regime had triumphed in England; it attempted to create a new public morality, although the extent to which it sought a new social structure remains ambiguous. Ireland came closest to being revolutionized. The transfer of over half of the country to newcomers had profound social and political consequences, for a new land-owning elite was created which was to provide the basis of the later Protestant ascendancy. In the economic sphere, the civil war may be seen to have accelerated existing commercial trends in England rather than to have initiated them. Some radicals advocated the common ownership of property, but this was a programme without measurable contemporary effect. The question of whether a 'revolutionary' British culture emerged remains problematic. Certainly much of the poetry and prose of Milton deals with religious and political themes, while the contribution to political thought of Thomas Hobbes ranks among the highest intellectual achievements of the era; but these were writers who were attempting to understand their times as much as propagate particular religious or political philosophies. It has also been claimed that the practice of science in England in the 1650s was inspired in part by a 'Commonwealth ideology', and that the foundation of the Royal Society in 1660 was an attempt by scientists with a suspect past to ingratiate themselves with the restored Charles II. Such claims remain fascinating contributions to a debate which must be taken much further, and must take much more account of 'popular culture', before definitive answers can be supplied.

England, Scotland and Ireland were revolutionized in certain and particular spheres only. There remains to be discussed later the subject of how far the Restoration period retained or reversed changes inherited from the 1640s and 1650s. When Charles II returned in 1660, it was unrealistic to suppose that he could simply restore pre-war conditions in any of the three kingdoms. He had to arrive at a compromise capable of commanding the acquiescence, if not the consent, of the majority of his subjects. In England, the civil war confronted him with a three-fold heritage to which he had to respond: his subjects were monarchists but were also committed to parliament; they had a horror of 'papistry'; and they were opposed to the army playing a role in politics. Whatever concept of 'restoration' he adopted, it had to take account of these legacies of civil war.

## THE UNITED PROVINCES, 1609–1654

Across the North Sea from Britain lay the United Provinces or Dutch Republic. Having asserted their independence from Spain in the sixteenth century, the Provinces were the youngest state in western Europe.[10] In their constitutional arrangements, they simply adapted traditional municipal and provincial institutions to new circumstances; at no stage did any 'constitutional congress' gather to devise new structures for the republic. Its political institutions emphasized the local over the federal. Each of the provinces had its governing body or states.[11] Those of the wealthy maritime provinces were dominated by urban and mercantile interests. In the states of Holland, for example, eighteen towns had a vote each, while the nobility had only one; in the states of Zeeland the proportions were seven votes to the towns and one to the nobility. The urban members of the maritime provincial states, often referred to as 'regents', came from a small number of wealthy families engaged in commerce and law. It should not be presumed that the rule of these tightly knit oligarchies was governed by self-interest; on the contrary, the regents exhibited a patrician sense of public responsibility and proved more than capable of governing to serve the public good. One can still find no better representations of regents in their oligarchic solidarity than the group portraits which they commissioned from Hals, Rembrandt and other artists, wherein one can observe images of intelligent, soberly dressed burghers who combined a hard-headed business sense with civic pride.

The decisions of the provincial states were carried out by small executive bodies headed by a senior officer, the stadtholder.[12] By 1609, the house of Orange, which had provided much of the leadership in the revolt against Spain, monopolized the stadtholderates. In that year, Maurice of Nassau, prince of Orange, held the stadtholderates of five provinces, the other two being with a cousin. Maurice also served as Captain-General of the army and Admiral-General of the fleet. After his death in 1625, his brother Frederick Henry held most stadtholderates, and when he too died in 1647 they passed to his son William II. The office was abolished in 1651, but was revived in 1672 in favour of William III, later king of England. The Orange dynasty may be compared to the Habsburgs in the Holy Roman Empire: it was the only family with the resources and prestige to make the political 'system' work; in lesser hands the stadtholdership would have been enfeebled, perhaps irreparably. Maurice of Nassau and his successors thought in federal rather than provincial terms and in times of war exercised a military authority which greatly enhanced their political standing. Attached to the states of Holland was also a powerful legal officer, the Grand Pensionary or Lands Advocate; no other province had an equivalent figure. It was he, not the stadtholder, who presided over the states of Holland and headed its deputation in the Estates General. The Grand Pensionaries saw themselves as upholders of provincial rights against federal authority. In practice, this frequently led to uneasy relations between themselves and the stadtholder. In 1609, for example, it was the Pensionary Jan van Oldenbarneveldt who negotiated the truce with Spain against the will of Maurice of Nassau, who wanted to keep on fighting.

The main federal institution was the Estates General, a small assembly of twenty-four deputies from the provincial states who met in The Hague. Their meetings resembled gatherings of ambassadors, for they constantly had to refer back to the provincial states for instructions, not being empowered to speak or vote according to their own judgement. Their ability to pass federal laws was limited, for unanimity was normally required. In extreme circumstances they could act on a majority vote; in 1648, for example, Utrecht and Zeeland opposed the Peace of Münster, but were overridden by the other provinces. The Estates General was concerned mostly with finance, foreign relations and military affairs, in which latter spheres it appointed ambassadors, the Captain-General and Admiral-General. The federal executive body was the Council of State comprising twelve members; its meetings could be attended by the stadtholder. The principal task of the council was to raise quotas from the provinces for military defence. Holland usually contributed between 55 and 60 per cent, Friesland and Zeeland about 11 per cent each, Gelderland, Gröningen and Utrecht 5 or 6 per cent and Overijssel 3 or 4 per cent.[13] These figures not only bear out the primacy of Holland in military affairs, but exemplify one of the chief reasons why the republic was able to survive. Because Holland had no rival in the republic, it was capable of holding all else together, even though the poorer provinces not infrequently resented its ascendancy. Had any other province been in a position to challenge Holland, Spain would have exploited the inevitable tensions, and the capacity of the republic to remain united would have been weakened.

## The Commercial Prosperity of the United Provinces

The survival of the republic is also to be explained by its prosperity. Once again, Holland led the way. This great maritime province, whose population of about 672,000 in 1622 was 45 per cent of that of the republic (1,500,000), was one of the most economically dynamic regions of Europe; we have already seen that many Neapolitans aspired to imitate the example which it set. The republic dominated the carrying trade of western Europe. Dutch ships in the Baltic and North Sea were more numerous than those of any other country, and Dutch fishing fleets were to be seen in the most lucrative fishing grounds of the North Sea and Atlantic. Holland became a financial centre of international importance. In 1609 the Bank of Amsterdam was founded; by the mid-1630s others had been established at Dordrecht, Middelburg and Rotterdam. Dutch banks facilitated large-scale borrowing and investment, while the Amsterdam stock exchange had become the leading financial market in Europe by 1620. Holland was a highly urbanized province. The population of its largest city, Amsterdam, rose from 60,000 in 1600 to 140,000 by 1647; in the same period the population of Haarlem rose from 30,000 to 45,000 and Leiden from 26,000 to 60,000.[14] People moved into the cities of Holland and other provinces from rural areas of the republic, the Spanish Netherlands and Germany; they usually came in search of better employment and wages than were available in their own regions, but many Germans came as refugees from the Thirty Years War.

The Dutch created an extensive overseas commercial network. Their principal instruments were trading companies, several of which were founded in the first two decades of the seventeenth century: the East Indies Company (1602), the Greenland Company (1613), the New Netherlands Company (1614) and the West Indies Company (1621). The East Indies Company was the most profitable of all, and in many ways served as a model adopted throughout Europe. Based in Amsterdam, it amalgamated several smaller enterprises, and through its board of directors concentrated its efforts on the spice islands of Malaya and Indonesia. The company aimed to control as much territory as possible, forcing local rulers to yield to its authority and trade exclusively with its agents. Representatives of the company had political as well as commercial credentials, and were empowered to act on behalf of the government. In commercial terms, this strategy proved outstandingly effective. The company controlled much of the importation into Europe of rare and luxury goods, especially pepper, other spices, silks and precious cloths, which were sold at handsome profit. The Dutch also moved into Portuguese South America. After a brief occupation of Bahia from 1624 to 1625, they seized Pernambuco in 1630, holding it until 1654. The West Indies Company was ordered to exploit the resources of Pernambuco – principally timber and sugar, but also leather and pelts – but the profits were never as abundant as those in the East Indies. In part, this was because the company held a monopoly only of slaves and timber, other commodities being bought and sold also by independent merchants.

By 1618, the Dutch Republic had established itself as a viable political entity based on a flourishing maritime economy. The latter enabled the republic to support many years of warfare (in the 1630s and 1640s, some 90 per cent of the federal budget went on war) without having to resort to bankruptcy, as did Spain on several occasions, France in 1648 and Denmark in 1660. Proportional to its size and population, the Dutch Republic maintained armies larger than those of most other European states in the seventeenth century. Its ability to do so is to be explained mainly by its sophisticated financial and economic systems. International financiers had confidence in the Dutch government, and afforded it both easy access to credit and lower interest rates than those demanded of less reliable governments. The republic created a successful long-term public debt. That of Holland, for example, grew from 5 million guilders in the decade of the 1600s to over 190 million in the 1690s, while rates of interest fell from 8.5 to 3.75 per cent over the same period.[15] This is not to say that the republic was without economic problems. The prosperity of Holland and Zeeland was not matched by the inland provinces – Utrecht, Overijssel and Gelderland – or even by the northern maritime provinces of Gröningen and Friesland. Traditional industries in the republic, such as textiles or brewing, suffered the decline that was endemic throughout most of Europe in the early 1600s. The agricultural sector was also having to adjust to new conditions. As cheap grain became available in the Baltic region, and the adverse effects of centuries of over-exploitation of arable land in the Netherlands manifested themselves, farmers turned increasingly to livestock and dairy produce.

## Religious and Political Tensions

In the sixteenth century, the Netherlands became one of the great centres of Calvinism, along with parts of France, Germany, Switzerland and Scotland. By the 1580s, the northern and southern provinces were dividing along religious lines, although significant minorities of Catholics or Protestants remained; about a quarter of the population of the Dutch Republic in the seventeenth century was Catholic. The Union of Utrecht (1579) had left the question of religious conformity to individual provinces; the pattern of religious life therefore varied according to the attitudes of different provincial states and municipalities. A major split with political implications developed over the theological question of predestination. Orthodox Calvinists maintained that God predestines some people to salvation – the elect – while denying it to others. The orthodox position had been formalized by Guido de Brès in his *Confessio belgica* of 1561. Adopted by Dutch Calvinists in 1571, all pastors and professors of theology were required to abide by its provisions. In 1581, the newly appointed professor of theology at the University of Leiden, Caspar Coolhaes, refused to subscribe to the *Confessio*. He contended that God does not actively predestine. God desires that all should be saved, but many reject salvation, and through His ineffable foreknowledge God knows who they are. Predestination exists only in this sense of divine prescience. The controversy ran on, and in 1588 the Amsterdam Consistory appointed Jakob Armenzoon (Arminius) to prepare a comprehensive rebuttal of Coolhaes. As he prepared his refutation, however, Arminius found it decreasingly persuasive; he changed his mind on predestination and abandoned the very orthodoxy which he had been called upon to defend. He too concluded that God bestows salvation on all who repent of their sins and believe in the redemptive power of Christ. In His omniscience, which transcends the limitations of time, God knows who will respond positively and who will not.

Arminian and orthodox divisions were accentuated after 1603 when Arminius was appointed professor of theology at Leiden. One of his orthodox colleagues, Francis Gomar, publicly denounced him; their theological differences soon were taken up by Calvinist congregations and the wider public. Arminians were in a minority, but argued that they sought a church which was moderate in its theology and pluralistic in its social appeal. Gomarists, who included many young pastors trained in Geneva, accused them of compromising their theological principles, and even of having pro-Catholic and pro-Spanish leanings. This latter charge was given substance, at least to Gomarists, when Oldenbarneveldt, an Arminian, negotiated the truce with Spain. The quarrel raised political issues of a deeper nature. Orthodox Calvinists, inspired by the example of Geneva, thought in theocratic terms and regarded the state as the servant of the church, an instrument through which the elect might create a Godly society. Arminians, on the other hand, saw the state as a mediating agency which must regulate relations between the many groups, religious and otherwise, of which society was composed. The Arminian stance on church–state relations was expounded in 1610 by Johan Uyttenbogaert in his *Treatise on the Authority of the Christian Magistrate in Ecclesiastical Matters*, and in 1614 by Hugo Grotius in his *Resolution for the Peace of the Church*. Both authors pressed the argument that the secular authorities are representatives of God on earth and have a duty to hold religious controversy in check. They must not allow it to turn into socio-political conflict; if ecclesiastical leaders cannot agree among themselves, the secular authorities are justified in imposing order.

In 1610, Arminians in Holland, seeking the protection of the states, drew up a Remonstrance outlining their position. Gomarists presented a Counter-Remonstrance. The quarrel between Remonstrants and Contra-Remonstrants became increasingly bitter as each side accused the other of fomenting religious and social division at a time when the young republic should be concentrating upon cohesion. The reaction of provincial and municipal governments varied, for they too held either Remonstrant or Contra-Remonstrant convictions. However, all shared a desire to maintain social order, and it was often this that determined their stance. The states and towns of Holland mostly sympathized with Arminianism, although Amsterdam remained Contra-Remonstrant. Elsewhere, Utrecht and Overijssel favoured the Arminian stance, while Zeeland, Friesland, Gröningen and Gelderland remained orthodox.

It was in the hope of securing agreement between the contending parties that the Estates General agreed to a synod which met in Dordrecht from November 1618 to May 1619. Contra-Remonstrants looked to the stadtholder, Maurice of Nassau, to support them in erasing Arminian 'heresy'. He sponsored the Contra-Remonstrants, but for political rather than theological reasons. Maurice was in conflict with Oldenbarneveldt over military affairs. The states of

Holland, under Oldenbarneveldt's influence, was attempting to raise its own militia. Maurice rejected the right of provinces to act individually in military matters, and concocted a charge of treason against Oldenbarneveldt who, after being arrested in 1618, was tried and executed in 1619. It was amidst the political tension surrounding the trial that the synod met. It too turned into a form of tribunal. Attended by observers from England, Germany and the Swiss Cantons, commissioners from the states and elders from provincial synods called thirteen Arminian pastors and theologians to account for themselves. In May 1619 the synod denounced Arminianism and ordered the dismissal of some 200 pastors. Maurice took the opportunity presented by this victory of orthodoxy to strengthen his political position. He purged the states of Holland and limited tenure of the office of Lands Advocate to five years. In major towns of the republic he used his influence to introduce councillors who were beholden to him. Maurice did not attempt drastic constitutional change (he rejected those who urged him to convert the republic into a monarchy), preferring to manipulate existing institutions by the placing of his 'creatures'.

The orthodox triumph was short-lived. The next stadtholder, Frederick Henry, disliked the exclusivity of high Calvinism; still less did he sympathize with the orthodox proposition that the state should devote itself to the interests of the church. During his years as stadtholder he allowed Arminian pastors quietly to return and take up the ministry again. The religious pluralism which had emerged in the 1580s and 1590s reasserted itself.

### Dutch Cultural Achievements

An assessment of the movement of Dutch history in the seventeenth century must pay attention not only to the defining features of the government of the republic, the dynamism of economic activity and the contributions which Dutch theologians and pastors made to the development of Calvinism, but also to the extent to which this small country of 1.5 million inhabitants excelled in certain spheres of cultural life. Of course, there is no necessary connection between the size of a country and the quality of its achievements in literature, the visual arts and so on; it is the nature of its social system and society's attitudes towards particular forms of cultural endeavour which count. In these regards, the United Provinces shared features in common with Italy: its most populous provinces were highly urbanized, cosmopolitan and well educated, and the republic, like several of the states of Italy, possessed numerous printing presses, both legal and clandestine, and a flourishing book trade. As regards education, there were five universities in the United Provinces – Leiden (founded 1575), Franeker (1585), Gröningen (1614), Utrecht (1636) and Harderwijk (1648) – and an array of good schools, usually founded through civic initiative. Leiden and Utrecht established themselves as the leading universities, the medical school of the former acquiring an international reputation and drawing students from across Europe. Wealthy merchants and regents sent their sons to these universities, but also hired teachers to provide education at home in subjects such as literature, mathematics, geography and philosophy. The mercantile and regent classes of the United Provinces regarded a 'modern' education as an essential prerequisite to worldly success.

One broad intellectual field in which the Dutch excelled was the experimental and applied sciences. Much traditional scientific

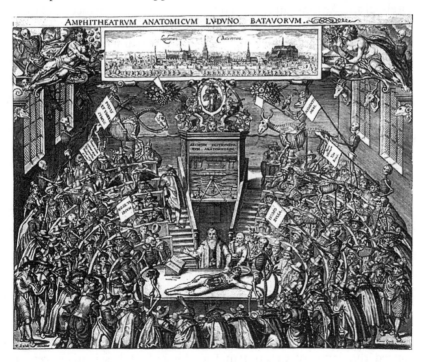

**Figure 3** The Anatomy Theatre at Leiden

thought was being challenged in the early 1600s, and one important source of scepticism was 'experimental learning' which, as the phrase indicates, advocated the study of the natural and material world through empirical research rather than through pure speculation. The United Provinces provided a congenial environment for experimental learning, not only because of the educational opportunities which they offered, but because of the expertise which they possessed in their extensive maritime enterprises: ship-building and its associated industries, the design and publication of maps or charts, the manufacture of navigational or surveying instruments, telescopes, glass and highly polished lenses, all of which served scientists as much as seamen. The towns of Holland possessed numerous workshops which made globes, sextants, quadrants, astrolabes, clocks and telescopes of the highest quality. One of the best known in Amsterdam in the 1620s was that of Willem Blaeu, while in Leiden the most prestigious was the house of Musschenbroek. Samuel van Musschenbroek and his brother Johan manufactured not only navigational aids, but scientific instruments such as microscopes and air pumps. In Hans Lippershey, Cornelis Drebbel and Antoni van Leeuwenhoek, the United Provinces had three of the leading designers of telescopes and microscopes in Europe.

Supported by an ample supply of good instruments, Dutch scientists in the first half of the century made a distinctive contribution to experimental learning. The outstanding figure was Isaac Beeckman of Middelburg, who did much fine work in mathematics and mechanics, in addition to his studies of navigation and optics. His interest in this last subject was inspired at Leiden University by Willibrodus Snellius, who discovered the law of refraction. Beeckman worked closely with Descartes on problems of motion and the acceleration of falling bodies. Using the newest microscopes, Leeuwenhoek and Jan Swammerdam were leaders in the study of capillary circulation of the blood, and in the study of corpuscles and bacteria in the blood. The rise of experimental learning posed difficult epistemological problems in the sciences; if newly acquired empirical evidence, especially if it could be replicated through repeated experiments, was in conflict with received theory, how should the two be related? Much scientific and philosophical controversy was generated by this question, for 'experimental learning' was not value free; and if received theory had to be revised or even abandoned, that could have implications for theology, and for social and political thought. In so far as they advanced the cause of experimental learning, Dutch scientists were at the centre of a wider European intellectual phenomenon.

On a more practical level, Dutch engineers were at the forefront of applied scientific knowledge, undertaking vast schemes with direct economic benefits. Jan Leeghwater was the outstanding expert in Europe in the drainage of lakes and swamps, and in converting the recovered land to agricultural use. Between 1612 and 1640 he directed the drainage of most of the lakes of Holland – Wieringer-waard, Purmer, Wormer and others – and was invited to France to undertake similar projects.

Another realm in which the Dutch proved to be masters was that of painting, and, as with the sciences, the nature of the Dutch social system had strong relevance for the visual arts. Calvinist churches contained little decoration and eschewed the paintings and statues that were to be found in Catholic churches; thus, Dutch artists not only lacked the ecclesiastical patronage that was crucial to artists elsewhere, but had no incentive to produce the large numbers of religious paintings that were a staple in Spain, France, Italy or else-where in Catholic Europe. In the predominantly Calvinist republic there was, for instance, little call for pictures of the Virgin or the saints. This is not to say that Dutch artists avoided religious subjects, but they normally chose them from the Bible. Nativity and crucifix-ion scenes were popular, and Rembrandt's *Belshazzar's Feast* attempts a dramatic representation of the appearance of writing on the wall as told in the Book of Daniel. Again, in a republic with no royal court or royal palaces (although Frederick Henry did construct a passable imitation of such a setting), there was no monarchic patronage to which artists could turn, but neither was there a dominant 'courtly' style to which they were expected to conform. Dutch artists were relatively free to experiment, and they did so to remarkable effect. It is difficult to identify a 'Dutch style' in painting; many styles were developed, and in so far as common traits did appear, it was in re-sponse to artistic problems rather than to the demands of patronage.

In the absence of ecclesiastical and royal patronage, Dutch artists compensated by the availability of a popular market for paintings. From the wealthiest burghers and merchants to people of modest financial means, the commercially minded inhabitants of the Dutch Republic had a liking for paintings, which guaranteed a healthy market for artists. Since most purchasers wanted pictures to hang on the walls of their houses, paintings often had to be small and cheap. Artists obliged by producing – indeed, almost mass producing – what the public wanted. The subject matter frequently came from familiar, everyday life: landscapes, river scenes, harbours, still lives, the interiors of houses, churches, inns and shops, scenes of urban life, views of towns or villages. Dutch painters certainly produced the kind of 'high' art that their counterparts did throughout Europe – great historical or mythological subjects – and like artists everywhere they were commissioned to paint portraits either of individuals or of groups such as trades guilds or town councils; but it was in their ability to turn the apparently commonplace into artistic masterpieces that Dutch painters created such a prodigious heritage. Quite apart from purely artistic considerations, Dutch artists left a pictorial record of their country, its people and their occupations, which is a first-class historical source. Even if no written records had survived, the historian would be able to construct a tolerable version of Dutch social and economic history from the visual record alone. Paintings of the interiors of houses frequently illustrate furniture, ornaments, wall decorations (maps making a frequent appearance), musical instruments, globes and scores of other artefacts. Scenes of rivers, harbours or the high seas show the mercantile community at work. Even winter scenes, so popular in the first half of the century, often depict people and children at leisure as they skate on the ice, play in the snow or otherwise divert themselves.

Yet while it is true that much of the work of Dutch artists was descriptive, it is also the case that, in the hands of the finest masters, common subjects were treated to uncommon effect. Thus, many church interiors by Pieter Saenredam or domestic interiors by Jan Vermeer are exercises in illusionist design, wherein more than one viewing point is adopted or human figures and objects are placed in overlapping planes. Adrian van de Velde transformed landscape, partly by his approach to design (he created a sense of spaciousness by dropping the horizon, devoting some three-quarters of a painting to the sky and keeping detail to a minimum), but also by an illusionist use of light: his monochrome tonalities related objects and colours, and turned his landscapes into powerfully atmospheric statements. His ideas were taken up by artists who painted domestic interiors. Rembrandt in the 1630s and 1640s, Adrian Ostade, Gabriel Metsu, Jan Steen and others, likewise used light to create atmosphere rather than simply illuminate and model people and objects. Similarly in portraiture, Dutch painters helped to raise the genre to new levels. Here the student can do no better than study the evolution of Rembrandt's treatment of the portrait (not least through the scores of self-portraits which he executed, tracing his own growth from young man to old). Therein can be seen the development of an artist who attempted to do more than create a 'photographic' effect; he aspired to convey something of the inner man or woman whom he was depicting.

In recent years, Dutch culture in the seventeenth century has proved a fruitful and profitable subject for historians, whose books are a timely reminder that, to understand civilizations of the past, it is certainly necessary to know something of their social, political and economic developments, but also to appreciate that those developments both affected, and in turn were affected by, particular cultural contexts. As we turn now towards the measures adopted by the government of the United Provinces to preserve the interests of the republic in the wider European setting, we should bear in mind that the governing elites thought of the republic, not just as a territory, but as a society which, having won its independence, was defining itself through particular forms of cultural expression.

## The Thirty Years War and the United Provinces

The Bohemian rising of 1618, its collapse in 1620 and the advance of the Spanish into the Palatinate confronted Maurice and the Estates General with a daunting challenge. In the short run, only two states realistically could give help to Frederick of the Palatinate: England and the Dutch Republic. The former proved ineffective; the chief burden therefore fell upon the republic. Frederick of the Palatinate was a Calvinist, and the Contra-Remonstrants called upon the stadtholder to go to his help. The Spanish truce was to expire in 1621, and a decision was also needed as to whether to seek to prolong it or return to war. The question was settled by the pressure of external events. The new king of Spain, Philip IV, was persuaded by his advisers that the time was ripe to attempt the reconquest of the republic, and the occupation of the Palatinate by his troops made war against the republic inevitable.

It began badly for the Dutch. Although the republic signed an alliance with Britain and France in 1624, little help was as yet forthcoming and the Spanish invaded the country, capturing Breda in 1625. In that year Maurice died, leaving his brother, Frederick Henry, as the main candidate to the stadtholderates. For several weeks, Frederick Henry had to concentrate on persuading the provincial states to elect him. By the summer of 1625 five had done so and he could now turn his full attention to the war. He proved to be a fine leader, he and his fellow commanders gradually driving out the

Spanish. By the end of 1627 both Overijssel and Friesland were relieved, and in 1629 Den Bosch was taken. At sea, the Spanish treasure fleet was captured by the Dutch at Havana. These were rare episodes of success in a decade which was generally dismal for Protestant states in the Thirty Years War. By 1630, the Danes had been defeated, the Holy Roman Emperor had issued the Edict of Restitution, and the entire Habsburg cause looked unstoppable. Then came the thunderbolts launched by Gustavus Adolphus of Sweden, who rapidly rolled back the Habsburgs. The crisis in the Habsburg camp allowed Frederick Henry to think in more ambitious terms. So far his war aim had been to expel the Spanish and secure the survival of the republic, but increasingly he believed that it might be possible to expel the Spanish from the southern Netherlands as well. He invaded the Spanish Netherlands in 1631, almost reaching Dunkirk; in the following year, the Dutch captured the fortress at Maastricht. Frederick Henry's expanding war aims were encouraged further when France declared war on Spain in 1635 and renewed the alliance with the Dutch Republic. France's human and financial resources were a match for those of Spain, and Frederick Henry could envisage some kind of 'United Netherlands' emerging from the war, with himself or a member of his family at the head.

His tendency to think in terms of the dynastic interests of his family as much as those of the republic caused misgivings within the states of Holland, to whom the war was being fought for security. It was costly both financially and in its harmful impact on overseas commerce; it had to be fought, but if Spain showed any readiness to sign peace, the states of Holland contended that the opportunity should be taken. In 1631 a new Lands Advocate was elected: Adrian Pauw. His relations with Frederick Henry at first were good, but he became unhappy at the stadtholder's confirmation of the alliance with France. Pauw felt that the stadtholder should have used the French declaration of war on Spain in 1635 to approach Spain with proposals for peace: Frederick Henry should have secured a treaty with Spain, and concentrated on economic rehabilitation while the Spanish and French fought each other. Instead, he had committed the republic to an alliance which would serve French interests more than Dutch, and in which the republic would be the junior partner. Frederick Henry engineered Pauw's dismissal in 1636 in favour of Jacob Cats, but Cats too became critical of the stadtholder's conduct of war.

Even the spectacular victory of the Dutch fleet at the battle of the Downs (1639) could not quell the disquiet in the states of Holland.

The suspicion was growing that the stadtholder was prolonging war for dynastic purposes: perhaps he aimed to turn the republic into a monarchy. Frederick Henry's son, William, had been born in 1627. In a procedure which resembled that whereby the imperial diet elected the emperor's son as king of the Romans, in 1629 the states of Utrecht and Overijssel recognized the infant as successor to his father as stadtholder, and in 1630 Holland and Zeeland followed suit. In 1641, William married Princess Mary, daughter of Charles I of England. This marriage into a royal family was a triumph for the Orange dynasty, for it raised the possibility that the house of Orange one day might rule Britain, as indeed transpired in 1689, although in circumstances not foreseen in 1641. More immediately, it gave succour to those 'Orangists' in the republic who were contemplating a possible 'kingdom of the Netherlands'. The Anglo-Dutch marriage alarmed supporters of the republican ideal, not only because it raised the possibility of an Orange king, but because it threatened to embroil the republic in the British civil war. In 1642 the Estates General banned the sending of money, supplies or troops to either side in England, but Frederick Henry clandestinely supported Charles I financially and materially; he allowed Prince Rupert and Scottish and English officers in the Dutch army to go to England to fight for the king.

By the mid-1640s the peace negotiations which had begun in Münster in 1643 were making progress. The Spanish government, whose war against France was proving difficult, was anxious to detach the republic from its French ally by making peace; the French government, on the other hand, was urging Frederick Henry to abide by the terms of their alliance, which prohibited either partner signing a separate peace. These and other matters became the focus of national and international attention in the autumn of 1646 when Frederick Henry fell seriously ill. In the event of his death, would the republic continue the negotiations at Münster, since it was known that his son and successor, William, was anti-Spanish and advocated the continuation of war? The states of Holland, which had borne most of the cost of war, wanted to press ahead with negotiations; if Frederick Henry died, would the states find themselves in conflict with the new stadtholder? The French government, which was in secret contact with William, was not distressed at news of Frederick Henry's illness; Cardinal Mazarin anticipated that, if the stadtholder died, William could be persuaded to abandon the Münster talks and pursue the war against Spain. Frederick Henry died on 17 March

1647. The question of the stadtholderate had been settled in 1629 and 1630; William II assumed his responsibilities, although the states of Holland did not confirm him as stadtholder of the province until after the Peace of Münster.

In the first test of strength with the new stadtholder, it was the states of Holland which prevailed. Through the Estates General it put pressure on the Dutch plenipotentiaries in Münster to settle terms as quickly as possible before William II, with French support, could wreck the talks. The Spanish government also recognized the danger, and moved towards a settlement. A Dutch–Spanish peace was signed on 3 January 1648 and confirmed by the more general Treaty of Münster in October. The Dutch secured recognition by Spain of the independence of the United Provinces, the transfer of land in Brabant to the republic, the closure of the river Scheldt in the Spanish Netherlands to all except Dutch ships, the introduction of Dutch tolls in the ports of Flanders, and the recognition by Spain of Dutch conquests in Portuguese overseas possessions. Whether or not these terms were to be welcomed in the republic was a matter of judgement. To the states of Holland and the mercantile community in general, they were excellent. An eighty-year conflict with Spain had ended, the republic was at peace and could now concentrate on economic and financial recovery. Provincial rights would again come into their own and the powers which the stadtholder had accumulated would be diminished. However, to William II, many nobles and even the states of smaller provinces, the peace was premature. The readiness of Spain to sign showed how vulnerable it was; could not even better terms be achieved by continuing the war in alliance with France? By pursuing the war to victory over Spain and driving the Spanish out of the southern Netherlands, it might be possible to create a greater, united Netherlands, although territorial concessions would have to be made to the French on the border of Flanders. Dutch opinion was divided over the merits of the 1648 peace, although the force of the 'Williamite' argument was weakened by the outbreak of the Frondes and the collapse of France into near anarchy.

## The Stadtholderate of William II and Emergence of Johan de Witt

William was stadtholder for three years before his death in 1650. However, this young man of decided opinions came close to achieving a revolution in the constitutional life of the republic. He regarded the peace of 1648 as a betrayal of its best interests and placed the blame on the states of Holland. He also recognized the constitutional assumptions behind the peace: the states of Holland regarded him as politically dangerous, suspecting him of monarchic ambitions; those suspicions were heightened even more when William gave shelter to the young Charles II after Charles I's execution in 1649. William played upon the execution of Charles to propagate anti-republican sentiments; he represented the beheading of the king of England as the kind of excess which befell a country where republicanism, as represented by the states of Holland, was unrestrained by a superior authority.

William's dispute with the states of Holland centred on the army. Now that the republic was at peace, the states of Holland contended that there was no need to maintain the army at war-time levels. Within the states, sentiments were expressed similar to those in the English parliament some years before: a large army might be used by the stadtholder to impose his political will on the country. In a republic whose 'constitution' had evolved in an *ad hoc* manner, the question of who had ultimate authority was exceedingly difficult to resolve. Was the army ultimately commanded by the Captain-General (the stadtholder), the Estates General or the individual provincial states? The states of Holland proceeded to demobilize regiments over which it claimed authority. Other provinces protested and William decided upon drastic action. In July 1650, he arrested six deputies from Holland in the Estates General and attempted to seize Amsterdam by force. The attack failed, but the city fathers sought a compromise. A settlement was mediated by representatives from the Estates General: anti-Orange elements were removed from the municipality of Amsterdam and other towns, and the states of Holland modified its demobilization programme. If anybody won in 1650, it was the Estates General.

Whether or not the compromise over the army would have simply been an armistice in the struggle between William II and the states of Holland was rendered academic by his death. His son, William III, was born later in the year, but meanwhile the Orange family quarrelled over who should assume the stadtholderate and Captain-Generalship of the army. In 1651 the states of Holland used the hiatus to call an extraordinary general assembly of the provinces. Five provinces abolished the office of stadtholder (Friesland and Gröningen retained it), while that of Captain-General likewise was revoked and the provinces assumed command of their own troops. Provincial authority had been endorsed, and with it the economic and political programme of the regents of Holland. For the next twenty-one years the republic was governed by the Estates General working through the provincial estates; the stadtholderate was not restored until the crisis of 1672.

During most of that period the single most influential figure in the republic was Johan de Witt, who was elected Lands Advocate in 1653. He epitomized the regent class and its political attitudes. He was born in 1625 into regent circles, his father Jacob being burgomaster of Dordrecht on several occasions and representing Dordrecht in the states of Holland, as did Johan's elder brother, Cornelis. Johan studied law at the University of Leiden, but also showed an exceptional aptitude for mathematics. After he and his brother undertook a grand tour in 1645 which took them to Switzerland, France, Italy and England, Johan worked as a lawyer at The Hague. He went into public life, and in 1650 was appointed leader of the Dordrecht representatives in the states of Holland, just when the conflict with William II was at its height; indeed, his father was one of the five delegates to the Estates General arrested by William in July 1650. They were released after William's death and, as has been said, the regents revised the institutions of the republic in accordance with their principles.

When he became Lands Advocate in 1653, de Witt inherited yet another war, this time against Commonwealth England. The regents hoped that, after peace with Spain in 1648, the republic could concentrate on economic recovery, but the British government turned hostile for the economic reasons that were discussed above (see pp. 177–8), and the Navigation Act (1651) deprived Dutch shipping of much lucrative business. War had broken out in 1652. De Witt was in office when the Rump proposed that the two states should unite. It was an idea which to de Witt lacked any shred of merit; his main purpose, which he failed to achieve, was the repeal of the Navigation Act. The war, as stated above, hit Dutch commerce hard. In 1653 there were riots in many towns of Holland and Zeeland at the scale of the losses and at the crippling decline of commerce. The poor performance of the Dutch fleets in home waters gave a renewed stimulus to Orangism in the republic. Orange factions asserted that had a stadtholder been in office, the war effort would have been better coordinated.

When de Witt discussed with England the terms that resulted in the Peace of Westminster, he bore the revival of Orangism in mind as much as the economic questions that had to be settled. The eventual terms were more favourable to England than to the republic, but in addition to the preservation of the Navigation Act and the precedence afforded by Dutch ships to English in the North Sea, there was another clause which was political in intent: the English demanded that the Orange family should be excluded from the stadtholderate, should that office ever be revived. Although in formal terms it was the English who insisted on the exclusion clause, there is circumstantial evidence that it was from de Witt himself that the idea came. It suited his republican and provincial ideals to neutralize the house of Orange as a force in Dutch political life, while placing the responsibility on others. When news of the exclusion clause reached the republic there were widespread protests, and it was dropped from the formal treaty of peace. However, de Witt and the English government had a secret agreement that nevertheless it should be enforced. The Peace of Westminster was ratified by the Estates General, whereupon de Witt introduced the exclusion clause into a meeting of the states of Holland. The states accepted it in spite of a vigorous Orangist campaign throughout the republic; over the next few years de Witt quietly persuaded other provinces to follow the example of Holland.

By the mid-1650s, the Dutch Republic was still a troubled state and society in many respects, yet it had assured its independence from Spain and established itself as a major regional power. Its economy remained among the most vibrant in Europe in spite of the impact of warfare, and there seemed every reason for that prosperity to continue. Yet the Estates General was very conscious that, to be a small state in the Europe of the seventeenth century was a perilous condition; should a major war break out again, the republic could scarcely remain neutral, and risked being exploited by larger powers to their own ends. For the time being, however, the republic was at peace, and could concentrate on the economic benefits to be derived therefrom.

# 6

# Northern Europe, 1618–1660: Scandinavia, Russia and Poland

That vast arc of territory from the Baltic countries into Russia and thence to the Black Sea and the Ottoman Empire, was affected by, and in some senses contributed to, the formative episodes of central and west European history, but it also had its own priorities. The historian must resist the temptation to suppose that central, southern and western Europe represent a norm against which the rest of Europe should be assessed. Nor should the north and east be seen as 'peripheral' regions, not least because they cover much larger areas than central, southern and western Europe. By the seventeenth century, most printed maps had adopted the convention of placing the north at the top, but the periphery was a cartographic illusion, not a representation of historical reality.

The north was thinly populated and suffered the hostile climatic changes which made this century a 'little ice age'. Winters were exceedingly long, the food-producing season was short, and famine and disease were common. Nature determined the patterns of socio-economic life in northern Europe more than in any other part of the continent. Most people lived near the coastline and the sixtieth parallel was the *de facto* northern limit of cities. Oslo and Stockholm lie close to this line of latitude, as do Helsinki (Helsingfors), founded by Gustavus I in 1550, and St Petersburg, built by Peter the Great at the beginning of the 1700s. Much of the history of Baltic Europe and Russia during this period may be interpreted in economic terms, as governments fought for control of material resources in a hard environment. As a major seaway, the Baltic provoked rivalries among would-be monopolists of its commerce. In the Middle Ages, the Hanseatic League predominated, but in the seventeenth century the Dutch gradually took over. Ports on the southern coast – Lübeck, Rostock, Stettin, Danzig, Königsberg, Riga and others – gave access to the hinterland of Germany and Poland, as did the Sound to the North Sea. Grain, iron, copper, fish and timber were the principal exports from the Baltic; wine, cloth, spices and manufactured goods were imported.

## SWEDEN

The kingdom of Sweden had a population of just over a million in the early 1600s, including those who lived in Finland. Between 1611 and 1660 it became the premier power in the Baltic, and did so by military conquests through which it annexed Carelia, Ingria, Estonia, Livonia and West Pomerania. Sweden also acquired Bremen and Verden in north-west Germany. Expansion exposed Sweden to the hostility of other Baltic states, and it spent most of the post-1660 period attempting to preserve earlier gains against retaliatory measures taken by the Danes, Poles, Russians and Germans. The preservation of a Baltic 'empire' imposed considerable strains upon the internal political and social stability of Sweden. The crown had to contend with frequent popular protest, and made generous concessions to the nobility in order to buy their continuing loyalty.

### Gustavus Adolphus and his Inheritance

Much of this territorial expansion was accomplished by Gustavus II Adolphus, whose reign began in 1611. Although only seventeen years of age when he succeeded, he had been thoroughly prepared for government by his father, Charles IX. As a boy, he met ambassadors, discussed politics with his father's advisers, and at the age of fifteen began to administer his duchy of Vestmanland. His education was based on the classics, but he was also fluent in Swedish, German, Italian and Dutch, and he acquired a grounding in Russian, Spanish and Polish. He also studied warfare and generalship. Charles IX had been a controversial monarch, accused by the aristocracy of autocratic tendencies. There was more than a little vindictiveness in this charge, for Charles had undermined the influence of the Riksråd, the aristocratic king's council, by working more frequently with the Riksdag, an assembly of nobles, clergy, burghers and free peasants. When Gustavus Adolphus succeeded to the throne, he made a point of improving relations with the aristocracy. He accepted a charter which listed the 'abuses' committed by his father, and which imposed on Gustavus the obligation to restore the aristocracy to their 'rightful' place in government. It also constrained him to introduce no new taxes without the consent of the Riksråd and Riksdag. One important source of revenue available to Gustavus was the iron and copper mines of Sweden. Copper was especially profitable: in 1623 he obtained over 23 per cent of his revenue from the copper mines at Falum, a proportion unmatched by any other single source.[1] Recognizing the contribution which copper and iron could make not only to the treasury but to the production of war materials, the king induced the finest mining engineers in Europe to work in Sweden. Several came from the Spanish Netherlands, including Anton Monier and, most celebrated of all, Louis de Geer.

Gustavus also inherited an efficient system of military recruitment. Since the 1540s the Swedish crown had practised national conscription. In 1617 Gustavus revised the system by dividing the kingdom into eight regions, each of which raised troops in numbers decided by the crown. Exemptions were granted to certain towns and occupations such as mining or ship-building; peasants living on the land of great aristocrats could also be excluded. This scheme, suitably modified as time went by, remained the basis of Swedish military recruitment throughout the century. The armies which Gustavus commanded were highly trained and equipped with the most modern weaponry. He had studied military techniques developed by Maurice of Nassau, but adapted them to his own requirements. The weapons which his troops used were supplied mainly from Sweden itself, where the metallurgical industries excelled in the production of light field guns. This was an area in which Gustavus surpassed Maurice of Nassau. Whereas Dutch armies usually took a handful of cannons into battle, Gustavus's troops had scores of light as well as heavy artillery, the former being transported and manoeuvred quickly around the battlefield.

Gustavus Adolphus inherited three wars from his father. One, against Denmark, was economic in origin. In 1570, Sweden had secured from Denmark exemption from the tolls which the Danes imposed on ships passing through the Sound between Elsinor and

Helsingborg. In 1607 Charles IX sought to expand upon this concession by creating a port at Göteborg, on the west coast of Norway, in territory which belonged to Sweden. His intention was that English, Dutch or other ships heading for the Baltic from the North Sea would discharge their cargoes at Göteborg, thus avoiding the tolls in the Sound. Swedish ships would then transport the cargoes to their destinations. Christian IV of Denmark, whose royal finances were heavily dependent on the tolls, saw this as an act of economic aggression. A Danish force attacked Göteborg and destroyed most of the installations. During the ensuing war, Charles IX died, but his son turned the tide on his Danish enemy. Peace was signed at Knared in 1613. Gustavus Adolphus made territorial concessions to Christian IV and agreed to pay an indemnity, but he recovered Göteborg and the exemptions which Swedish ships enjoyed in the Sound. The second war was against Russia,[2] which was just emerging from the Time of Troubles. Sweden used this period of anarchy to invade Russian provinces on the Baltic coastline. Carelia and Ingria fell to Gustavus. To the new tsar, Michael Romanov, whose priority was stability at home, peace with Sweden had to be signed at any price. By the Treaty of Stolbova (1617), Michael ceded these provinces to Gustavus. Russia was deprived of its outlet to the Baltic, whose eastern reaches were now controlled by Sweden.

The third conflict, between Sweden and Poland, continued a struggle which had been going on since 1601 when Charles IX attempted to seize parts of Polish Livonia. He suffered defeat at Riga in 1605, but pursued the war intermittently. Enmity between Sweden and Poland was fuelled by dynastic tensions, for the king of Poland, Sigismund III, was a member of the Vasa family and had designs on the throne of Sweden. Religious rivalries between Swedish Lutherans and Polish Catholics also contributed to hostilities. Gustavus Adolphus brought new vigour to the conflict. After his victories over Michael Romanov, he resumed the campaigns against Poland, concentrating on Livonia. He supplemented his military efforts with diplomatic moves. He signed an alliance with Tsar Michael, and in 1620 married Mary Eleanora of Brandenburg, sister of the elector, George William. The elector was duke of Prussia, and as such was a vassal of the king of Poland; through his marriage, Gustavus secured the neutrality of the elector. This latest phase of warfare between Poland and Sweden was fought concurrently with the Thirty Years War in Germany. Gustavus captured Riga in 1621 and completed the conquest of Livonia by 1626. Thereafter he invaded East Prussia and occupied several ports including Pillau and Elbing. The English and French governments attempted to mediate in both the Swedish–Polish war and the conflict in Germany. In 1629 their efforts bore fruit when peace was signed at Lübeck, ending the war between Christian IV of Denmark and the emperor (see above, p. 56), and the truce of Altmark suspended fighting between Sweden and Poland. Sweden retained most of the Prussian ports which it had occupied, and it secured a toll on shipping on the river Vistula. The truce was turned into a formal peace in 1635: Sweden returned all the Prussian ports in exchange for its complete occupation of Livonia.

### Oxenstierna and the Government of Sweden

When Gustavus Adolphus was absent from his kingdom on military campaigns, government, at least until 1626, was handled by his chancellor, Axel Oxenstierna. Appointed in 1612, Oxenstierna enjoyed the utmost trust of the king; indeed, their relationship bears comparison with those between Louis XIII and Richelieu and Philip IV and Olivares. Eleven years older than Gustavus, Oxenstierna came from one of the most distinguished aristocratic families in Sweden. His pedigree in itself rendered a service to Gustavus: that somebody of his status was at the centre of government exemplified the improving relations between crown and aristocracy which Gustavus desired. After university studies in Germany, Oxenstierna returned to Sweden in 1603 and entered the service of Charles IX. Charles used Oxenstierna's first-hand knowledge of Germany by sending him on diplomatic missions to Mecklenburg in 1606 and Denmark in 1610. Even after Oxenstierna's appointment as chancellor, Charles continued to employ his expertise in foreign relations. It was he who in 1620 headed the mission to Berlin which led to the marriage of Gustavus and Mary Eleanora, and he accompanied the king on some of the campaigns in Livonia. He was made governor general of the newly conquered Prussia in 1626, and negotiated the Truce of Altmark in 1629. The Prussian post kept him out of Sweden for ten years; he did not return until 1636.

Within Sweden, Oxenstierna introduced extensive constitutional and legal changes. He did so partly because he thought in terms of 'modern' and 'efficient' government, but also because he was convinced that Sweden could only undertake an expansionist foreign policy if its domestic affairs were in order. Warfare would impose financial and social strains; it was essential to anticipate them by reorganizing the principal branches of government, which still relied on improvisation. Many of the ideas which he adopted had been developed in the sixteenth century, but it was he who put them into effect. One realm in which he moved quickly was that of justice. Sweden lacked a supreme court which could take final decisions in cases which moved from one tribunal to another through successive appeals. This problem not only caused interminable delays and consumed large amounts of money, but occasioned disputes between courts regarding their respective spheres of competence. Cases eventually could go to the king himself for settlement, but this procedure only lengthened delays. In 1614 Oxenstierna drafted the Judicature Ordinance which created a supreme court based normally in Stockholm and empowered to pass final judgment. The effect was not immediate, for it took time to install the new court and agree its procedures. Even when it was operational, it too found itself weighed down by the number of cases requiring judgment. However, the new system was an improvement on the old, and other supreme courts were created for Finland (1623) and the Baltic provinces (1630). In an attempt to lessen the burden on the Stockholm court, another body was created for southern Sweden in 1634.

Like every government in Europe, that of Sweden had to grapple with complex financial problems. One major difficulty was that the king lacked a comprehensive accounting system whereby he could distinguish with tolerable accuracy the revenue actually received as against what was sought. Charles IX had taken steps to remedy the situation, but it was not until the Exchequer Ordinance (1618) created a 'college' of fiscal administrators, whose duty was to establish and maintain records of receipts and expenditure, that a reasonable system of accounting was established. The college was also instructed to conduct a review of the royal domain, identifying its existing possessions, and listing royal lands which had been alienated since the 1520s. Oxenstierna also reformed the Chancery. This body drafted all laws, royal correspondence and state papers, and its responsibilities touched almost every branch of government. In Oxenstierna's view it needed to be regularized in its structure and responsibilities. In 1618 the Chancery Ordinance clarified the membership of the Chancery: it was to comprise the chancellor, an archivist, six secretaries and a team of clerks. Each secretary was given charge of a defined geographical region. The ordinance was modified in 1626 when the number of secretaries was reduced to four, their respective responsibilities being: archives; domestic affairs and Denmark; Poland with Russia and the Baltic; and, finally, a secretary for relations with other foreign governments.

The Riksdag itself was not immune from change. This assembly, whose origins went back to the fourteenth century, was called by the king when he wanted advice or consent from the wider community; in the sixteenth century it had proved invaluable to Gustavus I when he broke with Rome and adopted Lutheranism as the religion of his kingdom. Such fundamental questions as the composition of the Riksdag, its functions and procedures had never been answered in the abstract; like other aspects of Swedish government, it had developed organically over time. In 1617 Oxenstierna presented it with proposals clarifying its composition and functions. The Riksdag Ordinance fixed the number of estates at four (nobles, clergy, burghers, peasants), laid down rules of procedure and decided who was eligible to attend the Riksdag; although membership fluctuated, it was usually above 500. During wartime, there arose the problem of what could be discussed in the Riksdag, for there was a self-evident danger that agents of enemy governments could secure sensitive information. To circumvent this problem, there was created in 1627 the Secret Committee composed mainly of representatives from the Riksdag. It dealt with subjects which were militarily or politically secret; although it began as an *ad hoc* committee, it became a fixed branch of government by the middle of the century.

Oxenstierna's reforms extended elsewhere – for example, into local government – and were coordinated and systematized in his Form of Government of 1634. This document of sixty-five clauses amounted almost to a written constitution confirming a mixed monarchy for Sweden. It divided government into five branches or colleges: the Supreme Court, a War Council, the Admiralty, the Exchequer and the Chancery. It defined their structures and procedures, and combined them into a coordinated system. It dealt with such questions as religion (the official status of the Lutheran church was confirmed), legislation (for the first time the role of the Riksdag was officially recognized), and how the country should be governed in the absence of the monarch (the heads of the five colleges would form a regency). The Form of Government was much admired outside Sweden for its modernity and clarity, but it also contained the potential for future tensions. Since much power was vested in the heads of the colleges (the 'Regents'), could they be relied upon to collaborate, or would rivalries develop? What would be the relationship between the Regents and the Riksdag? Would this latter body develop ambitions of its own and seek to expand the range of its competence? If it did, would it come into conflict with the king and the Regents? And what were the implications of this document for the monarch? Had the Form of Government in any sense imposed new limitations on the monarch? Was it a device to reaffirm aristocratic government in the aftermath of the death of Gustavus Adolphus?

## Social Consequences of Warfare

We saw in chapter 2 how, after the wars of the 1620s, Gustavus Adolphus was drawn into the Thirty Years War, and how Sweden remained involved until the Peace of Westphalia. In one sense, warfare brought bountiful rewards as Sweden imposed its hegemony throughout much of the Baltic, but at home a price was paid in terms of social division and hardship. The peasantry were especially vulnerable. They fell into three main strata. The free peasants (*bönder*) were *de facto* owners of their farms, although they paid a small annual sum – a form of ground rent – to the crown, usually in kind. They were represented in the Riksdag, their deputies being chosen by royal agents on the basis of between two and six per county. The *kronöbönder* worked the royal domain as tenant farmers, and it was from their ranks that most of the soldiers were recruited. The *frälsebönder* leased farms from aristocratic land-owners, and although in theory they were liable to be recruited into the army, it was possible for their masters to secure their exemption. There was also a floating population of itinerant labourers.

The burden of military service, which fell mainly on the *kronöbönder*, increased as the army grew in size. In 1621 the army had about 17,800 troops, but the numbers rose to 42,100 in 1630, 83,200 in 1631 and 149,000 in 1632.[3] The rapid expansion between 1630 and 1632 was achieved mainly by recruiting foreign mercenaries who, in 1632, accounted for 82 per cent of the Swedish army; this still meant that about 26,800 Swedes and Finns were in service. The annual levies of men in Sweden rose from about 10,000 a year in the early 1620s to perhaps 15,000 in the middle of the decade. After the death of Gustavus Adolphus, levies were less frequent, for by 1632 he had not only bound several German princes to Sweden through treaties which transferred much of the cost of war to them, but he and the regency which governed after 1632 used the financial resources of Sweden's Baltic provinces to continue hiring mercenaries, thus easing the pressure on the population at home. Even so, recruitment could not but have serious consequences for a country with such a small population. The experience of the village of Bygdeå in northern Sweden may not be typical, but it is a concrete example. Between 1621 and 1639 the village sent 230 men into the army, of whom 215 were killed or died on active service; five returned as invalids. The exodus of young men distorted the demographic structure of Bygdeå: the adult male population during this period declined by 40 per cent and the number of households headed by women rose by 700 per cent.[4]

The escalating financial cost of war forced the government to increase taxes, which fell mainly on the peasants. Gustavus Adolphus also resorted to the farming of direct taxes: groups of financiers paid him an annual sum and then collected revenue themselves. Such arrangements suited a money-starved government, but left scope for abuses by tax farmers and their agents. There were frequent complaints from peasants that the agents of tax farmers were assessing them at excessive levels or were demanding bribes in return for lower assessments. In Finland, cases arose of criminal gangs collaborating with tax collectors to extort protection money from peasants. There was much rural unrest in the 1620s, hardly a year passing without anti-tax riots. Nevertheless, peasant violence in Sweden was less serious than, for example, in France. One principal reason was the presence of peasants in the Riksdag, where they could voice their protests. The government heeded their demands, and in 1635 ended the farming of direct taxes.

Among the new taxes which Gustavus Adolphus introduced were duties on livestock and land in 1620, on food sold in markets in 1622, and on grain taken to be ground at mills in 1625. These tariffs affected the nobility as well as commoners, in spite of the fiscal privileges which nobles in Sweden enjoyed. This was the kind of issue which provoked crises between crown and nobility elsewhere in Europe, but it was balanced in Sweden by Gustavus's practice of granting or selling royal land to the nobility. In a sense a bargain was struck: nobles would tolerate the inroads which the crown made into their fiscal privileges, provided that it rewarded them with land. Gustavus Adolphus was not the first king of Sweden to alienate royal land in this way, but it was a feature of the 1620s explained chiefly by the exigencies of warfare.

## Queen Christina, 1632–1654

Under Gustavus Adolphus, the organization of the Swedish war effort, with all of its drawbacks, was probably the most effective in Europe; but his death at Lützen illustrated the danger of a king personally commanding his troops. He was succeeded by a daughter, Christina, who was only six years old. Because she could not rule personally until her eighteenth birthday, 8 December 1644, a regency governed in her name during these twelve years. When she did assume personal rule, Christina displayed nothing like the political acumen of her father. She dismissed Oxenstierna in 1645, and urged the Swedish negotiators in Westphalia to settle peace as quickly as possible. She accepted terms which, in Oxenstierna's opinion, were less favourable than could have been achieved by a more robust stance. She proved to be controversial in other respects. She made it clear that she had no intention of marrying, and proposed that her successor be her cousin, Charles Gustavus. Resisting pressure to the contrary, she persuaded the Riksdag in 1650 to declare the Swedish crown the hereditary possession of Charles and his line. On the question of religion, she came to reject Lutheranism and embrace Catholicism. These and other factors, such as her growing weariness with the demands of government, led her to the most dramatic decision of all, to abdicate in 1654. She left Sweden, travelled Europe, returned to Sweden on two occasions in the futile hope of resuming the crown, and finally settled in Rome where she died in 1689.

After his return from Germany in 1636, Oxenstierna was the commanding presence in the regency. He owed his authority in part to his unrivalled political experience and prestige, but also to the members of his wider family whom he brought into government. Three members of the Riksråd bore the name Oxenstierna, and at least eight senior councillors and administrators were linked to him by marriage. The domination of this 'clan' provoked resentment in other aristocratic circles. A group led by Carl Gyllenhielm (an illegitimate son of Charles IX) and John Casimir (Christina's uncle; it was his son who became Charles X in succession to Christina) accused Oxenstierna of exploiting the regency to turn Sweden into an 'aristocratic republic' run by his own house. The power of the Oxenstiernas alienated Christina, and was one factor in her decision to dispense with him in 1645.

Although Oxenstierna had persuaded Richelieu to continue French subsidies to Sweden, the regency had to adopt other measures for funding war. Oxenstierna was reluctant to increase the burden of direct taxation further, for it had already led to social unrest; it was the regency which, as stated above, ended the farming of direct taxes in 1635 in an attempt to placate the peasantry. Oxenstierna was well informed about civil disturbances elsewhere in Europe (he received reports on the revolt of the Nu-pieds in France), and took care not to provoke similar crises in Sweden. When it was necessary to raise taxation, he did so on customs duties or consumer goods; he preferred indirect to direct taxation on the ground that it was socially less divisive. His other favoured method of raising money was to distribute yet more royal land, either through sales or gifts in return for cash or favours. The scale on which Oxenstierna alienated royal land should not be exaggerated, but it was a device which he employed to considerable effect.

### War between Sweden and Denmark, 1643–1645

In foreign affairs, the regency had to direct Sweden's participation in the Thirty Years War, but in 1643 it committed the country to another war against Denmark. For several years, Emperor Ferdinand III had been attempting to bring Denmark and Poland into league against Sweden, and in 1643 these two kingdoms formed a defensive association. However, as in the past, this new war was triggered by disputes over tolls in the Sound. The Danes respected the exemption enjoyed by Swedish ships, but refused to extend the same right to ships from ports seized by Sweden during the Thirty Years War. They also raised the rates to be paid by Dutch ships, which by now were the most numerous in the Baltic.

Aware of the emperor's diplomatic efforts, and anxious not to wait until Christian IV of Denmark had built up his armed forces, Oxenstierna decided on a pre-emptive strike. In the autumn of 1643, he diverted Swedish troops from Germany into an attack on Denmark; a supporting fleet came from the Dutch Republic. Swedish forces occupied the Danish provinces of Schleswig and Holstein, and proceeded to invade Jutland. Although the Danish fleet performed well against the Swedes and Dutch, Christian IV knew that he could not prevail against the superior Swedish forces. He requested the French government to initiate peace negotiations. Cardinal Mazarin agreed, for he resented French subsidies being 'wasted' by the Swedes to fight Denmark. Christian IV satisfied the Dutch by lowering the charges imposed on their ships, and through French mediation signed the Peace of Brömsebro with Sweden in 1645. By its terms, he ceded two large islands in the eastern Baltic to Sweden: Gotland and Osel (although Sweden had been occupying the latter since 1570). As a guarantee of these terms, and as a warning to Sweden to remain at peace with Denmark, Mazarin signed an alliance with Christian IV later in 1645.

## Domestic Tensions in Sweden

By this time, Christina was ruling personally, having dismissed Oxenstierna, but her policies and conduct undermined the social stability which the chancellor had striven to preserve. At a time when governmental finances were strained to the limit, she built up a lavish royal court, the cost of which rose from about 3 per cent of national revenue in 1644 to over 12 per cent by 1654. She entertained large numbers of foreign visitors at court, patronized scholars, artists and writers generously, and tolerated luxury and scandalous conduct on a scale which evoked widespread condemnation from the clergy. In order to raise money, she resorted to the sale of noble titles as the Stuarts had done in Britain and the Bourbons in France. Among her new creations were seventeen counts (there were only three in 1632) and forty-seven barons, of whom over half were foreigners. The sale of titles provoked the kinds of protests from the older nobility that were expressed in England and France: the crown was subverting authentic noble lineage. Most serious of all was the scale on which Christina alienated royal land. Ironically, the Peace of Westphalia made the financial problems of the Swedish government worse rather than better, for the French subsidies ceased and the cost of administering the newly acquired territories had to be met. Between 1648 and 1654, Christina sold or donated land to nobles on a colossal scale; many of the gifts went to soldiers returning from the wars. By 1652, the amount of land in Sweden held by nobles had doubled since 1611, and in Finland it had gone up by 600 per cent. Revenues to the crown from the royal domain decreased as a result.

The alienations brought forth a rising tide of protest from peasants and clergy. When royal land passed into noble ownership, its peasants lost their status; the smaller the royal domain, the fewer the number of free and crown peasants. Quite apart from their concerns over their loss of status and rights, they could perceive a social revolution with political consequences taking place. In this they were supported by clergy who also feared the socio-political consequences of the alienation of the royal domain. They foresaw the possible disappearance of the free peasantry, the enserfdom of other peasants (as happened in Russia and Poland), and the loss of peasant representation in the Riksdag. Since the beginning of the century, the lower estates in the Riksdag had demanded Reductions: that is, a resumption by the crown of its alienated land. To the lower estates, a large and flourishing royal domain was the best guarantee of the monarch's independence, and therefore of his or her ability to uphold the rights and privileges of commoners, including peasants. The loss of royal land increased the influence of the nobility over the crown and upset the 'balance' which, to burghers, clergy and peasants, constituted 'authentic' Swedish society. Such concerns were expressed widely from the pulpit, but also in a pamphlet campaign which broke out in 1649. Oxenstierna, and the expansion of aristocratic power which he exemplified, were attacked. Like the Mazarinades in France, this pamphlet campaign called for a return to an idealized past when a prosperous monarch protected the rights and privileges of subjects.

When the Riksdag met in 1650, the lower estates formed an unprecedented alliance to defend their 'liberties' against the nobility. They issued a Protestation declaring that too much royal land had been alienated, extraordinary fiscal measures had become permanent and the liberties of the monarch's subjects had been sacrificed; to remedy these grievances, the Protestation sought an end to the alienation of royal land, a programme of Reduction, greater financial contributions by the conquered lands, equality before the law and appointments to public offices according to merit, not social status. Only one person could enforce these demands, the queen, but she was in no financial or political position to consent. However, she did exploit the Protestation to her own constitutional ends. Having refused to marry, the question of her successor was paramount. This was settled in 1649 when the Riksråd agreed that her cousin, Charles Gustavus, would succeed, but it refused to accept him as hereditary king; in that case, the crown would become elective again. Christina outwitted the noble opposition by expressing sympathy with the Protestation. Aristocrats fearful of losing land pleaded with her not to proceed with a Reduction. Her price was their recognition of Charles Gustavus as hereditary king. Faced with this choice, aristo-

cratic resistance collapsed, and in 1650 the Riksdag acknowledged
Charles Gustavus and his line as hereditary monarchs.

Having secured her purpose, Christina withdrew her support for
the Protestation, effectively rendering it null and void. The Riksdag
met again in 1652, but she still refused a Reduction. By now social
distress had risen to dangerous levels, made worse by the exceptionally hard winter of 1652–3, which was accompanied by disease and
famine. In February 1653, revolts and army mutinies spread across
southern Sweden. At Närke, peasants elected a 'king', a 'chancellor'
and a 'marshal'. This was an act of derision at the perceived ineptitude of the government, not an attempt at alternative government,
but it signalled the depth of popular discontent. Sweden in the early
1650s was experiencing social turmoil in common with other parts of
Europe. It never threatened to turn into a Fronde or a civil war, not
least because the nobility and urban elites played little part, but it
demonstrated that Christina left her successor, Charles X, an impoverished government beset by a fearsome array of domestic problems.

## Charles X, 1654–1660

Charles X Gustavus, cousin of Christina, was thirty-two when she
abdicated. For several years he had fought in the Swedish army and
had attended the royal court. He had discreetly withdrawn as she
prepared her abdication, only returning to Stockholm after she left the
country. Brief as it was, his reign exemplified the strategic dilemma in
which Sweden now found itself. From certain perspectives, Sweden
was the success story of the Baltic, but its imperial edifice rested on
dangerously slender foundations. War had created Swedish hegemony,
and it was only by further war that hegemony could be preserved.
Charles hoped to repair the finances of the crown by taking up again
the question of a Reduction. After the meeting of the Riksdag in
1655, he created a Reduction College which would oversee the return
of one-quarter of lands alienated to the nobility since 1632. The necessity for measures of financial rehabilitation was all the more pressing because Charles, who had been following international affairs in
the Baltic closely, came to the throne persuaded that the years of peace
which Sweden had enjoyed since 1648 must come to an end: war
must be undertaken again, this time against Poland.

The two states had been at peace since 1635, but Charles regarded
Poland as presenting a danger to Sweden which, although indirect

rather than direct, could not be ignored. When Charles ascended the throne, Poland was in the midst of an internal crisis. A great Cossack rising had occurred in Poland in 1648, and in 1654 it led to intervention by Russia. There seemed every prospect that Russia would seize Polish territory and secure an outlet into the Baltic. This was the prospect which alarmed Charles X, for in his own mind he saw Russia as presenting a greater long-term threat to Sweden than either Denmark or Poland. He decided to forestall further Russian advance, not by offering aid to King John Casimir of Poland, but by invading and occupying part of Poland himself, and erecting a barrier against further Russian advance. In 1655 he invaded Poland and in the first twelve months of campaigning enjoyed remarkable success. He took Warsaw and Cracow, and forced the Polish army to surrender. John Casimir fled to the Austrian Habsburg province of Silesia. The commander of the Swedish army, Magnus Gabriel de la Gardie, signed a convention with representatives from the Grand Duchy of Lithuania, who ended their union with Poland in favour of one with Sweden. Charles X now had the barrier against Russia which he desired.

Swedish victories caused other governments to reassess their positions. The tsar now sought a *rapprochement* with John Casimir. Knowing that a Swedish-occupied Poland would be a much tougher prospect than one ruled by John Casimir, he suspended operations to allow John to recoup his forces. Encouraged by the latest news from Poland, John did so, returning to Poland in January 1656. By this time, the conduct of the Swedish army had provoked outrage in Poland, not only because of its brutality against the civilian population, but because of the spoliation which it inflicted on Catholic churches, monasteries and convents. Although it was not Charles X's intention, the invasion assumed features of a religious war. The first check to Swedish advance occurred in the autumn of 1655 at Czenstochowa, a town with a strong cult of the Virgin Mary. After a siege of seventy days, the Swedes retreated. Poles attributed their victory to the intervention of the Virgin Mary, and were inspired by confidence that she would continue to assist them to repel the Swedish heretics. When John Casimir returned to Poland, he recruited troops fired by a powerful religious and national fanaticism.

The elector of Brandenburg, Frederick William, also observed Swedish advance with concern. One of the Swedish armies which invaded Poland had passed through Brandenburg without his consent, and by the Treaty of Königsberg (1656), Frederick William was forced by Charles X into an alliance. Frederick William was obliged to send soldiers to assist the Swedes. They fought well, helping Charles X to recapture Warsaw in July 1656 after John Casimir had briefly reoccupied it. By the Treaty of Labiau (November 1656), Charles X continued to buy Frederick William's support by promising to recognize his full sovereignty over Prussia. In 1657, however, Frederick William changed sides. An imperial representative, anxious to secure his electoral vote for the Habsburg candidate in the next imperial election, offered to secure Polish acceptance of Brandenburg's sovereignty over Prussia in return for Frederick William's transferring his support to John Casimir. By the secret Treaty of Wehlau (1657), the elector agreed and got the recognition of his sovereignty over Prussia that he sought. The attitude of the Holy Roman Emperor, Ferdinand III, to events in Poland was likewise ambivalent. Although he signed an alliance with John Casimir in 1657 and sent him subsidies, he also exploited John's difficulties by occupying certain frontier towns over which they were in dispute. Ferdinand died in 1657 and his successor, Leopold I, adopted a more resolute position. He collaborated fully with John Casimir and Frederick William in attempting to drive out the Swedes.

The war extended with the entry of Denmark. Hoping to reverse some of his country's earlier losses to Sweden, Frederick III of Denmark took the opportunity of Charles X's absence in Poland to declare war in 1657. It was a bad miscalculation. Charles diverted troops from Poland and, in a brilliant campaign, invaded Denmark and forced Frederick III to accept the Treaty of Röskilde (1658). Denmark ceded the eastern side of the Sound to Sweden. This was a heavy blow to the Danes, and when they proved reluctant to implement the treaty, Charles X laid siege to Copenhagen. This 'Northern War' now acquired wider ramifications, for the Dutch Republic, England, France and other countries with commercial interests in the Baltic were unwilling to tolerate the seemingly relentless extension of Swedish power. A Dutch fleet was sent to support the Danes, and the French, having ended their war against Spain in 1659, used their influence to restrain Charles X. Meanwhile, a combined Polish–Austrian army had invaded Swedish Pomerania and threatened the port of Stettin. Charles X recognized that he would make no further military gains and that it was time to discuss peace. Two sets of negotiations were set in motion. One took place at Oliva near Danzig, with France serving as mediator. A treaty was signed on 3 May 1660 by which the king of Poland renounced his claims to the throne of Sweden, Sweden retained Livonia, and Poland confirmed the sovereignty in Prussia of Brandenburg. The other discussions took place in Copenhagen, where the Dutch government was chief mediator. Denmark and Sweden signed peace on 4 June 1660. The terms of Röskilde were confirmed, with the additional proviso that the Sound must be open to international shipping. Peace had come to the Baltic, thanks to the diplomatic interventions of the French, Dutch and other non-Baltic governments. Sweden remained the chief power, but the question of how long it could do so remained. It was a question for Charles X's successor. Charles had died on 13 February 1660 in his thirty-eighth year. He left a five-year-old son as Charles XI, and it would be for him, after a period of regency, to consider how Sweden might uphold its Baltic hegemony.

## DENMARK

The expansion of Swedish power in the Baltic had obvious implications for its great rival Denmark, and was an important contributory factor in the royal coup which took place in 1660. Before his decision to enter the Thirty Years War, Christian IV of Denmark enjoyed considerable domestic independence of action, even though in theory royal authority was circumscribed by that of the Rigsdag, composed of nobles, clergy and burghers, and the Rigsraad, the aristocratic inner royal council. The king was elected by the Rigsdag (although the eldest son of a deceased king was normally chosen), which also required him to agree to a charter guaranteeing the rights and liberties of his subjects. The king needed the consent of the Rigsdag before introducing taxation or undertaking major policy initiatives. Until his intervention in Germany in 1624, Christian IV nevertheless was free from excessive control by the Rigsdag and Rigsraad because of the healthy financial position in which he found himself. He enjoyed his favourable position for two main reasons. One was that the crown had appropriated church lands in the sixteenth century, as the Tudors did in England; by selling or leasing the land, it kept the royal coffers reasonably full. The second, and more important, reason was the tolls which the king derived from shipping passing through the Sound; these latter revenues were the most lucrative single source of royal income.

Warfare, however, wreaked havoc with crown finances. After his intervention in Germany in 1624, Christian IV was obliged to invent numerous extraordinary levies which required the consent of the

Rigsraad and Rigsdag; he also had to raise the levels of regular taxation. Since the nobility enjoyed exemptions from most direct taxes, higher taxation affected commoners, whose resentment towards noble privileges increased. The military failures of Christian IV led to the invasion of Jutland by Wallenstein, whose army left a trail of destruction, impoverishing a population from which higher taxes were being demanded. Just as harmful to the socio-economic structure of Denmark were the disastrous harvests of 1629–30, which caused serious shortages of food, and the outbreak of bubonic plague in 1629 which swept through Jutland and into the islands. In 1629, Christian IV signed the Peace of Lübeck, and although it did not impose particularly punitive terms on Denmark, it did add to the country's desperate predicament by obliging Christian IV to pay an indemnity to the emperor. Bitter soul-searching followed the peace. The crown blamed the Rigsraad and Rigsdag for the recent failures, while they blamed the crown; among clergy, burghers and peasants there was much popular hostility towards a political system which manifestly had failed to uphold the interests of Denmark. Sympathy lay mostly with the king who, in the popular imagination, had been frustrated in his attempts to defend the kingdom by self-interested nobles, more concerned to preserve their fiscal privileges than to save the country from invasion.

In spite of this sour atmosphere, the crown had to continue to impose extraordinary taxes throughout the 1630s in order to pay off debts accumulated during the war. As part of his plans for financial recovery, Christian paid special attention to the efficiency with which Sound tolls were collected. His measures provoked the Dutch and Swedes in particular. Disputes over Sound tolls were behind the war of 1643–5, when once again Danish territory was invaded, this time by Swedish forces. On this occasion, Christian, as was seen above, was saved by the French, whose diplomatic pressure upon Sweden led to the Peace of Brömsebro (1645), another humiliation for Denmark.

Christian died in 1648; the Rigsdag elected his son as Frederick III and, as was the custom, the Rigsraad insisted that he consent to a charter before ascending the throne. It removed ambiguities in the relationship between crown and nobility, by affirming that Denmark was a country in which the latter held the upper hand. The charter of 1648 constituted an unequivocal statement of noble power over the king. It did so by proclaiming the right of nobles to resist Frederick if he departed from the terms of the charter, and of the Rigsraad to take over the running of the kingdom should such an eventuality occur. In short, the monarchy was subjected to the 250 wealthiest noble families, who between them owned about half of Denmark, and especially to about forty families who together owned about 40 per cent of the country.

The triumph of the Danish nobility over the crown was to rebound on them with a vengeance. When, in 1657, Frederick III declared war on Sweden, the Danish forces collapsed again. Charles X invaded Denmark, which had to accept the Treaty of Röskilde (1658) and that of Oliva (1660). Denmark lost its exclusive control of the Sound, and had to make further concessions to Sweden. Within Denmark, there was no question as to who bore the responsibility for these further defeats: the nobility, who had imposed restrictions on the king by the charter of 1648, and the Rigsraad. A mood of popular hostility towards the nobility developed, which Frederick III quickly exploited. In 1660 he called an extraordinary assembly of nobles, clergy and burghers in Copenhagen, and formed an alliance with the last two orders against the first. Demonstrations took place in favour of the king, and the militia imposed its control over the city. The nobility surrendered to its opponents. The assembly annulled the charter of 1648, and turned the crown into a hereditary possession of Frederick and his successors. The king undertook to replace the charter with new provisions, incorporating tax reforms and measures to reduce crown debt. The king and his advisers worked at this over the next few years until, in 1665, they produced what was, in effect, a new constitution for Denmark. They turned Denmark into an absolute monarchy, the king enjoying powers to which even Louis XIV never aspired. The king was acknowledged as being above the law; he embodied the state, and henceforth was authorized to create and promulgate all law without consultation. Such claims were bound to be provocative, and it was for this reason that the provisions of this constitution were kept secret until Frederick's death (1670), and it was his successor, Christian V, who openly adopted them. Thus, although Denmark was spared the civil wars of France or Britain in the 1640s, the powers of its monarchy were limited in 1648, but, as in those two other countries, the monarchy revived around 1660. The Danish form of absolutism lasted until 1848.

## RUSSIA

The term 'Russia', although used in the seventeenth century, was strictly speaking inexact; contemporaries also employed the more accurate 'Muscovy'.[5] The Muscovite state had expanded and consolidated itself in the fifteenth and early sixteenth centuries. Its heartland was defined by its river system, and its eastern limit by the Ural mountains which run from the Kara Sea in the north almost to the Caspian Sea in the south. In the seventeenth century, another period of expansion began as the state extended its authority east of the Urals into Siberia. The three principal rivers were the Neva, which flowed into the Baltic and had Novgorod as its principal city; the Dnieper on which stood Kiev (a Polish city in the early seventeenth century) and which flowed into the Black Sea; and the Volga, which flowed into the Caspian Sea. In the middle of the country, on a tributary of the Volga, stood Moscow. Other networks of rivers ran through the low-lying heartland and carried most of the commerce of Muscovy. Russian rulers pushed west towards the Baltic in the sixteenth century, but by the Treaty of Stolbova in 1617 the tsar abandoned the Baltic provinces to Sweden, and in 1618 signed a fourteen-year truce with Poland whereby several towns, including Smolensk, were surrendered. Russia accepted these humiliating terms in order to concentrate on internal recovery after the Time of Troubles (1598–1613).

These years of anarchy were composed of dynastic struggles which coincided with a calamitous famine arising from general harvest failures between 1601 and 1604. The dynastic rivalries can be traced to the death of Ivan IV ('the Terrible') in 1584. His successor was his simple-minded son Fedor, during whose reign government was run by Fedor's brother-in-law, Boris Godunov. Fedor had a half-brother, Dmitri, whom he exiled to the provinces. In 1591 news arrived in Moscow that Dmitri, aged nine, had been found with his throat cut; murder was suspected, but an inquiry concluded that he had committed suicide. Thus, when Fedor himself died without an heir in 1598, the main line of the Riurik dynasty – like the Valois in France (1589) and the Tudors in England (1603) – expired. To settle the succession, a Zemsky Sobor[6] met and elected Boris Godunov as tsar. Boris would not concede the principle of election. For several days he rejected the adjurations of the Zemsky Sobor, then announced that, in a vision, God had called him to be tsar. He accepted the throne, not, he insisted, by election, but in obedience to God.

During his reign the great famine occurred. Amidst the socio-economic crisis which it created, groups of disaffected nobles (*boyars*) plotted to overthrow Boris, and various 'false Dmitris' appeared, a phenomenon similar to Sebastianism in Portugal. Rumours spread that Dmitri had not died, but had emerged from hiding to claim the throne. The first such 'Dmitri' appeared in Poland in 1603. Sigismund III of Poland allowed him to raise troops, and for two years the pretender campaigned against Boris, who died in April 1605. Boris's son succeeded as Fedor II, but *boyars* overthrew him, admitted the self-styled Dmitri into Moscow and had him crowned tsar. However, the new tsar failed to dispel the impression that he was a pawn of Polish policy. He married a Polish princess, whose arrival in May 1606 with a large train of nobles and Catholic priests, provoked the kind of hostility in Moscow that Henriette-Marie of France was to arouse in London twenty years later. A group of *boyars*, led by Prince Basil Shuisky, who objected to the influence of the Poles, incited mobs to attack the palace in 1606; in the violence, the tsar was killed.

Shuisky, who belonged to a cadet branch of the Riurik dynasty, assumed the crown by succession. He reigned until 1610, but faced constant rebellion in the provinces as more rumours spread that Dmitri miraculously was still alive. A second 'Dmitri' emerged in Poland in 1607; he too received military support from Sigismund III and invaded Russia, which collapsed into anarchy again. More Polish forces advanced into Russia, and as they approached Moscow, Sigismund decided to abandon the second Dmitri, who retreated south, and impose his own son, Wladislaus, upon the throne. In 1610 Sigismund's army occupied Moscow, forcing Shuisky to abdicate. Now that he controlled much of Russia, Sigismund withdrew his son's candidature and presented himself as prospective tsar. This provoked a violent reaction throughout the country and at every level of society. Church leaders called upon Russians to resist the Poles, and nobles led an army which drove them from Moscow in 1612. In 1613 another Zemsky Sobor met. It chose as tsar a sixteen-year-old aristocrat who had marriage links to the Riurik dynasty: Michael Fedorovich Romanov. Although the circumstances of his ascension to the throne were unpropitious, Michael not only was to survive, but was the first of a family which ruled Russia until 1917. The dynastic conflict was over.

This brief summary cannot convey the brutal reality of the violence and anarchy which accompanied the Time of Troubles. Wide tracts of Russia were devastated by the passage of soldiers and bands of brigands, whose depredations added to the socio-economic havoc wreaked by famine. Villages and towns were destroyed or sacked, and much of Moscow was burnt when the Poles defended it against the Russian counter-attack. A desperately weakened Russia was exposed to the aggression of neighbours, who exploited every opportunity to appropriate Russian territory; hence the treaty of 1617 and truce of 1618.

## Sources of Revival: the Church

The Time of Troubles was a catastrophe, yet the Muscovite state survived. One source of preservation was the Orthodox church. The Orthodox and Catholic churches had split in 1054. The main territorial distribution of Orthodoxy coincided with the boundaries of the Byzantine empire, but also extended into Russia. The fall of Constantinople in 1453 confronted Orthodoxy with a crisis, for the Ottoman Turks were Muslim. It also forced the church in Russia to reassess its situation, for after 1453 it was the only branch of Orthodoxy to be independent of Islam. It steadily acquired a sense of destiny which had implications not only for the church but for the Muscovite state as well. The Russian church came to see itself as called to preserve the purity of Orthodox faith and worship in a hostile world wherein Catholicism, Islam and, in due course, Protestantism endangered true belief. This notion expressed itself in the idea of Moscow as the 'Third Rome'. According to this thesis, Rome had lost its spiritual authority in the schism of 1054, Constantinople had lasted as the second Rome for four hundred years, and now the mantle had descended on Moscow. The theory was millenarian in character. Russian spiritual leaders believed that the Second Coming was imminent and that the 'Third Rome' must prepare the faithful to be gathered up by Christ; heretics and infidels would be consigned to perdition. In order to fulfil this great task, the church needed the backing of the tsar. The Orthodox church proclaimed that the tsar had spiritual as well as secular authority; he was a quasi-religious figure entrusted by God to share in fulfilling the divine will. He must receive the complete obedience of his subjects, over whom he exercised unquestioned control.

The growing self-assurance of the Russian Orthodox church and the religious importance of Moscow found expression in architecture. Splendid churches were built, notably the Cathedral of the Assumption in the Kremlin in the 1470s, and in the 1550s the church of Basil the Blessed in the Red Square of Moscow. In 1589, the metropolitan of Moscow was elevated to the rank of patriarch; thereby the entire Orthodox church acknowledged the spiritual authority of Moscow as equal to that of Constantinople.[7] In the sixteenth century, the Russian Orthodox church engaged in extensive missionary work, pushing north into Lapland and east into the middle Volga region. By the 1620s, archbishoprics were established at Kazan and Tobolsk, and by the middle of the century, the church was established on the Pacific coast. During the Time of Troubles it suffered as much as every other section of society, but it preserved its hold on the mass of the population, who looked to it as a source of consolation and, in the war to liberate Moscow from the Poles in 1612, inspiration.

### Sources of Revival: the Tsar

Another institution which enabled Russia to survive was that of tsarism, in spite of its chequered history during the Time of Troubles. The prestige and authority of the office were such that nobody could rule other than the tsar. The emergence of pretenders was in itself a tribute to tsarism as a concept. There was no organizational or institutional alternative to tsarism (the Zemsky Sobor was called only in times of emergency; it lacked any potential to develop into a regular parliamentary body); the Time of Troubles confirmed the universal view that, in the absence of a strong tsar, Russia would fall prey to internal chaos and foreign invaders. All in all, tsarism had an enormous capacity for survival, even if its powers for practical jurisdiction might be emasculated. The title was of relatively recent origin, having emerged in the aftermath of 1453. In 1472, Grand Duke Ivan III married the niece of the last emperor of Byzantium. By a process which was the secular counterpart of the claims of Moscow to be the third Rome, Ivan and his son, Basil III, designated themselves 'tsar' ('caesar'), thereby unilaterally assuming attributes of the Byzantine emperor. As a symbol of this self-ascribed status, they added the two-headed Byzantine eagle to their state seals. When Ivan IV was crowned in 1547, in a ceremony which drew extensively and consciously on Byzantine coronation ritual, he officially took the title of tsar. In 1561 the patriarch of Constantinople conferred his recognition.

In his correspondence, Ivan III further appropriated the imperial tradition by referring to himself as 'autocrat', by which he meant that, like the emperors of Byzantium, he was independent of all earthly authority, be it secular or religious. Ivan IV expanded the concept to incorporate the notion that he was proprietor of the state. To this end he conducted a long and sustained assault on the princes and old aristocracy. His principal weapon was the Oprichnina. In 1565 he divided Russia into two unequal parts: in the larger, the Zemschina, existing land-owners were permitted to retain their estates, but the smaller, the Oprichnina, was designated the personal land of the tsar. Aristocratic land-owners whose estates fell within the Oprichnina were dispossessed and their land redistributed by Ivan, mostly to lesser nobles who had served him. These newcomers – Oprichniki – became tenants of the land, holding it at the pleasure of the tsar. During the rest of his reign he extended the Oprichnina at the expense of the Zemschina until, by his death, about half of Russia had been transferred. This process was not pursued peacefully. Dispossessions took place by force and were resisted violently. For several years large segments of Ivan's Russia were in a condition of civil war as Oprichnikis and land-owners fought. In 1572, Ivan IV nominally abandoned the scheme, but in practice it continued. In the longer term it facilitated the triumph of the principle that Russia was a service state: social status and the occupation of land depended on service given to the tsar.

## Sources of Revival: the Army

Since the Muscovite state was extended by the wars of the fifteenth and sixteenth centuries, the question of military organization was crucial to its ability to continue expansion and resist foreign enemies. Geopolitical facts dictated that the latter would be numerous. In the south and south-east, the Muscovite state had a string of fortifications near its indeterminate borders with the Tatars. The military servitors who were stationed there were mostly cavalry supported by foot soldiers. They made little use of modern weapons, and fought what was essentially guerrilla war against the Tatars. As compensation, they received grants of land. Russians and Tatars were locked in permanent conflict, and the concept of a frontier had to be extremely flexible. Even Ivan IV tolerated this situation, for a systematic attempt to overcome the Tatars could have brought him face to face with the Ottoman Empire, a much more formidable foe. Irritating and destructive though they were, the Tatars were a useful barrier between Russia and the Ottoman Turks. The tsars made use of Cossacks against the Tatars. Cossacks were mainly peasant refugees from Russia who had fled warfare, famine and the assaults of the Oprichniki. Leading a semi-nomadic life, they organized themselves into bands, each of which elected its leader (*hetman*). The tsars rewarded them with grants of land, and immunity from being returned to the estates which they had left.

Wars against western enemies required a different military structure from that in the east. Polish and Swedish forces were more highly organized than were the Tatars, and made systematic use of gunpowder weapons. The Russian armies which fought in the west also employed artillery; the heaviest guns were limited to the defence of cities, but lighter cannon were occasionally used in the field. However, even the Russian armies which fought in the west continued to rely on cavalry, and were largely ineffective against enemies deploying up-to-date weapons and infantry tactics. The recruitment of the Russian army was also archaic by comparison with, for example, Sweden. It still relied heavily on nobles being called by the tsar and bringing servitors with them. In the minutely stratified society of the nobility, there were frequent quarrels over rank and precedence of command, to the extent that military efficiency sometimes was sacrificed. It was not until the 1630s, when a New Model Army began to be formed, that Russia consciously sought to imitate western military organization.

The New Model Army emerged in the 1630s, at first through the initiative of Patriarch Filaret, father and chief minister of Tsar Michael Romanov. Filaret recognized that if Russia were to fight western enemies on their own terms, it must adopt western military structures, weapons and tactics. Moreover, this was a propitious time to do so, for the Thirty Years War had created a pool of mercenaries and military expertise which could easily be recruited. Between 1630 and 1634, the government created ten regiments of foreigners. More were recruited in the 1650s, and some 60,000 foreign mercenaries were in service by the 1660s. Some mercenaries such as the Scot, Alexander Leslie, trained the Russian army in modern, western warfare. The government paid for the translation into Russian of western military manuals. The first, available in 1647, was *The Art of Infantry Warfare*, a German text written by Johann von Wallhausen in 1615; in 1649 a set of *Military Instructions*, based on those of Maurice of Nassau, was adopted by the Russian army as its basic training manual.

## The Russian Peasantry

The dynamics which affected state and church in the sixteenth century contributed to important changes in the condition of the Russian peasantry. Even at the best of times Russia was sparsely populated, but the social and political crises of the late 1500s made the situation worse. In the late 1500s the average distribution of population was only about three or four people per square kilometre, whereas that of France was about forty.[8] Like their counterparts elsewhere, the peasants of Russia were far from uniform either in social status or economic standing. Most prosperous were the 'black peasants' who worked the tsar's personal domain, and tenant farmers who leased land either from the church or nobles; beneath them were assorted groups of landless labourers, some residing permanently in villages, other itinerant; below them were bondsmen of lords, working their land in return for maintenance; at the bottom of the social hierarchy were the slaves. In north-west Russia, slaves constituted about 7 or 8 per cent of the population, whereas they could rise to almost 50 per cent of the labour force on the eastern and southern frontiers.[9] Peasant farms were grouped into communes, whose area often corresponded to the parish. Communal affairs, including the distribution and collection of taxes, were overseen by peasants elected from within the commune.

The principal change to affect peasants was the rise of serfdom and its formalization by the code of 1649. Serfdom was not a phenomenon peculiar to Russia; it also emerged in Germany east of the Elbe and Poland. The civil disruption and social distress of the mid- and late 1500s caused heavy depopulation in the Russian heartland. Peasants fled from war zones, and, in times of famine, many of those who survived did so by moving south in the direction of the Black Sea and Caspian Sea. The Time of Troubles further increased peasant dislocation. Population statistics for Russia can only be impressionistic, but if the area around Novgorod is taken as an example, the population fell from about 396,000 in 1500 to 95,000 in 1582, and to 42,000 by 1620.[10] Similar stories could be told about other parts of Russia. Farms and villages were abandoned by the thousand, until some areas of the Russian heartland were wastelands by the end of the century. The movement of population from the centre benefited the south and south-east, and was one of the factors behind the expansion of the Muscovite state in those directions in the seventeenth century; but the demographic structure of Muscovy itself was transformed between the mid-1550s and about 1620, after which slow recovery began.

If the land and rural economy were to recover, it was essential to keep a working population there. Both landlords and the state had an interest in so doing. The former needed their estates to be cultivated, while the latter needed to build up its tax-paying base. Ivan IV had converted almost all peasant dues into taxes paid in cash. The depopulation of the land drastically reduced the state's revenues; a stable peasant population was essential to financial recovery. Ivan IV tried to stem the loss of population by introducing 'forbidden years' when, in theory, peasants were not allowed to leave their estates or villages; and it was from this principle – that the state could fix peasants to the land – that legal serfdom emerged. In the 1580s and 1590s registers of male peasants and their places of residence were drawn up, and forbidden years continued to be announced with increasing frequency in the early to mid-1600s. In 1649, the government gave serfdom legal status by the law code: peasants henceforth were obliged to remain on the farm or village of their birth; moreover, the law was retrospective: peasants not living in their place of birth in 1649 were to return.

Although the code formalized what was a growing social reality, its implications were considerable. It represented an admission that the economic and financial needs of nobility and state required a fixed rural population. If the nobility were to be sufficiently prosperous to serve the tsar, and if state authority were to recover from the disasters of the Time of Troubles, a guaranteed rural population was necessary. Russia, in other words, could not tolerate the kind of rampant peasant mobility of the 1500s. Serfdom reinforced the theory of a tsar with proprietorial rights over his subjects. A proprietor, by definition, can dispose of his possessions as he wishes; through serfdom, the tsar accordingly arranged rural society in conformity with his autocratic ideal. Serfdom made a certain economic sense as it would also revive the market economies which had collapsed. Towns and villages would recover as the rural population was stabilized; commercial and artisanal activities would flourish as peasants supplied food and other raw materials to the towns, and then consumed the commodities which towns produced.

The implications of serfdom for peasants themselves were mixed and, on the whole, deleterious. If the state could provide security and social stability, and if disease and harvest failures could be avoided, serfs could expect to share the economic advantages of a fixed rural population. However, nobody could guarantee such idyllic conditions; war, civil conflict, pestilence and famine remained harsh realities. If serfs could no longer flee from these scourges, the likelihood was that they would rise in rebellion. Within a couple of decades of 1649, Russia indeed was to face a serious rising of serfs, for whom traditional escape routes from crisis were now closed. Again, the imposition of serfdom blurred the distinctions which earlier existed between peasants. In particular, there was little difference between serfs and slaves after 1649, especially as slaves were made to pay taxes. The law code had the long-term effect of breaking down the distinctions between peasant ranks, reducing them all to that of serf. Even so, the law code of 1649 could not be enforced comprehensively. Russia lacked the means of policing serfdom, and the economic self-interest of nobles caused them to harbour fugitives in spite of the proscriptions of the law. Nevertheless, in spite of anomalies and evasions, most Russian peasants were turned into serfs in the middle of the century. Russia had created a social system which endured to the nineteenth century.

## Michael Romanov, 1613–1645

When Michael Romanov came to the throne in 1613, the enormity of the social, economic and political realities which awaited him threatened to make a mockery of the claims to autocracy and spiritual authority with which he was buttressed. His courtiers might prostrate themselves before him, but the recent past showed how vulnerable the tsar was to intrigue, rebellion and assassination. Michael received invaluable assistance from his father, who had become a monk under the name of Filaret. Captured by the Poles in 1610, he was released in 1619 and was appointed patriarch of Moscow. Filaret not only advised Michael, but was in effect co-ruler until he, Filaret, died in 1633. Without pushing the parallel too far, Filaret was the 'Richelieu' of Russia. This austere, over-powering man not only guided his son but attracted to himself, rather than to the tsar, any potential opposition to policy. He used his ecclesiastical authority to bring the resources of the church to the task of disseminating respect for, and obedience to, his son. The church urged upon the faithful the virtues of cooperation, unity, concord and obedience to the tsar.

The process of deflecting criticism from Michael was helped by the fact that the Zemsky Sobor, which elected him in 1613, continued to meet until 1621. Although an advisory, not legislative, body, it conferred upon his policies an element of consent which was necessary to gaining general acceptance of the terms reached in 1617 and 1618. The Zemsky Sobor rarely met after 1621, for Michael and his father were determined to avoid any suggestion that it might become a permanent body or acquire claims to formal status. The possibility that it might do so was real since there was no gainsaying the fact that Michael was tsar because of his election by the Zemsky Sobor; unlike Boris Godunov in 1598, he had not been able to devise an alternative source of legitimation. Again, whereas the Sobors of the sixteenth century had usually been little more than meetings of state and church officials, the Sobor that met in 1613 also included members elected by the provinces and towns. Some among them demanded that Michael agree to a charter requiring him to consult the Zemsky Sobor on matters of high policy, and to govern through *boyar* advisers. Michael, at least during the first few years of his reign, conformed to the latter provision, but *boyars* themselves resisted any suggestion that a Zemsky Sobor might share in government. To the *boyar* mentality, the political, economic and social recovery of Russia could be achieved only by an autocratic tsar; it was unthinkable that a Zemsky Sobor could become a permanent body. After 1621, Michael did not call it until 1632 when Russia went to war with Poland, after which it met in 1637, 1642, 1648 and finally in 1654; it never met again. When Michael died in 1645, his son Alexis succeeded by hereditary right; no Zemsky Sobor was called to elect or acknowledge him.

An immense task of socio-economic reconstruction awaited Alexis. It was aided by the fact that, since most of the recent fighting had occurred in the southern half of Russia, the more northern regions had retained sufficient social cohesion and economic productivity to provide the foundations of recovery. The devastated parts of Moscow were rebuilt and foreign merchants were encouraged to settle there and conduct business. This was a sensitive issue on social and religious grounds. Recent history had left many Russians with a strong xenophobia, and the Orthodox church was nervous about admitting heretics into the holy city. Nevertheless, a sizeable foreign merchant community grew (it consisted mainly of Dutch, English and Germans) and helped the recovery of Moscow. By mid-century this community had become so numerous that it was considered to be potentially disruptive to the ethnic and religious purity of Moscow. In 1652, the foreigners were removed to a designated suburb which became popularly known as the German Quarter. There they conducted their business affairs and created western life-styles. Foreign merchants established themselves in other Russian towns, and although Russia did not become a major force in European economic life, it did develop exports mainly of flax, timber, copper, animal pelts and grain. Some went through the Baltic, Riga being the main port, but there were drawbacks. During the Thirty Years War, merchant ships were vulnerable to unprovoked attack, while duties had to be paid to the Danes if exports went through the Sound. Other exports took the northerly route from Archangel. Although the distances to western Europe were longer, the route was safer than the Baltic, and it avoided the Sound tolls. On the other hand, for climatic reasons Archangel was open only during the summer months, and Christian IV of Denmark added to problems by claiming suzerainty over the White Sea and demanding tolls from ships which passed through it.

For several years after 1618, Michael pursued a hesitant foreign policy, not being willing to risk another disastrous war. He and his father, like many of their advisers, regarded the loss of Smolensk as a humiliation. In 1621, when Poland was at war with the Ottoman Empire, the sultan sent a mission to Moscow proposing that they join forces, with the restoration of Smolensk being the main prize for Russia. The Zemsky Sobor urged Michael to agree, but he and Filaret temporized: was Russia in any condition to undertake war? The question was settled when news arrived of peace between Poland and the Ottoman Empire; there was now no question of the Russians alone attempting to recover Smolensk. A similar reticence governed Michael's attitude to Denmark. He objected to Danish claims in the White Sea, and approached James I of England with a proposal that they sign an anti-Danish alliance. Although James was supporting Christian IV in the Thirty Years War, he too resented the financial demands being placed by the Danes on English shipping coming from Archangel. The English government made a positive response, but Michael let the matter drop; once again he was reluctant to enter into a commitment which might lead to war. It was not until 1632 that he abandoned his cautious stance. In that year the truce signed with Poland in 1618 expired and Sigismund III died, to be succeeded by his son as Wladislaus IV. Urged on by the Zemsky Sobor, Michael judged that here was a coincidence of favourable circumstances which he could not forgo. He dispatched an army to retake Smolensk. It besieged the city, but failed to complete its mission. After two years of futile attempts to invest Smolensk, there was no option but to seek peace, which was signed in 1634. Poland kept Smolensk and received a large financial indemnity from Russia; however, Wladislaus renounced his claim to the throne of Russia, and recognized Michael with the title of tsar. After this new defeat by the Poles, Michael purged the high command of the army, several of whose members were executed, and ordered further military reforms along western lines, but he never again went to war.

By the time Michael died in 1645, he had given Russia almost thirty years of respite, although even this was relative, for the southern and south-eastern frontiers remained extremely volatile. By comparison with the thirty years before his reign, however, the period from 1613 to 1645 was one of stability and recovery. The population of the heartland of Russia steadily recovered from about 700,000 in the 1620s to over 2 million by the end of the century, and in 1628 the state began to sell unused land on condition that the purchasers bring in settlers to cultivate and exploit it. Meanwhile the trend towards the enserfdom of the mass of the rural population went ahead, to be completed in the reign of his son Alexis by the law code of 1649.

## Alexis, 1645–1676

Alexis adopted the practice of other seventeenth-century monarchs by allowing leading advisers to run government and draw upon themselves, rather than himself, opposition and criticism. During Alexis's reign, three figures dominated day-to-day government. Boris Morozov, who was linked to the tsar by marriage, served as principal minister until 1648; he was dismissed amidst widespread riots (although he secretly returned to Moscow and continued to advise Alexis). Morozov was replaced by the Patriarch Nikon, who ran government for ten years, after which the tsar relied on Athanasy Ordya-Nashchokin.

Within three years of the start of Alexis's reign, social turmoil broke out again. The deeper causes lay in the grievances of the merchant communities of Russia. They sent frequent protests to Moscow that foreign traders were receiving preferential treatment from the government, and that churchmen, *streltsy* (musketeers) and even nobles were engaging in trade and depriving merchants of income without paying the taxes and fees which merchants themselves had to pay. In the short term, the riots were provoked by a sudden rise in taxation. In 1646 the government augmented the tax on salt by one-third; many fishermen working the great rivers of Russia, and who used salt to preserve fish which was then transported to distant peasant communities, could not afford to buy salt in the same quantities as before. The supply of preserved fish – crucial to the diets of many peasants and poorer town-dwellers – suddenly diminished and caused food shortages, which in turn provoked riots, especially as the government continued to export much-needed grain to Sweden and Germany. The riots began in Moscow in 1648, but soon spread to the countryside and the commercial cities of Novgorod and Pskov. The tsar placated the merchant community by dismissing Morozov, expelling English traders from Russia (the pretext was the execution of Charles I) and forcing everybody who engaged in trade to pay the same fees as merchants. Soldiers had to be sent to Pskov, which held out for several months and only surrendered on the promise of an amnesty. Russia was not the only country in Europe to experience popular rebellion in 1648; one has but to recall Britain, France and Spain in that year, and, as will shortly be seen, Poland too collapsed into chaos in 1648. This, the year when peace was signed at Westphalia, was also one of popular revolt in many parts of Europe as governments confronted risings by almost every section of society.

The violence of 1648 caused Alexis to call a Zemsky Sobor, and it was this body which adopted the law code of 1649. The code has already been referred to in the context of serfdom, seen as a means of disciplining an unruly rural population, but the code sought to stabilize society in other ways. It imposed restrictions on townspeople similar to those affecting the peasants: they had to remain in the town where they were residing in 1649, and could not move or marry somebody from another town without permission. The code also reinforced the privileges of church and nobility, two groups with whom the tsar regarded it as essential to form an alliance. Thus, the ownership of serfs was limited to nobles and gentry, and officer ranks in the army were reserved for nobles. The governing principle of the 1649 code was cooperation between crown, nobility and church to hold state and society together.

## The Great Schism

The Orthodox church was integral to the political and social life of Russia as well as to the spiritual. It had helped tsarism to come through the Time of Troubles, it had provided national leadership when the country was all but prostrate before the Poles, and it continued to proclaim the message of Moscow as the Third Rome, with all the wider religious significance that this formulation implied. Around mid-century, however, it experienced a division which in some sense was to last into the nineteenth century, and which became known as the Great Schism. It was a crisis compounded of many elements: religious, ecclesiastical, political and social; moreover, the conflicts which it generated were often conducted violently: beatings, imprisonment, torture, exile and execution were all employed by the contending parties.

Since at least the early seventeenth century, there had been quiet pressure from some monks and liturgical experts for changes to Russian Orthodox worship. In the Orthodox church, each detail in the conduct of worship is doctrinally significant; the reform movement contended that errors inadvertently had crept into Russian Orthodox liturgy, taking it away from Greek Orthodoxy, and hence incorporating doctrinal error. Such arguments remained a matter of strictly ecclesiastical concern until the nomination, in 1652, as patriarch of Moscow of a remarkable figure, Nikon, who, without too much distortion, may be seen as the William Laud of Russia. This energetic and charismatic figure championed the reform movement, partly for reasons of genuine concern for the purity of worship, but also for broader political reasons. Nikon placed the cause of reform at the forefront of his patriarchate, and divided the church of which he was leader.

His own origins were humble. The son of a peasant, he became a priest, then a monk. His talents attracted his ecclesiastical superiors, and in 1648 he was made metropolitan of Novgorod. This was, of course, the year when the city collapsed into violence, and Nikon was instrumental in eventually pacifying the populace. Four years later he was made patriarch of Moscow at Alexis's insistence. Nikon brought to the patriarchate a well thought out and consistent strategy. He took the idea of the Third Rome very seriously; however, if he were to persuade the international Orthodox community to acknowledge Moscow as the seat of supreme ecclesiastical authority, Russian

Orthodoxy must conform to Greek in matters of liturgy; hence a programme of change was necessary. There was another theme in his strategy. The church, in his view, had a mission to shape the political evolution of Russia. Not only must there be no division between state and church, but the state, in the person of the tsar, must submit itself to the authority of the church, in the person of the patriarch. Nikon's model was Patriarch Filaret, who had in effect ruled jointly with Michael. However, Filaret was Michael's father, whereas Nikon came of peasant stock: was it appropriate that he should rule alongside the tsar?

As regards liturgy, Nikon brought Greek Orthodox scholars to Moscow, and between 1653 and 1656 instituted changes to prayer books and worship in conformity with their recommendations; but in so doing he provoked strong reaction, much as Laud's reforms had done in England and Scotland two decades earlier. Resistance came from many quarters, both ecclesiastical and lay. The essence of their censure was that it was the Greek Orthodox church which was in error; indeed, the fall of Constantinople in 1453, and the continuing subjection of Greek Orthodoxy to Islam, were nothing less than God's judgement upon an apostate church. If Russian Orthodoxy were to adopt Greek ways, divine judgement likewise would strike down both church and the state which had harboured it; the fate which befell the Byzantine empire would be visited upon Russia. The anti-Nikon movement found its spokesman in the Archpriest Avvakum, a man as stubborn and resolute as Nikon himself. Avvakum composed a journal of his life and experiences, which is often regarded as the first masterpiece of Russian literature. As an historical source, it bears all the hallmarks that one would expect of somebody of Avvakum's uncompromising views and character: it is written with passion, it describes in grim detail the suffering which Nikon and his supporters inflicted on Avvakum and his family (Avvakum was beaten, imprisoned and exiled to Siberia with his wife and children), and it execrates Nikon and his henchmen as blasphemers, idolaters, hypocrites, whose sacrilegious ways will bring down God's fury. It is precisely through its partiality and anger that Avvakum's journal conveys the emotions generated by Nikon's liturgical reforms.

The changes remained, and were adopted formally by a general church council which assembled in Moscow in 1666, but a large section of the church – the Old Believers – refused to submit, and, in the face of continuing persecution leading to executions, mass suicides and imprisonment, maintained their stance until the nineteenth century, when they were eliminated in another outburst of suppression. Nikon himself was coming under political pressure in the 1650s, as *boyars* and princes resisted the authority which he wielded over the tsar. Alexis himself increasingly made it plain that he was losing patience with Nikon's overbearing conduct. In 1658 Nikon suddenly announced his retirement from his political and ecclesiastical activities. It is possible that in so doing he was challenging the tsar to admit that he, Nikon, was indispensable, by calling upon him to return; in that case, Nikon's critics would be silenced, and his authority in state and church would be total. If so, Nikon miscalculated. Alexis accepted his resignation. Nikon withdrew to a monastery near Moscow. He was nominally still patriarch, and Alexis assumed temporary direction of church affairs. The church council of 1666 adopted the reforms of Nikon, but also denounced him for having abandoned his duties. It stripped him of the rank of patriarch and exiled him to a monastery in northern Russia. He died in 1681, and there was perhaps a bitter coincidence in that his inveterate opponent, Avvakum, was burned at the stake in the same year.

The long-term consequences of the Great Schism extended to the sphere of relations between church and state. Never again did a tsar permit a patriarch to exercise the authority of Nikon. If anything, the reverse happened. Tsars increasingly subjected the church to state authority, turning the church into a branch of the state. Peter the Great at the end of the seventeenth century was to accelerate this process by deliberately leaving the patriarchate vacant. No patriarch was permitted after the 1720s, and the patriarchate was revived only after the February Revolution of 1917.

By the 1660s, tsarism had engaged upon a process of territorial expansion which would bring numerous non-Russian peoples under its rule. The ideologies of Russia as successor to Byzantium, and Moscow as the Third Rome, were, at one and the same time, causes and signs of the imperial enterprise to which Russia was now committed. One might interpret Russian history from the mid-sixteenth to the mid-seventeenth century thus: the tsars could have concentrated on Muscovy itself, turning it into a modern state with a prosperous and free peasantry, a thriving commerce, and a nobility and church which conformed to the needs of a specifically Russian state. However, Ivan IV opted to expand the frontiers in every direction, and imposed upon his subjects intolerable burdens which resulted in the Time of Troubles. The motives for his expansionism undoubtedly included a rapacious appetite for land, but also reflected an obsession with security from foreign invasion. This meant pushing back the frontiers from Moscow as far as possible. In 1613, the Romanovs possibly had an opportunity to reject the imperial path and concentrate upon Russia itself; however, the memory of the Polish invasion was too recent and vivid. In their turn they yielded to the temptation to create an empire which necessitated the preservation of serfdom and autocracy, and drove their subjects into periodic explosions of rebellion. Russia was locked into a rigid social and political system because of the needs of empire. The church, or at least the majority which followed Nikon, lent itself to this strategy. The liturgical changes which Nikon introduced aimed to place the Russian church at the head of all Orthodoxy, in what was the religious equivalent of Romanov territorial expansion. The Old Believers stood for a national, Russian church; the reformers for a church suited to the imperial needs of the state. Such an interpretation doubtless can be criticized on the ground that it is excessively schematic, but it has the virtue of indicating the long-term significance of those crucial first few decades of Romanov rule.

## POLAND

Unlike Russia, whose political, religious and social cultures were European only in limited senses, Poland emphatically was a European country. Like Britain and Spain, it was a composite kingdom, and as in Bohemia and the Holy Roman Empire its king was elected. Poland comprised two territories: the kingdom of Poland and the Grand Duchy of Lithuania. It had a diet (*Sejm*) which, unlike the Zemsky Sobor, was a permanent, and even over-ambitious body. The two parts first came together in 1386 when a Polish princess married the Grand Duke of Lithuania, but what began as a family compact turned into a formal, constitutional union in 1569 when the Republic or Commonwealth of Poland was created. The union confirmed the elective status of the king, who would be chosen by the *Sejm*; a common currency was established, but Poland and Lithuania retained their independent legal and administrative systems. The open frontiers to east, west and south forced Poland to scrutinize the course of international relations in Europe closely, and since the Muslim Ottoman Empire to the south and Orthodox Russia to the north-east differed from most of Poland in religion, many Poles, rather like the Spanish in other contexts, felt themselves to be a

frontier people with a mission to defend Catholicism. King Sigismund III, who ruled from 1587 to 1632, was a devout Catholic
committed to the Counter-Reformation. His main strategy was to
make common cause with the Austrian Habsburgs, turning Poland
into the Spain of the north as together they contrived to uphold
Catholicism in Europe. Both of Sigismund's wives were Austrian
princesses: Anna whom he married in 1592 and, after her death, her
sister Constantia, who became his wife in 1602.

Sigismund may have entertained lofty ambitions, but his powers as
king were meagre. He was dependent on the diet, whose authority
covered both Poland and Lithuania. The diet was composed of three
orders: the king himself, the senate whose members were great aristocrats, and representatives of provincial assemblies. All decisions of
the diet had to be unanimous. The king was forbidden to name his
successor, who would be elected by the diet. He required the consent
of the diet before declaring war or peace, and before raising an army
or imposing taxes. He required the consent of the senate before
marrying; and a council of six senators kept a permanent watch on
the king to make sure that he did not exceed his powers. The king of
Poland, in short, was mainly a war leader who executed the will of
the diet. The diet, in turn, was dominated by the aristocracy, who
were renowned for their sense of individualism and independence.
Unlike most other parts of monarchic Europe, where the general
trend was towards the augmentation of royal authority, Poland
remained a kingdom run by semi-autonomous aristocrats.

The basis of their power was the vast amounts of land which they
had accumulated in the sixteenth century. In the Middle Ages,
Poland had been composed mostly of small to medium-sized noble
estates, but during the sixteenth century much larger estates emerged
in response to three main forces: favourable economic trends; increasing rights of landlords over peasants; and opportunities to
occupy land in the Ukraine.[11] By displaying a strong sense of commercial enterprise, unlike many western European nobles whose
social values discouraged their participation in trade, astute aristocratic families and also some monasteries gradually bought out lesser
nobles and peasants, and coerced the latter into working land on
their behalf. Some of the great aristocratic dynasties of Polish history
emerged as large estate owners in this way: Leszcynski, Lubomirski,
Radziwill, Sapieha and others.

The principal economic trend to which aristocrats responded was
the expansion of the Polish grain trade. This came in response to

increasingly buoyant demand from the west because of the growth in the European population in the sixteenth century. Forests in Poland were cleared and land turned mainly to the cultivation of cereals, especially rye; but profits were also to be made from industrial crops such as timber and flax, which were also exported to western Europe. The principal outlet was the river Vistula, linked to the hinterland by a network of tributaries. Danzig, at its mouth, became a flourishing port. By the early seventeenth century, it was exporting some 70,000 tons of rye each year. Most of the merchants who organized the commerce were Swedish and German, and the majority of the ships exporting grain were Dutch.

The Polish grain trade, supplemented by timber, flax and tar, generated unprecedented wealth for aristocratic and ecclesiastical landowners, who used the profits to accumulate yet more land; by contrast, peasants derived little financial reward. Historians have shown that, as the sixteenth century progressed, aristocrats imposed control over their peasants by converting former cash rents into service and by tying peasants to the land. The precise processes whereby this was done are still not entirely clear, although they did involve legislation by the diet and the use of seigniorial courts by the magnates. Polish peasants increasingly fulfilled their obligations by labour service, and because they were fixed to the land, evolved towards serfdom similar to that in Russia. The availability of a cheap labour force obviated the necessity for land-owners to invest in expensive agricultural equipment, hence the large profits which they made. Then there is the question of the availability of land in the Ukraine. Many Cossacks inhabited this large, open plain, but after the creation of the Commonwealth in 1569, Poland engaged upon a policy of systematic occupation. Polish aristocrats treated the Ukraine as an empty land waiting to be colonized. They carved out immense tracts as far as the Dnieper, which became an unofficial frontier between Polish Ukraine and the remainder, where Cossacks continued to resist further Polish advance.

## Religion and Culture

Sigismund III's desire to turn his kingdom into the northern Spain inevitably raised the question of religion. On this subject any comparison with Spain breaks down, for Poland was that rarity in the early modern period, a kingdom willing to permit religious diversity.

This stance had been adopted by the Confederation of Warsaw (1572), which had created a regime of religious coexistence. The confessional composition of Poland consequently was complex. The majority of the population was Catholic, and was touched by the spirit of renewal which emanated from the Council of Trent. Indeed, Polish representatives had made a significant contribution to the discussions at Trent, and Stanilaus Hozjusz, bishop of the Polish diocese of Warmia, had presided over the council at one stage. The Jesuits were admitted to Poland in 1565, and they opened a string of colleges wherein were educated the sons of the nobility and aristocracy; but they existed alongside well-established older orders (Benedictines, Dominicans, Franciscans) as well as more recent foundations, such as the Lazarists of St Vincent de Paul. Among the laity, the Counter-Reformation found particular expression in the cult of Mary the Virgin, who was revered through thousands of shrines, both public and private, which appeared in the late 1500s and early 1600s. However, the Polish diet, while recognizing the revival of Catholicism, adhered to the principle adopted in 1572: the state would not assist the Catholic church to coerce non-Catholics into conversion. The Catholic church in Poland therefore had to rely on persuasion and negotiation as it faced those whom it regarded as heretics or infidels.

The religious minorities of Poland included Jews, for unlike the king of Spain, the king of Poland never forced them to convert to Catholicism or leave the country. Indeed, many Jews who were refugees from persecution elsewhere had settled in Poland. Synagogues and centres of Talmudic studies multiplied, and Jewish communities enjoyed considerable administrative self-control. A central council, the Vaad, supervised their corporate interests. The generally favourable circumstances under which Jews lived in Poland were to change in the great Cossack rebellion of 1648, when thousands of Jews were massacred. In the second half of the century, they were to experience sustained popular hostility whose effects could not be prevented by the crown, which still afforded them its protection. Protestants constituted another minority. The Reformation in both its Lutheran and Calvinist forms reached Poland, which contained both faiths by the second half of the sixteenth century. The key to the spread of Protestantism was the land-owner, for those who became Protestant were followed by their tenants. The port of Danzig, where Protestant merchants from Germany, Sweden and the Netherlands operated, was a source through which German Protestant literature entered the country.

The religious complexion of Lithuania differed in significant re-spects from that of Poland. Here, Catholicism in the sixteenth cen-tury was the minority faith; moreover, the church still had to combat a residual and stubborn paganism. Lithuania was the last part of Europe to convert to Christianity at the end of the fourteenth cen-tury; one condition of the Polish–Lithuanian marriage of 1386 had been that the Grand Duke and his subjects become Christian. Pagan traditions, rituals and beliefs continued, and Lithuanian Catholicism in some respects depended on a compromise with older practices and belief systems. After the Council of Trent, the Catholic church set about combating residual paganism in Lithuania. The church insisted that Catholics adhere to doctrine as defined at Trent, the training of priests conformed to the rigorous provisions of Trent, and the teach-ing of the church made no concessions to non-Christian beliefs.

In the context of Lithuania, the phrase 'Counter-Reformation' is inappropriate for another reason: it was not Protestantism that Cath-olicism faced, but Orthodoxy. If the population of the whole of the Polish Commonwealth is taken into account, then about 40 per cent belonged to the Orthodox church, but in Lithuania itself the Ortho-dox were the majority. The Orthodox church was also dominant in the Polish Ukraine, with Kiev at its centre. The encounter between Catholicism and Orthodoxy in Lithuania in the sixteenth century resulted in the most important change to affect both churches: the creation of a united church in 1596. One section of the Orthodox church leadership entered into theological discussions with Catholic representatives in the 1590s, with a view to overcoming the division that had existed since the eleventh century. In 1596, by the Union of Brest-Litovsk, the Orthodox church, or a significant part of it, was reconciled to Rome in a Uniate church. An agreed liturgy was estab-lished which retained many elements of Orthodox worship, Ortho-dox priests entering the union kept the right to marry, and the united church formed part of the Catholic church under the author-ity of the pope. Rome regarded this as a triumph and the beginning of further advance in Lithuania. However, the union caused a crisis within Orthodoxy. Constantinople and Moscow denounced what they regarded as an act of apostasy, while within Lithuania and the Polish Ukraine, the Orthodox church split. For many years there were bitter and often violent disputes between Uniates and Dis-uniates for control of Orthodox churches. Sigismund III withdrew recognition from the Disuniates, refusing to acknowledge their legit-imacy. The social unrest which the division provoked was such that in

1633, Wladislaus IV, who had just ascended the throne, recognized the Orthodox church once again, although its division from the Uniate church remained.

Kiev was the centre of the Disuniate cause, to which theological and practical leadership was given by Peter Mohyla, metropolitan of Kiev. This resolute opponent of the Uniates published in 1640 a *Confessio fidei orthodoxiae*, a catechism of Orthodox belief. He also founded the Kiev Academy in 1632 to teach and disseminate Orthodox theology. It acquired an international reputation, as students came from across the Orthodox world, including Russia, to study. It became the most important academic institution in the Ukraine, lectures being given in Greek, Latin and various Slavic languages. The academy was associated with a Kievan literary revival, which expressed itself mainly through mystery and miracle plays, several of which were written by a German pastor, Gregory. The movement was short-lived, dying out in the 1670s, but its influence extended beyond Kiev into Russia: young men preparing for the priesthood came from Russia to study in Kiev, where they made contact with the new drama.

The churches in Poland were agents of cultural activity. The Catholic church, for example, supplied channels through which Italian baroque architecture entered Poland. Until Sigismund III transferred his capital from Cracow – the traditional capital of the old kingdom of Poland – to Warsaw in 1611, Cracow was the principal city of Poland. It had a fine university which sustained humanist scholarship during the Renaissance (its most celebrated graduate being Nicholas Copernicus) and had links with Italy: it was the custom for young Polish noblemen to study first at Cracow, then to go to Italian universities to continue their education. In Cracow itself, several churches were built in baroque styles. Probably the best known is the Church of Saints Peter and Paul, constructed between 1597 and 1619 by Jan Travano after plans by Bernadoni, but other examples were the façade of the Ursuline Convent and the reredos of the Church of the Immaculate Conception, either of which would not have been out of place in Italy. The transfer of court and government to Warsaw stimulated building there, much of it again adapting baroque to native needs. The royal palace was embellished and the university provided with new buildings; St John's Cathedral had already received a baroque façade in 1602, and the Jesuits, Carmelites and other religious orders built churches or chapels in baroque styles. Aristocrats too patronized Italian architects and artists, there being no better example than the magnificent Wilanow Palace, close to Warsaw, built by Giuiseppi Bellotti.

## War and the Monarchy

While it would be dogmatic to claim that long wars automatically enhanced the powers which a king exercised over his subjects (they could equally provoke socio-political turmoil which subverted royal authority), Sigismund III and Wladislaus IV did regard warfare as a means of weakening the grip in which the diet held them. For that very reason, the Polish diet was chary of providing the king with an army for longer than was necessary. When, for example, Sigismund proposed in 1606 that a standing army be created, the diet refused to comply; it also rejected his plan to substitute majority voting for unanimity in the diet. Sigismund entertained exalted ambitions for his family. He coveted the Swedish throne, and when his forces occupied Moscow in 1610 he attempted to become tsar. War, in other words, fed Sigismund's appetite for dynastic grandeur; he never abandoned the hope that he or his son simultaneously might be king of Poland, king of Sweden and tsar of Russia, thereby equalling, if not surpassing, the dynastic achievements of the Habsburgs.

Such aspirations were frustrated by the military failures against the Russians and the Swedes, and between 1629 and 1635, Sigismund and Wladislaus signed a series of agreements creating peace between Poland and its neighbours: the truce of Altmark with Sweden in 1629, peace with Russia in 1634, a truce with the sultan in 1634, peace with Sweden in 1635. These settlements were strongly approved by the diet, which continued to suspect that foreign military adventures too easily encouraged the king to enhance his domestic powers. For several years after 1635, Wladislaus IV acquiesced in the limitations which the diet placed upon him; however, his marriage to an Austrian princess, Cecilia Renata, and the birth of a son, Sigismund, in 1640, caused him to attempt to revive the royalist cause. In that year he announced the creation of a new chivalric fraternity, the Order of the Immaculate Conception. It would consist of seventy-two young nobles who would swear allegiance to the king. Fearful that the order could turn into a powerful personal following of the king, the diet vetoed the idea. Again, Wladislaus contemplated war as a means of augmenting his authority within Poland, and he approached the Republic of Venice with the offer of an alliance against the Turks; this too came to nothing. Wladislaus died in 1648 having kept the kingdom at peace for most of his reign, but at the price of having failed either to enhance the powers of monarchy or to modify the procedures of the diet.

## The Cossack Rising, 1648

In the last year of Wladislaus's life, there erupted a Cossack rising in the Ukraine which spread into Poland itself, turned into an international war, and subjected Poland to 'the deluge', an experience similar to that of the Time of Troubles in Russia. Wladislaus was succeeded as king by his brother John Casimir, and it was he who had to contend with the multiple crises that followed on the rebellion. He was to abdicate in 1668 after a reign in which one frustration followed another, until he could take no more. The rising in its early stages may be represented as a reaction by Cossacks, supported by peasants and other refugees who had come to the Ukraine, against the growing authority of the Polish state and the extension of Polish landed estates into the Ukraine. There was also a religious aspect to the rising. The Counter-Reformation was moving into the Ukraine as Catholic priests sought to bring the predominantly Orthodox population into the Uniate church; most Cossacks were Orthodox, and violently resisted the missionary enterprise of the Catholic church.

The leader of the rising was Bogdan Chmielnicki, the elected head of the Cossacks, whose family had suffered at the hands of Polish nobles and who felt that Wladislaus had gone back on certain promises regarding land. He gathered a Cossack army, formed an alliance with groups of Tatars, and set out to seize control of the Ukraine. Emissaries of the Cossacks travelled throughout Poland and urged peasants to join the rising. The whole of the Ukraine and parts of Poland were quickly engulfed by the rebellion. At the beginning of the revolt, Bogdan overcame a Polish force, which lost some 10,000 men in the slaughter that followed. Throughout the Ukraine, peasants rose against the land-owners, whose houses and castles were destroyed. There occurred widespread destruction of towns and villages, thousands were massacred including Catholic priests and Jews, whom the Cossacks associated with landlord exploitation. John Casimir tried to buy off Bogdan with offers of an amnesty and the recognition of certain Cossack rights, but Bogdan imposed his control throughout the Ukraine, which he proceeded to rule as an independent prince, dividing the country into sixteen provinces and dealing with local communities as their overlord.

However, Bogdan knew that he could not hold it indefinitely against a Polish government bent on reconquest, especially when the Cossack army suffered a heavy defeat by the Poles at Beresteczko in 1651. Moreover, some of his erstwhile friends began to desert him, and in 1654 he approached the tsar, Alexis, to seek assistance. He invited Alexis to become protector of the Ukraine. The argument was political: here was an opportunity for Russia to extend its influence into a region which it had long coveted; and religious: Bogdan called upon the Orthodox tsar to save the faithful in the Ukraine from Catholicism. At first Alexis demurred, for if he accepted, Poland would declare war. However, the Zemsky Sobor urged him to agree, and in 1654 an accord was signed between Bogdan and Alexis. The tsar took the Ukraine under his protection, but recognized it as an autonomous region; the Cossacks swore allegiance to Alexis and promised to have no separate dealings with Poland or the Ottoman Empire.

The Russian decision led to the internationalization of the Cossack rising (as described earlier in this chapter). There followed the occupation of Warsaw and Cracow by Swedish forces, John Casimir's flight, Polish recovery, John Casimir's return, the ambivalent policies of the elector of Brandenburg and the emperor, and the war between Denmark and Sweden, all of which led to the Peace of Oliva in 1660 by the terms of which John Casimir surrendered Livonia to Sweden and Prussia to Brandenburg. Now relieved of the Swedish burden, John Casimir concentrated on the war against Russia. Bogdan Chmielnicki had died in 1657, and the unity which he had imposed on the Cossacks disintegrated under the weight of internal feuding. The war now turned increasingly in Poland's favour. By the end of 1662 the Russians were driven from most of the eastern provinces of Poland, and in 1664 peace negotiations were opened. At this juncture the Polish position once again was undermined when another rebellion broke out, this one led by Prince Jerzy Lubomirski, a great magnate and marshal of the crown. John Casimir had attempted to impose majority voting on the diet and had tried to create a central treasury which would weaken the power of the diet to control crown finances. This conflict between crown and social elites over financial and constitutional issues resembled those in Britain and France in the 1640s and early 1650s. In the fighting which followed, neither side could defeat the other; in 1667 the civil war ground to a halt and Lubomirski went into exile. Meanwhile, the Russians had used the hiatus to press tougher claims in the peace discussions. A truce was signed at Andrusovo in 1667. Russian conquests west of the Dnieper were returned to Poland, but Smolensk and the whole of the eastern bank of the Dnieper were ceded to Russia. The Cossacks were placed under the joint dominion of the tsar and the king of Poland. The Russians were to occupy Kiev for two years; in fact, they retained it permanently.

By 1667 Poland had suffered almost twenty years of civil war, rebellion and foreign invasion. The Vasa kings of Poland – Sigismund III, Wladislaus IV and John Casimir – had ruled in tempestuous times, and while some of the violence can be attributed to their ambitions, notably Sigismund's hopes to acquire the throne of Sweden, much was a consequence of the wider Baltic struggles that were taking place. Poland's international standing by 1667 had suffered as a result of territorial losses, but it was still a leading force in the region. Nevertheless, a thoroughly disillusioned John Casimir abdicated in 1668; the diet elected as his successor a Polish magnate, Michael Wisnwiecki, and the Vasa phase of monarchy came to an end. The rebellion which began in 1648 led to no positive results for the mass of the peasantry. Land-owners reinstated their legal and service control, and the enserfdom of the Polish peasants continued unabated. The diet retained its authority and continued to insist upon unanimity when decisions were taken.

The political, constitutional and religious conflicts of the Baltic and northern regions had much in common with those elsewhere, even though they were played out on a much vaster geographical stage. Some of the consequences of those struggles had no exact parallels farther west, especially the widespread imposition of serfdom in parts of Germany, Poland and Greater Russia; nevertheless, in its broad features, the history of northern Europe to the 1660s was of a piece with the rest of the continent. One might even extend the comparison to the movement of peoples. Although overseas colonies are incidental to the main subject-matter of this book, the emigration of Spaniards, Portuguese, French, English and others to the Americas had its equivalent in the flight (in spite of serfdom) of refugees to the Ukraine or the lands around the Black and Caspian seas, or in the acquisition and settling of land by Polish and other magnates. Although accurate figures cannot be established, it is a fair conjecture that between 1600 and the 1660s, more Europeans went to these eastern regions than to the Americas. The large Cossack bands which they joined or formed contrasted with, rather than resembled, American colonial societies, being 'northern' answers to 'northern' problems; but the essential point remains, that emigration was not a phenomenon peculiar to western Europe. In the decades after the 1660s, the dynamism of northern history continued unabated. The great powers fought for possession of land, people and economic resources, and substantial changes in the distribution of power were to occur. These, however, are topics for a later chapter; by the early 1660s, many of the internal and international problems of the north European states had been brought to resolution, albeit on a temporary basis.

# *Interlude*

---

This is an appropriate juncture at which to take stock of Europe in 1660 and indicate some of the challenges awaiting the generation which came to maturity at this time. By 1660, key questions relating to the territorial structure of central Europe had been resolved. The Thirty Years War had assured the preservation of the Holy Roman Empire, but on terms which conformed to the views of princes, bishops and other heads of the imperial territories. Whatever aspirations the Austrian Habsburgs had cherished towards an integralist empire, wherein the kind of authority which they exercised in their patrimonial lands might be extended, had receded. Provincial particularism continued to flourish in lands adjacent to the empire, notably in Italy and the Dutch Republic. In this latter country, the issue of provincial rights as against federal authority remained volatile, and before long was to come to the fore again when the republic was invaded by France in 1672. France and Spain survived internal crises which, in varying degrees, threatened to turn those monarchic states into variants of the Holy Roman Empire. In France, provincial liberties were defended energetically by local elites, and until 1629 some Protestants harboured autonomist tendencies. Spain in particular strained under the pressure of centrifugal forces, and although Catalonia was forced back under Spanish Habsburg control, Portugal recovered its independence. Ironically, the civil wars in England, Scotland and Ireland had the contrary effect of bringing the former three kingdoms together in close constitutional bonds under the Commonwealth. Although the Commonwealth proved to be transient, it did anticipate the unions between England and Scotland in

1707, and Britain and Ireland in 1801. In Scandinavia, Russia and Poland, many boundaries remained flexible and undetermined, as did those between the Ottoman Empire and its neighbours. The Ottoman Empire has made but incidental appearances in this book so far; it will receive more systematic treatment in the second part.

International relations in Europe were more stable by the 1660s than for many decades. The peace settlements of Westphalia, the Pyrenees and Oliva had pacified central, southern and northern Europe, but had also generated portentous questions for the future. Had Spain and France reached a durable *modus vivendi*, or was the Peace of the Pyrenees but a temporary truce during which the Habsburg and Bourbon regimes would compose themselves for a renewed struggle? Similarly, in the Baltic, could the hegemony which Sweden had achieved be maintained, or would that country's territorial conquests prove ephemeral? And, further east, could Poland and Russia coexist in peace, or would their attempts to resolve their steppe frontier problems occasion more conflicts? Such questions were predictable, but other post-1660 international developments were less so. During the first half of the century, England had exercised relatively little influence on continental Europe. It had made desultory contributions to the Protestant cause in the Thirty Years War and fought brief wars as occasion demanded, but it had collapsed into civil war itself. British political instability was still not cured by 1660. Charles II was restored, and although he proved an astute politician who handled his kingdom with skill, his brother and successor, James II, proved so inept that he provoked the so-called Glorious Revolution of 1688, which not only admitted William of Orange to the throne of England, but had profound repercussions in Ireland and Scotland. Under William III, Britain exerted an unprecedented influence on European affairs. No major international peace settlement in western Europe thereafter was sealed without British participation. In collaboration with the Dutch Republic, it provided the core of anti-French alliances into the eighteenth century. The foundations of Britain's impact on the international stage were the increasing wealth coming from its North American colonies, the development of its naval power, and the emergence of financial institutions and techniques enabling it to create and manage a large public debt.

The preceding chapters have devoted much space to two interlocking themes: the incidence of rebellion and civil war on the one hand, and the endemic nature of international warfare on the other. Contemporaries were conscious that Europe was experiencing a disastrous conjunction of domestic and international strife. It was against this background that Thomas Hobbes wrote his *Leviathan*, published in 1651. Observing that the natural state of human beings is one of conflict and mutual destruction, and that for most people life is 'solitary, poor, nasty, brutish and short', he called for the creation of an all-powerful state able to force its subjects into obedience. In the 1950s and 1960s, some historians were impressed by the number of rebellions and wars that occurred in the first half of the seventeenth century, especially between the late 1630s and 1660. They sought causative factors which could explain an eruption of violence that stretched from Ireland to the Ukraine, and from Sweden to Sicily. They developed the theory that a general crisis swept Europe, manifesting itself in civil war, rebellion and international war. This is not the occasion to analyse the theory in detail: although its various advocates contended that a general crisis did occur, they were unable to agree on its character. Some saw it in economic terms, as marking a shift from feudal to capitalist modes of production, with profound and adverse consequences for traditional social structures. As primitive capitalism created new forms of social exploitation, the victims resorted to violent protest and rebellion. Other scholars depicted the crisis as a phase in the emergence of the modern state. Governments increasingly were asserting their authority over every section of society – elites as well as commoners – and were doing so mostly in the realms of finance and law. The escalating cost of warfare compelled governments to maximize the tax-paying potential of their subjects, who, when they reached breaking-point, rebelled. Not all historians conceded that a general crisis occurred. Sceptics argued that the differences between the insurrections and civil wars were so many and so diverse (even within countries, let alone between them) as to render the theory futile.[1] When studied in detail, so went the counter-argument, the risings in Britain and Ireland, France, Spain, Italy, Scandinavia, Poland, the Ukraine and so on, display so many unique features that they cannot be pressed into a theory of all-embracing crisis without distorting the historical evidence. As so often happens in historical debate, the issue was not resolved in the sense of a final consensus being reached. It did, nevertheless, force historians to think laterally about popular protest and revolt, and attempt to construct typologies.

The endemic international warfare of the period between 1618 and 1660 also commanded the attention of historians. They were impressed not only by the duration of war, but by changes in its conduct. Indeed, some contended that a military revolution was taking place; it began about 1560 and concluded about 1660. Any discussion of warfare must recognize that in the first half of the seventeenth century it could be difficult to distinguish between international and domestic conflict. This was especially true of Russia and Poland where, with the exception of occasional episodes of mass patriotic movement against an invader (such as Russian resistance to the Polish occupation of Moscow in 1610, or Polish reaction to the Swedish offensive of 1655), war and rebellion often merged. Spain and France, for example, intervened in each other's rebellions, thereby confusing domestic and international conflict. That having been said, what is to be made of the proposition that a military revolution occurred? The thesis originated with Michael Roberts in a lecture which he devoted to this theme in 1955.[2] He argued that, down to the early 1500s, European battles were dominated by knights on horseback, but that the emergence of massed ranks of pikemen – an innovation pioneered by the Swiss – ended their military superiority and transferred the initiative to infantry. The Spanish adapted Swiss methods, added musketeers to the pikemen, and arranged their troops into *tercios* of 3,000 men. In a *tercio*, a square of pikemen was surrounded by musketeers who fired at the enemy, then retired behind the pikemen to reload. Later in the century, Maurice of Nassau refined the tactic: he divided his troops into groups of 500 (thereby improving their flexibility and manoeuvrability), ranged them in linear formation rather than squares, and increased the proportion of pikes to muskets. Gustavus Adolphus added his own ideas (as outlined in chapter 6). Thus, the modernized, revolutionized Swedish army swept through Europe in the 1630s, overwhelming its opponents. There was more to the military revolution than changes in tactics, weaponry and organization, important though they were. Other ingredients included the expansion in the size of armies, the more systematic recruitment of soldiers than in the past, and the introduction by governments of financial and administrative measures to meet the escalating cost of warfare. This last facet of the military revolution had profound social consequences, as the taxpaying masses of Europe were subjected to ever-increasing demands which contributed to the social turmoil referred to above.

The thesis of military revolution, like that of the general crisis, has undergone considerable revision since its first formulation. Later commentators have pointed out that it paid too little attention to naval warfare and to forms of land war other than pitched battles (it was neglectful, for example, of the conduct of sieges). They have also argued that pikes and firearms were usually adapted to older tactical manoeuvres and did not necessarily initiate new ones. Again, while the knight in heavy armour might have lost his pre-eminence on the battlefield, the emergence of light cavalry, able to move and respond quickly to the changing fortunes of a battle, guaranteed that the cavalry would remain a significant force in warfare. The military revolution thesis is especially open to the charge that the dates between which it is alleged to have occurred are arbitrary. In the late 1400s in Italy, tactics and firearms were already being deployed in a 'modern' manner, while after 1660, warfare continued to mutate: armies grew even larger, so did navies, new tactics were developed, improvements continued to be made to weapons, and the administrative support given to armies and navies by governments constantly expanded in size and sophistication. In other words, the year 1660 has little significance in the history of war; perhaps the concept of a military revolution should be replaced by one of continuing evolution.

In a Europe where the forces of domestic and international instability were rampant, the task of instilling respect for government was inordinately difficult. The bold claims to absolute power made by monarchs often flew in the face of reality. A rapid scan of the preceding chapters will reveal numerous instances wherein monarchs died violent deaths, were deposed or abdicated. As an institution, monarchy was on the defensive in many parts of Europe, and by 1660 faced a massive task of rehabilitation. One self-protective device which monarchs employed in the first half of the century was to appoint a principal minister. The chosen person – Olivares, Richelieu, Mazarin, Buckingham and Oxenstierna come to mind – exercised enormous political influence, and could become immensely wealthy as he amassed land and money; he could also acquire noble titles for his family and retainers, placing them in influential political positions, and arranging marriage alliances at the highest levels of society. As a *quid pro quo*, the principal minister drew upon himself, and so deflected from the king, the opposition which controversial policies could generate; hence during the Frondes, the cry went up, '*Vive le roi sans Mazarin*', and, in England, Buckingham was murdered and Strafford executed (it says much for Charles I's lack of political finesse that he failed to extract political profit from these episodes). Another trend which monarchs encouraged was towards making the crown hereditary. They did so for mixed motives. They saw hereditary monarchy as a powerful agent of socio-political stability, but it also invested their own families with the mystique and glory that was attached to monarchy. Some monarchies had long been hereditary, but in northern and central Europe, the first half of the seventeenth century saw several elective monarchies become hereditary. That in Russia did so in 1613, Bohemia in 1627, Sweden in 1650 and Denmark in 1660; the principle of heredity was also crucial to the restoration of the Stuarts in Britain in 1660 and was to provide the rallying point for Jacobitism after 1688. By 1660, monarchic governments throughout Europe were turning to the question of how to restore political and social cohesion and recover from the divisions bequeathed by the past. New strategies were necessary; the search for them will provide some of the themes in coming chapters.

Turning to the question of religion, its socio-political functions had been among the most divisive in Europe since the Reformation. In the seventeenth century, Catholic, Protestant and Orthodox churches continued to observe each other with, at best, a controlled suspicion and, at worst, an undisguised hostility. The same might be said about attitudes within the different confessions; all the churches had internal tensions which easily translated into confrontation, as the careers of Laud and Nikon illustrated. Faced with this spectacle, the historian can be tempted to treat religion as no more than a socio-political phenomenon, but it cannot be repeated too often that religious faith was at the centre of the lives of the overwhelming majority of Europeans. The precise nature of their faith, the extent to which they followed official church teaching, or to which they held on to non-Christian beliefs, is a subject of great complexity which cannot be treated here; but religious faith was not something foisted on gullible laymen by unscrupulous priests and pastors (although in the eighteenth century, some *philosophes* of the Enlightenment were to make precisely that charge). Religious faith and practice was a phenomenon in its own right. No historian can study the struggles of conscience, the heart-searching, the readiness to suffer persecution, and the ardent spiritual journeys undertaken by a host of Christians of all persuasions, without being conscious that, even though the churches were guilty of greed, fanaticism and aggression, and too often sought to justify questionable means by appeal to exalted ends, religion was among the most profound forces influencing people's conduct. In institutional terms, Catholicism recovered much lost ground in Europe, and continued to disseminate its influence across southern America. Protestantism too was becoming a world-wide movement, although its extension within the

Americas belongs more to the second than the first half of the seventeenth century; and Russian Orthodoxy experienced unprecedented growth as it spread into the far north and east. It is sometimes said that the Peace of Westphalia marks the end of the religious wars in Europe, which went back to the Reformation era. Whilst there is some truth in this assertion, particularly as regards the Holy Roman Empire and most parts of western Europe, it cannot be accepted as a definitive judgement. Later in this book we will see how the wars between the Holy Roman Emperor and the Ottoman Turks manifested elements of religious crusade, and, after the Revocation of the Edict of Nantes by Louis XIV (1685), even those conflicts between France, Britain and the Dutch Republic were inspired in part by religious purposes.

In the spheres of the visual arts, seventeenth-century Europe continued to sustain that astonishing vitality and innovation which went back at least to the Renaissance. Architects and artists, some of whom adopted baroque styles, others of whom followed alternative artistic routes, endowed Europe with a prolific and heterogeneous stock of buildings, paintings, sculptures and other artefacts which constitute a major treasury of European artistic achievement. The modern visitor to the churches, palaces and civic buildings constructed across Europe in the first half of the century can still sense something of the 'shock of the new' which they constituted in their day.

Equally, if not more, significant for the future of humanity were the changes taking place in scientific thought. This is a subject to which we will return, but the references made earlier to Galileo and the controversies which he provoked should be recalled here. By 1660, scientists were moving to a view of the world which sought explanations of natural phenomena in terms of mathematics and mechanics, not hidden spiritual powers. The transformations in scientific thought and method which contemporaries referred to as 'experimental learning', and to which we often attach the phrase 'scientific revolution', were commanding the allegiance of most scientists by 1660. The implications were to extend beyond the sciences themselves into theology, philosophy, political thought and action, education, economic life, and indeed almost every facet of human activity. In the first half of the seventeenth century, most people interested in natural philosophy could follow scientific controversies, for the sciences were not yet as abstruse as they were later to become. Contemporaries recognized that worlds of the mind were being opened up which were every bit as new and exciting as anything discovered in the New World of the Americas.

By 1660, some historical themes of the preceding six decades were close to resolution, others were in full flow, and yet others were in a state of gestation. Nevertheless, that year does represent a time when Europe, or a large part of it, was at peace. It was not long before conflict broke out again, yet while the origins of some wars can be traced to the 1648 and 1660 settlements, others arose out of new international circumstances. European history was entering another stage in its evolution.

# 7

# Central and Southern Europe with the Ottoman Empire, 1648–1720

## Post-war Recovery

After the Peace of Westphalia, much of Germany and central Europe turned to social and economic regeneration. The need for recovery was self-evident. In 1654, Ferdinand III, as king of Bohemia, ordered a census of the population. The results showed that it was only about half of what it had been in 1618, and that of Moravia about two-thirds. Other censuses were taken between 1654 and 1720, and it was only by this latter date that the population of Bohemia and Moravia had returned to the level of 1618. Much the same could be said about other parts of Germany and Central Europe in this period; it took about seventy years for demographic recovery to be achieved. Several factors assisted the process. The smaller population at the end of the Thirty Years War placed less pressure on the food supply; indeed, if anything, there were modest food surpluses in the 1650s and 1660s, which meant that food prices remained low and within the reach of most people. In Munich, Augsburg and Würzburg in the late 1660s and early 1670s, the price of rye was only a quarter of what it had been in 1618. An adequate food supply and low prices contributed to another factor: the rising birth rate as infant mortality declined and more children grew to adulthood than in the past. Immigration into Germany also helped. Protestant states in particular welcomed refugees fleeing religious persecution. Some 30,000 Huguenots settled in Germany in the mid-1680s (about

20,000 going to Brandenburg), many more following over the next few decades. In 1731 another wave of 20,000 Protestants moved north from Austria, having been driven out by the archbishop of Salzburg. Demographic recovery nevertheless was not constant; for example, the great epidemics which swept central Europe in 1679–80 and 1713–14 temporarily retarded progress.

The diminished post-war population confronted land-owners with the dilemma that the Russians had faced earlier in the century: how to retain peasants on the land and prevent them from emigrating to towns. Extensive tracts of rural Germany either had been abandoned or had pitifully small and poor populations in 1648. One answer was similar to that adopted in Russia: the strict application of seigniorial rights over peasants, particularly the imposition of labour service. Thereby a *de facto* serfdom spread across much of Germany, but especially the north. In Brandenburg, servile labour was compulsory by the early 1680s, and in 1685 the death penalty was introduced for any peasant who fled the estate where he was born and did not return within four weeks; even so, as in Russia, peasants did leave the land clandestinely and evade recapture.

Following the examples of the French and other governments, Ferdinand III, and later Leopold I, used state resources to stimulate industry and commerce in Austria and Bohemia. Leopold I attracted Italian merchants to Vienna and allowed his economic policies to be influenced by economic thinkers such as Johann Becher and Wilhelm von Schröder, both of whom advocated urban renewal and commercial innovation as keys to improved prosperity. Becher called for the foundation of commercial companies similar to those in the Dutch Republic, England and France; he even proposed the creation of overseas colonies in the Americas. One of his ideas, which the emperor did implement, was the creation of a council of commerce through which state aid might be channelled into selected sectors of the economy. Persuaded of the virtues of such a council, Leopold I in 1666 created the *Kommerzkollegium* with Becher as a member. Technically the council was a committee of the *Hofkammer*, the central body through which the financial profits of the emperor's personal domains in Austria and Bohemia, and returns on mineral rights in those countries, were administered. The *Kommerzkollegium* supervised links with foreign merchants, maintained a watch on the movement of prices, and granted privileges and monopolies to selected companies; in 1667, for example, it granted a privilege to a silk manufacturing enterprise at Wappersdorf. Again, in 1667 an Italian entrepreneur was authorized to set up the Oriental Company, whose ships would go to Turkey via the Danube; the company would carry metal goods and cloth from Germany to Turkey, and bring back silks, cottons and other high-quality cloth; it would also import beef from Hungary to be sold in the Vienna markets. In spite of these measures, the council failed to live up to Becher's expectations, principally because of its standing as a committee of the *Hofkammer*. The great aristocrats who monopolized the *Hofkammer* had little interest in commerce, which they considered socially demeaning, and they failed to develop a comprehensive commercial strategy. In 1674 Becher wrote a critical report advocating that the *Kommerzkollegium* be made independent and staffed with new personnel with commercial expertise. This plan was rejected, and Becher withdrew from the *Kommerzkollegium*. He travelled to the Netherlands and to England, where he died in 1688. His success had been limited, but he testified to a spirit of commercial innovation which still had to contend with deep-seated social prejudices.

Patterns of long-distance commerce after 1648 reinforced trends which had developed during the Thirty Years War. Hamburg and Bremen, with their outlets into the North Sea and their relatively easy access to a growing Atlantic commerce, continued to prosper; for ports in the Baltic it was a different story. Most of the major Baltic ports after 1648 belonged to Sweden which extracted tolls and other dues, while the Hanseatic League, which once had been the mainstay of Baltic commerce, was all but inactive, its governing diet meeting for the last time in 1669. Only Danzig enjoyed undiminished prosperity as it continued to export large quantities of Polish grain to other parts of Europe.

The process of socio-economic recovery after 1648 also owed much to initiatives taken by German princes to enhance their own urban and court life. This was a phenomenon driven by a complex interaction of motives involving economic revival, public duty, and the glory or reputation of individual princes. The prestige of a ruler depended not just on military success or strong government, but on patronage of high culture; and the settings wherein many of the fruits of patronage were displayed were capital cities and princely courts. The Peace of Westphalia had fortified the autonomy of the princes; their sense of identity and self-determination expressed itself through ambitious programmes of urban renewal and the construction of splendid palaces. Few individually could aspire to exert decisive political or military influence on European affairs, but many more could enhance their international reputations through architecture and patronage. As princes engaged upon their building programmes, fascinating stylistic cross-currents emerged. Three centres in particular were influential: Italy, Vienna and Versailles, as that immense palace was expanded by Louis XIV in the 1670s. However, these were not mutually exclusive models, for they too interacted and displayed features in common. The public buildings and palaces which German princes constructed, and the manner in which they were decorated by painters and sculptors, were eclectic in their styles, and defy such easy classification as 'classical', 'baroque', 'Italian', 'French' or 'Austrian'.

Some of the most enterprising patrons were ecclesiastical princes of southern Germany. Splendid churches and palaces combining all the visual arts were built in Franconia, Baden and Bavaria. No family made a greater contribution than the counts of Schönborn who, in the late 1600s and early 1700s, produced several bishops and archbishops of Mainz, Spire, Bamberg and Würzburg. They left an outstanding architectural bequest, including the castle of Würzburg, built by the Bavarian architect Balthasar Neumann. The electors of Bavaria, Ferdinand (ruled 1651–79) and Maximilian II (1679–1726), created a sumptuous court at Munich. Palaces were built nearby at Nymphenburg and Schleissheim, and numerous noble residences in the city were constructed. In the Palatinate, Mannheim was transformed after being destroyed by the French in 1689. It was rebuilt according to a regular plan. Twelve parallel streets were intersected by others at right angles, dividing the town into 136 square sections of equal size; a promenade formed a circle around Mannheim. In 1720 work began on a new palace for the elector, who in that year transferred his residence from Heidelberg. Another new town was Karlsruhe, which took its name from the margrave of Baden, Karl Wilhelm. In 1715 he built a hunting lodge (later turned into a palace) around which the town, parks and gardens were built. Urban renewal drew people back into towns and cities, but also created work for architects, artists, builders, artisans and a host of satellite traders, who benefited from the economic stimulus generated by large-scale private and public works.

Prague too was extended after 1648. Even though the imperial court no longer resided there, noble and ecclesiastical patrons built on a grand scale. Most of the new buildings were Italian baroque in style; indeed, several Italian architects found employment in Prague, including Carlo Lurago who was invited by the Michna family to complete the chapel of the Jesuit College (1648–51). Humprecht-Jan Cernin de Chudenic, who had been imperial ambassador in Venice and Rome, and was steeped in Italian baroque artistic values, built a palace on the Hradcany Hill between 1669 and 1687. His architect was an Italian, Francesco Carrati, who constructed an edifice which would not have looked out of place in Italy itself. One of the most popular architects was a Burgundian, Jean-Baptiste Mathey, but he too had spent many years in Italy and built in an Italian style. He was invited to Prague by the archbishop, Johann-Frederick von Wallenstein; among his more prestigious commissions were the archiepiscopal palace, the Bucquoy palace, and the Church of St Francis of Assisi, built for the Knights of the Cross. In the four decades after the Peace of Westphalia, much of the visual aspect of Prague was transformed as churches and palaces were built in profusion.

The slow socio-economic recovery of Germany and Bohemia was in its early stages when Ferdinand III died in 1657. He was succeeded by his younger son, Leopold, who was to be one of the dominant figures in European affairs over the next half-century. Leopold's reign was longer than those of his father and grandfather – it lasted until 1705 – and marks strategic shifts in Austrian Habsburg fortunes. He was to preside over a remarkable revival which, by 1720, left the Habsburgs masters of central Europe and Italy. In view of his achievements, a glance at his personality and commitments will be of help.

## Leopold I

The death of his elder brother in 1654 left Leopold as heir presumptive to the imperial, Bohemian and Hungarian crowns, as well as to Austria. Ferdinand III took steps to ensure his succession. Leopold was crowned king of Hungary in 1655 and king of Bohemia in 1656. When Ferdinand III died, Leopold, aged seventeen, was too young to be emperor and had to await his eighteenth birthday. During the intervening eighteen months there was much intrigue surrounding the impending imperial election (Mazarin was involved in attempts to put forward Louis XIV or Ferdinand, elector of Bavaria, as candidates), but the senior elector, John Philip von Schönborn, archbishop of Mainz, oversaw Leopold's candidacy. At a time when Poland was in turmoil, Turkey was showing signs of aggression and the outcome of the Franco-Spanish war was uncertain, it was essential to avoid the upheavals to which the election of a non-Habsburg would have led. Leopold became emperor in 1658.

Leopold is sometimes contrasted with Louis XIV, not least because their personalities differed (Leopold never indulged in Louis's self-glorification), they had differing attitudes to war (Leopold, unlike Louis, never led his troops into battle) and were opposed over many aspects of international relations. Although they never met, they developed a mutual antipathy, Louis XIV referring to Leopold slightingly as 'captain-general of the Republic of Germany', and Leopold resenting Louis's pretensions to rival him as the first prince of Christendom. On one point they agreed: they both ruled personally. After the death of Mazarin in 1661, Louis XIV assumed control of government; Leopold did so in 1665 after the death of his chief minister, Johann Ferdinand Portia.

Before he became heir, Leopold was intended for the priesthood. His religious convictions were genuine, and throughout his life he was noted for his piety and modesty. He remained committed to the Counter-Reformation, and to the end of his reign supported the Catholic church in its endless struggle to secure the conversion of Protestants. Likewise did he display strong family commitments, being warmly affectionate towards his three wives, especially the second, whom he married for love rather than for reason of state. The first was the Spanish princess Margaret (d.1673) (they had one daughter, Maria Antonia), the second was his cousin Claudia Felicitas of the Tyrol (d.1676), and the third was the Palatine princess Eleanor of Neuburg, whose two sons, Joseph and Charles, both became emperor.

Leopold was intelligent and cultured. He was fluent in classical and several modern languages (except French, which he refused to speak), and had a particular passion for music. He invited Italian musicians to his court at Vienna. Chief among them was Marc Antonio Cesti, who had studied under Carissimi and was master of choristers at the Collegium Germanicum in Rome. He composed operas and cantatas as well as instrumental and vocal pieces, and collaborated in compositions with the emperor himself. Leopold recognized the political as well as cultural significance of a large and flourishing court and capital city. Later, his encouragement of new ecclesiastical and secular buildings will be discussed. Behind it was a desire to ensure that Vienna should be comparable to Paris or Rome, and should be worthy of a Holy Roman Emperor. He was an admirer of Italian baroque in general and Venetian in particular. Cernin de Chudenic, referred to above, was Leopold's ambassador to Venice between 1660 and 1663, and he sent scores of detailed reports not only on the latest buildings that had been completed, but also on how the Venetians organized public festivities.

Of all the offices which Leopold inherited or to which he was elected in the 1650s, the most problematic was that of king of Hungary. Within a few years he faced major challenges there, arising, among other things, out of a renewed policy of aggression adopted by the Turkish government. During most of the first half of the century, the Ottoman Empire had been occupied with problems to the east, especially a war against Persia from 1623 to 1639, which forced the sultan to hold the line in Hungary rather than attempt further expansion. In the 1640s, the Turks began a long struggle with Venice for control of Crete, and this too occupied much of their military attention. However, by the early 1660s, Turkey felt able to resume its expansionist approach to central Europe, and in so doing helped to determine the principal themes in the history of that region over the next two hundred years. At this juncture, therefore, we will turn away from central Europe to Turkey itself, and examine the structure and character of the Ottoman Empire.

## THE OTTOMAN EMPIRE

The Ottoman Empire covered much of central Europe and the Balkans, extended east to Persia, north to the Black Sea, south through the Levant into Egypt and along the north African coast. The foundation of the empire was conquest in accordance with the Islamic precept of Holy War (*jihad*) against infidels. Since 1453 it had been based on Constantinople, and although various practical changes in the government of the empire had taken place, the idea of Holy War remained. The empire existed to secure an environment in which Islam could flourish. The empire therefore was an instrument of divine, not human, purpose. Unlike western states, where the ideal of one faith remained the norm, the Ottoman Empire was multi-religious as well as multi-ethnic and did not insist that Christians or Jews become Muslims. Some Christians did convert, for instance in parts of the Balkans, but this had more to do with local conditions than with a policy of forced conversion by the Turks. In Hungary, for example, there were almost no conversions by Christians to Islam. The Ottoman Empire required obedience from its non-Muslim subjects, not conversion. On the other hand, the Turks recruited

Christian boys for military and administrative service, and those who were chosen had to become Muslim. Even so, there was nothing in the Ottoman Empire resembling the religious persecution which happened in other parts of Europe. Those who remained Christian or Jewish paid taxes from which Muslims were exempted, and had to conform to certain modes of dress; they were also liable to be taken as slaves, something from which Muslims were excluded. Non-Muslims were allowed to organize their communal affairs on the basis of confessional allegiances. Officially, the Ottoman Empire was organized not on ethnic grounds, but religious. Five main non-Muslim communities (*millets*) were recognized: Orthodox, Gregorian Armenian, Roman Catholic, Protestant and Jewish. Of these, the Orthodox church was by far the largest, and the patriarch of Constantinople continued to be a figure of considerable political as well as ecclesiastical significance. In practice, the patriarchs generally cooperated with the government in order to secure the continuing security of the church and its members.

The empire was ruled from Constantinople, which could claim to be among the largest, economically most prosperous and aesthetically most imposing cities of Europe. At the beginning of the seventeenth century, it was one of only three cities with populations over 200,000 (the other two being Paris and Naples), and by the middle of the century, the city and its environs contained some 700,000 people. In its commercial activity, Constantinople was rivalled only by Cairo. Its geographical location at the junction of the Mediterranean and Black Sea, its fine port and its access by land to the Balkans, made it one of the great commercial entrepôts linking Europe and Asia. As the seat of the chief prelate of the Orthodox church, it contained numerous churches and monasteries. Until the Turkish conquest, the largest church had been Saint Sophia. The Turks converted it into a mosque. Numerous other mosques were built over the next two centuries, while in the seventeenth century mosques were built by the Sultan Ahmed I (1610) and Yeni-Validé-Jamissi (1615–65). Among the finest buildings in Constantinople was the sultan's palace, the Topkapu. It was organized around three courts, each known by its gate: Bab-i-Humayum (the court of the janissaries), the Middle Gate where the sultan held formal receptions, and the Gate of Felicity which led into the private apartments of the sultan. The concept of Constantinople as a capital city created tensions with the ideology of an empire created by, and existing to pursue, Holy War. Constantinople stood for government, administration and commerce, three spheres of activity which did not always relate easily to the pursuit of constant war. On the contrary, they flourished more under conditions of peace. The sultans were pulled in opposing directions by their religious obligation to conduct *jihad*, which drained financial and human resources, and augmented socio-political instability, and their desire for internal harmony and economic prosperity, which required peace. This was a paradox which they never fully resolved.

The sultan was a religious leader as well as ruler. He had unrestricted authority over his subjects, and owned the land of the empire as his personal domain; in these respects he resembled the tsar of Russia more than the monarchs of central and western Europe. The Ottoman Empire had no tradition of intermediate bodies, such as national or provincial assemblies, to stand between the sultan and his subjects. In this respect too, the Ottoman and Russian empires were similar. He was charged with preserving two categories of law, religious and civil. The religious law, or *sheriat*, was based on ecclesiastical texts, especially the Koran, and applied only to Muslims; it covered a host of subjects, including religious observances, pilgrimages, marriage, divorce and inheritance. Civil laws, or *kanuns*, were created and announced by the sultan as decrees. He received advice from the imperial council (*Divan*), but took decisions himself. In its idealized form, the Ottoman Empire was a community of Muslims and non-Muslims, held together in a just balance through which God could fulfil His will. The imperial succession was thought to rest with God. Although it was accepted that the sultan should come from the house of Osman, until 1617 there was no suggestion that the eldest son automatically should succeed. The sultan had many wives and large numbers of children. When a sultan died, God in His wisdom chose the most appropriate successor, who could be any of the brothers or sons of the former ruler. In practice, a succession occasioned deadly family and court intrigue, and the one who triumphed usually did so because his backers outwitted rivals. A new sultan usually eliminated his many brothers and sisters so as to weaken hostile powerbases; thus, Mehmed III, who became sultan in 1595, had nineteen brothers and over twenty sisters killed.

In 1617 this sanguinary practice was abandoned in favour of the principle that the eldest son of a sultan should succeed and, having done so, would confine his brothers to the royal palace, limiting them to innocuous activities. The consequences for the qualities of rulership shown by the sultans were disastrous, for in practice several sultans were succeeded by brothers, not sons. Their enforced political naïveté left them as pawns of particular factions. This was especially true in the early seventeenth century, when sultans came and went with as much frequency as tsars.[1] Sultans often were made or broken by the army. Given the Ottoman emphasis on war, the army naturally assumed a position of primary importance in the life of the empire. In the sixteenth century, sultans personally led their armies on campaign, but their successors in the early seventeenth century usually remained in Constantinople, entrusting command to their generals.

The elite foot soldiers of the army were the janissaries, recruited mostly through the *kul*, or slave system. Officials made tours of non-Muslim regions of the empire, mostly the Balkans, to select boys between the ages of eight and twenty. After this collection (*devshirme*), the recruits were taken to Constantinople where technically they became slaves. Some were trained as administrators, others were prepared for service in the royal palace, and the majority went either to work on Turkish farms or to join the janissaries; all converted to Islam. About a thousand boys a year were collected in this way. While training they lived in barracks wherein was fostered the *esprit de corps* and regimental pride which made them such a formidable fighting force. When training was completed they were allowed to marry, wives usually being found in the palace harem. By the early seventeenth century, other recruits were joining the janissaries. Some were prisoners of war taken by the Turks (the sultan had the right to receive one-fifth of such prisoners), and others were free-born Muslims seeking a military career. The janissaries were a political as well as military force: they provided the royal body guard and were heavily implicated in the political infighting which was such a feature of court life. They were by no means the only infantry. Some regiments in the frontier regions were formed out of Muslim recruits, and, in the Balkans, pioneer corps of Christian volunteers were created.

Fine soldiers though the infantry were, they were not feared by western forces as much as the Turkish cavalry (*sipahis*), who were generally considered to be superior to their European equivalents. *Sipahis* lived on land granted to them by the sultan; as landlords, they were responsible not only for exploiting their estates (*timars*), but for collecting taxes, administering justice and ensuring that Muslims obeyed the *sheriat*. By the end of the sixteenth century, the government was trying to arm the cavalry with pistols as a means of redressing the adverse military balance created by western infantry tactics based on the use of pikes and muskets, but there was much resistance in the Turkish cavalry, who despised firearms as unworthy of a true warrior. In addition to the principal infantry and cavalry regiments, the Turkish army made extensive use of auxiliaries and military engineers (the Turks had a long tradition of siege warfare), and had at its disposal splendid fortifications in frontier regions. Some were built at the mouths of rivers flowing into the Black Sea; at Azov, for example, the fortress had a 4,000 strong garrison. Others were constructed near the Persian frontier at Erivan and Tabriz; in Rumania, the great fortress of Sibiu was built.

For purposes of government, the empire was divided into provinces, the largest of which – such as Egypt and Syria – were administered by governors (*pashas*), who were moved from one province to another to prevent them developing provincial loyalties. The Balkans were sub-divided into smaller areas, whose governing officers often remained for long periods. At the centre, the sultan was advised by the *Divan*, but for the execution of policy he relied on four principal figures. First and most important was the grand vizier. He was *de facto* chief minister of the sultan, exercising authority over every aspect of government. The other principal ministers were the judge advocate, the minister of finance and the secretary of state. The central government of the Ottoman Empire may be envisaged as a group of power blocs, held in check by the sultan; if the sultan failed to do so, then it was up to the grand vizier to impose his authority. During the first half of the century, however, the office of grand vizier succumbed to the faction fighting at court, and one vizier after another rose and fell, unable to impose his authority. It was not until 1656, when the remarkable Mehmed Köprölü was appointed, that Turkey finally discovered its 'Richelieu'.

Mehmed Köprölü illustrates a feature of the Ottoman Empire which differed from other parts of Europe: it was possible to rise from the humblest of origins to the very summit of political power. Born into a peasant family which had migrated to Asia Minor from Albania, he was chosen in a *devshirme* and taken to Constantinople where he was attached to the imperial palace. He proved to be exceptionally intelligent and ambitious, and worked his way up to be a financial adviser to the grand vizier. He served as governor in Damascus and Jerusalem, and in 1656, at the age of seventy, was appointed governor of Tripoli. Before he could leave for Africa, however, he was appointed grand vizier amidst yet another crisis. Since 1645, the Ottoman Empire had been at war with Venice, and while in one theatre, Crete, the war was progressing satisfactorily, at sea it was not. In 1656 a Venetian fleet overwhelmed a Turkish force in the Dardanelles. This humiliation provoked riots in Constantinople and raised the threat of another janissary revolt. In response, Mehmed IV appointed Köprölü as grand vizier. Köprölü agreed on condition that he be given unlimited authority. Thus began a period of some forty-five years during which this family dominated the office.[2]

Köprölü gave priority to the suppression of rebellion, the elimination of corruption and insubordination in provincial and central government, and of mutinous groups in the army and navy. His first act was to crush the rioters in Constantinople, after which he executed opponents at court. Early in 1657 he suppressed a rising of *sipahis*, but caused a sensation by executing the patriarch of Constantinople, who had prophesied the downfall of the Ottoman Empire. During his five years in office (he died in 1661), Köprölü hammered into submission those whom he regarded as opponents. He showed little mercy. Some 36,000 victims of his purges were executed, and many thousands more were imprisoned or dismissed. He justified his actions by appeal to necessity: efficient government, administration and military organization would be restored only when disaffected elements had been destroyed. At the same time he pursued an energetic programme of fortifications. The Ottoman Empire already possessed a string of fortifications running from the Adriatic to the Sea of Azov via Slovenia, Hungary, Transylvania, Moldavia and the Ukraine. He strengthened defences by the construction of castles at the mouths of the Don and the Dnieper, and closer to home on either side of the Dardanelles. Before he died, he recommended to the sultan that Mehmed appoint Köprölü's son Ahmed as grand vizier. The Sultan complied. Ahmed proved to be a statesman of outstanding ability, whose influence on European history was no less than that of his contemporaries, Louis XIV of France and Emperor Leopold I.

### The Ottoman Empire and its Western Neighbours

During most of the first half of the seventeenth century, Turkish governments had rested content with holding their position in central Europe rather than attempting further advances. The political instability in Constantinople and the war against Persia from 1623 to 1639 left the Osman dynasty with no option; and the autonomy of the princes of Transylvania, nominally subjects of the sultan, was further evidence of the inability of the Turks to sustain a westward thrust of policy. Even the decision to attack Crete in 1645 can be interpreted in defensive rather than aggressive terms: as a means of securing approaches to the Dardanelles, and of keeping a politically dangerous army occupied. By mid-century, however, domestic and international circumstances were changing. Ottoman dynastic instability had been overcome and the Köprölü family brought a consistency to domestic and foreign policy which hitherto had been lacking. The risings in the Ukraine and, as will be seen, Hungary provided both challenges and opportunities; there was a danger that social conflict would extend into the Balkans, but equally, the Turks could exploit the troubles in the Ukraine and Hungary to their advantage. The possibility of rebellion in the Balkans was heightened by religious factors. The claims of the Russian Orthodox church to be the Third Rome, and the reforms associated with Nikon whereby Russian liturgy came closer to that of Greek Orthodoxy, carried the danger, from the Turkish point of view, that Orthodox Christians in the Ottoman Empire would become reinvigorated and look to Russia to liberate them. Again, the Peace of Westphalia released the Austrian Habsburgs from the German conflict, and left them relatively free to turn their attention to Turkish Hungary. A combination of positive and negative factors therefore persuaded the Turks that central Europe must become a priority once again.

Events in Transylvania stimulated the Turks into action. The prince of Transylvania, George II Rákóczy, developed ambitions towards independence from Turkey, and even sought the aid of some Balkan Christian princes to that end. He conducted foreign policy as if he had no obligations to the sultan, for example by invading Poland in 1655, in collaboration with Charles X of Sweden, without consulting or receiving permission from Mehmed IV. This was the kind of behaviour which the grand vizier, Mehmed Köprölü, found intolerable, and as part of his assault upon insubordination he deposed Rákóczy, replacing him with an obedient prince, Michael Apafy. The Transylvanian diet at first refused to acknowledge Apafy and a war broke out between the Turkish-backed Apafy and Rákóczy, who appealed to the Holy Roman Emperor, Leopold I, for assistance. The emperor refused to become involved, but the Turkish forces which defeated and killed Rákóczy in 1660 also occupied the Austrian imperial stronghold of Grosswardein. Between 1660 and 1662, the Turkish army, which included large numbers of marauding Tatars and Cossacks, completed the subjection of Transylvania, even though Leopold belatedly sent forces against them.

It was the very ineffectiveness of Austrian intervention which persuaded Grand Vizier Ahmed Köprölü to add to the success in Transylvania by renewing the assault on the Austrian Habsburgs. In 1663 he declared war on Leopold and personally headed an invasion which went from Constantinople through Belgrade and Buda to invade Habsburg or Royal Hungary. The campaign was notable both for its Turkish military successes, especially the capture of Neuhäusel after a siege, and for the efforts which the Turks made to depict themselves among the Hungarian population as their liberators from oppressive Habsburg rule. At the end of the year, when fighting had to be suspended during the winter months, Köprölü returned to Turkey well satisfied with his achievements. Meanwhile Leopold called a meeting of the imperial diet to appeal for military assistance. He was supported by the pope, who added his call for a renewed crusade against the Muslim invader. Thus, when the Turks reopened their campaign in 1664, they faced an imperial defence backed by princes of the Holy Roman Empire, and even by Louis XIV of France, who sent troops to assist Leopold. Significantly, Leopold received no assistance from Spain. In their defence it could be said that, in 1663 and 1664, the Spanish were fighting a war against Portugal; even so, Leopold felt badly let down by his Spanish cousins. Thereafter he felt fewer obligations towards them, and increasingly treated them in the light of political necessity rather than family commitment. The Turks still outnumbered the imperial forces, and while their main line of attack was against Styria, their Cossack and Tatar allies invaded Wallachia and Silesia, carrying off some 80,000 Christians as slaves. As the main Turkish army approached Styria, it was met by a mixed force of imperial and French troops headed by Marshal Montecuccoli. On 1 August 1664 they fought at St Gotthard, a battle in which the numerically inferior, but tactically superior, joint imperial forces achieved a decisive victory. It was a battle which showed that the Turkish army had fallen behind those in the west in matters of weaponry and infantry tactics, and that some urgent military rethinking was required by the Turkish commanders.

Leopold desired peace for he had urgent problems to the west, and did not want to become involved in a long war against Turkey. A few days after victory at St Gotthard, he signed the Peace of Vasvar with the Turks in which he yielded on almost all points. Leopold recognized Michael Apafy as prince of Transylvania, agreed to pay an annual subsidy to the Turks and conceded most of their territorial gains; in return, he secured a twenty-year truce. Contemporaries regarded Vasvar as an unnecessary humiliation for Leopold and a triumph for Ahmed Köprölü. The Turks were firmly re-established in central Europe, and had a guarantee of twenty years of peace with the Holy Roman Emperor. The 1660s finished with another victory for the Turks. They had been fighting a somewhat desultory war against the Venetians in Crete since 1645. The Turks held most of the island, but still the main Venetian fortress of Candia held out. After Vasvar, Ahmed Köprölü pursued the siege of Candia with greater resolution, and the fortress capitulated in 1669. By the end of the 1660s, the Ottoman Empire gave every appearance of having recovered from the political instability and military languor of earlier decades. It had a sultan and grand vizier who, between them, were capable of restoring the balance between the power blocs upon which the empire depended. The prestige of the Ottoman Empire stood high, and it was once again a major factor in European international relations.

## Leopold I and Hungary after the Peace of Vasvar

In Hungary, the Peace of Vasvar was seen as a humiliation. Both Catholic and Protestant nobles accused Leopold of having failed to take the opportunity of victory at St Gotthard to recover at least part of Turkish Hungary, and of having made unnecessary concessions to the Turks. Powerful aristocrats, such as Ferenc Wesselényi (palatine of Royal Hungary),[3] Ferenc Nádasdy (head of the judiciary), Miklós Zrinyi (ban of Croatia)[4] and his brother Peter, were but the most prominent figures in a wider movement of those whose frustration drove them into resistance. This group became the core of a movement to end Habsburg rule in Royal Hungary, and replace Leopold with either a Polish or a French prince. Beyond that, however, they had few concrete plans. Some were thinking only of an independent Royal Hungary, others of a Hungary united to Poland, while the Zrinyi brothers contemplated a separate Croatia under the suzerainty of Turkey. This confusion of aims was to undermine the effectiveness of the cabal.

Through their foreign contacts, they approached French diplomats in Warsaw and Venice to raise the possibility of Louis XIV supporting them in a rising against Leopold. The emperor had informants through whom he followed the intrigues of the aristocrats; his tactic was to allow them enough rope with which to hang themselves. Even though Louis XIV gave no encouragement, they took up arms against the emperor in 1670, but the rebellion was a fiasco. The imperial forces were well prepared; they quickly suppressed the rising and proceeded to occupy the whole of Royal Hungary. Leopold viewed this victory as his 'White Mountain', and proceeded to subject Hungary to the kinds of policies which Ferdinand II had imposed upon Bohemia in the 1620s. The ringleaders of the rising were tried by a special tribunal headed by Austrians, and several, including Peter Zrinyi, were executed. Next, a commission of Hungarians loyal to the emperor was appointed to investigate the conduct of some 2,000 mainly Protestant nobles, about 300 of whom had their estates confiscated. The Jesuits, supported by senior members of the Hungarian ecclesiastical hierarchy, began a new phase of forced conversion. Protestant churches and schools were closed, and pastors driven into exile. In Croatia, several hundred pastors were arrested and tried; some were executed, and others either banished or sent to the galleys. Leopold suspended the office of palatine and refrained from calling a meeting of the diet. He imposed punitive taxes upon Hungary, and suspended the fiscal immunity which nobles hitherto had enjoyed.

However, the Hungary of the 1670s was not the Bohemia of the 1620s, and Leopold's heavy-handed policies and military occupation of the country provoked stiff resistance. There were popular riots, particularly in reaction to Leopold's religious policy, and bands of dissident nobles and ex-soldiers took refuge in Turkish Hungary, from where they launched guerrilla attacks upon the Habsburg forces. This resistance, or *Kuruc*, movement received external help. One source was France. In 1672, Louis XIV invaded the Dutch Republic. Louis knew that Leopold might intervene in the international war that ensued, as indeed he did in 1674; it was in Louis's interest to keep Leopold enmeshed in Hungary as long as possible. Assistance to the *Kuruc* also came from Transylvania, where Prince Michael Apafy feared that if Leopold succeeded in subjugating Royal Hungary, he might be tempted then to invade Transylvania.

The *Kuruc* found an inspirational leader in a young Protestant nobleman, Imre Thököly. Born in 1657, he belonged to a wealthy family with estates in Upper Hungary, and displayed a capacity to hold together nobles of all religious persuasions and often of volatile temperament. He brought an impressive military coordination to the attacks on Habsburg forces, which, by the mid-1670s, were doing little more than hold key strongholds. So effective were Thököly's tactics that the French ambassador to Poland contacted him and, by the Treaty of Warsaw (1676), agreed on a plan of joint action. France would supply Thököly with money and military equipment, the *Kuruc* would pin down as many Habsburg regiments as possible (thus preventing them from fighting the French in the Rhineland), and together France and the *Kuruc* would aim to replace Leopold as king of Hungary with the king of Poland, John III Sobieski. Reinforced by French help, Thököly continued to harass the Habsburgs until Leopold accepted that his attempt to turn Hungary into a version of Bohemia in the 1620s must be abandoned. Leopold as yet would not negotiate with Thököly directly, but in 1681 he recalled the diet, which met at Sopron, mid-way between Vienna and Buda. Leopold made concessions which went a long way towards restoring the traditional constitution of Hungary and would, he hoped, reconcile the majority of the nobility to Habsburg rule. He reinstated the office of palatine, reduced the levels of taxation, acknowledged the fiscal privileges of the nobility, reintroduced liberty of worship, and promised to withdraw his armies and Austrian administrators who had flooded into Hungary since 1670. On the other hand, there was no question of returning confiscated estates.

These measures won the approval of most nobles, but were rejected by Thököly, who judged that the international situation of 1681 placed him in an unusually advantageous position. In that year, Louis XIV was implementing a policy of Reunions in the Rhineland whereby he annexed certain imperial territories to which he laid claim. This was Leopold's chief problem in 1681, and contained the potential for another Franco-Austrian war. Thököly calculated that Leopold would not risk heavier involvement in Hungary and might make even more concessions. Another factor was the attitude of Turkey. The truce established by the Peace of Vasvar had only three years to run, and there were signs that the Turkish government was preparing another war against Leopold: increasing numbers of sorties by Turkish raiders into Royal Hungary took place, and the advances which Leopold made, suggesting that the truce be extended, were rejected. The grand vizier, Kara Mustafa, was known to be bitterly anti-Christian and anti-Habsburg, and it was he who precipitated a crisis. In 1682, he approached Thököly with a bold offer: if Thököly would transfer his allegiance, and that of Upper Hungary which he controlled, to the sultan, the territory would be recognized as a formal protectorate of the Ottoman Empire with Thököly at its head. Thököly agreed, and accepted his appointment from Mehmed

IV later in the year. When Leopold again sought the renewal of the twenty-year truce, the Turks refused, and instead gathered an army under the command of Kara Mustafa. In 1683 he launched an invasion of Royal Hungary in support of the *Kuruc*; he was joined by Thököly with his own troops.

## The Siege of Vienna, 1683

The army commanded by Kara Mustafa was composed of a kernel of some 60,000 regular troops, including janissaries and *sipahis*, accompanied by some 80,000 Tatars and auxiliaries from the Balkans. The Tatars roamed far and wide in Hungary, causing widespread havoc and fear. Leopold's army, commanded by Charles V of Lorraine, retreated towards Vienna, which 20,000 of his infantry occupied in readiness for a Turkish assault. Disobeying orders from the sultan, and ignoring the advice of his generals who were aware of their lack of equipment to conduct a long siege, Kara Mustafa decided to besiege Vienna. He arrived before the city on 13 July. He formally invited it to surrender and submit to Islam. Upon its refusal, he began the siege, which lasted almost two months. Leopold and his court had left the city, settling in Linz. The prospect that Vienna might fall alarmed all the governments of central Europe. If Kara Mustafa succeeded, the whole of Hungary would be lost, and Poland and many parts of Germany would be vulnerable.

Leopold was promised aid from princes of the Holy Roman Empire (several, including Saxony and Bavaria, sent contingents); on 31 March, John III Sobieski of Poland had signed an alliance with Leopold. He mustered an army and in mid-August marched south. Louis XIV offered assistance, but it was refused by Leopold. Vienna was well defended, but by early September the Turks were close to a breakthrough. The Polish and German armies finally arrived and on 12 September, at the battle of Kahlenberg close to Vienna, their joint forces, commanded by John Sobieski and Charles of Lorraine, inflicted a heavy defeat on the Turkish army. The siege was broken and the Turks retreated, suffering another defeat at Sczecsen on 11 November. When word arrived in Constantinople of the failure at Vienna, there were demonstrations against the grand vizier and even against the sultan. Mehmed IV discussed Kara Mustafa's fate with the *Divan*, and it was decided that the grand vizier must pay with his life. Emissaries and an executioner went to meet him in Belgrade. On

25 December, Kara Mustafa handed over the symbols of his office and submitted to death by strangulation.

The relief of Vienna was celebrated in the city itself and throughout Europe, not only because it was a dramatic military triumph, but because of its symbolism. In the eyes of contemporaries it was a triumph of Christianity over Islam (even though the Turkish army contained a high proportion of Christians), of the Holy Roman

**Figure 4**   John Sobieski, king of Poland

**Figure 5**   The execution of Kara Mustapha

Empire over the Ottoman Empire, and of Leopold over Mehmed IV. Even though Leopold personally had not relieved Vienna, he was seen (and he depicted himself through the issue of prints and medallions) as the monarch who, with divine assistance, had overcome overwhelming odds. Henceforth he was seen as a man of power as well as prestige. The reputations of John Sobieski and Charles of Lorraine likewise shone in the aftermath of Kahlenberg; so did that of the pope, Innocent XI. Ever since his election in 1676, Innocent had been trying to revive the crusading ideal in Europe, and it was his mediation which brought about the alliance between Leopold and John Sobieski. One leading monarch whose reputation failed to be enhanced by the defeat of the Turks was Louis XIV. Louis did seek a share in the glory by claiming that he temporarily suspended military action in the Rhineland so that Leopold might concentrate on Vienna, but this assertion only served to highlight the contrast between a victorious Leopold and a piqued Louis XIV.

Leopold was urged by John Sobieski and other commanders to pursue the Turks into the Balkans, but he refused on the ground that the Ottoman invasion had wreaked such devastation in Hungary that peace was necessary. He contacted the Turkish government and offered to renew the Peace of Vasvar, but his proposal was rejected. John Sobieski had continued harrying the retreating Turkish army, but he returned to Poland in November. It looked as if the *status quo ante bellum* might prevail, but Pope Innocent XI would not let matters rest. Still fired by a crusading zeal, he mobilized his considerable diplomatic resources and in 1684, on the promise of large financial subsidies, persuaded Leopold, John Sobieski and the senate of Venice to form a Holy League. Its purpose was to restore as much of Christendom as possible, Orthodox as well as Catholic. To this end Innocent also attempted to persuade Russia to join the League; at first the tsar refused, but did join in 1687. On behalf of the League, Venice declared war on the Ottoman Empire in 1684; the war lasted fifteen years.

## The Holy League versus the Ottoman Empire

The war may be divided into three phases. In the first, which lasted until 1689, the allies achieved notable successes; in the second, to 1696, the Turks launched a counter-offensive which won back much lost ground; in the third, the allies advanced again until the Peace of Carlowitz was signed in 1699. Geography seemed to ascribe each of the members of the league a specific role. Venice would concentrate on the war at sea and on the Dalmatian coast, the Austro-Hungarian forces of Leopold on Turkish Hungary, and John Sobieski would attack from the north. In practice, the allies acknowledged no neat division of labour, apart from the maritime war, which was left to Venice. Leopold had designs on the Dalmatian coast which came into conflict with those of Venice, and John Sobieski planned to occupy Transylvania and Moldavia, two territories which Leopold regarded as his by right.

In phase one, the allies advanced on all fronts. At sea the Venetians steadily gained control of the Adriatic and Ionian seas, and in 1687, supported by troops from several German states, launched their most audacious attack of all upon Athens. They bombarded the city (a shell hit the Parthenon, which was used by the Turks as a gunpowder store; the ensuing explosion left the Parthenon a ruin). In Hungary, the armies of Leopold took most of Hungary and Croatia, although Thököly remained at large. Buda was taken in 1686, and a symbolically important victory won at Mohács in 1687: it was there in 1526 that the Turks had crushed the Hungarian army and, as a result, went on to occupy most of the country. Mohács 1687 was revenge for 1526. The imperial armies also invaded Transylvania and forced Michael Apafy to acknowledge Leopold as his master. Leopold guaranteed religious liberty for Transylvania, but Michael also had to accept imperial garrisons in the principality. Having driven the Turks from most of Hungary, the imperial armies moved into the Balkans, and in 1688 achieved one of their most notable successes, the capture of Belgrade. They then pushed into Bosnia and Serbia, but by now were in danger of coming up against the Venetians, who regarded the Balkans as their field of operations. Further north, the Poles had been fighting to recover Podolia from the Turks, but the major change was the entry of Russia into the war in 1687. The immediate object of their attack was not the Turks themselves, but the Crimean Tatars who had fought with the Turks in 1683. The effects within Constantinople of the allied advances were considerable. In 1687 the Sultan Mehmed IV was overthrown and replaced by his brother Suleiman II, who, although he ruled only until 1691, oversaw a short Turkish revival. He was assisted by his new grand vizier, Mustafa, appointed in 1689. Mustafa was another member of the Köprölü family, and, like his forebears, he made rapid strides towards improving Turkish military organization. It was a tragedy from the sultan's point of view that Mustafa was killed while fighting in Hungary in 1691.

The complexion of the war was affected also by developments in western Europe. In 1688 a war broke out between France and the League of Augsburg, of which Austria was a member. Leopold was now faced by war on two fronts, and had to divert forces from Hungary to the Rhineland. Again, in 1689 Innocent XI died. He had been the mainstay of the Holy League, and although his successor, Alexander VIII, continued support for the war, his relations with Leopold were cool, not least because the war funds which he gave to Venice, of which he was a native, were more generous than those granted to Leopold. Alexander died in 1691, but his successor, Innocent XII, gave greater attention to the war in western Europe than to that against the Turks. In the 1690s, therefore, the papacy was not the driving force within the Holy League that it had been in the 1680s.

Phase two of the war opened with the death of Michael Apafy in 1690. Grand Vizier Mustafa nominated Thököly as prince of Transylvania, and equipped him with an army with which to tie down imperial troops while Mustafa himself led a larger force against Belgrade. The strategy worked, Mustafa recovering Belgrade later in the year. In 1691 Mustafa followed up his victory with an invasion of Hungary, but he was defeated and killed by an imperial force at Szalankemen. The Turkish advance halted, and for the next three years neither side made much progress, for Leopold's armies by now were concentrating on the war against France. The accession to the sultanate of Mustafa II in 1695 marked another revival of Turkish fortunes. He quickly recovered part of southern Hungary, his cause being helped when John Sobieski died in 1696. The commander of the imperial forces, Frederick-Augustus, elector of Saxony, was a candidate for the Polish crown and left his post in Hungary to go to Warsaw for the election, which he won, then taking the name King Augustus II. The Turkish position in the Adriatic and Ionian seas also improved. The Venetians had abandoned Athens, for they lacked the military strength to hold it; and even though they captured the island of Chios in 1694, the Venetians once again relinquished it after a short occupation. By contrast, the Russians continued to make important advances: in 1695, Tsar Peter I captured Turkish fortresses at the mouth of the Dnieper, and in 1696 he took Azov at the mouth of the Don. Russia was now poised to extend its influence across the Black Sea.

The final phase of the war saw renewed allied victories. In western Europe, peace was signed at Ryswick in 1697, allowing Leopold to concentrate once more on Turkey. Already he had transferred troops from Italy under the command of Prince Eugene of Savoy; on 29 August 1697, Eugene heavily defeated the Turks at Zenta. In the Black Sea region, Russian power continued to expand at the expense of the Turks. By now there was talk of a peace settlement, the initiative being taken by the Dutch and English governments, Leopold's allies in the War of the League of Augsburg. A new crisis over the Spanish succession was looming, and there was a possibility of yet another war against France. It was essential, in the view of the Dutch and British, and indeed of Leopold himself, to extricate the emperor from the Turkish war. The Dutch and English mediated peace talks at Carlowitz in Croatia, against the wishes of the Russians, who wanted to continue fighting. Peace was signed on 26 January 1699 between Turkey on one side and, on the other, Venice, Poland and Leopold as king of Hungary. Leopold retained most of Hungary and Transylvania (although part of southern Hungary remained in Turkish hands). Venice kept most of its conquests in Dalmatia and the

Adriatic. Poland held on to Podolia and part of the western Ukraine. Peter I did not sign peace in 1699, but did so at Constantinople in 1700. A truce of thirty years between Turkey and Russia was agreed, forts at the mouth of the Dnieper were to be destroyed, and Peter retained Azov.

The War of the Holy League showed that it was possible to achieve major territorial changes in central Europe by sustained military effort. Turkey's presence in central Europe had been all but eliminated, and for the first time in some 175 years the Habsburgs ruled almost the whole of Hungary. The Peace of Carlowitz, and indeed that of Constantinople in 1700, marked a shift in the Turkish approach to international relations. The Turkish government gradually relinquished its long-held allegiance to the concept of continuous Holy War; increasingly it shaped its foreign policy in the light of the dynastic or strategic considerations which were followed by other European governments. The foreign policies of most Christian states had subordinated religious to secular imperatives by the mid-seventeenth century; the Turkish government did so after the treaties of Carlowitz and Constantinople.

## War, 1715–1718

It would be wrong to think that the reverses in Hungary placed the stamp of inevitable decline on the Ottoman Empire, for most of the Balkans remained in its hands, and the Turkish government was not reconciled to the losses at Carlowitz. The Turks had shown a remarkable capacity for revival in the past, and did so again. In 1715 they made another attempt to recover territory on the Dalmatian coast and in the Peloponnese. They declared war on Venice and, having established naval supremacy, attacked the Dalmatian coast and Corfu; most of the Greek inhabitants of the island were pro-Turkish, having been disillusioned by the fiscal pressures applied by the Venetian government. Venice was close to defeat, and was saved by the emperor, Charles VI, who intervened in 1716.

In that year, Charles VI was mostly concerned with affairs in Italy, but Eugene of Savoy persuaded him that, if the Turks succeeded against Venice, and especially if they recaptured the Dalmatian coast, Croatia and Styria once again would be vulnerable. In 1716, Charles VI signed an alliance with Venice and entered the war, to the consternation of Turkish ministers who had counted on the emperor's neutrality. A Turkish army of some 120,000 went to reinforce Belgrade, still in the sultan's hands, but *en route* attacked the fortress of Peterwardein, where Eugene was ensconced with 70,000 men. Eugene defeated the Turkish army, but the janissaries fought so well that Eugene dared not pursue them to Belgrade. Instead he invaded Turkish Hungary, which capitulated in October 1716. In 1717 Eugene at last besieged Belgrade. A Turkish army came to assist the city, but on 16 August was defeated by Eugene. Two days later, Belgrade surrendered. At this time, Charles VI was in conflict with Spain over the question of Italy, and was being supported by the British and Dutch. As in 1699, they offered to mediate peace talks between Venice, the emperor and Turkey, thereby allowing Charles to concentrate on Italy. The offer was accepted by the warring parties, and peace signed at Passarowitz in 1718. The Turks formally surrendered their last enclave in Hungary to Charles VI, who also retained Belgrade and most of Serbia. Passarowitz completed what Carlowitz had begun. Turkey no longer endangered central Europe.

## Constitutional and Socio-economic Consequences of War in Hungary

The recovery of Hungary unquestionably was the greatest achievement of Leopold I and his successors, but the constitutional and social problems which remained were fearsome. Under Turkish rule, Hungarian aristocrats had enjoyed much independence of action; would they continue to do so, or did the restoration of unity imply an unacceptable degree of control from Vienna? Aristocrats from the whole of Hungary now would take their seats in the diet; how would new members relate to old, and how would the king handle the diet of a united Hungary? Then there were the socio-economic consequences of the war to be confronted. Since most of central Hungary was a plain, it had experienced almost a non-stop passage of troops, both imperial and Turkish. Tatar bands had constantly been on the prowl, kidnapping even whole villages to be sold as slaves. By the early 1690s, wide tracts of central Hungary were deserted as people left the land in search of refuge in the northern mountains or encampments near towns. These latter were, in effect, immense refugee camps, one of the largest being at Kecskemet between the Danube and the Tisza. Elsewhere, land and livestock went uncultivated or untended, and agricultural production collapsed. The population of central Hungary had probably declined to under a million by the 1690s.

In 1686, after the capture of Buda, Leopold appointed a commission to investigate the question of socio-economic recovery. It was placed under the presidency of a priest and adviser to the emperor, Leopold Kollonics, later cardinal-archbishop of Esztergom. His task was to propose measures whereby Hungary could be repopulated and agriculture revived. The commission classified the reconquered areas of Hungary as *neo acquisita* (i.e. as now belonging to the king, to dispose of as he wished), but it did allow former land-owners to reclaim their estates, provided they had proof of ownership and on condition of payment of a fee. In practice, the crown rewarded its military commanders, many of whom were Germans, Austrians and Italians, with large tracts of land. Wealthy land-owners from Croatia and Slovakia also profited from the availability of land by buying estates from the crown; for example, the Grassalkovic family, of Croatian origin, thereby became one of the largest land-owners in central Hungary.

As military security in central Hungary improved in the late 1680s and 1690s, refugees returned from the Slovakian mountains and elsewhere. A flood of migrant peoples – not only returning refugees, but newcomers – entered central Hungary. Some came from Transylvania (and migrants from Rumania then moved into vacant land in Transylvania), but almost 200,000 Serbs settled in southern Hungary, the first wave having been led by their bishop in 1690. Kollonics himself was anxious to encourage German immigration into Hungary. He was suspicious of native-born Magyars, regarding them as politically untrustworthy. Germans, especially those from the south, he considered to be reliable and capable of exerting pro-Habsburg influences on their Magyar neighbours. He was also an admirer of German agricultural techniques which, he believed, would bring to Hungarian crop and livestock production the most modern methods. He took steps to attract immigrants from the Black Forest region, Franconia and Swabia. Favourable terms were offered: land, houses, livestock and financial loans at low rates of interest were available. Many Germans came, especially poorer peasants who, in Germany, had skills but lacked money and stock. The Kollonics commission also made proposals of an administrative and judicial nature which reduced the privileges of the nobility. A particularly contentious measure was the creation of royal law courts at Kosice, Zagreb and

Pest, to which peasants and others could submit appeals against the decisions of local courts, which were controlled by the nobility. Again, the commission introduced rules limiting the amount of labour which peasants owed to land-owners. Such measures elicited a hostile response from nobles, who viewed them as manifestations of Habsburg absolutist intent at the expense of noble rights and privileges.

The decisions of the commission were instrumental in provoking the last great Hungarian revolt of this period, in Transylvania from 1703 to 1711. Changes to the Hungarian constitution also lay behind the revolt. While his armies were advancing against the Turks, Leopold called a meeting of the Hungarian diet at Pressburg (1687). It was a momentous occasion, for Leopold's reputation stood unprecedentedly high, and many of the nobles at the diet, whose estates had been ravaged by war, were looking to him for economic assistance. Leopold seized this opportunity to accomplish a goal which the Habsburgs had long cherished: the diet agreed to transform the monarchy from an elective office into the hereditary possession of the male line of the Habsburgs. Secondly, the diet abandoned one of the oldest Hungarian noble rights, that of resistance to an 'unworthy' king. The diet of 1687 was a major victory for Leopold; in its own way it was just as portentous as that over the Turks. The relationship between king and subjects had been redefined, and Hungary joined Austria and Bohemia as a hereditary possession of the Habsburgs. Not all Hungarian nobles were reconciled to these changes, and in 1703 resorted to rebellion in an attempt to restore their traditional rights.

## The Rákóczy Revolt, 1703–1711

The rising began in Transylvania and was led by Ferenc II Rákóczy,[5] who was a member of the great family which had been prominent in Transylvanian affairs for several generations. He was steeped in the ideology of *Kuruc* opposition to Habsburg ambition, and in some respects became the Transylvanian Thököly. Exploiting noble suspicion of Habsburg constitutional intentions, popular discontent at high taxation and rising opposition to the influx of immigrants from Germany and the Balkans, he raised rebellion in 1703 in defence of what he considered Hungarian liberties. In 1704 the diet of Transylvania recognized him as prince. By now, Leopold was embroiled in the War of the Spanish Succession (he was allied to England and the Dutch Republic against France and Spain), and could not afford to bring upon Transylvania sufficient military force to crush the rebellion; he died in 1705, leaving his son Joseph with the task of ensuring election to the imperial crown, ruling Austria and Bohemia, and subduing Hungary. Rákóczy was recognized as prince of Transylvania by Louis XIV, whose ambassador in Sweden sought to secure Swedish help for Ferenc. The rising spread from Transylvania across many parts of Hungary, and acquired the character of a nationalist movement against supposed Habsburg absolutism. In 1707, an assembly of Transylvanian nobles issued a declaration of independence.

The prospects of Transylvania preserving independence depended on Rákóczy and the French constructing a regional power system, involving the Swedes, Poles and perhaps even the Russians, capable of defending it against the inevitable Habsburg counter-measures; but, as will be seen in due course, relations between these states were such that no viable system could be devised. Joseph I diverted more troops from the war against France, and in 1708 inflicted a heavy defeat on Rákóczy's army at the battle of Trencsén. Later in the year Rákóczy left Transylvania to seek further foreign assistance, and in his absence his commanders approached Joseph I requesting peace talks. The negotiations lasted three years and resulted in the Peace of Szatmár (1711). This effected a compromise by confirming Habsburg hereditary possession of the Hungarian crown, while Joseph agreed to restore the traditional rights of the nobility, including the principle of legitimate resistance and rights of worship. Thus, the Habsburgs retained Hungary, but at the price of restoring the ancient constitution with its protection of noble rights; the spirit of reform embodied by the Kollonics commission was set aside. At Szatmár, Joseph conceded that Hungary could not be treated as Bohemia had been after 1620; if anything, Szatmár may be seen as a Hungarian version of the Peace of Westphalia as it affected the Holy Roman Empire. The Hungary created at Szatmár balanced a monarchy which had reforming and modernizing instincts, with a diet which incarnated the traditional liberties of the nobility. The great question for the future was, would monarchy and diet collaborate to create a Hungary adapted to the demands of the eighteenth century, or would they fail to establish a mutuality of interest? Rákóczy felt betrayed by the Peace of Szatmár. He went into exile and became a Carmelite monk, first in France and then in Turkey, where he died in 1735.

## Vienna by 1720

As the reign of Leopold I progressed, his quest for glory, which was continued by his sons, found expression in the beautification of Vienna and the construction of notable buildings, both secular and ecclesiastic, in the provinces. The earlier section on Leopold's personality and artistic tastes referred to his liking for things Italian; he never abandoned this predilection, but after 1683 he showed a marked sensitivity towards more distinctively central European styles in art and architecture. The siege of Vienna, in other words, marks a juncture in the architectural and artistic history of central Europe as well as the political. Thereafter a new surge of building in Vienna turned that city into one of the glories of Europe. Italian influences certainly continued. Among the more prominent artists were Domenico Martinelli, who designed the Liechtenstein palace in Vienna, and Andrea Pozzo, former artist to Pope Clement XI. Pozzo's decoration of the ceiling of the Liechtenstein palace and of the university church (1702–9) were among his finest masterpieces.

However, Vienna and other parts of Austria and Hungary were increasingly adorned by churches and palaces designed by Germans and Austrians, who might have followed Italian styles, but adapted them to their own ends. Three such figures stand out. One is Johann Fischer von Erlach, whom Joseph I appointed as Inspector of Royal Commissions in 1705. Two of the finest churches in Salzburg were designed by Erlach: the Trinity (1694) and the Kollegienkirche (1696); in Prague he built the palace of Count Clam-Gallas, and in Vienna he built the imperial library. He collaborated with the second figure in this trinity, Lukas von Hildebrandt: together they worked on the Winter Palace built for Leopold's most famous general, Prince Eugene of Savoy. For a time Hildebrandt had a military career, serving as an engineer in the imperial army. He came to the attention of Prince Eugene, who brought him back to Austria and set him to work not only on the Winter Palace, but also on the prince's Summer Palace in Vienna, the Belvedere. This spacious building arranged around a series of pavilions is regarded as Hildebrandt's masterpiece of secular building; his finest church was the Karlskirche in Vienna. The third figure, Jakob Prandtauer, worked almost entirely on ecclesiastical architecture. He contributed to reconstruction work at the Klosterneuburg abbey, and between 1708 and 1726 helped to reconstruct the Abbey of St Florian, a long-delayed scheme to celebrate the liberation of

Vienna in 1683. His most dramatic and spectacular design was for the monastery at Melk on the Danube. Perched on a rock overlooking the river, the church and monastic buildings create one of the most imposing architectural effects in Europe.

The architectural adornment of Vienna and other areas, which was financed by emperor, magnates and prelates, turned Vienna and the Danube basin into one of the most artistically dynamic regions of Europe. The relative peace which central Europe enjoyed after 1683 was a time when the compromise reached between emperor, aristocrats and Catholic church to preserve a social and economic system based on hereditary Habsburg rule, noble privilege and Counter-Reformation Catholicism, expressed itself through secular and ecclesiastical projects such as those which have been outlined. Without claiming that the visual arts are nothing more than the cultural superstructure of a given socio-political system, there are grounds for arguing that, in post-1683 central Europe, patterns of urban and architectural development were conditioned by the social, political and religious principles of emperor, aristocrats and Catholic church. Those principles might now be an historical memory, but the architectural heritage which they left remains one of Europe's finest treasures, and the equal of anything produced by France, Spain, Italy or any other part of the continent.

## ITALY AT THE TURN OF THE CENTURY

The Peace of Westphalia brought peace to Germany, but also ushered in about forty years of relative stability in Italy. The incidence of military conflict between Italian states declined rapidly, and even though other international wars occurred, their direct effects upon Italy were few. During the war of 1672–8 arising out of France's invasion of the Dutch Republic, an anti-Spanish revolt occurred in Messina in 1674. Emissaries from the town went to France to request aid from Louis XIV. In 1675 a French squadron disembarked soldiers at Messina. They remained until the last months of the war in 1678, when they withdrew. Panic spread throughout the town, and some 4,000 managed to depart on the French troop ships. Fearful of the vengeance which the Spanish would take when they re-entered Messina, another 16,000 or so fled the city, going mostly to France, the Levant and even to Canada. The War of the League of Augsburg between 1688 and 1697 spread into northern Italy, but the Treaty of Ryswick (1697) by which it terminated did not alter the political map of Italy. Venice was involved in wars against Turkey between 1645 and 1669, and 1684 and 1699, but these were purely Venetian concerns which, again, did not implicate the rest of Italy.

It was the War of the Spanish Succession, from 1702 to 1713, which not only brought warfare to Italy again, but transformed the political map. The origins of the war are a subject for the next chapter, but the crucial point is that, in 1700, Charles II of Spain died without a male heir; in his will he left the crown to a French prince and grandson of Louis XIV, the duc d'Anjou, who became Philip V of Spain. After intense diplomatic wrangling and many misunderstandings, a war broke out in 1702 in which the emperor (still Leopold I at this stage), England and the Dutch Republic fought against France and Spain, with the object of replacing Philip V with an Austrian Habsburg prince. During the course of the war, which was joined by other states, the aims of the principal belligerents were modified, but for eleven years much of Europe, including Italy, was once again engulfed by a long and destructive war. In so far as it affected Italy, its main consequence was the gradual expulsion of the Spanish by the Austrians, and the replacement of the former by the latter as the chief power in the peninsula. The Austrians took Milan in 1706, Naples in 1707 and Sardinia in 1708; in this same year they annexed Mantua, whose duke was a partisan of the Spanish. Victor Amedeo II, duke of Savoy and an ally of the Austrians, occupied part of Lombardy.

The war ended in a series of treaties signed at Utrecht, Rastadt and Baden between 1713 and 1715; it was the Treaty of Rastadt (1714) which settled the future of Italy. Considerable changes were made to its political complexion. Milan, Naples, Sardinia, Mantua and several former Spanish ports in northern Italy passed into Austrian Habsburg possession. Victor Amedeo of Savoy acquired territory in Piedmont, but more significantly the island of Sicily and title of king. At Utrecht (1713), the Spanish had already ceded the southern Netherlands to Austria. Philip V remained king of Spain, but his European possessions were much reduced, the Austrian Habsburgs being the principal beneficiaries. The late 1600s and early 1700s were golden decades for the Austrian Habsburgs, as Hungary, part of the Balkans, much of Italy and the Netherlands came under their rule.

Just as the Turks attempted to reverse Carlowitz, the embittered Spanish took the first opportunity to overturn Rastadt. In 1714, Philip V's wife, Marie Louise of Savoy, died. Philip quickly remarried, his second wife being an Italian princess, Elizabeth Farnese of Parma;

the match was negotiated by Philip's chief minister, Giulio Alberoni, himself from Parma. One reason for Philip choosing Elizabeth was that the duke of Parma had no male heir; when, in 1716, Elizabeth gave birth to a son, Don Carlos, she and Philip claimed that Parma would devolve to him, thus restoring a Spanish presence in Italy. The duke of Tuscany, a member of the Medici family, also was without male heir. Since the Farneses had marriage links with the Medicis, Philip V and Elizabeth Farnese claimed that Don Carlos was also heir apparent to Tuscany.

Pending the opportunity to press these claims, Philip V attempted to reverse Rastadt by force. Alberoni had been rebuilding the army and fleet since 1713, and in 1717, when Austrian forces were fighting the Turks, decided on action. Spanish forces occupied the islands of Sardinia and Sicily. This unilateral move alarmed not only the emperor and Victor Amedeo, but the French and other governments. The French concern was dynastic. It will be shown in the next chapter that, following the death of Louis XIV in 1715, a French succession crisis was possible, since Louis XV was a sickly boy. If he died, Philip V might claim the French throne, and from the ensuing crisis, war might result. An aggressive, victorious Spain in 1717 therefore spelt possible danger for France. British concern at the occupation of Sardinia and Sicily was strategic. If the Spanish succeeded in their enterprise, it was only a matter of time before they invaded the Italian mainland, with calamitous consequences for European peace. At Utrecht in 1713, Britain had secured two Spanish possessions in the Mediterranean: Gibraltar and Minorca. The British government appealed to the Spanish to withdraw from Sardinia and Sicily in return for the restoration of Gibraltar. The Spanish refused.

Britain, France and the Dutch Republic responded by forming a Triple Alliance in 1717, joined by Austria in 1718. In July 1718, the British and Dutch mediated the Treaty of Passarowitz which freed Emperor Charles VI to move his troops to Italy. In August, a British fleet encountered the Spanish off Cape Passaro on the south-eastern tip of Sicily. It attacked and destroyed many of the Spanish ships. This action was followed by a declaration of war on Spain by the allies. Allied shipping transported Austrian forces to Sardinia and Sicily, and a French army crossed into northern Spain, destroying naval installations at Pasages. The Spanish attempted to strike back. They sent a fleet towards England in the hope of stimulating a Jacobite rebellion, but after the failure of the rising of 1715, the chances of success were small; and in any case the fleet was dispersed by storms. The Spanish urged the Turks to begin war against the emperor again; but after Passarowitz, they were in no position to renew hostilities. Having failed on all fronts, Alberoni was dismissed in December 1719. The Spanish government entered into peace negotiations in London, where peace was signed in February 1720. Charles VI and Philip V both accepted the principle of the division of Spain's territories. Austria and Savoy exchanged islands, Sicily now becoming an Austrian possession and Sardinia passing to Savoy. The right of Don Carlos to succeed in Parma and Tuscany was recognized, and as a guarantee of its acceptance of these terms, Spain joined the Quadruple Alliance of Austria, Britain, the Dutch Republic and France.

Central Europe and its two southerly projections, one into the Balkans, the other into the Italian peninsula, underwent profound political and social change in the forty years between 1680 and 1720. The Austrian Habsburgs, having accepted the 'solution' to German problems represented by the Peace of Westphalia, returned to the eastern challenges bequeathed by the sixteenth century: the power of the Ottoman Empire, and the presence of Protestantism. The first was overcome by 1720, and while Protestantism remained in Austria, Bohemia and Hungary, and helped to inspire the Rákóczy revolt, Joseph I restored freedom of worship in the Peace of Szatmár (1711), and effectively conceded that a mono-religious Hungary was not feasible. As the eighteenth century progressed, central Europe was to pose renewed political and economic problems to the Habsburgs in Vienna, and in 1740, when Emperor Charles VI died without male heir, the Habsburgs faced a succession crisis which led to war. As for Italy, it remained subordinated to Austria rather than to Spain after 1714 and 1720, but in 1731 Don Carlos acquired the territories promised to him in 1720. Within a few years he exchanged them with Austria in return for his becoming king of Naples, a title much more appropriate to his ambition than that of duke. Under his rule, Neapolitans made a distinctive contribution to the Enlightenment. Economists such as Antonio Genovesi, who advocated the virtues of free trade, were at the forefront of the new thought, and in Giovanni Battista Vico, Naples produced one of the outstanding philosophers of the century. Beyond Naples, the great Italian cities retained their artistic prestige and, of course, the religious authority of Rome kept Italy at the centre of international developments in Catholicism. The great powers still regarded the question of who controlled Italy as one of international importance; as in the seventeenth century, so in the eighteenth, the history of Italy was of more than parochial significance.

# 8

# Western Europe, 1660–1720: France and Spain

---

The marriage of Louis XIV and Maria Teresa in 1660 was celebrated throughout France and Spain as the dawn of a new era in Franco-Spanish friendship. Similar platitudinous sentiments had been expressed in 1615 at the marriages of Louis XIII to Anne of Austria, and Philip IV to Elisabeth of France, but in 1660 there were grounds for believing that, on this occasion, such avowals might possess more substance. The Peace of the Pyrenees afforded both countries an opportunity to recuperate from the socio-political wounds left by international and civil war, and in 1660, Spain was still fighting to recover Portugal. Yet within a few years France and Spain were at war again. The resumption of hostilities has sometimes been interpreted in terms of inevitability. Since the mid-1500s, so the argument goes, the two states had been locked in a struggle for preponderance in western Europe. Spain generally got the better of it down to the 1640s, but thereafter France made its greater demographic and financial resources tell. The Peace of the Pyrenees afforded Louis XIV an interlude in which to strengthen French sinews for the next round. Beginning in 1667, he dealt a series of hammer blows to Spain, and in 1700 enjoyed the final triumph when his grandson became king of Spain.

Recent scholarship has been sceptical towards this schematic interpretation. Without engaging in a lengthy discussion, some of the more weighty objections can be noted here. Although France and Spain did oppose each other, it was usually for dynastic rather than geopolitical reasons. After the partition of the Habsburg territories in 1556 between the Austrian and Spanish branches, the principal aim of the latter was to preserve its geographically dispersed European inheritance. The loss of the northern provinces of the Netherlands forced the Spanish Habsburgs to fortify the southern Netherlands, both to discourage further separatist tendencies and to be prepared to re-occupy the Dutch Republic. However, since dynastic honour obliged Philip III to maintain his claim on the north, he could not cut his losses, recognize the Dutch Republic and turn it into a satellite state as a policy based on hegemony might have indicated. As regards France, defensive motives, not aspirations towards hegemony, governed most Valois and Bourbon policy towards Spain. With Spanish territory bordering France's land frontiers, and Spanish ships plying between Spain and the Netherlands, French monarchs felt hemmed in; this was a situation which the Peace of the Pyrenees did not materially alter. As regards Louis XIV's resumption of war against Spain in 1667, it will be argued in due course that this too was for dynastic reasons; and, thereafter, necessity as much as ambition drove French policy. Moreover, although Spain and France were the major individual powers in western Europe, a third bloc emerged in the second half of the century as Britain, the Dutch Republic and the Emperor Leopold I increasingly collaborated. To interpret the period between 1672 and 1713 in terms of a Franco-Spanish struggle is to ignore this third force, whose effectiveness was seen in the international peace settlements of 1713 and 1714, when the Austrian Habsburgs acquired extensive territory in Italy and the Netherlands and Britain secured important concessions from Spain.

## FRANCE, 1661–1715

### Louis XIV and the Government of France

On 10 March 1661, the day after the death of Cardinal Mazarin, the archbishop of Rouen asked Louis XIV to whom he and others should go for instructions. The king replied, '*A moi, Monsieur l'archevêque!*' This incident has acquired the status of a defining moment in Louis's reign. Aged only twenty-two, he adopted a rigorous routine of work in fulfilment of his pledge to govern as well as reign. He presided over government councils, discussed matters of state with individual ministers, read endless reports and became probably the best-informed monarch in Europe, unsurpassed in his knowledge of government and administration. He is often dubbed an 'absolute monarch'. In so far as the epithet is justified, it owes much to his unremitting hard work. His decision to govern personally was not as radical as sometimes has been claimed. It is true that his father and grandfather employed principal ministers and that Louis did so until 1661, but this was in response to circumstances, not a matter of principle. Mazarin himself had urged the young Louis eventually to govern personally. Mazarin sensed that France was coming to the end of a century of endemic socio-political upheaval. The collapse of the Frondes and approaching end of the war against Spain created a context in which the kingdom was receptive to social healing. The time was right, judged Mazarin, for the king to govern personally. Herein lay the real significance of 1661. It was not that Louis XIV set out to create a new pattern of government; on the contrary, he believed that he was now in a position to restore a form of monarchic rule which had been rendered impossible by the crises of the past hundred years. Louis was a social and political conservative. His strategy was to recover an idealized past in which the king governed obedient subjects, the Catholic church commanded universal allegiance, and social hierarchies were respected. It was also a France in which the king's subjects enjoyed rights and privileges which Louis, in his coronation oath, had vowed to safeguard. Whatever happened in practice, Louis was conservative in intent.

To assist him in the formulation of policy, Louis XIV was advised by the *Conseil d'en Haut*. This was the only body in which policy was discussed; decisions rested exclusively with Louis. Its members in 1661 were all protégés of Mazarin: Jean-Baptiste Colbert who specialized in financial and economic affairs, Hugues de Lionne who was made secretary of state for foreign affairs in 1663, and Michel le Tellier, secretary of state for war.[1] The *Conseil d'en Haut* was the king's personal council. He kept it small – it rarely had more than four members – and drew its members from three main families: those of Colbert, Le Tellier and, in due course, Phélypeaux. Louis rewarded them with land and titles, and they formed marriage alliances between each other and with the aristocracy. Service to the king conferred prestige and wealth as well as political influence. Other councils existed, but they were executive in their functions, carrying out but never discussing the king's policies. Louis presided over two: the *Conseil des Finances*, which supervised revenue and expenditure, and the *Conseil des Dépêches*, which administered domestic policy. Others, which he did not attend, included the *Conseil des Parties*, whose functions were mainly legal, and the *Conseil de Commerce*, which Colbert revived in 1664. These councils had small staffs. Central government bore little resemblance to that of a modern state, and was not overloaded with a teeming bureaucracy; if anything, there were too few administrators for the enormous tasks in hand.

### Parisian and Provincial Institutions

By contrast, many Parisian and provincial institutions, such as municipal councils, law courts, tax offices and provincial estates, were staffed by a host of *officiers*. Chapter 4 has indicated how the fiscal needs of government forced the crown to multiply and sell offices. In 1664 Colbert calculated that there were about 46,250 *officiers* in France, far too many to be justified by the tasks they performed. Colbert persuaded Louis to begin reducing their numbers by buying back offices, and between 1665 and 1669 several edicts to that effect were issued. However, when the king's wars placed new demands on revenue, the crown reverted to the sale of offices. The continuing proliferation of *officiers* had social implications. One of the commonest complaints of the old nobility was that prosperous commoners invested in offices which carried titles (some offices in the *parlements* or great city institutions of France conferred nobility), or used the wealth acquired through offices to secure marriages with impecunious noble families. *Officiers*, in other words, were responsible for blurring the social distinctions between noble and commoner which Louis sought to clarify. His inability to reduce the number of *officiers* undermined his efforts to restore a clearly defined social hierarchy.

Another sensitive issue was that of the *parlements*, the most important of which was in Paris.[2] The *parlement* of Paris had been in the forefront of the Frondes, and the Chambre St Louis, comprising representatives of the *parlement* and other sovereign courts, had produced a programme of reform. Without saying so explicitly, Louis XIV in the 1660s adopted those demands of the Chambre which coincided with his own plans, especially in the realms of justice and taxation (although not with regard to the abolition of the *intendants*). One question that remained contentious was the role of the *parlements* in legislation. The king created law, but it only came into force when edicts or ordinances were registered by the *parlements*. If a *parlement* considered an edict or ordinance to be of questionable legality, it was empowered to 'remonstrate': that is, withhold registration and ask the crown to reconsider. By manipulating this right of remonstrance, *parlements* could frustrate the designs of the crown for many years. As a traditionalist, Louis never questioned the principle of remonstrance, but did resolve to impose his own interpretation of how it should work in practice. Already in 1655, at Mazarin's behest, he had forbidden the *parlement* of Paris to discuss the policy which lay behind a particular law; the *parlement* must limit itself to the law's content. Louis returned to the question in 1667. He informed the *parlement* of Paris (and the same applied to provincial *parlements*) that, if it wished to exercise its right of remonstrance over a particular piece of legislation, it must do so quickly and on one occasion only; if the king returned the law unmodified, it must be registered. Louis intervened again in 1673, when France was at war and the need for the rapid registration of fiscal legislation was imperative: he instructed the *parlement* of Paris to register laws first, and only then to remonstrate if necessary. This position held until the end of the reign, mainly because warfare continued almost unabated. Louis XIV acknowledged the *parlements* as integral to the process of legislation, but in his view they had accumulated excessive powers during the Wars of Religion and civil conflicts of the 1600s; it was necessary to restore a balance of which he approved. His successor, Louis XV, reverted to the position of 1667.

Some provinces, mainly on or near the frontiers, had their own assemblies or estates. In these *pays d'état* the crown transmitted its policies and laws through the estates. Richelieu had undermined these bodies by suspending them in several provinces, and Louis XIV likewise held others in abeyance. The estates of Normandy last met in 1655, Basse-Auvergne in 1672, Quercy and Rouergue in 1673, Alsace in 1683 and Franche Comté in 1704. On the other hand, the estates of Brittany, Burgundy, Provence and Languedoc continued to flourish, not least because these provinces were in militarily sensitive areas and Louis had no desire to provoke them unnecessarily. Although the provinces enjoyed a variety of fiscal privileges, the crown attempted to persuade the estates to contribute 'free gifts' (*dons gratuits*) to the national treasury. *Dons gratuits* amounted to taxation under another name, but were the subject of tough bargaining between the estates and royal commissioners. Louis conceded that it was not within his power simply to dictate to the estates how much they should contribute; he must, in effect, negotiate with them. Even when money was raised, Louis spent a sizeable proportion in the provinces themselves. Thus, in the 1660s and 1670s, about 60 per cent of the money raised by the estates of Languedoc, as 'free gifts' to the king, were spent within the province on public works such as a canal linking the Mediterranean and the Atlantic. Louis was anxious to avoid any suggestion that he simply milked the provinces of their finances; it was politically necessary that they derive visible benefits from royal fiscal policy.

Louis made increasing use of royal commissioners or *intendants* as his agents in the provinces. Richelieu had employed *intendants* spasmodically, but under Louis XIV they became permanent fixtures. By the 1670s, each *généralité* or *pays d'état* had an *intendant* in residence. The functions of the *intendants* revolved mostly around law, administration and taxation. Historians once depicted *intendants* as instruments of royal absolutism, enforcing the king's will against provincial resistance or procrastination, but scholars are now more disposed to understand them as intermediaries enabling collaboration between king and provinces. *Intendants* did impose the royal will by force if necessary, but surviving correspondence between them and their masters in Paris shows that the government was constantly urging them to avoid confrontation with town councils, trades guilds and other pressure groups. The crown preferred disputes to be resolved by negotiation. It is notable that the incidence of provincial rebellion in France declined after 1661. This was not entirely the work of the *intendants*, but there is no denying that they made a significant contribution by enabling grievances to be settled without resort to violence.

## The Royal Court

The key to Louis's strategy of creating social harmony in his kingdom lay in healing the breach between himself and the social elites, and to this end the royal court had a crucial role to play. The French court was already one of the most sumptuous in Europe; under Louis XIV it became the measure against which many others assessed themselves. The court traditionally moved between palaces which belonged to the crown – the Louvre, Fontainebleau, St Germain and others – but in 1682 Louis fixed his residence at Versailles. This relatively modest palace, built by his father as a base for hunting expeditions into the neighbouring forest, was expanded by Louis into the colossal structure which can be seen today.

To Versailles came the royal family, aristocrats, nobles, prelates, ministers of the crown, ambassadors and thousands of visitors. By the early 1680s, between 4,000 and 5,000 nobles attended the court, and if administrators, servants, gardeners and a host of others who found employment are added, then over 10,000 people were attached to the palace. Versailles was an open society. Then, as now, guided tours around the palace were available, and the gardens were open twenty-four hours a day. The king was at pains to be visible. During religious festivals, poor people came to receive alms from the king, and sufferers of scrofula presented themselves to receive the Royal Touch.[3] Louis made frequent appearances at military parades or religious processions. He often took his meals in public. In 1687, for example, an English visitor, Richard Ferrier, 'had the honour to see the king, Monsieur and the dauphiness at dinner with abundance of the nobility standing round the table',[4] and in 1698, the Danish physician Winslow and two German friends were admitted to the chapel of Versailles, where they observed the king at mass.

Versailles was more than a royal residence and seat of government. Among the hundreds of young people to be seen there were the page boys who served aristocrats and other notabilities. The pages received education at the charge of the king. Mathematicians, philosophers, masters of classical and modern languages, teachers of dancing and riding instructed them; and Madame de Maintenon, Louis XIV's second and morganatic wife, founded a school for the daughters of indigent nobles.

Plays and operas were presented at the palace. In 1664, there took place the Plaisirs de l'Ile Enchantée, an extravaganza of music, dance and theatre at which Molière and Lully presented *La Princesse d'Elide*, *Les Fâcheux* and *Le Mariage Forcé*; and in 1668, to celebrate the conquest of Flanders, a similar '*divertissement royal*' was held, with over 3,000 performers participating. There was a constant background of music at Versailles. In addition to choral music in the chapel, there were musical entertainments, and, when the king dined each evening, he was entertained by the '24 Violons du Roi'. During the day, violinists, singers and performers on wind instruments performed in the gardens and in the palace. By 1702, some three hundred musicians were employed at Versailles.

The life of the court was governed by rigid rules of etiquette whose purpose was to create a society serving as a model for the rest of the kingdom. The king was the focal point of court ritual;

everything revolved around the rhythm of his day, from the ceremony of his rising in the morning, to his attendance at mass, his work with councils of government and individual ministers, his lunch, his walking or hunting in the afternoon, the entertainments which he attended in the evening, his dinner, and the ceremony whereby he retired at night. The court nobility adjusted their daily routines to that of the king. They strove to be physically close to him and between themselves observed strict rules of precedence, a subject over which there were numerous disputes. The cost of residing at Versailles was considerable, for in addition to expenditure on food, servants, horses and carriages, courtiers had to provide themselves and their wives with new and expensive clothes, gowns and costumes for the balls and other court entertainments. Louis was well informed on the financial straits of his courtiers, and granted hundreds of pensions and gifts to help those who fell into debt. The court brought king and social elites together, and bound them in a relationship in which his mastery was proclaimed at every turn. At court, Louis was an absolute monarch *par excellence*; the entire ritual and life of Versailles proclaimed the submission of the nobility to the king.

Nevertheless, it would be a mistake to represent the court simply as a setting wherein Louis XIV subdued the nobility; it was also an instrument of collaboration between crown and nobility. Aristocrats were appointed by Louis as governors of the provinces, or ambassadors to foreign courts; others went to senior positions in the ecclesiastical hierarchy. By far the largest number joined the army and navy. The longer Louis's wars continued, the greater the demand for officers, almost all of whom were noblemen. By the 1690s, some 24,000 nobles were serving in the army and navy. Louis himself went on military campaigns, sometimes taking the court with him. This was not because he refused to forfeit his life of luxury (on other occasions, he left the court behind), but because he wished to affirm that in times of war, he, the court, the nobility and the army were bound together in a great enterprise. Aristocrats had châteaux and large estates; when they visited their provincial seats, they held courts in miniature, replicating the rituals of Versailles. Many had Parisian residences where they or their wives held salons wherein nobles, intellectuals, magistrates, clergy and other guests discussed subjects in literature, philosophy and the sciences. Courtiers did not regard Versailles as a gilded cage which reduced them to decorative ornaments; on the contrary, it was a setting wherein they shared the lustre which surrounded the king. Versailles became a model adapted, if not copied, by monarchs and grandees elsewhere in Europe. Thus, the approach to the palace along three broad avenues which converged on the château was followed at St Petersburg and Aranjuez, south of Madrid. The gardens at Versailles inspired those at Caserte near Naples and the Schönbrunn just outside Vienna. In England, Greenwich Hospital, Blenheim and Castle Howard revealed the influence of Versailles. Even the political enemies of Louis XIV had to concede that at Versailles he had created an environment perfectly suited to late seventeenth-century ideals of monarchy.

## Economic Reform

The need for economic and financial reform after the peace of 1659 was demonstrated by a crisis which hit northern France at the beginning of Louis's personal reign. In 1660 and 1661, harvests in Normandy, the Paris basin and the Loire valley were disastrous. Familiar consequences ensued: famine struck, food prices shot up (in 1661, the price of grain in Paris was 250 per cent higher than in 1655), widespread rioting occurred and people flocked into towns in search of sustenance. Louis responded by importing grain from the Baltic and forcing provinces with a sufficiency of grain to export it to areas of shortage. At his own cost, grain was distributed in Paris, Rouen, Tours and other towns. His response to rioters was harsh. The violence was especially fierce around Boulogne, to which Louis sent troops who crushed the rising amidst much bloodshed. Executions followed and over four hundred rioters were sent to the galleys. From 1663 the harvests steadily improved and northern France recovered, but the episode demonstrated how slender was the margin between sufficiency and insufficiency, social stability and instability.

The minister responsible for overseeing economic recovery was Colbert. The king afforded him a few years of peace in the 1660s, but when war resumed, Colbert was faced with fiscal and economic problems of daunting complexity. He shared the opinion of contemporaries, like Johann Becher in Austria, that government should stimulate economic activities which directly enhanced the wealth of the state. The word wealth, however, meant bullion; the more bullion in the country, the greater the power of the state. Economic policy must concentrate on sectors which attracted bullion and prevented it leaving. These mercantilist principles also included the premise that the volume of economic activity in Europe was limited; if one state increased its wealth through economic growth, it must be at the expense of rivals. Such principles had a certain grounding in theory (developed by writers such as Barthélemy de Laffemas in *Les trésors et richesses de la France* [1597] and Antoine de Montchrestien in his *Traité de l'economie politique* [1615]), but found practical justification in the example of the Dutch Republic. Here was a small country which, through mercantilist policies, had become the wealthiest in Europe in relative terms.

The instrument through which Colbert executed policy was the *Conseil de Commerce* (1664). In the 1660s and 1670s it issued some two hundred laws on commerce and industry, such as that of 1669 which imposed uniform measurements and standards of quality upon the cloth industry. Certain industries, classed as *manufactures royales*, received government subsidies. They usually produced luxury goods which could be sold abroad at high prices and attract bullion into France. The first was the Gobelins on the outskirts of Paris, founded in 1662; it produced tapestries, furniture, paintings, statues and other ornamental works. In 1663, the Savonnerie, also near Paris, was reorganized. Founded in 1626, it manufactured carpets of the highest quality. The *Conseil de Commerce* granted monopolies to selected companies in the cloth manufacturing towns of northern France, the metallurgical industry in Champagne and Burgundy, and the silk industry at Lyon. To assist him in enforcing regulations, Colbert made use of *intendants* but also appointed general, regional and local inspectors. Like the *intendants*, they were not simply enforcers; they cooperated with local industrial and commercial interests, and transmitted to Paris information and advice. Of course, governments elsewhere were attempting to attract bullion into their own countries. Colbert thus resorted to import duties to discourage the movement of goods into France. In 1664, he reorganized tariffs on imported goods, concentrating on any which rivalled those made in France. Cloth was his principal target. He set duties on Dutch, English and Spanish cloth, and in 1667 raised the rates even higher. Tariffs had to be handled judiciously, for other states responded in like manner, and tariff wars hurt everybody.

On the commercial front, Colbert followed current practice by creating trading companies, the most important being the West Indies Company (1664), the East Indies Company (1664), the

Northern Company (1669) and Levant Company (1670). None performed as well as Colbert hoped, partly because of a lack of capital, but also because they alienated vested interests. Although the crown put money into them, the companies found it difficult to raise sufficient funds from private investors. Thus, it was calculated that the East Indies Company would need about 15 million livres, but by 1668 it had raised only 5 million. Although it established bases in India, it struggled for several decades and it was only in the eighteenth century that it prospered. The Northern Company, intended by Colbert to compete with the Dutch in the Baltic, foundered under the pressure of war and disbanded in 1684. The West Indies Company at first attracted investment, but the supply dried up as the company encountered hostility from French settlers in the Americas, who resented the government's attempts to limit their trade to the new company. French merchants who formerly traded independently with the colonies also tried to circumvent its monopoly. Illegal commerce continued on such a scale that Colbert had to lift the company's monopoly with Canada in 1669 and the West Indies in 1674. The Levant Company too proved a disappointment, not least because it imported luxury silks and cloth which were paid for in cash; this ran contrary to Colbert's economic principles. The company was disliked by Marseille merchants whom its monopoly excluded from the Levant. Although the monopoly was renewed in 1678, the company had almost ceased trading by the mid-1680s.

Although his achievements were mixed, Colbert, when he died in 1683, left France economically stronger than he found it. Even so, most economic activity remained local, and it is only in a limited sense that one can speak of a 'French economy' at this time. Colbert did contribute to the longer-term emergence of a national economy through the improvements he made to internal communications. In 1669 he created a commission to oversee improvements to the main highways and river systems. Stretches of the principal rivers – the Seine, Loire, Garonne and Rhône – were improved to allow easier passage for boats. The Montargis canal was built, linking the Seine and Loire, and the canal joining the Mediterranean to the Atlantic was completed in 1681. Even so, a national economy did not yet exist, and most activity continued in traditional ways. Colbert was not a *dirigiste* in a modern sense; he was selective in his economic intervention, his principal motivation being to enhance the wealth, and hence the power, of the state.

## Fiscal Reform

This does not mean that the improvement of the socio-economic lot of the king's subjects counted for little. The means whereby Louis XIV and Colbert sought to *soulager le peuple*, as Louis referred to it, was by fiscal reform. Peasants were encumbered by numerous fiscal demands. They owed dues to their land-owners which could consume up to 10 per cent of peasant income. To the church they paid the tithe or *dîme*; this was paid in kind, and was usually about 7 per cent of the harvest. Tenant farmers paid cash rents, and many peasants had individual debts to pay. Then there were the fiscal demands of the state. The direct tax which rural and urban masses paid was the *taille*. Colbert was extremely conscious that large numbers of wealthy people were immune from this tax (notably, but not only, the nobility and clergy), and that it fell predominantly on the poorer sections of society. He knew too that there was much corruption in its assessment and collection. Colbert sent a stream of letters to *intendants*, urging them to keep a vigilant eye open for abuses. His main strategy was to reduce the amount of *taille* which people had to pay by controlling government expenditure and shifting the tax burden from direct to indirect taxes. For a time he succeeded. In 1661 the government raised 42 million livres through the *taille*, but by 1665 reduced the sum to 34 million. However, in 1667 Louis XIV went to war and, apart from a few years between 1668 and 1672, was at war almost incessantly until 1713. War drove up expenditure. From 77 million livres in 1670 it rose to 96 million in 1680 and 198 million in 1685; it dropped to 182 million by 1700, but during the War of the Spanish Succession went as high as 264 million in 1711.[5]

As expenditure rose, so did the *taille*, and with it social distress. Fiscal grievances led to riots, although on a much-reduced scale by comparison with the 1630s and 1640s. The troubles around Boulogne in the early 1660s have already been noted. In 1675 the so-called '*révolte du papier-timbré*' (the paper stamp rebellion) occurred in Brittany. The immediate trigger was the imposition by the government of a stamp duty on legal contracts and on the sale of tobacco and pewter, but other local grievances were involved: rumours that the province's exemption from *gabelle* was to be ended, peasant resistance to seigniorial obligations, and disputes between the estates of Brittany and the crown. The revolt began in Rennes in April 1675 and lasted about six months. It fell to the governor, the duc de Chaulnes, to suppress it by armed force. This was not the last of the popular movements, for another occurred around Quercy in 1707; these and other insurrections testified that it was extremely difficult to attain social harmony in times of protracted warfare.

From 1690 to 1692, France experienced probably the worst natural disaster of the century: across the whole country harvests failed, the weather was extraordinarily inclement, and a national famine occurred. Roughly 10 per cent of the population died between 1690 and 1692. This catastrophe was one of the factors which forced the government to attempt radical fiscal changes aimed at tapping the resources of the wealthier sections of society. The first was the introduction in 1695 of a new tax, the *capitation*. This was assessed on social status and income; everybody apart from the clergy would pay, and even the clergy paid the equivalent in special *dons gratuits*. A commission divided the population into twenty-two classes, which paid the tax on a sliding scale. Even members of the royal family were included. In its first three years, the *capitation* raised 93 million livres; this compared with about 63 million in *taille* in the same period. The tax was suspended after the Peace of Ryswick (1697), but was reintroduced during the War of the Spanish Succession. The second new tax was also a wartime measure: the *dixième*. Introduced in 1710, it lasted until 1717. It was a straightforward annual levy of 10 per cent on wealth and income. Once again, everybody had to pay. The tax raised between 22 and 28 million livres a year.

It cannot be said that the standard of living of the majority of Louis's subjects underwent any marked improvement during his personal reign. At times of natural disaster, the state could do little other than stave off the worst of the consequences. The wars in which Louis engaged prevented him from easing the financial burdens borne by his subjects. His personal reign never reconciled the paradox that the king, whose political philosophy emphasized the paternal element in monarchy, imposed heavy and relentless sacrifices on his hard-pressed people.

## Catholic Church and State

One aspect of life in which Louis took a personal interest was that of religion. Well over 90 per cent of his subjects were Catholic, the ideology of French monarchy incorporated religious categories of thought, and Louis was punctilious in his religious devotions. He regarded the Catholic church as an ally in controlling the country. In their Easter messages, bishops reminded people of the duty of obedience to the king, and priests frequently preached sermons on the subject. In return, the General Assembly of the Clergy, meeting usually every four years, called on Louis to wipe the stain of heresy from France by revoking the Edict of Nantes.

It is difficult to generalize about the spiritual condition of the Catholic church in France. The Catholic reform movement attained its greatest influence in France in the early seventeenth century, producing outstanding individuals such as St François de Sales, St Vincent de Paul and Ste Jeanne de Chantal, but also exerting on the laity an influence which manifested itself through heightened spirituality and social action. As an institution, the church was wealthy, but bore heavy social responsibilities: many of the schools and hospitals of France were run by religious orders, and the church was the largest source of charitable work. The king drew on its financial resources, even though it was immune from direct taxation. When the General Assembly of the Clergy met, it was faced by requests from the crown for a *don gratuit*; the clergy would negotiate with royal commissioners, but almost invariably paid. Senior prelates had the right of attendance at provincial estates and the Estates General (although after 1614 this body did not meet until 1789), and thereby influenced public affairs. Most archbishops, bishops and heads of prominent monasteries and convents were noblemen, although commoners did rise in the hierarchy.

One subject on which the Catholic church in France was sensitive was that of Gallican rights. Since the fifteenth century, the French church had maintained that it possessed certain rights for which it was not beholden to the pope. Some were confirmed by the Concordat of Bologna (1516), wherein the pope agreed that the king of France, not the pope, would nominate incumbents to the prelacy, the pope then formally appointing them; the pope also recognized the *droit de régale* whereby, if a benefice was vacant, the king, not the pope, received its revenue. The church in France considered that Gallican rights also included the principle that the temporal power of the king was not subject to any spiritual authority, and that the pope exercised spiritual, not temporal, authority over the French clergy. The question of Gallican rights was raised during Louis XIV's war against the Dutch Republic. In 1673, when he needed revenue to fight the war, Louis XIV extended the *droit de régale* to provinces which France had acquired since 1516. Two bishops challenged the legality of the move, and when Innocent XI was elected pope in 1676, he supported their stance. Innocent insisted that the *droit* applied only to territory ruled by the king of France in 1516. Louis sought the help of the French bishops who, in an assembly in 1682, proclaimed that the *droit de régale* was a temporal, not spiritual, issue and therefore not subject to papal authority. The assembly also adopted four Gallican articles: the king was supreme in temporal affairs, the spiritual authority of the pope was subject to a general council of the entire Catholic church, Gallican rights were valid, and in matters of faith the pope was not infallible but required the consent of the church. Innocent rejected the articles and refused to ratify the appointment of bishops who subscribed to them. This created a conflict of authority between the French crown and the pope. By 1688, thirty-five bishoprics in France were vacant as neither side would yield. In January 1688, Innocent secretly informed Louis XIV that he was excommunicated. Innocent died in 1689 without the deadlock being broken; it lasted through the pontificate of Alexander VIII (1689–91) into that of Innocent XII. It was he who reached a *rapprochement* with Louis XIV in 1693. The French bishops would withdraw the Gallican articles, and the pope recognized the *droit de régale* throughout France.

One of the most controversial movements within the wider Catholic church was Jansenism. Inspired by Cornelius Jansen, bishop of Ypres, whose theological treatise, *Augustinus* (1640), espoused a doctrine of predestination similar to that of John Calvin, the movement found much support in the Spanish Netherlands and France. His theology was critical of the Jesuits who, in his eyes, deprived Christianity of much of its spiritual and moral essence by accommodating it to contemporary social values. The socio-political thought of Jansenism denied that political institutions were reflections of the divine order; rather were they imperfect instruments created by fallible human beings to manage public affairs; as such, they could not command unquestioning obedience. Although the *Augustinus* was condemned by Pope Urban VIII in 1642, Jansenism found converts among the social and intellectual elites of France. Many nobles and magistrates became Jansenists, and among the intelligentsia who converted were Blaise Pascal, whose *Lettres provinciales* (1656–7) brilliantly explained Jansenist thought, and Jean Racine, several of whose plays dealt with themes arising from the doctrine of predestination. Several leading Frondeurs such as Cardinal de Retz and the duc de

Luynes were Jansenists, and it was this, as well as its doctrinal hetero-doxy, which turned Louis XIV against it. He never lost his conviction that Jansenism fostered political resistance and questioned the ideo-logical foundations of his regime.

The institutional centre of French Jansenism was the Cistercian convent of Port Royal. Originally located near Versailles, it moved to Paris in 1625. In 1633, Jean Duvergier de Hauranne, the abbé de Saint Cyran, a friend and disciple of Jansen, became spiritual director of Port Royal. Under his influence the convent embraced Jansenism. It founded schools in Paris through which it disseminated Jansenist influences. The abbess, Mère Angélique Arnauld, belonged to a leading family of the *noblesse de robe*;[6] other members of her family became Jansenists, including her brother Antoine, whose *De la fré-quente communion* (1643) became one of the great texts of Jansen-ism. In 1648, as the Fronde was beginning, Mère Angélique took some of the nuns back to the site near Versailles, where the revived convent – known as Port Royal des Champs to distinguish it from Port Royal in Paris – became another focal point of Jansenism.

In 1651 a papal commission reported that Jansen's *Augustinus* contained five heretical propositions, and Innocent X issued a bull to that effect. Jansenists countered by claiming that, although the prop-ositions listed by the commission were heretical, they were not in the *Augustinus*; the commission had misrepresented Jansen. In 1661, the General Assembly of the Clergy in France sought to bring Jansenists back into the orthodox fold by adopting a formulary to which all priests and members of religious orders must subscribe. It included an oath of obedience to the pope, and agreement that the five heret-ical propositions were in the *Augustinus* and must be condemned. Most priests conformed, but Jansenists were divided. Some con-sented to the formulary, but the nuns at Port Royal and a handful of bishops refused. In 1668 a 'peace of the church' was reached in France: the wording of the formulary was modified to enable most of the remaining Jansenists to subscribe. Port Royal held out.

In 1679, the archbishop of Paris, frustrated by Port Royal's resist-ance, barred the convent from recruiting any more novices. In effect, this condemned it to closure. Several leading Jansenists were driven into exile. Among those who left was the priest Pasquier Quesnel, who went to the Spanish Netherlands. Quesnel sought to demon-strate the compatibility of Jansenism with orthodox Catholic doc-trine by publishing in 1692 a new edition of his *Réflexions morales*. He was encouraged when the *Réflexions* won the praise of no less a figure than the new archbishop of Paris, Louis-Antoine de Noailles. However, Noailles was involved in disputes with the Jesuits, and his support for Quesnel implicated Jansenism in his anti-Jesuit stance. In 1703 Quesnel was arrested in the Spanish Netherlands – now allied to France in the War of the Spanish Succession – and his correspondence was handed over to the French government. To a state obsessed by conspiracies, the letters provided evidence that Jansenism remained strong in France, and that Jansenists remained a danger to the unity of state and church. In 1705, Louis XIV persuaded Clement XI to publish the bull *Vineam domini*, which reaffirmed that Catholics must subscribe to the formulary of 1661; in 1708, also in response to a request from Louis XIV, the pope condemned Quesnel's *Réflexions morales*. In 1709, Louis had the nuns of Port Royal des Champs dispersed among other religious houses and the convent destroyed.

So far, there was a certain, if perverse, logic to Louis's actions. However, he increasingly allowed personal feelings to overrule calculation, and pursued the Jansenists to the point where he alienated even orthodox Catholics who had earlier sympathized with him. Encouraged by his Jesuit confessor and by Madame de Maintenon, Louis sought from the pope yet another condemnation of Jansenism. Clement XI complied in 1713 by issuing the bull *Unigenitus dei filius*, which condemned as heretical 101 Jansenist propositions in Quesnel's *Réflexions morales*. The bull split the Catholic church in France. Louis called a meeting of bishops to receive it, but Noailles refused to publicize the bull in the archdiocese of Paris. He was supported by the Sorbonne and the *parlement* of Paris, who interpreted *Unigenitus* as a contravention of Gallican rights. They saw the question of Jansenism as one of church discipline – and therefore a matter for the crown alone – and not of spiritual authority; the *parlement* even called for a general council of the church to discuss Jansenism and other matters of faith. Under royal pressure, the *parlement* and Sorbonne eventually withdrew their objections to *Unigenitus*, but they resumed their criticism after Louis's death in 1715.

Louis's policies on religion undermined the social harmony which he was so anxious to restore, and forced him into contradictory positions. His defence of Gallican rights brought him into conflict with Rome, but his attacks on Jansenism drove him into the arms of the pope to the extent that the Sorbonne and *parlement* of Paris objected. His inability to come to terms with Jansenism was especially portentous, for the movement continued into the eighteenth century and is seen by some scholars as one of those subterranean forces which steadily undermined the ideological foundations of the Bourbon regime, and thereby contributed to the crisis of 1789. Even setting aside such longer-term speculations, Louis's handling of both Gallicanism and Jansenism showed an ineptitude rarely matched in other spheres of government. It was as if Louis, in spite of his protestations to the contrary, was incapable of subjecting his policies towards the Catholic church to political criteria. A similar judgement may be made about that other great branch of his religious policy, his treatment of the Huguenots.

### The Huguenots and the Revocation of the Edict of Nantes

Politically, the Huguenots presented no danger, yet they too faced mounting pressure from Louis XIV, culminating in the Revocation of the Edict of Nantes. Their 'offence' was ideological: they were an embarrassment to the majesty of a crown which had failed to keep France wholly Catholic. It must be stressed that the anti-Huguenot measures which Louis adopted were popular among his Catholic subjects; indeed, in many respects his policy was a response to calls to eliminate Protestantism. As was noted earlier, the General Assembly of the Clergy regularly called on Louis to eliminate heresy, and provincial estates frequently issued similar demands. As early as 1661, Louis appointed commissioners to investigate alleged abuses of the Edict of Nantes by Huguenots. The commissioners closed about half of the Huguenot churches in Languedoc, and large numbers of Protestant schools throughout France.

Over the next twenty-five years, Louis constructed a body of anti-Huguenot legislation based on three strategies. One was to weaken the religious foundations of Protestantism. Churches were closed (there were about 800 in 1660, but only about 240 by the early 1680s), the national Huguenot synod was banned (it last met in 1659), and from 1669 provincial synods were debarred from communicating with each other. In 1676 the government created a 'treasury of conversion', which granted payments and tax concessions to Huguenots who became Catholics. A second strategy was to undermine Huguenot family life. Intermarriage with Catholics was forbidden if an objection came from the Catholic side, and children born of mixed marriages had to be raised as Catholics. From 1681, Huguenot children could convert at the age of seven, whereupon they would be taken from their parents and placed in Catholic boarding schools. Huguenots on their death-beds were to be visited by magistrates, who could seek last-minute conversions. The third strategy was to exclude Huguenots from a wide range of careers, especially in the law and crafts. Huguenots were debarred from sitting on municipal councils in Montpellier and other towns, and from participating in the estates of Languedoc.

In 1681, anti-Huguenot policy acquired new features. Emigration by Huguenots had already begun, but Louis forbade them to leave the kingdom; they must remain and convert to Catholicism. This led to charges that Louis was a tyrant, for he contravened the custom followed by European governments since the Peace of Augsburg (1555) whereby subjects who in all conscience could not conform to the established church were allowed to emigrate; and, as other chapters in this book have shown, tens of thousands of Europeans did so. By preventing his subjects from leaving, Louis exposed himself to international criticism, especially from Protestant states. Pamphlets appeared, depicting Louis XIV as a latter-day pharaoh whose refusal to permit the People of God to leave would bring divine retribution. The other change in 1681 was the adoption by the government of violent methods to secure conversions. First in Poitou, then in Languedoc, Provence, Béarn and Dauphiné, the intendants billeted soldiers on Huguenot families. This practice, known as *dragonnades*, caused terror among Huguenots, for in addition to having to bear the cost of lodging and feeding soldiers, they were subjected to widespread atrocities in which the military authorities colluded. Only if Huguenots converted were they excused the *dragonnades*. By the end of 1682, the *intendant* in Poitou boasted that the *dragonnades* had led to 30,000 conversions in his area, and it is thought that by 1685, the billeting of soldiers led to almost 400,000 Huguenots becoming Catholic. Other Huguenots disobeyed the king and resorted to flight, even though capture carried heavy penalties. From the late 1670s to the late 1680s, about 200,000 escaped from France (about 27 per cent of the Huguenot population). Some 60,000 went to the Dutch Republic, 50,000 to Britain and Ireland, 30,000 to Germany (of which 20,000 went to Brandenburg), 22,000 to Switzerland and the remainder to other parts of Europe, the Americas and southern Africa.

On 15 October 1685, Louis XIV issued the Edict of Fontainebleau which proclaimed that, since the Huguenots had been reduced to a remnant, the Edict of Nantes served no further purpose and was

revoked. Anti-Huguenot legislation remained in force and Huguenots continued to leave France. There also developed a movement of
resistance in the mountainous areas of Languedoc, where pastors and
people continued to meet in secret for worship. Pursued by the authorities, they turned to armed rebellion in 1702. This 'revolt of the
Camisards' was concentrated in the Cévennes mountains. It lasted
until a truce was signed with the government in 1704; even so, some
Camisards continued a sporadic guerrilla warfare down to 1713.
Louis was proud of the revocation. A few pockets of Huguenot resistance apart, he had restored to France the religious position of
the early 1500s. Yet in so far as he hoped that the revocation would
take the shine off Leopold I's triumph over the Turks, he was dis-
appointed. Huguenot refugees disseminated horrific tales of persecution, and the governments of Protestant states criticized his
heavy-handed policies. Even the pope deplored the violence with
which Louis treated his Huguenot subjects, fearing that few of their
so-called conversions were likely to be genuine. When Louis lay on
his death-bed, he expressed regrets over his excessive love of warfare,
but no contrition for his persecution of the Huguenots. It was not
an episode for which he felt it necessary to apologize.

## State and Culture

By the 1660s it was axiomatic that one mark of modern kingship was
its patronage of scholarship and the arts. That Louis XIV should have
been a lavish patron therefore is unexceptional. What is notable is the
extent to which that patronage was channelled through state academies founded for the purpose. His guide in this respect was Colbert
who, as *surintendant des bâtiments,* acted as an unofficial minister for
culture. Colbert's experience of service under Mazarin convinced
him of the political importance of patronage; he therefore took
advice from several quarters as to the most effective means of pursuing a cultural policy. For guidance on the visual arts he looked to
Charles Lebrun, director of the Gobelins and one of France's leading
painters; with respect to literature, philosophy and the sciences, Colbert's chief mentor was Jean Chapelain, a member of the *Académie
Française.* In 1663, Colbert announced that the government had
created a fund from which selected scholars, both at home and
abroad, would receive gifts and pensions; in return they were
expected to laud the glories of the king of France. He also

**Figure 6**  Louis XIV at Maastricht, by Pierre Mignard, *c.* 1670

contemplated the formation of a General Academy which would incorporate scholars from many disciplines. Had it been realized, the
scheme would have furnished France with the largest learned academy in Europe, but Colbert encountered opposition from bodies
such as the University of Paris, the *Académie Française*, the royal
botanical gardens and other institutions which felt themselves
threatened by such a foundation. He abandoned the idea of a General Academy, and instead created individual academies.

The first was the *Académie des Inscriptions* (1663), a small group
of four members who designed the medals issued to commemorate
notable events in the reign of Louis XIV, and recommended the

Latin inscriptions to be inscribed on public buildings. Also in 1663 the *Académie Royale de Peinture et de Sculpture*, which had been founded in 1648, was reformed. Lebrun was made director, and under his leadership painting was rooted in classical theory. Students had to study mathematics, optics and geometry, and become familiar with themes in classical mythology. Painting in the academy empha-sized design over colour, and appealed to the intellect rather than the emotions. To enhance French students' encounter with classical art, a French academy was opened in Rome in 1666, where selected artists, architects and sculptors were sent to study. In 1671 the *Aca-démie d'Architecture* was founded under François Blondel. He too emphasized the classical, but also encouraged his students to under-stand baroque buildings. He sought to develop a distinctively French architectural style in which grandeur and austerity prevailed over the decorative and the dramatic. Such features characterized the great public buildings erected in Paris after 1661: they included the eastern colonnade of the Louvre, the Observatory, the Invalides and the Porte Saint Denis, all of which are still to be seen.

Colbert recognized that changes in the sciences were such that the state ought to take a direct interest in their further development. Scientific societies already existed in Italy, and in 1662 the Royal Society in London received its charter. Since at least the 1640s, groups of natural philosophers had been meeting in Paris to discuss scientific subjects; some of the better known included the circles around Louis Habert de Montmort and Pierre Michon, the Abbé Bourdelot. The Dutch scientist Christiaan Huygens, who visited Paris in the 1650s and 1660s, attended these meetings, and became well known in French scientific circles. In the early 1660s, scientists met Colbert, arguing that a state-sponsored scientific society would advance the sciences even further, but would also serve the utilitarian needs of France and contribute to the glory of the king. Colbert was persuaded, and in 1666 announced the names of twenty-one scien-tists who would constitute the Academy of Sciences.[7] Huygens was a member, and other notable names included Roberval the mathemat-ician and Auzout the astronomer. The academy was provided with a laboratory in the royal library, but Colbert also paid for a large obser-vatory just south of Paris. Designed by Claude Perrault, a member of the academy, it was completed by 1672. The academy engaged in collaborative research programmes whose results the government published at its own expense. They included the *Mémoires pour servir à l'histoire naturelle des animaux* (1671) and the *Mémoires pour servir à l'histoire des plantes* (1676). Colbert regarded the academy as a source of utilitarian advice. He consulted it on such matters as navigation (especially the search for a method of calculating longitude at sea), military and civil engineering, and the invention of agricultural and industrial machines. The academy undertook the preparation of a new atlas of France, free of the errors which distorted existing maps. It was completed and presented to Louis XIV in 1684. The Academy of Sciences remained a relatively small body of between twenty and thirty members until 1699, when it was reformed. Its size was increased to seventy, its financial organization was regularized, and for the first time it was granted statutes spelling out its structure and functions. The revitalized academy entered upon a period of remarkable scientific activity which made it, in the opinion of many, the foremost scientific society in Europe.

Voltaire, writing in the eighteenth century, referred to 'the Age of Louis XIV' as if the study of this king could encapsulate the essence of the history of the period. Modern historians might be reluctant to make such a confident claim, but nevertheless concede that the long-term history of France was profoundly affected by his reign. Certainly, Louis himself went to great lengths to ensure that he would command a towering position in the historical memory, and he was not fanciful in agreeing that, in the paintings and sculptures which adorned Versailles, he should be represented as a latter-day Roman emperor or reincarnation of Alexander the Great. To modern eyes, it was the scale on which he operated, rather than the principles by which he did so, that look exceptional. His 'absolutism' relied more on impressive demonstrations of monarchic glory combined with an astute willingness to compromise with powerful provincial bodies, than on putative 'modern' techniques of bureaucratic, centralized government. His greatest asset was the immensity of the human and financial resources on which he could draw, even if he did so with a marked lack of efficiency. The foregoing discussion of France under Louis XIV has concentrated on internal affairs, but his impact upon Europe was no less profound. This is a subject to be discussed in due course, but at the present juncture we may say that, internally, Louis's greatest achievements were to enhance the prestige of the crown, stabilize French society after the upheavals of earlier decades, lay the foundations of the economic prosperity of the eighteenth century, and oversee a remarkable efflorescence in French cultural activity. To this list, Louis himself doubtless would have added the Revocation of the Edict of Nantes and the persecution of Jansenism, although these are achievements which few modern commentators would admire.

## SPAIN, 1660–1720

### Socio-economic Developments

General accounts of the social and economic history of Spain usually peter out in the middle of the seventeenth century, the assumption being that decline – as exhibited by depopulation, government bankruptcy, the collapse of trade between Spain and the Americas, and the fiscal deprivation suffered by the government – was so deep-rooted that nothing more need be said. This now looks a greatly simplified interpretation, and while it would be unjustified to go to the other extreme and argue that economic life in Spain experienced widespread recovery in the later seventeenth century, there is evidence that revival of a modest order was achieved during the reign of Charles II. Although reliable figures are impossible to establish, there seems to have been a steady rise in the population after 1660, albeit with regional variations and temporary interruptions, as when plague struck in the ten years between the mid-1670s and mid-1680s.

On the economic front, the creation in 1679 of the Committee of Trade signalled a serious attempt to introduce modern economic techniques. The committee was founded by the *valido* Don Juan of Austria, and was the Spanish equivalent of the French *Conseil de Commerce* or the Austrian *Kommerzkollegium*. Like the French and Austrian bodies, its remit extended to industry as well as commerce. When founded in 1679, it was composed of four ministers from the councils of Castile, War, Finance and the Indies. It was suspended in 1680 because of chaos created by a devaluation of the currency, but was revived in 1682 with additional members coming from Madrid and Aragon. Regional committees of trade were established in Granada (1683), Seville (1687), Barcelona and Valencia (both 1692). The committee pursued measures similar to those of its counterparts in France and Austria. It issued grants and monopolies to selected industries (usually in the silk or woollen trades), and attracted foreign entrepreneurs and workers by tax concessions and other financial allurements. English, French and Flemish artisans moved to Spain, Flemish wool manufacturers set up in Valencia in the mid-1680s, and a Flemish-owned paper mill opened in Segovia in 1686. Given the number and enormity of Spain's economic problems, the Committee of Trade could not expect to transform the country into a model of prosperity and initiative, but its work did lay the foundations of the country's recovery in the eighteenth century.

Positive remarks may also be made about Spain's trade with its colonies in the Americas. Once again, the traditional view was that this commerce had all but collapsed by the 1660s, and that very little bullion thereafter crossed the Atlantic. Recent scholarship suggests that, if anything, Atlantic commerce improved from the 1660s onwards, but that it was carried in ships from countries other than Spain. The government attempted to stimulate Atlantic commerce by ending the privilege of Seville as the only port into which ships from the Americas might bring their cargoes. Merchants were demanding the right to sail into Cádiz, which was more accessible than Seville, and the government made the concession in 1680. Cádiz steadily overtook Seville as the favourite port of entry for ships from the Americas, and in 1717 the government transferred the House of Trade, which oversaw Spanish Atlantic commerce, from Seville to Cádiz. The amount of bullion leaving the Americas rose from the late 1660s. Before that, the maximum quantity entering Spain had been attained in the five years from 1591 to 1595, when gold and silver worth about 35 million pesos was imported. By 1631–5 the amount had dropped to about 17 million, and by 1656–60 to about 3.5 million. Most historians assumed that decline continued, but more recent figures indicate that the amount of bullion leaving Spanish America increased from the late 1660s, varying between 50 and 60 million pesos in any five-year period between 1660 and 1700; in the decade after 1700, the amount dropped to about 25 million pesos per quinquennium.[8] Most bullion was carried in foreign ships which, after arriving in Spain and discharging other commodities, carried the bullion elsewhere. The problem for Spain was not one of the supply of bullion, but of the domination of the carrying trade by vessels from other countries.

After the waves of unrest and rebellion towards the middle of the seventeenth century, Spain, in common with other parts of Europe, experienced relative social calm. Even so, outside the cities and towns, brigandage and violence were common and resentment at royal taxation and seigniorial exactions could easily turn into resistance. Towards the end of the century, two rebellions occurred on a grand scale. The first lasted from 1688 to 1689 and affected most of Catalonia. It resembled earlier insurrections in being provoked by a combination of food shortages, the billeting of soldiers and high taxes. In 1687 the harvests throughout Catalonia failed, crops having been consumed by swarms of locusts. Meanwhile, in anticipation of a possible new war against France, the government increased the number of troops in Catalonia and billeted them on the impoverished civilian population. In the autumn of 1687 clashes between soldiers and civilians occurred, but in the spring of 1688 the incidence of peasant resistance rose until it coalesced into a general movement which gained the sympathy of townspeople, priests, lawyers, tradesmen and artisans. In April a large peasant force converged on Barcelona to demand a reduction of taxes and of the billeting of troops. By the summer, most of Catalonia had passed under the control of the peasants. In autumn they returned home to collect the harvest, and since it proved much better than in 1687, social tensions temporarily eased. They rose again in 1689, for Spain went to war against France and the government imposed more taxes. On this occasion the peasants failed to retain the sympathy of other social groups. Now that the country was at war and an invasion of Catalonia by the French was possible, urban and rural elites were reluctant to expose themselves to charges of treason. The crown organized a counter-attack on the rebels, and in November 1689 arrested several leaders and dispersed their followers. By the end of the year the rebellion had collapsed. Not wanting to provoke further trouble, the crown issued a general pardon, excepting a handful of rebel leaders who fled to France.

The second rising, in Valencia in 1693, was different since it arose out of a sense of long-term social injustice rather than immediate material concerns. In Valencia, land-owners, including the church, imposed upon peasants exactions which could take up to a third of farm and crop produce. Many peasants were heavily in debt and had no prospect of paying off their landlords. In the 1670s and 1680s, lawyers, rather than peasants themselves, protested against such practices on the ground that they were unjust and possibly contravened royal authority. In 1693, lawyers, clergy and administrators from many towns in Valencia drew up a statement of grievances, and elected three representatives to put their case to the viceroy. When he turned them down, they appealed to the Council of Aragon in Madrid, but became bogged down in legal procedure. Frustrated at the lack of progress, villages and peasant communities in 1693 refused to pay their dues to landlords; rioting began and spread quickly. The viceroy responded with force, securing the main towns and engaging the rebels in battle on 15 July. The peasant army was overwhelmed, and by the end of the year the insurrection was over. Like that in Catalonia, the Valencian movement of 1693 remained localized and never looked like igniting a pan-Spanish rising.

## Spain to 1680

The beginning of the reign of Charles II in 1665 resembled that of Louis XIV in 1643: Charles was only four years old when his father, Philip IV, died, and his mother, Mariana, had to govern as regent, just as Louis's mother, Anne of Austria, had done in France. Mariana was assisted by the Committee of Government comprising five advisers. Anne of Austria had relied on the Italian-born but naturalized Cardinal Mazarin as chief minister; Mariana turned to her Austrian-born and naturalized Jesuit confessor, Johann Eberhard Nithard, who was made Grand Inquisitor, a post which allowed him to attend meetings of the Committee of Government. After his dismissal in 1669, she looked to a Spanish courtier, Fernando Valenzuela and his wife, for companionship and advice. However, whereas the young Louis XIV grew into a resolute, self-controlled adult capable of governing as well as ruling, Charles II remained a physical and mental weakling. When he reached his majority in 1675, the regency nominally ended; in reality, Charles remained dependent on his mother. We should not leap to the conclusion that the king's condition reduced Spain to political confusion. The royal councils in Madrid, and the network of local political and legal institutions throughout the composite kingdom, ensured that government and administration continued.

Two chief political problems arose from Charles II's numerous frailties. One was his inability to provide an heir. By the end of the century, the question of who would succeed him had become the most urgent political issue in western and central Europe, and was to trigger the War of the Spanish Succession in 1702. Secondly, aristocratic factions exploited the opportunity presented by the incapacity of the king to exert their political influence in Spain. The most powerful faction was that around Don Juan of Austria, the king's half-brother. Born in 1629, Don Juan was the son of Philip IV and one of his mistresses, an actress. Philip eventually recognized the son and made him a prince, but never legitimized him. There was therefore never any question that Don Juan might become king. He was everything that Charles II was not: he was physically strong, intelligent, and an experienced soldier who had fought in Flanders and Italy, and commanded the army fighting in Portugal. He was such a contrast with his younger half-brother that Mariana viewed him with anxiety and ensured that he was excluded from the Committee of Government. Don Juan deeply resented his mistreatment, as he saw it, and placed much of the blame on Nithard; indeed, in 1668, he was implicated in a plot to kill the Grand Inquisitor. In that year, Don Juan travelled in Aragon and Catalonia, raising support among the nobility and councils of major cities such as Barcelona, and denouncing the allegedly iniquitous influence of Nithard on the queen.

In January 1669, Don Juan left Barcelona with a small force and marched towards Madrid with the intention of forcing the dismissal of Nithard. There was consternation in the capital. Many nobles and soldiers deserted to Don Juan, and the possibility of civil war looked real. Mariana had no option but to yield to Don Juan's threat and dismiss Nithard, who was eventually sent to Rome as ambassador extraordinary. Meanwhile, the queen recalled regiments from Portugal and placed them around Madrid. Don Juan denied that he had any aspirations towards political power and, faced by the strong defences at Madrid, agreed to be appointed Vicar General of Aragon, where he remained until 1675. The crisis of 1669 resembled that in France some twenty years before: a regency in which an unpopular foreign-born adviser dominated the queen, military failure in Portugal and (as will be seen) in Flanders, an alienated nobility and provincial suspicion of Castile, combined to enable Don Juan to overthrow Nithard. However, Spain escaped its own version of the Frondes mainly because Madrid did not rise against the queen, and Don Juan allowed himself to be bought off with his post in Aragon; but the affair showed how vulnerable the regency was to aristocratic resistance.

With some variations, the events of 1669 were repeated seven years later. After the *de facto* exile of Nithard, the queen fell under the spell of Don Fernando Valenzuela and his wife. Valenzuela was a social adventurer who had found a place at court and married a lady-in-waiting of the queen; Mariana made him marquis of Villasierra in 1675, the year in which Charles II reached his majority. Because of the king's physical and mental condition, the Committee of Government remained in existence, but Charles attempted to release himself from his mother's influence by calling Don Juan of Austria to Madrid with the intention of making him first minister. Mariana intervened, and forced her son to drop his plan. Once again a political crisis was in the making, for Don Juan still commanded much support and sympathy among Spanish nobles, who regarded the rise of the up-start Valenzuela with distaste. The situation was temporarily relieved when two central councils, the Council of State and the Council of Castile, advised that both Valenzuela and Don Juan be removed from Madrid: the queen's favourite was sent to Granada and Don Juan retired towards Saragossa. However, in 1676 Mariana abolished the Committee of Government and recalled Valenzuela as principal min-ister. The court nobility was outraged at the further elevation of Valenzuela, and by the end of the year was issuing calls for his dis-missal and exile. In December 1676, Don Juan once again marched on Madrid. He was joined by supporters from many parts of Spain, and within the capital city itself the Council of Castile urged the king to dispense with Valenzuela. Royal resistance collapsed: in January 1677, Valenzuela was arrested and Don Juan appointed *valido*. As news spread throughout Spain, it was received with celebrations and rejoicing, for Don Juan was a national hero. The new *valido* removed his enemies from court: the queen was sent to Toledo, Valenzuela was deported to the Philippines, and others whom Don Juan did not trust were dismissed.

The prince served only two years as chief minister, for he died at the age of fifty in September 1679, but displayed administrative qual-ities which suggest that, had he lived longer, he might have become an outstanding statesman. He assumed his position at a time of diffi-cult socio-political circumstances. Spain was involved in a war against France again, and the Peace of Nijmegen (1678), which ended the war, was humiliating for Spain. In 1676, Spain was hit by an epi-demic of plague which, with a few periods of respite, lasted for about ten years and touched most parts of the country. In 1677 and 1678 there were general harvest failures which led to famine. One of Don Juan's first acts was to persuade the king that he must visit his various kingdoms. In 1677, the king accordingly made a formal visit to Aragon, and at Saragossa swore to respect and defend the rights of the kingdom. Don Juan had plans for further such journeys, but died before he could organize them. Another question affecting the king was that of his marriage. Charles II was now in his mid-teens, and it was necessary that he produce an heir. The Spanish Habsburgs nor-mally married Austrian Habsburg or French princes and princesses.

In 1677, Don Juan and the Council of State identified two candidates as suitable wives for Charles II: Maria Antonia, daughter of
Emperor Leopold I, and Marie Louise d'Orléans, daughter of the
duc d'Orléans. The choice fell on the latter, mainly because the
former was only eight years old in 1677, and it would be several
years before she could bear a child; Marie Louise, on the other hand,
was only a few months younger than Charles II. Louis XIV agreed to
the match, and the marriage took place in 1679.

Government finance faced Don Juan with a daunting situation.
Inflation was rampant, and for many years the Spanish government
had run up deficits, occasionally resorting to bankruptcy as a means
of staving off disaster: most recently Philip IV had declared bankruptcy in 1662, and Charles II did so again in 1666. The principal
sources of revenue available to the crown were the taxes paid by
Castile (the other kingdoms yielded negligible sums), money received
from the church, and the tax on bullion from America. Expenditure
permanently outstripped revenue, forcing the government to borrow
heavily. The chief explanation for the crown's financial difficulties was
its international military commitments: Spanish armies were based or
fought in the Netherlands, Italy, Germany and Portugal as well as
Spain itself; the fleets defended Spanish interests in the Atlantic,
Mediterranean and North Sea. Don Juan took steps to rectify the
financial situation. He ordered reports on the state of the economy
and the condition of the rural population (the former resulted in the
creation of the Committee of Trade), and concluded that the only
way to tackle the financial crisis in the short run was by a devaluation
of the currency; this undoubtedly would hit the value of private
fortunes and would provoke protests, but it would also reduce inflation and ease the government's debt. He made the necessary preparations, and in February 1680 a 75 per cent devaluation of currency
was imposed. As anticipated, it led to short-term confusion and social
protest. Financiers claimed that they faced ruin, merchants saw
profits decline, unemployment rose and there were demonstrations
in major towns. Within a few years, however, inflation had dropped
markedly, and internal markets adjusted to the new currency.

## Spain in Europe to the Peace of Ryswick, 1697

When Maria Teresa married Louis XIV she renounced her claim to
the throne of Spain, but a dispute arose when Louis refused to

acknowledge the validity of the renunciation until Philip IV paid his daughter's dowry. Philip refused to pay until Louis publicly accepted the renunciation. The birth of the future Charles II in 1661 rendered the question academic, but if he died, insisted Louis XIV, Maria Teresa should succeed as queen of Spain, with himself as her consort. Louis pressed a second claim which did not depend on Charles II's death. Maria Teresa was the daughter of Philip IV by his first marriage, and Charles II his son by the second. In the province of Brabant and elsewhere in Flanders, inheritance rights followed the Law of Devolution which stated that children of a first marriage had precedence over those of a second. When Philip IV died in 1665, Louis XIV proclaimed that the Law of Devolution applied to the whole of the Spanish Netherlands, which should pass immediately to his wife. The Spanish government spurned the claim. In 1667 Louis sent an army into the Spanish Netherlands to take what, in his view, legitimately belonged to Maria Teresa. In 1668 another French army occupied the Spanish territory of Franche Comté on France's eastern frontier.

The implications of Louis's actions were considerable. To Spain they threatened the loss of the Netherlands, but the Dutch Republic also viewed these developments with alarm: if the southern Netherlands fell to the French, this would create a dangerous new neighbour. Emperor Leopold I also reacted. His motives concerned less the Netherlands than the throne of Spain. The sickly Charles II of Spain was not expected to survive childhood. Leopold was resolved that Charles would be succeeded, not by Maria Teresa, but by her younger sister Margaret, who was Leopold's wife. Louis's invasion of the Netherlands showed that he was intent on the Spanish succession; if Leopold were to secure it for Margaret, it would have to be by war. However, Leopold faced challenges in eastern Europe and had no desire to fight France. He made secret approaches to Louis XIV with a bold proposal: rather than fight for the Spanish succession, should they not share it in a partition agreement? The French consented, and by the secret Treaty of Grémonville (1668) agreed that, if Charles II died childless, Maria Teresa would receive the Spanish Netherlands, Franche Comté, Navarre, Naples and Sicily, while Margaret would be queen of Spain and would retain other Spanish possessions in Europe and the Americas. Unaware of the treaty, the Dutch in 1668 persuaded the British and Swedish governments to form a Triple Alliance to mediate peace between France and Spain; if France failed to comply, they would join Spain in war against

Louis XIV. In February 1668, the Spanish conceded independence to Portugal, and withdrew their forces in preparation for the relief of the Netherlands. Safe in his knowledge of the partition treaty, Louis was conciliatory. He accepted the mediation of the Triple Alliance, and signed the Treaty of Aix-la-Chapelle with Spain later in 1668. Louis returned the Franche Comté and the Netherlands, apart from some frontier towns. Spain and its allies mistakenly supposed that their stance had cowed Louis XIV.

Within a few years, Spain was drawn into war against France once more. In 1672, for reasons to be discussed later, Louis XIV invaded the Dutch Republic. He anticipated a short, triumphant campaign, for his army greatly outnumbered that of his enemy. Yet he bungled what should have been an easy conquest. Instead of pushing on to Amsterdam, whose occupation would have forced the republic to surrender, Louis halted his advance expecting that he would simply dictate terms of surrender to the Dutch. They used the interval to open dikes near Amsterdam, flooding the countryside and securing the city against the French. Louis was in possession of most of the republic, yet was unable to force its government to surrender. A *coup* brought William III of Orange to power in the republic, and he set about mustering Dutch resistance and international help. In 1672–3, Leopold I, Charles II of Spain and several German princes formed an anti-French coalition – joined later by Denmark and Saxony – whose aim was to drive Louis out of the Dutch Republic. He did leave by the end of 1673, but now concentrated his attention on the Rhineland and the Spanish Netherlands. Most of his victories were at the expense of the Spanish. In 1674 he occupied Franche Comté again, and defeated a joint Spanish and Dutch force near Mons. In 1677, Cambrai, Valenciennes and Saint Omer fell to the French.

The war spread to the Mediterranean. In Sicily, rebellion against Charles II broke out in Messina in 1674, and the leaders appealed to Louis XIV for help. French ships evaded the blockade which the Spanish had imposed, and in 1675 landed troops to assist the rebels. In 1676 a combined Dutch–Spanish fleet was sent to Sicily, but was defeated by the French, who now enjoyed maritime superiority in the Mediterranean. In Catalonia, Spanish troops, who had not been paid for months, deserted to the French, leaving Barcelona exposed. Diplomatic moves were afoot to end the war. In 1676 negotiations opened in Nijmegen, where peace was signed in 1678. The terms imposed territorial losses on Spain. It surrendered Franche Comté, part of Flanders and Hainault to France; on the other hand,

Spain did recover Courtrai, Oudenaarde and Charleroi. The loss of Franche Comté was especially serious: it had long served as a conduit through which Spanish troops passed between northern Italy and the Netherlands. The land route between Spanish-held Milan and the Netherlands was now compromised.

The 1680s proved no more successful for Spain's position in Europe. In the early years of the decade, Louis XIV engaged in 'Reunions'. He appointed *chambres de réunion* whose purpose was to scour major treaties in which France recently had been involved – Westphalia (1648), the Pyrenees (1659), Nijmegen (1678) – for evidence that France might lay claim to territory in Germany or Flanders. The *chambres* came up with the desired recommendations; acting on their basis, from 1680 to 1684 he occupied much of the region between the Moselle and the Rhine, including most of Luxembourg and Alsace with its city of Strasbourg (1681). In an attempt to restrain the French, the Dutch and Swedish governments signed the Treaty of the Hague (1683): they formed an association, joined later by the Holy Roman Emperor and Charles II of Spain, to restore the frontiers agreed in 1648 and 1678. However, in 1683 Leopold I's attention was monopolized by the siege of Vienna, and only the Spanish took action by trying to relieve Luxembourg. They received no support from other governments, and by the truce of Ratisbon (1684) had to consent to the French Reunions for twenty years.

French aggression in the Rhineland, and the failure of the Hague powers to halt it, demonstrated the need for more concerted action. After his success against the Turks, Leopold I could devote more resources to Germany. In 1686 there was created the League of Augsburg: Austria, Spain, Sweden, Saxony and Bavaria promised mutual assistance should any of the signatories be attacked by France. Within three years, the league was embroiled in the War of the League of Augsburg (1688–97), to be discussed in chapter 9. In this war too, Spanish interests suffered. The French moved into the Spanish Netherlands and defeated a combined Spanish–Dutch army at Fleurus (1690); they also invaded Catalonia and in 1695 occupied Barcelona. Elsewhere, the war turned into a stalemate, and when Sweden offered to broker peace, the belligerent powers agreed. Negotiations took place at Ryswick near The Hague, and peace was signed in 1697. For once, Spain got off lightly and recovered everything lost since Nijmegen. The French withdrew from Catalonia, and returned all the Reunions on the frontier with the Spanish Netherlands and Luxembourg. France also gave way on the successions to the Palatinate and Cologne. France's lenient treatment of Spain had little to do with altruism, and much to do with the subject that was now paramount: the Spanish succession.

## The Spanish Succession Crisis, 1697–1702

In February 1689, Charles II's French wife, Marie Louise d'Orléans, had a riding accident which proved fatal. She and Charles had no children. Charles II's Council of State sought a second wife for him in Germany, where Spain's prestige needed to be restored after recent military failures. The choice fell on a Bavarian princess, Marian of Neuburg, who married Charles in 1690. However, this marriage too proved to be childless, and by the time the War of the League of Augsburg came to an end in 1697, the question of who would succeed Charles had become urgent. His health was giving cause for deep concern, and if he died, who would become king of Spain and its many European and overseas possessions?

The secret partition treaty which Louis XIV and Leopold I had signed at Grémonville in 1668 was by now redundant, not least because Leopold's position had changed. He now had three children: Maria Antonia – married to Maximilian of Bavaria – Joseph and Charles. Joseph eventually would be Holy Roman Emperor, but Leopold coveted the Spanish throne for his younger son, the Archduke Charles. Louis XIV would not countenance such an outcome, for he still contended that Maria Teresa's renunciation in 1660 had been invalid, and that the Dauphin Louis should be king of Spain after Charles II's death. In short, all the indications were that France and Austria would fight over the succession. After three decades of conflict this was an appalling outlook, not only for France, Austria and Spain, but for their respective allies who were bound to become embroiled. To forestall such a conflict, the English and Dutch governments in 1698, without consulting the Austrians or Spanish, signed a treaty with France based on the principle of partition. When Charles II died, Spain and its empire would go neither to a French prince nor to the Archduke Charles, but to Joseph Ferdinand, the son of Maria Antonia and Maximilian of Bavaria. France and Austria would be compensated from Spanish possessions in Italy. France would receive Naples and Sicily and Austria would obtain Milan. Whether the Austrians and Spanish would have consented is immaterial, for Joseph Ferdinand died in 1699, nullifying the partition treaty of 1698. In

1700 the English, Dutch and French governments agreed a second plan. The Spanish succession would go to the Archduke Charles (which should satisfy Leopold I), but Louis XIV would be compensated by the whole of Spanish Italy – Milan as well as Naples and Sicily.

Nowhere was the Spanish succession discussed with greater urgency than in Madrid itself, where the French and imperial ambassadors were hard at work cultivating factions favourable to their respective monarchs. The Council of State, in consultation with Charles II, arrived at a principle which must govern all others: Spain and its possessions must remain intact and partition be avoided. To the Council of State, the question of the succession therefore translated into that of who could best guarantee the Spanish inheritance in its entirety. Within the council, the prevalent view was that only one monarch possessed the resources to do so: the king of France. On 1 November 1700, the event which Spanish and European statesmen had been expecting for over thirty years occurred: Charles II died. His will announced a French prince as his successor: Philippe, duc d'Anjou, the younger grandson of Louis XIV. To the Spanish, the preservation of Spain's territories in their entirety was a more demanding imperative than family loyalty towards the Austrian Habsburgs. After some hesitation Louis XIV accepted the will (thereby reneging on his partition treaty with the English and Dutch), and his grandson duly travelled to Spain to be king. Leopold I disapproved of Charles II's decision, and likewise the British and Dutch were unhappy, but it had the backing of the powerful Council of Castile, and within Spain itself the seventeen-year-old Philippe was welcomed as legitimate king.

To all appearances the Spanish succession question was answered. Why then should a war have broken out in 1702? The answer is found less in the accession of the French prince than in actions taken by Louis XIV between 1700 and 1702, actions which, in the extremely tense international atmosphere created by the Spanish succession, persuaded the Austrians, Dutch, English and others that Louis was preparing either the unification of France and Spain or a power bloc which could hold the rest of western Europe to ransom. In February 1701 Louis announced that, although Charles II's will required the duc d'Anjou to renounce his claim to the throne of France, no French prince could be held to such a commitment. In the same month French troops took over fortresses on the frontier between France and the Spanish Netherlands (the 'barrier forts') which the Peace of Ryswick had conferred on the Dutch, who were driven out. Later in 1701 Philip V of Spain granted to a French company the monopoly to sell African slaves in Spain's American colonies, which perhaps indicated a coordinated Franco-Spanish colonial policy. On 5 September, the exiled James II of England died in France. Louis XIV recognized his son as James III in defiance of the Peace of Ryswick wherein Louis had withdrawn recognition from the Stuarts. Modern scholars can find explanations for these actions which negate any suggestion that Louis was intent on creating a super-state. If Philip V ever became king of France, it was in the expectation that he would abdicate as king of Spain; the seizure of the barrier forts was a measure to deter any independence movement in the Spanish Netherlands; and the commercial treaty simply formalized what was already a fact, namely that the French played a prominent role in Spanish overseas commerce. Leopold I nevertheless reacted with extreme hostility. Convinced that Louis had long-term plans for the coordination of Franco-Spanish policy in Europe, and perhaps even the union of the crowns, the emperor in 1701 sent troops to occupy northern Italy, then built an alliance of German states which, by the Treaty of the Hague (September 1701), was joined by Britain and the Dutch Republic. The English government reacted with extreme hostility to Louis's recognition of James Stuart, and even though William III died on 8 March 1702 as a result of a riding accident, his successor Anne continued with England's commitment to the Grand Alliance. The alliance declared war on France on 15 May 1702.

### Spain under Philip V

The new regime had only just settled in at Madrid when war broke out. During the first ten years or so of his reign, which was to last until 1746,[9] Philip V had to cope with the double challenge of ruling his composite kingdom and defending its interests in war; he was more successful in the first than the second. His approach to government reflected his French upbringing. He made use of French advisers, of whom two were especially important. The first was Jean Orry, a businessman and financier sent by Louis XIV to bring order to the Spanish crown's finances. By making the church and the kingdom of Aragon contribute more to the royal treasury, Orry raised its income by about one-third; he also introduced intendants into Spain, using them to supervise the implementation of royal policy. The other adviser was Michel-Jean Amelot, marquis de Gournay who, as Louis XIV's ambassador to Spain, helped Philip V to undermine the political privileges of the non-Castilian kingdoms, and to extend the political and judicial structures of Castile. Another French influence upon Philip came as a result of his marriage in 1701 to Marie Louise of Savoy; this was a match which Louis XIV had encouraged as he worked to bring Marie Louise's father, Victor Amedeo II of Savoy, into the French camp (in fact Savoy joined the allies). When she arrived in Spain, the entourage of Marie Louise included the French-born Marie-Anne de la Trémoïlle, princess of Orsini. Madame Orsini was to be a significant power behind the throne, at least until the queen died in 1714. When Philip married again at the end of the year, his second wife, Elizabeth Farnese, dismissed Madame Orsini. Philip V's use of French advisers caused resentment among some Spanish grandees, but others such as Cardinal Portocarrero and Manuel Arias, president of the Council of Castile, favoured the introduction into Spain of French techniques of government, being convinced that they held out the best prospect for the future. Under the influence of French advisers, Philip V changed the respective importance of the councils of central government.[10] The most significant development was the decline of the Council of State and the expansion of the powers of the Council of Castile. The former administered Spanish possessions in Italy and the Netherlands, but as control over them gradually was lost during the war, a loss confirmed by the Peace of Utrecht (1713), the council became almost redundant. The Council of Castile, on the other hand, served as the principal instrument of internal government, the supreme court of appeal and the chancery drafting laws and proclamations; it also supervised the universities and the secular interests of the church. When, in 1707, the Council of Aragon was disbanded, its functions were assumed by that of Castile.

The constitutional changes which Philip V wrought were closely linked to the fortunes of the war, especially the invasion of Spain itself by the allies. Although the Bourbon cause fared reasonably well in 1702 and 1703, it suffered setbacks in Spain in 1704 and 1705. In the former year Gibraltar was captured by the English, who used it as the base from which to launch a bigger allied campaign in Valencia and Catalonia in 1705. The Archduke Charles – the candidate of the allies to be king of Spain – had joined the allied forces, and in 1705 sailed to Catalonia to foment rebellion there and in Valencia. In October 1705 the allies captured Barcelona. Almost the whole of

Catalonia, Aragon and Valencia rose against the Bourbon regime in Madrid; by the end of the year Spain was in a state of virtual civil war as Castile remained mostly loyal to Philip. In 1706 the allies invaded Castile, and for a few weeks in summer even occupied Madrid itself, where they proclaimed the archduke as Charles III of Spain. This was the high point of the allied campaign, for they could not hold Madrid permanently. Philip V retrieved the capital in August 1706, after which the Bourbon position in Spain began to recover. In April 1707 occurred the most decisive battle of the war in Spain, when the Bourbon forces defeated the allies at Almanza. Thereafter, Philip gradually reoccupied Aragon and Valencia, but Catalonia held out and it was not until 1714 that Barcelona was retaken.

The failure of the resistance of Aragon, Valencia and Catalonia placed Philip V in a position to diminish their privileges. In 1707 the political privileges of Catalonia and Aragon were abolished and important changes were imposed on the legal systems of Valencia and Aragon. In these latter regions, new supreme courts of law were created to judge criminal cases according to the law of Castile, not of Valencia or Aragon. When Barcelona surrendered in 1714, similar legal changes were introduced into Catalonia; in the following year a high court for Majorca was created. In 1708 the customs barriers between Castile and Aragon were dismantled, thereby encouraging the emergence of larger internal markets. In finance, the crown simplified taxation by imposing new, comprehensive taxes on Aragon (1714), Valencia (1716) and Catalonia (1717). The attack on Catalan particularism was continued in 1716 by the New Plan (*nueva planta*): the Catalan language was no longer to be used in law courts or in public administration, and the councillors of the leading cities and towns, including Barcelona, were to be chosen by the king. The War of the Spanish Succession, which in Italy and the Netherlands was to result in the collapse of Philip V's power, had the contrary outcome within Spain itself. There it led to the enhancement of the control of Madrid over the other kingdoms, and the creation for the first time of a unitary, as against a composite, kingdom of Spain. If the consequences of the war in Italy and the Netherlands corroborate the notion of the decline of the Spanish empire in Europe, its course within the Iberian peninsula led to the rise of the kingdom of Spain.

In 1700, Franco-Spanish rivalry was transformed into amity and alliance, but it is one of the ironies of this shift that, far from securing the entirety of the Spanish succession as Charles II had intended, it resulted in Spain's network of European possessions being shattered. Whether the alternative to Philip V – the Archduke Charles with the backing of the Holy Roman Emperor – would have been a better option is a matter for speculation; it might even be that, in the Europe of the late 1600s and early 1700s, the Spanish 'empire' in Europe was beyond preservation, and that it was simply a question of whether the Austrian Habsburgs or the French Bourbons dismembered it. These are matters which will emerge again later; for present purposes it is sufficient to note that Philip V survived in his new kingdom, defeated the allied invaders, and exploited the opportunity presented by his victory to come closer than any of his predecessors to the ideal of a kingdom of Spain.

# 9

# *Western Europe, 1660–1720: Britain, the United Provinces and War*

## BRITAIN, 1660–1688

### The Restoration of Charles II, 1660

During the civil war, Charles, prince of Wales, fought in military campaigns until he departed for France in 1646. He was then involved in royalist naval raids on England, and after the execution of his father in 1649, assumed the title of king. Chapter 5 described how he went to Scotland in 1650, was crowned in 1651, but after his defeat at Worcester retreated again to France. As long as Cromwell was alive there was little prospect of Charles's return, but when the Lord Protector died, the subsequent political factionalism created a climate favourable to the restoration of monarchy. Charles II travelled to Breda in the Netherlands and in April 1660 issued a conciliatory declaration promising a general amnesty for former opponents of the monarchy (excepting such persons as parliament might decide) and freedom of religious conscience. A new ('Convention') parliament proclaimed Charles king. He travelled to Dover where he was met by General Monck, and he arrived in London to a tumultuous welcome on his thirtieth birthday, 29 May. Measures were taken to reassure Charles's subjects that he had no vengeful intentions: only eleven regicides were executed, and the pacific tones of the Declaration of Breda were seconded by parliament which passed the Act of Indemnity and Oblivion (1660), making it an offence to resume former quarrels. Problems which had precipitated the civil war – for example, royal prerogative or the validity of fiscal measures imposed by the crown without reference to parliament – had never been solved. Charles was conscious that, as far as possible, he must therefore avoid unnecessary confrontations with parliament. Accordingly, he left the assessment and raising of taxes to that body. On the other hand, he did act independently of parliament in religious affairs, eventually raising fears that he had long-term ambitions to dispense with his reliance on parliament once monarchy was firmly re-established.

In 1660 the Church of England was recognized again as the established church, and it recovered lands lost in the 1650s. At Breda, Charles had promised religious toleration, but after an abortive religious conference failed to agree on the extent to which it could be extended to non-Anglicans, parliament in 1662 passed the Act of Uniformity requiring all Anglican priests to be ordained by bishops and to conform to the Prayer Book; it outlawed all other denominations. Some clergy could not accept the new provisions, and when the deadline of 24 August 1662 arrived (the date by which clerics had to subscribe to the act), they were deprived of their livings. By 1663 about 1,760 clergy in England and 120 in Wales had lost their parishes, and about 200 university and school teachers had been dismissed. By driving the 'Puritan' element out of the ranks of the clergy, the act reinforced the distinction between Anglicans and dissenters, who were subjected to yet more discrimination. The Quaker Act of 1661 tried to suppress that movement, the Conventicle Act of 1664 outlawed non-Anglican religious assemblies of more than five persons, and the Five Mile Act of 1665 forbade dissenting ministers from living any closer to a town than that distance. In Scotland, the covenants were abolished and the episcopacy restored, the latter also being reintroduced into Ireland in 1661. In 1666 the Act of Uniformity was adopted in Ireland.

Another aspect of restoration that had to be dealt with concerned land which had been transferred during the civil war and revolution. Charles accepted that a comprehensive restoration of property would invite political disaster. He compromised by allowing the Anglican church and prominent royalists to recover property, but most people who had sold land, even under pressure, got nothing. In Ireland, where the Cromwellian land settlement had transferred extensive tracts of territory to English adventurers and soldiers, the Act of Settlement (1662) and the Act of Explanation (1665), which were passed by the Irish parliament, forced the beneficiaries to surrender a portion of their land to compensate royalists, most of whom were Catholics. The Cromwellian land settlement of Ireland nevertheless remained largely intact; even after compensation was made, Catholics still owned only 20 per cent of land as against 59 per cent in 1641.

There was a cultural dimension to restoration. The Commonwealth had tried to improve the moral as well as spiritual condition of the country by banning or controlling activities which were considered subversive of moral standards, especially theatre, popular festivities and music. After the restoration, theatres reopened, drama flourished, and all forms of music found expression. The sciences too prospered after 1660. There had been no attempt to place the sciences under the kind of scrutiny to which theatre and music were subjected during the Commonwealth period, even though scientists themselves showed differing political loyalties. When Charles II was restored, however, a group of scientists in London deemed the atmosphere right to create a formal society. The result of their endeavours was the foundation of the Royal Society.

**Figure 7**    Greenwich Royal Observatory

## The Royal Society

The Royal Society bears comparison with the French Academy of Sciences in its origins, but thereafter the two bodies contrasted with, rather than resembled, each other. Like their French counterparts, the founders of the Royal Society were inspired by the example of earlier private 'academies' in Italy and in France itself, and indeed as early as the 1630s and 1640s English scientists too were holding informal gatherings at Gresham College in London. In 1648 and 1649, when Oxford and Cambridge universities were purged of royalists, some of the London group were transferred to Oxford. They continued their meetings, which were attended by other colleagues in the university, including Thomas Willis, professor of natural philosophy, Seth Ward, professor of astronomy, and his successor in that post, Christopher Wren. When the universities were counter-purged at the Restoration, some of the Oxford group returned to London. With other interested persons they founded a formal scientific society on 28 November 1660, their intention being to concentrate on experimental learning. Numbers quickly grew to over seventy, and by the end of the decade the society had over two hundred members from many walks of life and of varied religious and political opinions. This mixture was deliberate, for whilst the primary purpose of the society was to conduct scientific research, the founders also perceived it as helping to heal the division and conflict which the country had experienced.

Some early members, who were courtiers, knew that Charles II personally was interested in the sciences. With the agreement of their colleagues they approached him with a proposal that he become their patron. Charles II agreed and in 1662 the Royal Society received its charter. From an early stage, therefore, it was governed by statutes, unlike the French Academy which had none until 1699; on the other hand, the London society received no financial subsidies comparable to those enjoyed by the Parisian academy. The majority of members were, in present-day parlance, interested amateurs rather than practising scientists, but they testify to an abiding feature of the early Royal Society: its determination to preserve the diversity of its social composition, and its intention of disseminating scientific information as widely as possible. This task was advanced by one of its secretaries, Henry Oldenburg, who in 1665 began to publish the *Philosophical Transactions*, a journal which included not only articles on every

**Figure 8**   Robert Boyle

aspect of science, but also information on books and scientific news from Europe and overseas.

One of the most distinguished founders of the Royal Society was the Anglo-Irish scientist Robert Boyle, who had been a member of the Oxford circles in the 1650s. In his research he was assisted by Robert Hooke, with whom he made improvements to the recently invented air pump and conducted experiments on the elasticity of air; in 1662 Boyle devised the law named after him. In *The Sceptical Chemist* (1661), he attacked many of the principles of alchemy, and

**Figure 9**   Robert Hooke's microscope

in his *Origin of Forms and Qualities* (1666) proposed instead a corpuscular theory according to which the structure and motions of matter are the product of the mechanical actions of minute, elemental particles of which all matter is composed. Boyle was a deeply religious man who worried that the corpuscular theory might lead to materialism. He wrote numerous works of theology, contending that modern science, far from undermining faith, reinforced Christianity by providing evidence of the works of a creator.

His assistant, Robert Hooke, served as curator and, from 1677, secretary to the Royal Society. His scientific reputation owed as much to his skills as an instrument designer as to his research. He constructed fine telescopes and microscopes, and in 1665 built a lens-polishing machine which he presented to the society. Among his more notable inventions were the compound microscope, the first reflecting telescope, and the wheel barometer. Hooke was more than a skilled craftsman. He studied the problem of terrestrial motion, presenting his hypotheses in his *Attempt to Prove the Motion of the Earth* (1674). He defended the reality of earthly motion, and explained it – and that of other heavenly bodies – as the product of gravity, a mutually attractive force acting across space; he surmised that the strength of this force was inversely proportional to the square of the distance between bodies. In 1679 he communicated this idea to Isaac Newton, who independently had reached a similar conclusion.

Newton, who was professor of mathematics at Cambridge, had been elected to the Royal Society in 1672 in recognition of experiments he had performed on the refraction of light. He worked in many branches of physics and mathematics, and was fascinated by alchemy. His interests also extended to theology, especially the interpretation of biblical prophecies. Although Hooke contacted him in 1679 on the question of gravity, Newton did not take it up systematically until the following decade. In 1684, the astronomer Edmond Halley approached Newton with a problem in celestial mechanics relating to the inverse law of attraction, and sought Newton's help in solving it. For the next two and a half years Newton worked on this and, encouraged by Halley, published his conclusions in his *Philosophiae naturalis principia mathematica* (1687), which provided a comprehensive explanation of all forms of celestial and terrestrial motion. It argued that motion is governed by universal gravity as all bodies exert attractive forces upon each other. It is, argued the *Principia*, the immensely intricate attractions and counter-attractions of material objects in the universe which determine the orbits and velocities of the planets and stars, and the nature and limits of motion on earth. The *Principia* is one of the supreme scientific texts of modern science, and over the next sixty years the theories which it defended became accepted by scientists everywhere as the definitive account of the structure and motions of the universe.

This and other contributions which fellows of the Royal Society made to their disciplines placed Britain and Ireland at the forefront of scientific achievement. Yet the significance of the Royal Society was more than the sum of its most talented individuals. It acted as an agent encouraging the propagation of scientific knowledge and habits of mind, and it endeavoured to reassure the social, religious and

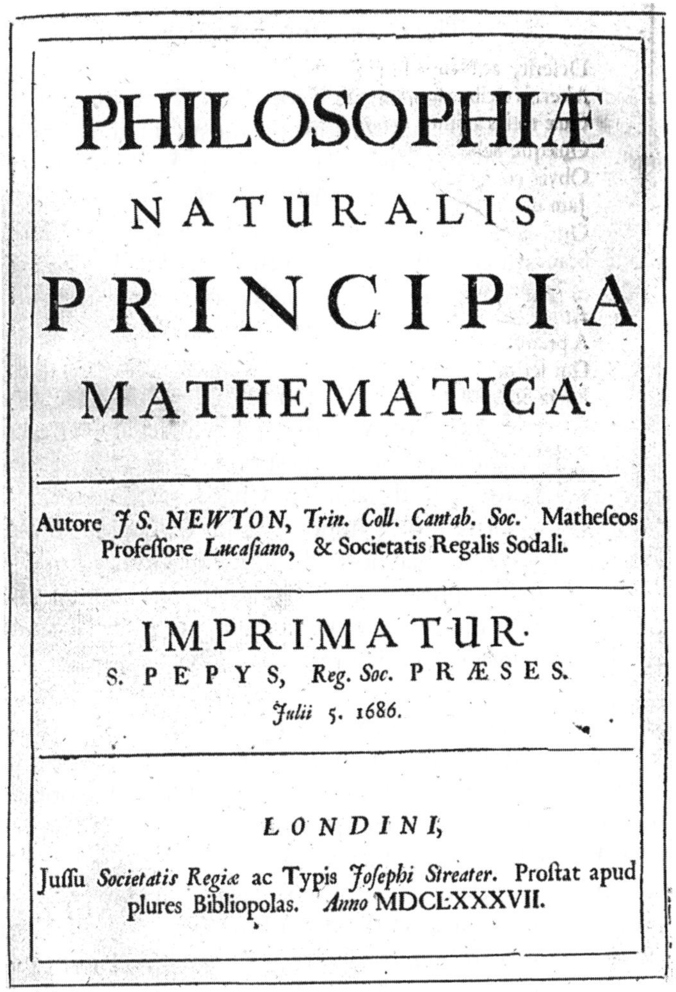

PHILOSOPHIÆ
NATURALIS
PRINCIPIA
MATHEMATICA.

Autore *JS. NEWTON*, *Trin. Coll. Cantab. Soc.* Mathefeos
Profeffore *Lucafiano*, & Societatis Regalis Sodali.

IMPRIMATUR·
S. P E P Y S, *Reg. Soc.* P R Æ S E S.
*Julii* 5. 1686.

L O N D I N I,

Juffu *Societatis Regiæ* ac Typis *Jofephi Streater.* Proftat apud
plures Bibliopolas. *Anno* MDCLXXXVII.

**Figure 10**   Title page of Isaac Newton's *Principia mathematica*, 1687

political elites that the sciences did not undermine – indeed, they
legitimated – royal political authority, religious belief as expounded
by the Anglican church, and conventional moral values. In an age
when, at so many levels, European civilization was fractured by contending socio-political forces, the Royal Society attempted to explain
the unity, balance and harmony of the physical universe which, by
implication, provided a model to which human societies ought to
conform.

## The Clarendon Years

Charles II proved to have little taste for the daily routine of government. Until 1667, he left administration mostly in the hands of his chancellor, Edward Hyde, earl of Clarendon. Hyde, who came of gentry stock, had entered parliament in 1640, where he became a prominent royalist. In 1642 he followed Charles I to Yorkshire, then accompanied the prince of Wales – the future Charles II – to France. At the Restoration, he was confirmed as chancellor and made earl of Clarendon. His position was strengthened by the marriage of his daughter to the king's brother, James, duke of York. The character of Restoration government owed much to Clarendon. He advised Charles II to avoid constitutional controversy and adhere to legal procedures in government; there must be no suggestion of the alleged arbitrary measures which had proved fatal to Charles I. However, moderation did not, in Clarendon's mind, extend to religion. He viewed dissenter churches as potential hotbeds of political radicalism which, if left unchecked, might present a challenge to monarchy in future. Hence he favoured the Act of Uniformity and other legislation which imposed religious and civil restrictions on dissenters as well as Catholics.

Religion was a topic on which Clarendon and the king disagreed. Charles II favoured the broad-church strategy of his grandfather, James I, and hoped that the Church of England would adopt a broad theology and be advisory rather than prescriptive in its approach to liturgy; he also took seriously the promise of religious liberty which he had made in the Declaration of Breda. This tolerant stance was a matter not only of principle on the part of the king but, with regard to the Catholic minority in England, gratitude. Catholics had been royalist in the civil war, and it was Catholics in the west of England who had helped him to escape to France after his defeat at Worcester in 1651. In December 1662, he issued a declaration proclaiming that he would, as he thought fit, exempt his dissenter and Catholic subjects from the Act of Uniformity. In 1672 he was to go further still, issuing a Declaration of Indulgence which, while confirming the status of the Church of England, allowed dissenters to worship in public and Catholics in private. Parliamentary opposition forced him to suspend this declaration in 1673. Such proclamations by Charles endangered his relations with parliament, for they raised the question of how far the king, by a royal declaration, could countermand its will. Most members of parliament agreed that, if temporary reason of state required it, the king could absolve individuals from the law, but the declarations on religion looked like much more: an attempt to subvert the entire will of parliament in matters of religion.

The reputations of the king and his chancellor were further damaged by England's unsuccessful war against the Dutch Republic from 1665 to 1667, and perversely by the plague and fire which devastated London in 1665 and 1666. The war was fought for commercial reasons. In 1660, parliament renewed the Navigation Act which required imported goods to be carried either in English ships or in ships of the country where goods originated. It was aimed chiefly at the Dutch, who carried much of the commerce between England and the continent. Parliament went further in 1662 by banning imports from the Dutch Republic. Meanwhile, violent clashes were occurring between Dutch and English traders in West Africa, the West Indies and the Americas. By 1664 a state of undeclared war existed between the two countries, and in that year the English seized the Dutch possession of New Amsterdam in North America; they renamed it New York. War officially broke out in 1665. In its early stages the English fleet proved superior, but gradually the initiative swung to the Dutch. The greatest humiliation for Charles II came in June 1667, when a Dutch fleet destroyed naval installations at Chatham and towed away the *Royal Charles*, the flagship of the English fleet. An Anglo-Dutch peace was signed at Breda in July 1667, and although Britain retained New York and a few other Dutch possessions, these gains were minute in comparison with the cost and humiliation of the war. Powerful enemies blamed Clarendon. Charles II sacrificed the chancellor, who was sent into exile. He was not replaced by a single chief minister. Charles relied on a loosely associated group of politicians, five of the more prominent being nicknamed 'the Cabal'.[1]

In fact, Charles II was playing a cleverer game than his critics realized. By now Louis XIV had invaded the Spanish Netherlands, to the consternation of the Dutch as much as the Spanish. In the recent Anglo-Dutch war Louis XIV had given modest help to the Dutch, but when Louis invaded the Spanish Netherlands in 1667, de Witt had no option but to turn to Britain in search of the alliance which was later joined by Sweden. Officially this Triple Alliance, which brokered the Peace of Aix-la-Chapelle (1668), took a dispassionate stance between the French and Spanish, making no pronouncement on the merits or otherwise of Louis's claim based on devolution; in practice, the allies had a secret agreement to declare war on France if Louis did not agree to peace. Charles II informed Louis XIV of this secret clause. The king of France was furious over this betrayal, as he saw it, by his former Dutch ally. Louis did sign peace in 1668, but emerged from the War of Devolution strongly anti-Dutch. Charles II, by contrast, continued to develop his relations with Louis XIV, and so confronted the Dutch with the threat of Anglo-French collaboration in the Netherlands and North Sea.

### Foreign and Domestic Tensions, 1667–1685

Charles's francophile tendencies had already appeared while Clarendon was chancellor. In 1662 Charles married a Portuguese princess, Catherine of Braganza, daughter of John IV of Portugal, and since Portugal was anti-Spanish and pro-French in its foreign policy, the marriage implied similar intent on the part of Charles II; also in 1662, Charles sold Dunkirk to Louis XIV, the resultant influx of money easing his dependency on parliament. Having split France from the United Provinces in 1668, Charles in 1670 signed two treaties of Dover with Louis. By their terms, Charles agreed to convert to the Catholic church, support Louis XIV's claims to the Spanish succession and back him if Louis went to war against the Dutch Republic; in return, Charles received further subsidies from France. These two treaties were secret, parliament being neither consulted nor informed. Charles was straying into dangerous constitutional territory, for he showed an increasing tendency to bypass parliament, as he had already done over the Act of Uniformity. The more French money came into his coffers, the more he dispensed with parliament: between 1671 and 1673, and 1675 and 1677 it did not meet; it was prorogued again after a brief session in 1677.

When parliament assembled in 1673, it did so at a time when domestic tensions were heightened by the questions of war and Catholicism. When Louis XIV invaded the Dutch Republic in 1672, Charles II supported him as he had promised in the secret treaties of Dover. In 1672 Charles also issued the aforementioned Declaration of Indulgence. The concurrence of war and indulgence had the opposite domestic effect from what Charles had intended. As the French devastated the Netherlands, forcing the Dutch to open the dikes, and as Louis XIV demanded full religious toleration for

Catholics in the republic, while at the same time persecuting his own Protestant subjects, he became perceived in Britain much as Philip II of Spain had been in the preceding century: the hammer of Protestantism. Charles II's support for Louis cast Charles as the potential reincarnation of Queen Mary Tudor, ready to do the bidding of a foreign monarch; this fear was enhanced by the fact that Charles's heir, his brother James, duke of York, had publicly converted to Rome in 1668. Parliament replied to the perceived Catholic threat in 1673 by proclaiming the Declaration of Indulgence illegal, and passing the Test Act: all holders of public office must take oaths of supremacy and allegiance in open court,[2] take communion in the Church of England (producing certificates from church ministers attesting that they had done so), and publicly reject the Catholic doctrine of transubstantiation. The Test Act forced several high-ranking Catholics to resign their offices, including James, duke of York, who was High Admiral; and although it was aimed at Catholics, it applied to dissenters too, who found themselves excluded from public office.

Popular anti-Catholic feeling in England was rife, even though in 1674 Charles II withdrew from the war against the Dutch and the Cabal was driven from office. The new chief minister, Thomas Osborne, earl of Danby, sought to calm popular fears by applying the Test Act rigorously and, in 1677, negotiating what was to be a marriage of historic significance between Mary, the Protestant daughter of the duke of York, and the stadtholder, William III of Orange. Even so, he could not prevent the outbreak of anti-Catholic hysteria known as the Popish Plot. The main instigator of the affair was Titus Oates, the son of an Anabaptist preacher. He became an Anglican clergyman, but was dismissed from his curacies for irregular behaviour. With the Reverend Dr Israel Tonge he set out to accuse Catholics of a plot by concocting a tissue of false evidence. He pretended to convert to Catholicism, and studied at Jesuit seminaries in Spain and the Spanish Netherlands. He returned to London in 1678 and informed the authorities of a plan involving a rising of Catholics throughout Britain, the assassination of Charles II and his replacement by James, duke of York. Oates swore to the truth of the plot before a magistrate, Sir Edmund Godfrey. In the investigation that followed, correspondence was found between Edward Coleman, secretary to the duchess of York, and the confessor of Louis XIV, suggesting that Louis might furnish money to be used to advance the

Catholic cause in parliament; the correspondence also referred to the conversion of the three kingdoms and the elimination of Protestantism. When Godfrey was later found murdered, panic gripped London, and Oates and his associates became popular heroes supposedly defending England against the Catholic menace. Catholic suspects were tried and some thirty-five were executed. The government and parliament were alarmed at Oates's actions, which threatened to let loose popular anarchy. When, in 1683, he accused the duke of York of treachery, he was arrested and imprisoned, and the hysteria gradually subsided; but the episode demonstrated the volatility of anti-Catholic sentiment in England.

In parliament, a group of ardent Protestants led by Anthony Ashley Cooper, earl of Shaftesbury (the Ashley of the Cabal), attempted to debar James, duke of York from the throne and transfer the succession to Charles II's illegitimate son, James, duke of Monmouth. The necessary Exclusion Bill passed the House of Commons in 1680, but was rejected by the Lords. When parliament reassembled in Oxford in 1681, Shaftesbury and some of his armed followers demanded that Charles II be forced to agree to the exclusion of his brother. The prospect of violent conflict over the succession appalled most of the king's subjects. Loyal addresses poured in to Charles II from all over the country. Shaftesbury was seized and imprisoned and the king dissolved parliament. Judicial proceedings were instigated against Shaftesbury, who fled abroad, and also against some of his supporters. Monmouth also fled to the continent. Charles had surmounted the exclusion crisis. Even so, other dangers arose, notably the Rye House Plot of 1683 whose aim was to assassinate him. Its leaders were discovered and executed.

Charles II's reign lasted two more years; he died in 1685. His brother succeeded unopposed, in spite of his Catholicism. For all Charles's failings and his tendency to overrule parliament, he had sufficient political acumen to remain within the bounds of acceptable monarchic practices, even if, at times, he extended them to the limit. His notoriously spendthrift and morally corrupt court scandalized much contemporary opinion, but this too was no cause for serious political objection. Although not a king capable of inspiring adulation, he did at least furnish his subjects with twenty-five years of relative stability; and he preserved the succession for his brother. Given the range and complexity of the problems facing him in 1660, Charles had performed creditably as king. If he was not a Louis XIV, neither was he a Charles II of Spain.

## James II, 1685–1688

In spite of his Catholicism, James II was in a strong position in 1685, for he overcame two rebellions in that year: one, in England, led by Monmouth, attempted to overturn the succession by force, and the other was led in Scotland by Archibald Campbell, earl of Argyll. Monmouth and Argyll were executed, and hundreds of Monmouth's followers were executed, transported or otherwise punished by the 'bloody assize' presided over by Judge George Jeffreys. Yet even though he had had ample time to study the political realities of the three kingdoms to which he succeeded, James II proved to have learnt remarkably little. To the modern observer equipped with hindsight, James's greatest mistake was probably to have misunderstood the importance of cultivating the nobility. The success with which Louis XIV re-established royal authority in France owed much to the care with which he restored relations between crown and nobility; James II neglected this segment of society which was wealthy and politically powerful, and paid a heavy price. He seems to have forgotten that it was to the House of Lords that he owed the crown: in 1680 the Commons had voted to exclude him, and it was the Lords which had voted against exclusion and preserved his inheritance. Yet when parliament met in 1685 and speeches critical of him were made in the Lords, he prorogued parliament and never called it again. Far from forming an alliance with the nobility, James seems to have gone out of his way to alienate them. He dismissed several from their offices at court, and in 1687 and 1688 discharged almost twenty from the post of lord lieutenant in the counties.

At the same time he promoted followers who had stayed with him loyally over the years. Many were Catholic, and their elevation by a king who himself was openly Catholic revived popular and constitutional fears that he was working towards the restoration of Catholicism as the established faith. When he issued another Declaration of Indulgence in 1687, absolving all Catholics and dissenters from the penal laws, he added constitutional to religious controversy: was he aiming at personal rule and the defiance of parliamentary will, especially since parliament remained prorogued? Nowhere were such implications more evident than in Ireland where, because Protestants were the minority, they suspected that he was intent upon a full restoration of Catholicism as a preliminary to that in England. Relying on the advice of the native-born Richard Talbot, earl of

Tyrconnell, whom he made Lord Deputy of Ireland in 1687, James agreed that the Protestant militia in Ireland should be disbanded, the army there purged of politically unreliable Protestant elements, Catholics promoted as officers and large numbers of Catholics recruited as rank-and-file soldiers. To Protestants in both Ireland and England, James looked to be equipping himself with a powerful military weapon which could be used to enforce his will on England. The civil administration of Ireland likewise was transferred into Catholic hands, and when Tyrconnell called a meeting of the Irish parliament in 1687, there were rumours that he intended pushing through legislation to restore land to Catholics.

In 1688, two developments occurred which cost James his throne. First, he issued another Declaration of Indulgence, and ordered Anglican bishops and clergy to read it from the pulpit. Seven bishops refused, and were tried on a charge of seditious libel; when they were acquitted, there was widespread rejoicing in England. Secondly, there was born on 10 June a son to James II and his Italian wife, Mary of Modena. From his first marriage, to Anne Hyde in 1660, James II had two daughters: Mary, now married to William III of Orange, and Anne, later to be queen. Anne Hyde had died in 1671, and in 1673 James married Mary of Modena. The marriage was childless until 1688, and until that point James II's heiress presumptive was his elder daughter. All was now changed, for the son, also named James and baptized as a Catholic, became heir apparent. From the Dutch Republic, the Stadtholder William III – himself a grandson of Charles I and nephew of James II – and his wife Mary, whose chances of succeeding in England had now diminished, followed events in England closely. Aware that another war against France was looming, William feared that the Catholic James II might support Louis XIV as Charles II had done. He was in touch with English nobles such as George Savile, marquess of Halifax and Daniel Finch, earl of Nottingham, but was reluctant to intervene unless sure of wider support among the nobility. On 30 June, seven nobles sent an invitation to William to come to England and rescue law and religion.[3]

Having secured the invitation, William gathered his forces. In order not to be seen as the puppet of an English noble faction, he sailed not to the east coast, where supporters waited for him, but to the west country and landed at Torbay, from where he advanced with his army towards London. Caught off their guard, most noblemen and county elites procrastinated, waiting to see what would happen; but as James's attempts to stop William failed, increasing numbers swung over to William's side. James sent his wife and son to France, and when it became clear that all was lost, he too fled. A Convention parliament, summoned without royal writ, met: it declared that James had abdicated and on 13 February 1689 proclaimed William III and Mary joint rulers. A Convention parliament in Scotland followed suit in April 1689.

These events were later dignified by the term 'Glorious Revolution', a national rising in which a tyrant was overthrown and liberty secured. In reality there was little glory. This was a *coup d'état* rather than a revolution. It was also a *coup* which, by the usual criteria, ought not to have succeeded. William III wanted as little as possible to do with the English lords who invited him; most English nobles stood aside from the crisis, at least until the outcome was clear; there was certainly no national rising; and parliament was not in session. But nobody expected James II to collapse so supinely. He appeared to hold most of the advantages: he was legitimate king, the nobility was divided and William was an invader; even so, James failed. His flight was a damning indictment of him as a king and a leader. He left behind an unexpected political vacuum. William, whose invasion was probably intended to wrest political and military concessions from James in the coming war against France, found himself king of England; the nobility and parliament found themselves with new monarchs. Parliament went on to impose conditions on William and Mary, but these were hastily concocted measures aiming to restore what members considered a right relationship between crown and parliament, not an attempt to create something new. In short, 1688 was less a Glorious Revolution than an unexpected *coup d'état*. Its effects in Ireland, on the other hand, were more dramatic, as will appear later in this chapter.

In a matter of eighty-five years, the Stuart kings gained and lost three kingdoms. James I/VI and Charles II exhibited a certain capacity to rule their composite inheritance, but Charles I and James II proved ill-suited, both in their obstinate temperament and in their lack of political aptitude; when it came to ruling diverse and contrasting lands, Stuart kings were not in the same class as the Austrian and Spanish Habsburgs. When James II sailed for France in 1688, he consigned himself, his son and the young James's descendants to a life of exile, punctuated by vain attempts to return. However, 1688 did not mark the end of Stuart rule, for both of James's daughters reigned: Mary, jointly with William III until her death in 1694, and Anne, from William's death in 1702 until 1714. Their reigns coincided with a period of almost incessant war against France. The reasons have much to do with the accession of William III and his deliberate conjunction of British and Dutch interests. This is the point, therefore, at which to turn from Britain and look at the evolution of the Dutch Republic and its condition in the late 1680s.

## THE UNITED PROVINCES AFTER 1660

The restoration of Charles II in England was studied closely in the United Provinces. Johan de Witt, the Lands Advocate, hoped that relations with England would improve after the recent war. On the other hand, he was disturbed to see that the restoration encouraged Orangist sentiments in the republic, and was displeased when the cities of Amsterdam, Haarlem and Leiden invited Princess Mary, the widow of the former stadtholder William II, and her son to pay them official visits. In the event, Anglo-Dutch relations failed to improve, and the English parliament renewed the Navigation Act, which hit Dutch shipping badly. Since better relations with England were unattainable, it was essential to avoid disputes with France. In 1663 the French ambassador informed de Witt that, on the death of Philip IV, Louis XIV intended pressing the claim of Maria Teresa to the Spanish Netherlands. De Witt proposed a compromise whereby France and the Dutch Republic would partition the Spanish Netherlands, leaving a remnant as an independent state. The French rejected the idea. Meanwhile, clashes with the English turned into war in 1665, and the bishop of Münster, who claimed territory on the eastern frontier of the republic, took the opportunity to invade. After early reversals against England – the Dutch fleet suffered a heavy defeat near Lowestoft in 1665 – the position improved. Neutral states proved benevolent towards the Dutch (Denmark, for example, excluded English shipping from the Baltic), and in 1666 the bishop of Münster was forced to make peace. Then came the successes of 1667, notably the attack on Chatham and the peace signed at Breda. In 1667 de Witt's reputation, and the republicanism which he represented, stood high both at home and abroad.

He seized the opportunity to deal a blow at Orangism, for by now the son of William II was in his teens, and Orangism was reviving as a viable political force. In recent years it had found support from the Reformed Church. Church leaders in Holland were unhappy at the failure of the states of the province to prevent the University of

Leiden from permitting the 'dangerous' philosophy of Descartes to be taught; in Utrecht, former ecclesiastical lands were being acquired by nobles and regents in spite of protests from the church; in both cases, church leaders turned to William of Orange in the hope that he might use his influence in their favour. De Witt observed such trends with distaste and took steps to prevent Prince William becoming stadtholder. De Witt developed the 'concept of harmony' which, he hoped, would strike a compromise by going some way towards satisfying Orangist aspirations, but barring William from political power. By this plan, Prince William would sit on the council of state and might also be Captain-General, but in this latter eventuality he would be excluded from the stadtholderate of every province. In 1667, de Witt presented the concept to the states of Holland, which accepted it subject to yet more conditions: the office of stadtholder in Holland was abolished (the 'Perpetual Edict') and William would become Captain-General only when he was twenty-three (1673). The 'concept of harmony', as modified by the states of Holland, was placed before the Estates General which accepted it by four votes to three.[4]

Meanwhile, Louis XIV invaded the Spanish Netherlands. Once again, de Witt attempted to persuade him to desist from a full-scale war by offering to support the French retention of certain towns on the frontier of the Spanish Netherlands and its annexation of Franche Comté. Louis, of course, refused and de Witt went on to create the alliance with Britain and Sweden, as discussed earlier. De Witt regarded the Peace of Aix-la-Chapelle (1668) as a triumph.

## Franco-Dutch War, 1672

Within a few years, however, the Dutch Republic faced the greatest crisis in its history. The primary reasons for the French invasion of 1672 were diplomatic. Louis XIV viewed the United Provinces with a mixture of hostility and contempt after 1668, an attitude hardened by his recognition that when he annexed the Spanish Netherlands, as guaranteed by his secret partition treaty with Leopold I, the Dutch would attempt to resist. It therefore made sense to neutralize them as an effective force in international affairs. Economic considerations also contributed to the French decision to go to war. Colbert's plans for economic recovery meant reducing the prominence of Dutch carriers in transporting French wine, brandy, salt and other commodities overseas, and cutting back on imports from the United Provinces of silks, spices, tobacco and fish products. The tariffs which Colbert introduced in 1664 and 1667 were aimed mainly at the Dutch who, in 1669, responded in like manner. The trading companies which Colbert helped to found in the 1660s also had an anti-Dutch purpose, and implied growing Franco-Dutch rivalry in the East and West Indies and the Baltic.

Between 1668 and 1672, Louis made diplomatic and military arrangements which indicated that he intended further military action, although it was not self-evident that the United Provinces were his target. Louis was already cultivating good relations with Charles II of England; he also signed treaties with the bishop of Münster and the archbishop of Cologne, each of whose territory was contiguous to the United Provinces. In 1670, Louis occupied Lorraine, a territory through which routes from France to the Netherlands, both south and north, passed. In 1672 he signed an alliance with Sweden, thereby detaching it from the Dutch Republic. Meanwhile, the French army was expanded. During the War of Devolution it stood at about 134,000; it was reduced to 70,000 after peace in 1668, but was raised again to 90,000 in 1670 and 120,000 by early 1672.[5] To the Dutch and other governments unaware of Louis's secret agreements with Charles II of England and Leopold I, the precise implications of these developments were unclear. It seemed possible that he was preparing another invasion of the Spanish Netherlands, or perhaps he was simply reinforcing his north-eastern frontier; either way, there was an implied threat to the United Provinces.

The difficulty for foreigners in discerning Louis's intentions is understandable since within the French government itself there was uncertainty. Three options were available to Louis. The first was to use these diplomatic and military preparations as an elaborate form of sabre-rattling, so alarming to the Dutch and Spanish that they would acquiesce in France's annexation of the Spanish Netherlands when Charles II died. The second was to invade the Spanish Netherlands for a second time, and persuade Leopold I to impose the partition treaty. The third was to attack the United Provinces with the help of Britain and Louis's German clients, and turn it into a French satellite. Louis XIV discussed these alternatives with his advisers. The first was rejected since it meant waiting for the death of Charles II, an eventuality over which Louis XIV had no control. The second was discounted because it ran too many diplomatic and military risks (Leopold I might renounce the partition treaty and side with Spain in a war which inevitably would follow). This left the third. Accordingly, France and Britain declared war on the United Provinces in April 1672.

## The Dutch War to the Peace of Nijmegen

As Louis put in place the diplomatic and military designs just outlined, some observers in the United Provinces felt that it would be prudent to take precautionary measures; in 1671, for example, the states of Gelderland called for William of Orange to be appointed Captain-General immediately. De Witt disagreed, but in February 1672, when it was evident to everybody that Louis XIV was preparing for a war which could well involve the republic, the Estates General overrode de Witt's objections and made William Captain-General for life. It was none too soon, for the French, and before long the forces of the bishop of Münster and archbishop of Cologne, poured into the country, sweeping aside Dutch troops who were inferior in numbers, equipment and morale. One town after another capitulated, including the fortress of Maastricht and city of Utrecht. Only at sea did the Dutch prove a match for their enemies, and several crucial victories over Anglo-French fleets in 1672 saved the republic from invasion from that quarter. The decision to open dikes to isolate Amsterdam was a measure of the desperate situation facing the country.

The collapse of the Dutch army and the defeatism of town councils and provincial estates provoked a violent popular response which expressed itself in pro-Orangist rioting. The first demonstrations began in Dordrecht, where there were demands that William of Orange be made stadtholder of the republic. The demonstrations spread to Rotterdam, Amsterdam, Gouda and other towns as a general popular uprising against de Witt, the regents and the republicanism which they represented, developed. In July 1672, the states of Zeeland and Holland (which rescinded the Perpetual Edict) made William their stadtholder, and the Estates General appointed him Captain-General and Admiral-General. On 4 August, de Witt resigned as Grand Pensionary; on 20 August, he and his brother were trapped by a mob at The Hague and beaten to death. Against this turbulent background, William III launched a purge of 'republicans' throughout the country; they were driven from provincial estates, town councils and other public offices, to be replaced by

Orangist sympathizers. A veritable *coup d'état* took place, leaving William III in control of the United Provinces.

In spite of further military failures – Nijmegen fell to the French and much of Drenthe and Gröningen was occupied by the army of Münster – the first signs of Dutch revival appeared. In 1672 William III signed alliances with Leopold I and Frederick William, elector of Brandenburg; in 1673 Spain joined the anti-French alliance. The Dutch fleet continued to hold the Anglo-French at bay, particularly after victory off the Texel in 1673, while on land the invading forces steadily were driven back: by the end of the year the French retained only Grave and Maastricht. In 1674, the Holy Roman Empire as a body declared war on France, whereas Britain and Münster made peace with the United Provinces. William III continued to reinforce his political position: in 1674 the states of Holland vested the stadtholderate of the province in William and his male heirs as a hereditary possession.

The entry of Spain, the emperor and most of the Holy Roman Empire into the war changed its character. Having begun as an Anglo-French assault on the United Provinces, it became predominantly a struggle between Habsburg and Bourbon. Having been driven out of most of the United Provinces, Louis XIV concentrated on securing his northern and north-eastern frontiers by occupying Franche Comté (1674), borderlands between France and the Spanish Netherlands, and the Rhineland, especially Alsace, where much campaigning and counter-campaigning took place over the next two years; as was seen earlier, Louis also intervened in Sicily.

This theme of Habsburg versus Bourbon occasioned a subsidiary conflict in Germany, where fears were rife that another Thirty Years War might be starting. The declaration of war on France by the Holy Roman Empire was an exceptional manifestation of imperial unity, testifying to a widespread resolve that Germany would not become once again a vast battlefield for the conflicts of others. Already in 1673 an anti-French pamphlet campaign had broken out in Germany. Typical of the pamphlets, which came out in German, Latin and French, were the Baron de Lisola's *Bouclier d'état* and *Dénouement des intrigues du temps*, which accused Louis XIV of territorial ambition at the expense of the empire. On the German fronts, French armies fought in the Rhineland, while Louis's ally, Sweden, bore the brunt of the campaigning in northern Germany. After the territorial gains secured in 1648, Sweden had become a conservative power in northern Europe. It signed an alliance with France in 1672, not because it sought war, but because it knew that, if it refused, Louis would turn to the arch-enemy Denmark. Sweden tied down some of France's enemies in northern Germany, notably Brandenburg, but also attempted to expand its own Baltic possessions by invading East Pomerania. The defeat of the Swedish army by that of Brandenburg at Fehrbellin (1675) not only frustrated Swedish designs, but indicated that the great days of Swedish military strength perhaps were numbered.

The war proved extremely costly to all the states involved. It provoked internal disorders in France, where risings occurred in Guyenne, Roussillon and Brittany in 1674 and 1675. In the United Provinces, the war drove up taxes and hit commerce. Yet in its military aspects it demonstrated that, while Louis XIV could be checked by the allies, he could not be beaten; but neither could the French overcome coordinated resistance. Accepting English mediation, French and Dutch representatives held informal peace talks at Nijmegen in 1676, out of which came an international conference in 1678. By this time, William III had reinforced his association with England through his marriage to Princess Mary in 1677. The peace talks, quite apart from the terms which they reached, are revealing as an exercise in international negotiation, for diplomats had learnt how to circumvent problems which caused long delays at Westphalia in 1648. One innovation was to hold the congress in one city not two, a change which greatly accelerated proceedings. Participants agreed that, within the city of Nijmegen, English representatives, who were the official mediators, would have precedence over all others; this avoided controversies over the status of mediators which had obstructed progress at Westphalia. Within Nijmegen, members of the different delegations observed conventional courtesies towards each other rather than the diplomatic niceties which easily ended in deadlock; thus, no insult was implied if a French delegate entered a room before a Spaniard, or a Dutch carriage yielded right of way to a Swedish when they met in a street. Such pragmatic arrangements served their purpose, making Nijmegen a much more efficient congress than Westphalia. In the principal agreements, France restored all of the territory of the United Provinces, ended the tariff war and signed a commerical treaty with the Dutch. Spain and France agreed the terms outlined in chapter 8. As regards peace between France, the emperor and Sweden, it was not settled until 1679 after a further bout of fighting. France gave up Philippsburg but retained Freiburg, and agreed to the restoration of the duke of Lorraine. Brandenburg

**Figure 11**   The signing of the Peace of Nijmegen, by Henri Gascard

was forced by France to restore to Sweden the territory of West Pomerania, which the elector's army had occupied.

The conventional view is that 1678 and 1679 mark the summit of Louis XIV's influence in Europe. Spain had surrendered territory to him, the Dutch Republic had been chastised, and his prestige had risen at the expense of Leopold I as Louis's client, Charles XI of Sweden, recovered land from the emperor's client, Frederick William of Brandenburg. Certainly Frederick William concluded that France rather than the emperor now was the power to back, and later in 1679 signed an alliance with Louis. Yet there are grounds for querying the proposition that Nijmegen was a French triumph, for Louis XIV got little more than de Witt had proposed in 1668, an offer which Louis had rejected as insufficient. By this measure, the outcome of the Dutch War was disappointing; moreover, the war had restored the Orange family in the United Provinces, and, in William III, Louis had an opponent of rare talent. It is possible even to present the Reunions in which Louis now engaged as an admission that Nijmegen afforded less than the effort and expenditure on warfare warranted. Over the next few years he indulged in 'salami-slicing' tactics, gradually acquiring more territory in the name of Reunions, but stopping short of provocation which might lead to another full-scale war. The tactics worked, and by the truce of Ratisbon (1684), France retained the Reunions for twenty years. By this interpretation, Nijmegen was less the culmination of a phase of French policy than a juncture in a process which led to Ratisbon in 1684.

In the United Provinces peace was welcomed as an opportunity to concentrate on economic recovery; moreover, there grew among the regents, especially those of Amsterdam, a sense that the United Provinces had paid heavily in the recent war and in future should maintain neutrality towards the major states of Europe. Such aspirations may be understandable, but they were unrealistic in the Europe of the 1680s. In the early years of the decade, Dutch merchants and entrepreneurs once again made inroads into French markets and shipping, but the French interpreted the commercial treaty of 1678 in such narrow terms as to raise the political temperature again. In 1687, Louis XIV reverted to the protectionism of Colbert by reintroducing comprehensive tariffs on Dutch goods, even though this contravened the commercial agreement signed at Nijmegen. In September 1688, he ordered the seizure of all Dutch ships in French ports; over 100 vessels were affected. Developments on the international political front also made Dutch neutrality impossible. Succession crises occurred to which Louis responded once again with force; but the international configuration had changed to the point where his opponents responded, not with more concessions, but with a war in which the United Provinces could not but be involved.

### Origins of the War of the League of Augsburg

In 1685 international tension was heightened by developments in France, Britain and Germany. The Revocation of the Edict of Nantes aroused fears in Protestant states that Louis might bring the same ultra-Catholic spirit to foreign affairs, and the accession of James II in Britain raised the possibility that he too might adopt a pro-Catholic stance. He might even receive help from Louis XIV to restore Catholicism in Britain, and then collaborate with the king of France in extending it to other parts of northern Europe. Frederick William of Brandenburg, although allied to France, was incensed at Louis's treatment of the Huguenots; by the Edict of Potsdam (1685), the elector invited Huguenots to settle in Brandenburg. He also set about improving diplomatic relations with Sweden and the United Provinces – emphasizing the need to stand together in defence of Protestantism – and with the emperor. Frederick William abandoned his alliance with Louis XIV. In 1685 and 1686 he signed treaties with Sweden, the United Provinces and Emperor Leopold I.

The other major source of tension in 1685 was the Palatinate. Its elector, Charles II, died childless. His sister, Charlotte-Elisabeth, who was married to Louis XIV's brother, the duc d'Orléans, had a claim to the succession, but was bypassed in favour of Philip William of Neuburg, father-in-law of Leopold I.[6] Louis XIV protested on behalf of Charlotte-Elisabeth, and his recent conduct suggested that he might take the Palatinate by force. In response to this evolving situation, the anti-French alliances engineered by Frederick William were supplemented by the formation in Germany of the League of Augsburg (1686). The emperor, Spain, Sweden and most of the princes joined this association for mutual assistance against French aggression; England and the United Provinces joined in 1689.

By 1688, Louis was faced by two hostile and overlapping blocs bound together by religious and political fears of his intentions. The episode that triggered war concerned the archbishopric of Cologne. On 3 June 1688 the pro-French archbishop, Maximilian Henry of Bavaria, died. Louis XIV wanted him replaced by another French client, Wilhelm Egon von Fürstenberg, bishop of Strasbourg, but Emperor Leopold I had his own candidate: Joseph Clement of Bavaria, bishop of Freising and Regensburg. After much energetic diplomatic consultation and calculation, the papal choice fell on Joseph Clement. Louis decided on a course of action which would, he hoped, force his opponents to back down. On 24 September he issued a manifesto stating three main demands: first, the truce of Ratisbon must be turned into a treaty confirming France's annexation of the Reunions; second, Charlotte-Elisabeth must be paid an indemnity to compensate her for her loss of the Palatinate; third, Fürstenberg must be appointed archbishop of Cologne. Louis backed up the manifesto with a show of destructive force. His troops invaded Cologne and the Palatinate, taking the fortress of Philippsburg in October 1688. Under instructions from the French government, they laid waste to much of the Rhineland, especially the Palatinate and adjacent territories. Heidelberg, Worms, Spire and other towns were razed to the ground; Mannheim was left a smouldering ruin. Louis calculated that the pope, the emperor and German princes would yield to this onslaught and agree to his demands. He was mistaken.

This was not the only misjudgement Louis made in 1688. He anticipated years of collaboration with James II and the resumption of close Anglo-French ties. Then came the 'Revolution'. Even when Louis heard that William of Orange had landed in England, he was not unduly perturbed: he expected that William would be defeated by James and that another Anglo-Dutch war might follow, a war which would divert the United Provinces from continental affairs. In order to help James, Louis declared war on the United Provinces on 26 November, eleven days after William's landing at Torbay. However, the unexpected happened. The defeated James II fled to France, leaving Louis at war with the United Provinces and facing a Britain controlled by William III. Over the next few months alliances and declarations of war followed in rapid succession as resistance to France spread. The War of the League of Augsburg began, not with a single declaration but accumulatively, following the French invasion of Cologne and the Palatinate. The key stages were:

*26 November 1688*: France declares war on the United Provinces.
*18 December 1688*: William III enters London and James II flees.
*January 1689*: Britain and the United Provinces join the League of Augsburg.
*13 February 1689*: William III and Mary become joint rulers of England.
*March 1689*: James II begins his campaign in Ireland.
*16 April 1689*: France declares war on Spain.
*12 May 1689*: Treaty of Vienna: the emperor and United Provinces form an alliance, joined later by Britain and Spain.
*17 May 1689*: Britain declares war on France.

## War in Ireland, 1689–1691

Although Louis faced a hostile government in London in 1689, he and James II still had reason to feel optimistic, for Ireland and the northern parts of Scotland remained Catholic, and William III and Mary could not presume that England would remain loyal. James II exploited this uncertainty by sailing to Ireland, where Tyrconnell had transformed the army into a Catholic force. James's plan was to assume control of Ireland, cross to Scotland with his army, gather more forces and descend on England. Backed by French money, ships, weapons and army officers, James landed in southern Ireland in March 1689. Tyrconnell met him and together they proceeded to Dublin where James met parliament, now dominated by Catholics.[7] Time was not on his side, for although most of the country was in the hands of his supporters (Protestants having fled to England or retreated into a handful of strongholds such as Londonderry, Coleraine and Enniskillen), it was inevitable that William would take counter-measures. James marched north and besieged Londonderry, but the city held out for 105 days until it was relieved on 28 July. James retreated, and in August a Williamite force commanded by Frederick, duke of Schomberg, landed near Bangor. Schomberg took Carrickfergus and Belfast and moved south towards Dundalk.

After a lull during winter, both sides were reinforced in 1690. Louis XIV sent 7,000 infantry to reinforce James's Irish army, giving him a total of 25,000. In June 1690, William arrived in person at the head of an international force, which, combined with those already in place, came to 36,000. On 1 July[8] the kings met in battle on the banks of the river Boyne, a few miles inland from Drogheda. Although casualties were light – about 1,000 Jacobites and 500 Williamites were killed – James was defeated. To the shame of his men, he fled the battlefield and returned to France; the Jacobite army retreated towards Limerick. Four days after his victory, William entered Dublin; from there he advanced towards Limerick and laid siege to the city. He was no more successful than James had been at Londonderry, and, anxious to get back to England, William left Ireland in the autumn with Limerick still under Jacobite control. Meanwhile, a seaborne force commanded by the earl (later duke) of Marlborough seized Cork and Kinsale, closing them to further use by the French. The war in Ireland concluded in 1691. On 12 July 1691, the Williamite army inflicted a heavy defeat on the Jacobites at Aughrim. Galway and Sligo surrendered to the Williamites and Limerick was besieged again. Recognizing that James II's cause was lost, the defenders signed peace on 3 October. Jacobite soldiers who wished to go to France were permitted to do so; those who remained were offered a *de facto* amnesty. William III authorized generous terms for a mixture of military and political reasons. Since the main theatre of war was the continent, he could not afford large numbers of troops being tied down in Ireland; and since his allies included Catholic states, he did not want to put their cooperation at risk by engaging in the suppression of Catholics in Ireland, especially as he had recently criticized Louis XIV's persecution of Protestants in France.

Figure 12   The Protestant Grindstone

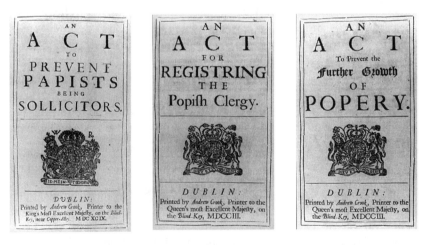

Figure 13   Anti-popery acts of parliament

Protestants in Ireland objected to William's leniency towards Catholics, and the Irish parliament, with a Protestant majority restored, went on to enact anti-Catholic legislation known as the Penal Laws.

Enacted between 1695 and 1709, the main laws forbade Catholics from going overseas for education or from bearing arms (1695); members of the Catholic hierarchy and the religious orders were banished, although ordinary priests could remain (1697); however, remaining priests were limited to one per parish and no more must enter the country (1704). Also in 1704 the Act to Prevent the Further Growth of Popery required Catholic land-owners to divide their property between all their sons, when they died, and not bequeath it intact to only one; Catholics were also forbidden to buy land from Protestants. A law of 1709 promised that any informant on Catholics who clandestinely bought land from Protestants would receive the land in question. Other laws debarred Catholics from public and legal offices, the army and navy and parliament.

In many respects the Penal Laws confirmed current practice rather than introducing something new, and they were applied selectively, not systematically; by the 1720s, for example, bishops had returned to Ireland and priests were practising again in most parts of the country. It was Catholic land-owners who potentially suffered most through the threat to their property; they protected their land by resorting to occasional conformity with the Church of Ireland, hence absolving themselves from the charge of Catholicism. The laws answered another imperative: as war lasted for most of the period between 1688 and 1713, the crown's need for money augmented; it had no option but to turn to the Irish and English (or British after 1707) parliament for financial grants. The Penal Laws were an affirmation of authority by the Irish parliament, a form of declaration that it, rather than the crown, would decide the pattern of sociopolitical life in that country. The English parliament asserted its authority in the aftermath of the flight of James II; the Irish parliament did so after the Treaty of Limerick.

## War on the Continent, 1688–1697

The War of the League of Augsburg lasted nine years and was even more destructive and costly than the Dutch War. It also lacked clearly defined purposes. The allies began by fighting to restore the frontiers of 1648 and 1659, yet as the war went on that purpose lost much of its relevance. As for Louis, he had stumbled into a war which he did not want, and his aim principally was to protect and preserve French territory. The armies which fought were larger than ever – some

400,000 on each side – and the areas in which the fighting was concentrated were traditional: the Netherlands, Flanders, the Rhineland
and northern Italy; as was discussed earlier, Spain itself was vulnerable,
for a French army invaded Catalonia and occupied Barcelona in 1695.
At sea, victory by the French over an Anglo-Dutch fleet at Beachy
Head in 1690 was countered by an Anglo-Dutch victory at La Hogue
near Cherbourg in 1692; neither side was able to achieve more than a
temporary mastery of the seas. As in the Dutch War, major battles and
sieges occurred, the allies wearing down France without being able to
defeat it. On several occasions, coalition armies attempted to invade
France, but were stopped in battles at Fleurus (1690), Steinkirk
(1692) and Neerwinden (1693). The war took a heavy toll on France.
Famine in the early 1690s hit the population hard, and the cost of war
forced the government into an array of loans, extraordinary taxes, and
the new tax of the *capitation*. As early as 1693, informal overtures
were made by French diplomats to imperial and other representatives,
but it was not until 1696 that serious discussions began. In that year
Louis made peace with the duke of Savoy, who was a member of the
anti-French coalition. The prospect of French troops being released to
fight the other allies caused them to agree to negotiations. With the
Swedish government as mediator, talks were held and concluded in
1697 at Ryswick near The Hague.

By the peace terms, Louis recognized William III as king of England, Scotland and Ireland (Mary had died in 1694) and promised to
withdraw support from the Stuarts. He satisfied the Dutch by evacu-
ating Luxembourg and several towns on the Franco-Flemish frontier;
he also agreed that the Dutch should occupy eleven towns on the
frontier (including Courtrai, Mons and Charleroi), and signed
another commercial treaty favourable to the United Provinces. As
regards Germany, Louis gave way on the successions to the Palatinate
and Cologne, although in the former case he did secure a financial
indemnity for Charlotte-Elisabeth. Louis also abandoned most of the
Reunions, the exception being Alsace, including Strasbourg, which
remained in French hands. In the agreement with Spain, Louis restored the territory which he had taken.

If France proved conciliatory at Ryswick, it was through a mixture
of necessity and calculation. French security had been preserved, and
it made no diplomatic or military sense to insist on terms which
might lead to another war. Furthermore, Louis concluded that
France must now work to re-establish the *ententes* with Britain and
the United Provinces which had served French purposes in earlier

decades. These two states had financed much of the allied war effort, and had prevented France from imposing hegemony at sea. Rather than have them as enemies, it made sense to have them as friends, especially as the Spanish succession question was looming. The news from Madrid was that Charles II's health was collapsing, and when he died, the question of his successor would involve France. Louis XIV therefore was determined to improve relations with the British and Dutch after 1697, for their hostility could prove fatal to his plans for the Spanish succession.

## BRITAIN AT THE TURN OF THE CENTURY

In and after 1689, the English parliament defined the powers of the crown with more rigour than in the past, and was able to do so because circumstances drove the crown into dependency on that assembly. In the short term, William III and Mary dared not challenge the body which could decide their survival; but even when their position was assured, the demands of fighting a sustained war forced them – and William alone after Mary's death – to cooperate with parliament. Throughout most of the century, Britain had intervened in continental wars only occasionally, but after 1688 it was at the centre of anti-French coalitions. In order to finance war, William III and his successor, Queen Anne, required parliamentary votes of money, which came at a price. In 1689, parliament issued the Declaration of Rights (turned into a bill at the end of the year), followed by the Mutiny Act. These removed the power of the crown to make or suspend laws independently of parliament (as in the Declarations of Indulgence) or impose taxation without its approval, and confirmed that no army could be maintained in peace time without parliamentary consent. The Triennial Act (1694) said that a parliament should meet at least once in three years, that there should be an election not later than three years after the dissolution of the previous parliament, and that no parliament should last longer than three years. Thereby ended the practice whereby the royal will decided the frequency with which it met; on the other hand, the corollary of the Triennial Act was that parliament was permanently implicated in royal policy, and the electorate had more opportunities to overturn unpopular ministries. It also followed that, because parliament now sat permanently, the significance of the House of Commons increased at the expense of the Lords. Great aristocrats, who sat in the House of Lords, had access to the king at any time and traditionally were not dependent on parliament as the arena in which to exercise political influence. Now that parliament was permanent, the Lords found themselves channelling their influence mainly through that body. The Act of Settlement (1701) reinforced a clause in the Declaration of Rights which said that an heir to the throne who married a Catholic should lose his or her right to succeed to the throne. The act was passed at a time when Mary's childless sister Anne was heiress; looking to the future, it proclaimed that if she still had no direct heir when she died, the succession would go to the Protestant Princess Sophia of Hanover (grand-daughter of James I) or her heir.

By these acts the English parliament, like that in Ireland, affirmed its authority and became a permanent fixture, central to the functioning of the constitution. It also exercised a high degree of financial control over the crown, for it created the 'civil list': a sum of money voted each year to the monarch. Yet parliament had made an important concession: it had accepted that the king or queen could no longer be expected to exercise monarchic functions solely on the resources of the royal estate. The civil list placed the monarchy on a sounder financial footing than ever before, and hence diminished the likelihood of serious rifts occurring over taxation. Monarchy and parliament were now bound in partnership, their mutual self-interest being served more by cooperation than by confrontation. Perhaps the most radical measure taken by parliament was the Act of Settlement, for the principle of hereditary succession was replaced by that of parliamentary will as the deciding factor in who should rule. The European convention whereby it was the monarch who decided the religion of his or her subjects had been reversed: the subjects – at least those represented in parliament – determined the religion of the monarch. To a king like Louis XIV, such principles were anathema; they were equally inadmissible to the exiled Stuarts, whose claim to the throne rested on heredity. Indeed, when James II died later in 1701, his son James claimed the succession and was recognized by Louis XIV as James III. This contravened the Peace of Ryswick, wherein Louis supposedly had withdrawn his recognition of the Stuarts. The English parliament reacted with indignation, and when war broke out in 1702, readily voted the necessary financial credits. The Act of Settlement, when added to the others, had the effect of reinforcing monarchy as an institution. Monarchy was now guaranteed by parliament, and it is no accident that it proved capable of surmounting the trials and tribulations of the next three centuries.

The other major constitutional change of these years was the Act of Union (1707) whereby the Scottish parliament ceased to exist, representatives going instead to Westminster in a British parliament. The two assemblies had already been conjoined under the Commonwealth, but the Scottish body had been restored in 1660. As in England, a Scottish Convention in 1689 offered the crown to William III and Mary, but the government of that country presented problems somewhat different from those in England. In Scotland, great magnates continued to wield immense political power. The struggles between the Hamilton, Queensberry, Atholl and Argyll factions threatened to render the country almost ungovernable. William III found that, if he favoured one group, the others would contrive to undermine it, if necessary by collaborating with Jacobites; indeed, the exiled James II maintained contact with supporters in Scotland in the hope of a restoration. To William III, who had seen factional in-fighting almost destroy his native United Provinces, Scotland faced a similar danger: internal political collapse could leave Scotland vulnerable to a Jacobite invasion backed by the French. His attempts to use the Scottish parliament to curb the magnates failed, and by the end of the century he was convinced that political union with England was the only way to keep Scotland secure. His death in 1702 in no way altered the situation, for Anne also advocated union from the beginning of her reign. Even in Scotland itself, a body of opinion was growing in favour of parliamentary union with England as the best guarantee of political stability.

Such sentiments were encouraged by economic considerations. The economies of the two countries operated independently, with Scotland (and, incidentally, Ireland) suffering the effects of the English Navigation Acts. The increasingly profitable colonial trade, from which English merchants prospered, was closed to Scots, and trade barriers between the two kingdoms heightened the sense of competition. In economic terms, the future looked to be served better by cooperation. The attractions to Scotland were especially strong, for the large neighbour to the south offered markets to Scottish cattle and other produce. When parliamentary union was enacted in 1707, Scottish economic life was a principal beneficiary. Although the effects were not immediately apparent, the increasing integration of the two economies – English capital moved north, Scottish agricultural and livestock exports increased, and Scottish merchants exploited colonial trade in tobacco and linens – created an economic environment in which Scotland prospered. By the Act of

Union, Scotland was to send forty-five members to the House of Commons at Westminster and sixteen elected lords. However, the church and legal system in Scotland were unaffected and were left with the same structures and prerogatives as before. There is no little irony in the fact that the union of England and Scotland occurred in the midst of a war whose purpose, from the British side, was to prevent such a convergence of France and Spain.

## THE WAR OF THE SPANISH SUCCESSION

Louis XIV's post-Ryswick intention of building close relations with William III worked in the short run, for he reached the partition agreements with William III in 1698 and 1700. However, as was shown earlier, when the Spanish succession devolved on his grandson, Louis helped him to succeed as Philip V of Spain, and engaged in a sequence of actions which convinced the British, Dutch and imperial governments that they must resist him by force. The Grand Alliance fought to replace Philip V with the Austrian Archduke Charles, and the British also fought to prevent the French from aiding a Stuart restoration. Some German states, Portugal, Denmark and Savoy also joined the Grand Alliance. France and Spain, supported mainly by Bavaria and Cologne, fought to keep Philip V on the Spanish throne.

The war followed the broad pattern of the War of the League of Augsburg, although on balance the French army performed less well than in the 1680s and 1690s; at Blenheim (1704) it suffered the heaviest defeat of Louis XIV's reign. In the final months of the war, however, it won several victories which enabled French negotiators to secure better terms at Utrecht than they had earlier expected. The war on land saw a mixture of rapid movement – in 1703, for example, Franco-Bavarian forces swept through southern Germany and even threatened Vienna itself – and sieges as heavily fortified towns and citadels slowed down military advance. The northern, eastern and southern frontiers of France were protected by a chain of fortifications built by Marshal Vauban, the greatest military engineer of the age; whilst they were not invincible (when the allies took Lille in 1708 there was alarm in Paris, for the road to the capital was now almost open), they did constitute a formidable defence. Both sides encouraged rebellion in the territory of the enemy. British and Dutch money went to the Camisards in the Cévennes mountains, while in

Hungary the French assisted the Rákóczy revolt against Leopold I. The war was fought also at sea, the principal operations being in the Atlantic, North Sea and Mediterranean.

Both sides had fine commanders. The outstanding French general was the duc de Villars. He had fought with the French army in the 1670s, but also gained experience in the imperial army against the Turks. He earned his marshal's baton after victory at Friedlingen (1702). He was appointed commander-in-chief in 1709 at an exceptionally difficult moment, for the northern frontier was under fierce pressure from the allies and the winter of 1709 had particularly ruinous effects in France. He was mainly responsible for the French victories at the end of the war; after defeating the imperial army at Denain (1712), he campaigned along the Rhine, forcing the imperial army to seek peace. The main imperial commander was Prince Eugene of Savoy. Born in Paris, he hoped to follow a military career in the French army, but was rejected by Louis XIV. He joined the army of Leopold I and excelled in the relief of Vienna in 1683. Although an outstanding military leader, he also had the ability to cooperate with the allied supreme commander in the War of the Spanish Succession, John Churchill, duke of Marlborough. Churchill came from an English royalist family, and even had suspicions of Jacobitism hanging over him in the 1690s. He owed promotion to his wife, Sarah Jennings, who was a confidante of Queen Anne and used her influence to have him appointed commander of the British and allied forces. Churchill, created duke of Marlborough in 1702, proved to be the greatest general of the war, for in addition to military leadership he too showed uncommon political tact: he had to coordinate British, Dutch and other armies whose sensitivities were easily offended. As a general he proved adept both in pitched battle – his principal victories occurred at Blenheim (1704), Ramillies (1706), Oudenaarde (1708) and Malplaquet (1709) – and in sieges: he captured over thirty fortresses. Political intrigue in England led to his dismissal in 1711, and it was then that the French recovered the military initiative.

The armies which both sides put into the field were on a scale commensurate with the conflict. The French armies rose to between 300,000 and 400,000, although normally they were around 270,000. Britain recruited an army of over 70,000 and the Dutch Republic some 150,000; this was an astonishing achievement for a small country, and was a tribute to its financial and economic strength. The Austrian army stood at about 150,000, and the lesser allies raised smaller, but significant, numbers. At any one time, over 500,000 soldiers were involved in the war.

After initial hostilities in Italy in 1701, the war gathered pace in 1702, the most notable victory being that of Villars at Friedlingen. Between 1703 and 1705 Bavaria was the centre of action. Campaigning also took place in Italy and the Low Countries, but was of secondary importance. Franco-Bavarian forces took control of much of southern Germany in 1703 and even threatened Vienna after defeating the imperial army at Höchstädt (20 September); these successes were matched in the Rhineland where they took Landau and Breisach. Franco-Bavarian victories obliged Marlborough in 1704 to leave the Low Countries and attack Bavaria. He was joined by Margrave Louis of Baden, who linked up with him near Ulm. Marlborough laid waste to much of Bavaria as the French had done in the Rhineland in the early 1680s, and defeated the Bavarians at Donauwörth (21 July); he was strengthened further when Eugene arrived with the imperial army at the end of the month. On 2 August they fought the main Franco-Bavarian force at Blenheim. The victory of the allies was the most spectacular of the war, but Marlborough could not remain in Germany: he returned to the Netherlands, for it was there that the war would be won or lost. Indeed, the campaigns of 1704 had so exhausted both sides that in 1705 they remained relatively quiet on the German and Netherlands fronts. On the other hand, in northern Italy in 1705 the French had the better of Savoy and Austria, while the allies invaded Catalonia and fomented rebellion against Philip V.

Over the next two years the French were driven on to the defensive. In the Low Countries, 1706 was a disastrous year for them. They were defeated again by Marlborough, this time at Ramillies, north of Namur (12 May); most of Brabant and Flanders subsequently fell into his hands. As the allied position in the Low Countries improved, the French concentrated on holding their northern frontier. In Italy, on the other hand, they defeated Eugene at Calcinato (19 April) and drove him up to Turin, but he recovered to win the battle fought there on 7 September. In Spain, the allies captured Madrid, holding it only for a few weeks before Philip V retook it. Throughout 1707, the defence of their northern frontier remained the top French priority, and it was only in 1708 that they went on to the offensive again. In May they advanced towards Brussels, retaking much of Flanders, including Ghent and Bruges. The next major stage on their route was Oudenaarde. Marlborough fought them there on 11 July and again proved superior. He and Eugene now combined to retake Ghent and Bruges, and they went on to besiege Lille which surrendered in December. Marlborough proceeded to besiege and take Tournai and Mons in 1709.

In May 1709, Louis XIV dispatched his foreign minister, Jean-Baptiste Colbert, marquis de Torcy, to the Netherlands where he met Marlborough, Eugene, Dutch and British representatives to discuss peace. The allies presented tough terms: Philip V must abdicate in favour of the Archduke Charles; Louis was to abandon his positions in the Spanish Netherlands; and if Philip V refused to surrender the throne, Louis must drive him out by force. So weak was the French position that Louis agreed, except for the last condition. The allies insisted on full compliance; rather than accept such humiliation, Louis opted to continue the war and placed Villars in command of the French forces. In the late summer, Villars advanced through the Spanish Netherlands and encountered Marlborough and Eugene – who had Dutch, Hanoverian and Prussian troops, as well as British and imperial, under their command – at Malplaquet, south-west of Mons. On 11 September they fought the bloodiest battle of the war. Marlborough won, but at crippling cost. Villars retreated, but whereas he had lost about 11,000 men, Marlborough had lost 21,000. The Dutch contingent had been cut to pieces, and the Hanoverians and Prussians suffered almost as badly. Given these losses, there was no question of Marlborough pursuing Villars.

In 1710 more peace talks took place, but once again they foundered on the allied insistence that Louis XIV should depose his grandson if Philip V declined to abdicate. The refusal of the allies to temper this demand was a mistake, for they had missed their best chance of dictating terms to Louis XIV. Villars had withdrawn behind a defensive line which he referred to as *ne plus ultra* (nothing further, or perfection), and although the allies did capture towns to the north, including Douai and Béthune, they dared not attack the line itself. Marlborough's position was now looking vulnerable. His losses at Malplaquet raised disquiet, and in England a peace party came into government in 1710: it objected to the financial strains which war was placing on Britain, and was critical of Marlborough's performance as commander-in-chief.

From the Franco-Spanish point of view, the position improved considerably in 1711. The emperor, Joseph I, died, leaving his brother, the Archduke Charles, as Habsburg candidate in the imperial election and as next ruler of Austria, Bohemia and Hungary.

Charles had been the candidate of the allies to replace Philip V in Spain, but it was inconceivable that they would now support him. While they were reassessing their attitude to Charles, Eugene departed for Germany leaving Marlborough alone to confront Villars, still entrenched behind his *ne plus ultra* line. Marlborough performed a set of complicated manoeuvres in an attempt to penetrate the line, but his political support in London collapsed and he was dismissed as commander of the British forces. The allied cause steadily disintegrated. In 1712 Britain secretly informed France that British forces would fight no more campaigns. Secure in this knowledge, Villars crossed his line and defeated Eugene at Denain. He went on to take Douai and Bouchain, and in 1713 he added Spire, Worms, Kaiserslautern, Landau and Freiburg to his conquests. By the time of this last victory (21 November), peace talks had begun at Utrecht, but other complications had arisen concerning the French succession. In 1711 Louis XIV's son, the dauphin, died, followed in 1712 by the duc de Bourgogne (elder son of the dauphin and brother of Philip V of Spain) and Bourgogne's own elder son, Louis. By the end of the year, the successor to Louis XIV was his great-grandson, Louis, duc d'Anjou, aged two years. If this infant died, next in line was Philip V of Spain. In other words, the problem of 1700 threatened to reappear: the possibility of the union of France and Spain.

## The Peace of Utrecht

The negotiations held in Utrecht led to several peace settlements signed between 1713 and 1715; there was no single treaty to which all the participants subscribed.[9] The broad thrust of the terms had already been decided in the secret Anglo-French talks which preceded the congress; the British and French then used their influence to have the terms accepted by their respective allies. This worked to France's advantage: although it had fought against a well-coordinated alliance during the war, it did not have to face a united diplomatic front in the negotiations. Britain's territorial gains at Utrecht, although few, laid the foundations of its future military and commercial role in the Mediterranean and Atlantic. Gibraltar and Minorca were secured from Spain, while Acadia, Newfoundland and Hudson's Bay in North America, and St Kitt's in the West Indies, were taken from France. A major bone of contention in Anglo-French relations was removed by Louis XIV's recognition of Queen Anne, although the Stuarts were allowed to remain in France. From Spain, Britain gained an important trading right, the *asiento*. This afforded Britain a thirty-year monopoly on the transportation of slaves to Spanish America, and a limited right to trade in other goods. Prospects of further Atlantic commerce appeared when Portugal also ceded to Britain trading rights in Brazil. With hindsight, we are aware that Utrecht was to launch a remarkable expansion in Britain's Atlantic commerce, but when the terms reached London, parliament complained that too little had been secured and that British honour had been betrayed.

The French negotiators could be satisfied with their work at Utrecht. Philip V was still king of Spain; and although he renounced his claim to the throne of France, nobody could be sure that he would abide by the promise if the infant duc d'Anjou died. Minor adjustments apart, the French frontiers in 1713 remained intact and this was a factor in Charles VI's decision to continue fighting, for he intended regaining Alsace. Villars's victories in 1712 and 1713 thwarted him, and at Rastadt – a peace negotiated in 1714 by Villars and Eugene – Charles conceded the retention of Alsace by France. After Utrecht, France was still a major power, although it had abandoned any pretensions to be the arbiter of western European affairs.

Spain was in a very different position in 1713. In effect it was partitioned. Most of its possessions in Italy and the Low Countries went to Austria as described in chapter 7 (see above, p. 284) while Piedmont and Sicily were conferred on Savoy. Humiliated at Utrecht, Spain within a few years attempted to recoup the losses in Italy. The Dutch at Utrecht were afraid that Britain would fail to stand by them, and this proved to be the case. The Dutch gained barrier forts on the border between the Austrian Netherlands and France at Furnes, Ypres, Menin, Tournai, Namur and Warneton, but they had hoped for more; they also coveted territory in Spanish Gelderland, but it went instead to Prussia, whose claim was backed by Britain. Many Dutch observers were left bitter at what they regarded as British perfidy. They had made military and financial contributions to the war proportionally greater than those of Britain, yet emerged with little. Other settlements affecting smaller powers were reached: the duke of Savoy not only acquired Sicily, but had his title of king recognized by the other signatories; the electors of Bavaria and Cologne were fully restored in their territories; the duke of Hanover was confirmed in his status of elector.

Taken in its entirety, the peace signified a reordering of western Europe. France remained a major power, but Britain now had attained that status. Austria also wielded considerable influence in western Europe through its acquisitions in Italy and the Netherlands. By contrast, the influence of Spain and the United Provinces diminished. In post-war Europe, France and Britain had more to gain by cooperation than by rivalry. Thus, when Anne died in 1714 and was succeeded by Elector George of Hanover, as provided by the Act of Settlement, the French government recognized George and refused to back the Jacobite rising of 1715. When Louis XIV died, he was succeeded by the duc d'Anjou. Louis XV was five years old and in poor health; his uncle Philippe, duc d'Orléans, was regent and, since Philip V of Spain had renounced his claim to France, was next in line of succession. However, in 1715 Philip V announced that he could not be bound by Utrecht, and would claim the throne if Louis XV died without an heir. If Orléans were to secure the throne himself in the event of Louis's demise, it would mean enforcing the terms of Utrecht, and that would require British support. Hence Orléans's self-interest as well as French interest of state was served by good Anglo-French relations. In 1716 the two countries signed an alliance, which became the basis of the Triple Alliance of 1717 which dealt with Spain's attempts to retake territory in Italy.

Utrecht is also significant for its espousal of the principle of 'balance of power'. In the negotiations, and in the decades which followed, statesmen approached international relations less through concepts of dynastic rights or the conventions governing earlier peace treaties than that of 'balance'. French, British, Austrian and other diplomats increasingly used the vocabulary of 'equilibrium' and 'balance' in their correspondence and negotiations; they came to envision Europe as a continent in a state of harmony and equilibrium, in which no state would have the capacity or have reason to overturn that balance. The origins of such notions are not easy to trace with exactitude, but they owed something to scientific habits of mind. The effects of the 'scientific revolution' of the seventeenth century went beyond the sciences themselves. Statesmen, many of whom followed scientific developments with a passion, came to apply scientific principles to international relations, and developed the concept of equilibrium analogous to that found in nature or the movements of planets and stars. It is, perhaps, no accident that negotiators from France and Britain in particular – two countries with leading scientific societies – were attracted to the 'balance of power';

the French foreign minister, Torcy, for example, was an honorary member of the Academy of Sciences, and brought scientific habits of mind to his diplomacy. In this regard, the Treaty of Utrecht was more than a conventional settlement: it was an attempt to create a balanced Europe in which no state aspired to preponderance. However, just as the scientist often has to manipulate nature to achieve a certain effect, so statesmen might have to resort to limited measures to preserve the balance of power. Thus the Anglo-French alliance of 1716, leading to the Triple Alliance of 1717, which in turn was joined by Austria in 1718, took action against Spain in Italy, but it made concessions in the Treaty of London (1720) to restore the equilibrium on which the new Europe rested.

# 10

# *Northern Europe, 1660– 1721: Scandinavia, Russia and Poland*

Without pushing the comparison too far, one might say that whereas international relations in western Europe in the early eighteenth century were determined by the Spanish succession question, those in northern Europe focused on Sweden's attempts to preserve its Baltic imperium. Sweden's dilemma arose not only because its traditional enemies, Denmark, Poland and Russia, sought to dismember its empire, but because the Holy Roman Emperor and most of the north German princes (notably the electors of Saxony and Brandenburg) no longer regarded the Peace of Westphalia (1648), in which extensive territory had been ceded to Sweden, as necessary to the peace of Germany. Thus, as the Danes, Saxons, Brandenburgers, Poles and Russians attempted to dismantle the Swedish Baltic empire, Sweden could not appeal to the sanctity of the Peace of Westphalia. France signed an alliance with Sweden in 1715, but could be of little practical use. The struggle was fought out mainly in the Northern War, 1700–1721, but was preceded by important changes in some of Sweden's rival states.

## BRANDENBURG–PRUSSIA

Among those states which sought to profit from Sweden's problems of imperial control was Brandenburg–Prussia (from 1701 known as the kingdom of Prussia). This north-German principality was in reality a collection of diverse and geographically dispersed territories which the ruling Hohenzollern dynasty had accumulated in the course of the century. Brandenburg itself was among the poorer regions of Germany, its chief distinction being that its prince was an elector of the Holy Roman Empire. During the Thirty Years War it suffered numerous depredations at the hands of invaders. When Frederick William succeeded as elector in 1640, much of Brandenburg was occupied by Swedish forces and his own army was mutinous. Justifying his policies on grounds of *raison d'état*, he set about preserving as much of Brandenburg's independence as possible and advancing its interests by whatever means necessary. In 1641 he signed a treaty of neutrality with Sweden, but managed to acquire Cleves, Mark and Ravensburg in west Germany and Prussia in the east. By the Treaty of Westphalia (1648) he received East Pomerania (which excluded the port of Stettin), Minden, Magdeburg, Kammin and a promise that Halberstadt eventually would pass to him. Paradoxically, these acquisitions were an indication, not that Brandenburg was an influential regional power, but that it was generally perceived to be impoverished, militarily weak, and could be granted territorial concessions without endangering regional stability. For many years after 1648, Brandenburg remained a minor force in international affairs. Frederick-William could never afford the luxury of a consistent foreign policy; he had no option but to react to that of others. This he did with considerable skill. In 1656 he joined Sweden in its war against Poland in return for Swedish recognition of his hold on Prussia, but in 1657 he changed sides when Poland made the same promise. He retained Prussia by the Treaty of Oliva (1660).

For the next fourteen years, Brandenburg was at peace and Frederick William (the 'Great Elector') turned his attention to problems of socio-economic regeneration. He encouraged immigration by Huguenots. The 20,000 or so who settled in Brandenburg received tax concessions and brought valuable economic skills in the design and making of jewellery, clocks and watches, in paper-making and the weaving and dyeing of cloth. Such economic recovery as Brandenburg–Prussia experienced in the later seventeenth century owed much to the contribution of immigrant workers. In his dealings with the great nobility and provincial estates, he had to strike a bargain: they supported his domestic policies on condition that he maintained their privileges. Thus, he permitted them to import and export manufactured goods and crops free of duty, and in 1653 guaranteed the supply of their rural labour force by designating all peasants as serfs unless they were able to prove their status as freemen. In 1644, disillusioned by the unreliability of mercenary soldiers, he created a new and permanent army. To pay for it, the estates of Brandenburg and Prussia agreed to financial subsidies, but only in return for guarantees of their privileges; such were the terms on which the estates of Brandenburg granted subsidies for a further six years in 1653. The estates of Prussia were noted for their attachment to their liberties. Although the Peace of Oliva confirmed the sovereignty of the elector-duke in Prussia, the estates withheld its recognition. By a mixture of threats and concessions, Frederick William gradually wore down the opposition, but it was only in the 1680s that it was fully compliant with his policies, especially in the realm of taxation.

In the administration of his territories, the elector moved towards a centralized structure based on the Council of State which, in 1651, he made responsible for all the lands which he ruled. Like Oxenstierna in Sweden, Frederick William favoured judicial centralization by creating a supreme court of appeal which was competent to give final judgement throughout Brandenburg–Prussia. Whilst the formation of the supreme court conformed in a general sense to Frederick William's purposes, its principal immediate aim was to stop appeals from Prussian tribunals to courts in Poland, as had happened previously. The assessment and collection of taxation was undertaken increasingly by centrally appointed commissaries in place of traditional municipal or rural officers. Brandenburg–Prussia did not adopt the practice of tax farming; revenue was assessed and collected by the state itself. Indeed, one of Frederick William's most abiding legacies was the principle of permanent taxation. He adopted the practice favoured by most European statesmen after 1660 of shifting as much of the tax burden as possible from direct to indirect levies. In 1661 he introduced an excise on a wide range of goods, and this became the basis of his revenue; it had become general throughout Brandenburg–Prussia by the early 1680s and provided the elector and his successors with a unified tax base. Income from the domain of the elector also occupied a prominent place in state revenue. Frederick William placed strong emphasis on the development and exploitation of his personal domain by such measures as stimulating mining and salt production. In 1640, he derived about 60 per cent of total income from this source, and still some 50 per cent when he died in 1688; the sums involved were one million *thaler* in 1640 and three million in 1688.[1]

The commanding imperative which drove almost all of Frederick William's domestic policies was the need to preserve the army in a high state of training and readiness. He normally devoted about 50 per cent of revenue to the army, and this he supplemented by loans during times of war. He had the highest respect for Sweden, whose ability to exercise hegemony over so much of the Baltic region, in spite of Sweden's small population and few natural resources, he attributed to its military prowess. Here was the inspiration for the strategies underlying his own policies, especially since he too governed scattered territories which were vulnerable to invasion. He placed overall administration of the army in the hands of a general directorate which transmitted its authority through provincial directorates. The General Director, who was an administrator, not a general in the field even though he held that rank, had direct access to the elector. Although small by the standards of some other countries – it stood at 2,000 in 1656, 12,000 by 1672 and 30,000 in 1688 – the army of Brandenburg–Prussia was well equipped, organized and trained. The victory over the Swedes at Fehrbellin (1675) was especially satisfying to Frederick William, for he had defeated those whom he regarded as the masters of warfare, and the triumph announced the arrival of Brandenburg–Prussia as a state whose interests and ambitions in northern Europe would have to be taken seriously by others. The growing international prestige of Brandenburg–Prussia was confirmed during the reign of Frederick William's son and successor, Frederick: in 1701 he was elevated by Emperor Leopold I to the status of king. However, the territory to which the title was attached was Prussia, which lay outside the Holy Roman Empire.[2] The only kingdom within the empire was Bohemia, whose king was Leopold himself. The emperor would not permit another imperial territory to attain that rank.

## RUSSIA

### Stenka Razin and the Peasant War, 1667–1671

Although Tsar Alexis could be well pleased with his territorial gains at the expense of Poland (see p. 244), the same year as the truce of Andrusovo (1667) saw the beginning of another general peasant revolt which began among the Cossacks of the Volga basin, and spread almost as far as Moscow itself. The revolt was headed by Stephen ('Stenka') Razin, a prominent Cossack leader, and arose from a blend of religious and social grievances. Most of the Cossacks not only were Orthodox, but joined the Old Believer cause; they detested the liturgical changes which Nikon had introduced, and fought to protect the true faith. They were able to exploit popular grievances which had grown in Russia over the government's monetary policy, which generated rampant inflation at a time of acute social distress. In 1656, following a year of plague in which some 800,000 Russians died, Alexis brought copper coinage into circulation; in theory it had the same purchasing value as existing silver coins. However, although the government settled its own bills in the new copper coinage, taxes had to be paid in silver coins. This transparent attempt by the government to amass silver and substitute cheaper and inferior coins, which poured into circulation, caused both popular hostility and inflation. Along the Volga, the price of rye more than quadrupled between 1658 and 1663, as an increased volume of cheap copper coins chased a limited supply of grain. In Moscow, the so-called Copper Riots broke out in 1662, forcing the government to recall copper coins and recirculate silver.

Into this atmosphere of socio-economic protest burst Stenka Razin and his horde of Cossacks. Razin, who as a young man made a thousand-mile journey to the famous Solovetsky monastery on the White Sea coast where he prayed and performed spiritual exercises for the good of his soul, resided near the mouth of the Volga, where he commanded a troop of pirates who lived by looting ships and barges. In 1667 he gathered an army and fleet, sailed up the Volga, captured several forts and laid waste to the countryside. After suspending operations to conduct a campaign on the Persian shore of the Caspian Sea, he returned to the Volga and in 1670 achieved his greatest victory: he took Astrakhan, which became his base. Again he transported his army up the Volga, calling on peasants to join him, and massacring those who resisted. The collapse of tsarist authority along the Volga forced Alexis to respond. Royal forces were sent against Razin, and a series of pitched battles followed. For a time, the Cossacks and peasants proved a match for the Russian army, but the violence and cruelty of Razin dissipated much of his support. In 1671 the patriarch of Moscow excommunicated him, and he was captured later in the year; he was taken to Moscow, tortured and publicly executed, but the insurrection which he led had caused some 100,000 deaths, and left much of the Volga basin in a state of devastation. Yet it acquired a mystique among the Russian peasantry, and public memory later idealized Razin and what he allegedly represented. Later generations saw him as the heroic

Cossack leader who resisted tsarist autocracy and fought for the liberties of his people and of the peasants who joined him, against Russian autocracy.[3] Shorn of its romanticized accretions, the rising now looks to have been one more example of popular resistance to fiscal exploitation by the state at a time of socio-economic hardship resulting from famine. The nature of Russia's south-eastern frontier, and the vast distances involved, ensured that Razin's rebellion and its suppression would take place on a grand scale; but, in its essentials, it was similar to popular uprisings elsewhere in Europe.

### Problems of Succession and Regency, 1676–1696

When Tsar Alexis died in 1676, he was succeeded by his son Fedor. Born in 1661, Fedor was fourteen and in poor physical and mental condition. He died in 1682 without an heir. A struggle ensued in which the families of Alexis's two wives contended for power. His first wife had been Maria Miloslavskaia, mother of Fedor; her second son, Ivan, was a candidate to succeed in 1682, but, like his deceased brother, he was a weakling. Alexis's second wife, Natalia Naryshkina, had a son, Peter, born in 1672. Given Ivan's infirmities, she had every intention of making Peter tsar. The rivalry between the Miloslavsky and Naryshkin families was complicated by a further factor. Ivan had an older sister, Sophia. The daughters of tsars were normally consigned to convents, but Sophia was determined to avoid this fate by contriving to place her younger brother on the throne, with herself as regent. Before he died, Fedor nominated the robust Peter as his successor, but the Miloslavsky clan allied with the *streltsy* (the permanent Moscow garrison) and attempted to seize power by force. Scenes of appalling violence took place (Peter saw members of his family and friends cut to pieces), and the outcome was a compromise: the sixteen-year-old Ivan and the ten-year-old Peter would rule jointly, with Sophia as regent.

To a dispassionate observer it seemed that as long as Peter was alive Sophia's long-term position was uncertain, yet she left the junior tsar largely to his own devices and there is no evidence that she tried to have him assassinated. Peter surrounded himself with friends, including foreigners, who encouraged him to break with many of the traditions of tsarism and get to know the outside world. One such figure was a Swiss adventurer François Lefort; others were the Dutchman Franz Timmerman and the Scottish mercenary, General Patrick Gordon. Timmerman taught Peter mathematics, geometry and the elements of navigation, three disciplines which later helped to inspire Peter's enthusiasm for ships and sailing. In 1689, Peter and his supporters felt sufficiently confident to challenge Sophia. In that year Peter married, and his wife soon announced that she was pregnant; by contrast, the sickly Ivan V had no heir. Peter called on Sophia to resign as regent, but she prepared to resist him by force. Although Peter fled from Moscow in August, his support was growing while that of Sophia was declining. In September 1689, Sophia gave up the struggle and was confined to a convent. Ivan V and Peter continued to rule jointly, with Ivan nominally the senior tsar. After his death in 1696, Peter ruled alone, although even before that he exercised the real authority.

In 1693, Peter made the first of several visits to the White Sea, which encouraged further his fascination for the design and construction of boats. His encounters with foreigners multiplied, and he took to visiting the foreign quarter of Moscow, where he met German, Dutch and Danish merchants; he also encountered French Protestant refugees and Scottish Catholics, some 3,000 Jacobites having moved to Russia after the 1688 'Revolution' in Britain. Peter's intellectual and personal development was strongly influenced by foreigners whom he continued to admit to his innermost circle throughout his life.

By his mid-twenties, Peter was at the height of his considerable physical powers – he stood almost seven feet high – and was possessed of a demonic energy which drove him incessantly. Restless, impatient towards the ritual and formality of the life of a tsar, Peter dressed and comported himself roughly; on his visits abroad he confirmed in the eyes of his hosts the stereotype of the wild, barbaric Russian. Yet he was also interested in ideas, especially those with practical application. Reference has already been made to his training in mathematics and navigation, and he collected navigational and scientific instruments, telescopes, globes and other utilitarian artefacts. The abiding passion of his life was ships and sailing. His papers and library were stocked with drawings and designs of ships, books on sailing, ship-building and naval manoeuvres; indeed, every conceivable facet of ships and the sea. The importance of the sea in Peter's foreign policy doubtless had strategic and diplomatic justification, but also owed much to his personal maritime obsessions.

## Russia, the South and West

It was the desire to extend the Russian presence in the Black Sea which lay behind Peter's first foray into war. He recognized that he could accomplish his goal only by subduing the Crimea Tatars and defeating their overlord, the Turkish sultan. Sophia had sent military expeditions into the Crimea, most recently in 1689, but without success. In 1695 Peter mustered another army with the aim of seizing the Turkish fortress of Azov at the mouth of the river Don. This campaign was no more effective than its predecessors. Peter besieged Azov from July to September 1695 but, unable to breach the walls, was forced to retire to Moscow. He spent the winter re-equipping his forces, this time with western help. He imported miners, engineers and carpenters from Austria and Germany, and ship designers from the Netherlands; he personally lived and worked with them at Voronezh on the Don, where he gathered a huge labour force which built a new fleet. In 1696 Peter launched his second assault on Azov, and this time it surrendered, on 18 July. The capture of Azov was the most spectacular Russian victory for many years; it was enthusiastically celebrated in Moscow and other towns of Russia.

Peter did not let the euphoria blind him to the fact that, if he were to retain Azov against an inevitable Turkish riposte, he needed allies. In 1697, he began a tour of selected western European countries to make them aware of his foreign-policy intentions and to cultivate diplomatic relations. In order to give himself maximum liberty of movement while abroad, he appointed Lefort head of the mission and Peter travelled 'incognito' (although everybody knew who he was) as a volunteer sailor. Politically the tour produced little of importance (in 1697, no western government wanted to become embroiled in the Black Sea), but in its effects upon Peter it was a seminal experience. Wherever he went he took the opportunity to study the most up-to-date techniques in ship-building, armaments and other facets of western military, economic and intellectual achievement. He inspected the manufacture of cannon at Königsberg, and ship-building in the Netherlands and England. He attended anatomy lectures at Leiden and took lessons in engraving at Amsterdam. He invited foreigners to enter his service; thereby the Scotsman Henry Farquharson became professor at the new Moscow school of navigation in 1701, and his compatriot Robert Erskine was appointed physician to the tsar. Peter had to break off the tour between

**Figure 14** The Peter-Paul Fortress with the Cathedral of Sts Peter and Paul, St Petersburg

Vienna and Venice in June 1698, for word arrived of a revolt of the *streltsy;* he returned to Moscow to complete the suppression of the revolt, which General Gordon had already crushed, and supervise the punishment of the perpetrators (over 1,200 were executed and the corps was disbanded); but he had seen enough on his travels to convince him of the superiority of western Europe over Russia in many facets of military and commercial life.

It is well known how Peter, on his return to Russia, launched an assault on traditional symbols or forms of dress in Russia. Over the next few years, he adopted, and insisted that his subjects also wear, western dress and hair-styles; beards were either forbidden or permitted only on the payment of a tax; in 1699 he transferred the beginning of the year from 1 September to 1 January in accordance with most western countries. His most ambitious and enduring attempt to force his subjects into western modes, however, arose from the foundation in 1703 of a new capital on the shores of the Baltic: St Petersburg, to which the court and government were transferred in 1713. The buildings, palaces and churches constructed in the course of this immense urban project would not have looked out of place in central, western or southern Europe. St Petersburg became the defining statement of the regime, proclaiming that Russia was committed to the path of modernization.

How should we interpret Peter's 'westernization' programme? Was it the key to his reign, or has its significance often been exaggerated? The practice of looking outside Russia for technical or military inspiration, and even of imitating foreign styles of dress, was not new. In the fourteenth and fifteenth centuries, grand dukes of Muscovy borrowed and adapted military training and forms of dress from Byzantium. In the sixteenth century, Ivan IV equipped his army with western firearms, and Italian fashions in clothing were to be seen in Moscow. In chapter 6 it was noted that young Russian men training for the Orthodox priesthood went to Kiev to study. In other words, Russia had a long tradition of opening itself up to external intellectual and cultural influences. This pattern was interrupted in the seventeenth century by the Time of Troubles and the Great Schism, both of which created an atmosphere of suspicion and hostility towards the outside world. Xenophobic attitudes penetrated deep into Russian society, but were the product of particular crises and contrasted with the norms of earlier centuries. When Peter's westernizing habits are viewed from such a perspective, they become an older norm, not an unprecedented innovation.

Even so, his intention was to turn upon his most powerful western neighbour, Sweden. He had enjoyed victory over the Turks and had plans to encroach upon the Baltic, but this meant war against Sweden. This could be undertaken only by a modern army and navy. Peter's 'westernization' therefore was not a manifestation of a starry-eyed awe towards things European; it was a selective adaptation of those features most necessary to his forthcoming campaigns in the Baltic region. In the two or three years before he began the Northern War in 1700, Peter carefully accumulated allies. In 1697 he met Frederick III, elector of Brandenburg, to plan joint action against Sweden, and in

1698 he had similar talks with Frederick-Augustus, elector of Saxony. Peter and Frederick-Augustus signed an alliance in 1699, which was soon joined by Denmark. The plan was that they would attack Swedish installations simultaneously: the Danes would hold the Swedes in the western Baltic and would attack Holstein (which had Swedish bases), the Saxons would invade Swedish Livonia, and the Russians would seize the gulf of Finland. Brandenburg–Prussia was not formally involved, but allowed allied troops to pass through its territory. Conditions looked propitious, for other major conflicts either had ended (Ryswick in 1697, Carlowitz in 1699) or were close to finishing (as by the Treaty of Constantinople between Russia and Turkey in 1700). There were no complicating impediments to forestall the allies, who anticipated a tough but victorious war.

## THE NORTHERN WAR

### The International Situation on the Eve of War

What about the condition of Sweden, and its hold upon its Baltic empire? Although defeated at Fehrbellin in 1675 and suffering the temporary loss of Bremen, Verden, Stettin and islands in the Baltic to Denmark and Brandenburg, Sweden was rescued by its ally France which, in 1679, forced Denmark and Brandenburg to restore these conquests. However, the implication was clear: Sweden could not preserve its Baltic supremacy without the help of a powerful ally. When relations with France soured in 1680 (as one of the Reunions, Louis XIV seized the Duchy of Deux-Ponts near Metz to which Charles XI of Sweden had a dynastic claim), Charles XI looked to the United Provinces as his main ally. Dutch prestige stood high after the Peace of Nijmegen, and Dutch ships were still the most common in the Baltic; both countries had an interest in preserving peace in that region. By the Treaty of the Hague (1681), they agreed on mutual assistance in time of war; however, when the War of the League of Augsburg began, Sweden declared itself neutral and remained so throughout the war, enabling it to mediate the Peace of Ryswick.

Shortly before it was signed, Charles XI died. His son and successor, Charles XII, was only fifteen. His youth and inexperience was one more factor convincing Peter I and his allies that the time was right to launch a concerted assault on the Swedish Baltic possessions. In the event, Charles XII proved to be a military commander of genius, comparable with the great Gustavus Adolphus himself. Although young, he was familiar with the demands of military life. His father personally had supervised his training, concentrating on generalship, military organization and administration. If there were any areas in which Charles's education was deficient, it was in politics and diplomacy. When he became king in 1697 the Riksdag conferred full sovereignty on him, and at his coronation he took no oath (an omission which implied that he was not bound by obligations to his subjects); yet even though he possessed more powers than most other monarchs, he consistently failed to exploit them in the realms of political and diplomatic dealing, preferring to rely on force. There were occasions during the Northern War when a more politically astute leader would have trusted his diplomats to secure advantageous peace terms, but Charles XII was wedded to war as the prime instrument of action; the harsh terms on which Sweden eventually had to settle in 1721 could have been avoided.

A key figure in the war, and the principal ally of Peter I in its early stages, was Frederick-Augustus of Saxony, recently elected king of Poland. When King John III Sobieski died in 1696, sixteen candidates presented themselves for election. The three most serious contenders were John III's son James, the French candidate François-Louis, prince de Conti, and Frederick-Augustus of Saxony who was backed by Peter. After an election marked by intrigue, threats and bribery (Frederick-Augustus pawned his jewellery and distributed the proceeds among the electors), the elector of Saxony was chosen; he converted from Lutheranism to Catholicism and was crowned Augustus II of Poland, 15 September 1697. However, in his discussions with Peter regarding an anti-Swedish coalition, he negotiated as elector of Saxony. Poland was inherently unstable (the magnates of Lithuania were in a state of almost permanent civil war), and to have committed the kingdom to a Russian alliance would have exacerbated an already dangerous situation. The tragedy for Poland was that, although it was nominally neutral during the Northern War, a high proportion of the fighting took place on its territory, which once again was devastated as armies crossed, recrossed and fought within the country.

## The Northern War: Part I, 1700–1709

In 1700 the allies began their campaigns against Sweden, and the first troops to move were those of Saxony, which crossed Poland and attacked Swedish Livonia, the port of Riga being the target. However, Charles XII decided to leave Riga to defend itself, and concentrate on removing the weakest of his enemies, Denmark. Before he did so, he entered into an accord with William III of England. In a remarkably audacious campaign assisted by an Anglo-Dutch fleet, Charles crossed the Sound, threatened Copenhagen and forced Frederick IV of Denmark to make peace at Travendal, 28 August 1700. Charles then proceeded to Livonia with the intention of relieving Riga from its Saxon besiegers, but he heard that Peter I had advanced on Narva in the Gulf of Finland. Against the advice of his generals, he marched his troops for a week through wasteland and reached Narva on 19 November. Next day he attacked the Russian encampment and all but annihilated the enemy. Charles lost less than 2,000 men. His generals advised him to pursue the Russians and remove them from the war as effectively as he had the Danes, but Charles refused. He dared not leave Augustus II besieging Riga, for if Riga fell while Charles was deep inside Russia, the Saxons could attack him from the rear. Thus, he returned to Livonia, cleared it of Saxon troops by the summer of 1701 and occupied the Polish Duchy of Courland. The first eighteen months of the war went emphatically in Sweden's favour. The defeat at Fehrbellin (1675) had been more than compensated for, and to all appearances Swedish ascendancy was confirmed.

William III of England counselled Charles to make peace with Augustus II. This would secure Sweden's victories and leave Russia diplomatically isolated; the tsar too might then sue for peace. However, the self-confident Charles rejected the advice and in 1702 invaded Poland with the intention of driving Augustus from the throne. If he succeeded, Augustus would have to rely exclusively on his Saxon resources, and Charles had no doubt that he was capable of overwhelming the Saxons. Charles entered Warsaw in 14 May 1702, and in July routed Augustus's Polish–Saxon force at Klissow. A few weeks later he took Cracow. Peace talks took place, mediated by Emperor Leopold I, but came to nothing. Over the next two years, Charles and Augustus continued fighting in Poland. The campaigns were brutal and destructive, and added to the anarchy which hit Poland as Polish and Lithuanian magnates fought each other. After the Swedish victory at Pultusk and capture of Thorn in 1703, rebellion began in the Polish Ukraine. In 1704 the cardinal of Warsaw called a specially convened assembly of aristocrats – the Confederation of Warsaw – to discuss Augustus's position. Charles XII urged

it to deprive Augustus of the throne, but the assembly was of a mind
to do so independently of any prompting from Sweden. In February
1704 it announced that Augustus II had forfeited the crown of
Poland. The diet met and elected as king the Polish-born, but
Swedish-backed, Stanislaus Leszczynski.

It had taken Charles four years to overthrow Augustus, but Peter I
had used the opportunity to strengthen his hold on the eastern ex-
tremity of the Gulf of Finland. In 1703 he began the construction of
St Petersburg, and in June defeated a Swedish force at Systerbäck.
He proceeded to devastate parts of Estonia and Livonia as a preliminary to another attack on Narva. Russian forces even penetrated as far
as Lithuania, forcing Charles XII to devote the autumn of 1705 and
spring of 1706 to expelling them. Once that had been accomplished,
Charles returned to his main objective, the invasion of Saxony. In
August 1706 he crossed the Vistula, cut through Saxony and by
September was almost at Leipzig. Augustus conceded defeat and
sought peace. By the Treaty of Altranstädt (24 September 1706), he
renounced his claim to the throne of Poland and broke off his ties
with Russia.

Charles's victories were attracting attention in western Europe,
where the War of the Spanish Succession was being fought. Representatives of various governments (including the duke of Marlborough on behalf of the allies) travelled to Altranstädt to gauge his
purposes. Although Charles disclaimed any intention of intervening
in that war, he did enter into a dispute with Emperor Joseph I which,
Britain and the United Provinces feared, might drive Charles into the
arms of the French. Joseph I was persecuting Protestants in his hereditary lands by closing their churches and multiplying the civil dis-
abilities under which Protestants lived. As long as he limited his
actions to Habsburg patrimonial lands he broke no treaty commitments, but he extended the oppression to Silesia where Protestant
religious liberties had been guaranteed by the Peace of Westphalia.
The Silesian Protestants appealed to Charles XII, and the threat
arose of Swedish intervention in Silesia. The British and Dutch governments urged the emperor to resolve the matter quickly. By
the Convention of Altranstädt (1 September 1707), Joseph restored
Protestant rights in Silesia and allowed the Swedish army right of
passage through that province.

With Poland under his indirect authority and Saxony out of the
war, Charles XII turned to his last enemy, Peter I of Russia. He
decided upon the most perilous campaign of his reign: an invasion of

Russia with Moscow as the target. Among the many problems to be overcome was the maintenance of lines of communication between Poland – from where Charles intended launching the invasion – and his army once it reached Russia. He found the solution in an unusual itinerary. Instead of taking the obvious and shortest route to Moscow, due east via Vilnius and Smolensk, he opted for a southern loop through the Ukraine. There he would be joined by Ivan Mazepa, leader of the Ukrainian Cossacks, who promised to provide up to 100,000 men. With the Cossacks protecting Charles's communications with Poland, he would lead this huge force against Moscow from the south. While Charles was executing these manoeuvres, his lieutenant, Count Adam Lewenhaupt, governor of Riga, would secure Courland against Russian attack and then march to meet Charles on the Dnieper.

Charles began the invasion early in 1708 and in July defeated a Russian army at Holowczn, a victory which opened the way to the Dnieper. From this point on, however, the campaign ran into difficulties. The retreating Russians adopted a scorched earth policy, destroying everything behind them. As Charles's army advanced it ran short of supplies, and to add to its difficulties the relief army led by Lewenhaupt was defeated by Peter I and lost the artillery intended for Charles. Peter's forces also attacked and dispersed the Cossacks. When Mazepa joined Charles at Horki in November, he brought not 100,000, but only about 1,300 soldiers to join the Swedes. The plan to attack Moscow was now unrealistic, and retreat along the original path of invasion too dangerous. Charles had no option but to spend the winter of 1708–9 in the Ukraine. This turned into the harshest winter in over a hundred years. Cold, hunger and disease reduced Charles's army from 50,000 to 28,000 by the spring of 1709. In May 1709, he resumed his march south. His intention was to take the Russian fortress at Poltava and hold it until reinforcements came from Poland and Sweden.

He began the siege of Poltava at the end of May, but Peter arrived with a relieving force which attacked and harried the depleted Swedish army. Charles decided on a pitched battle. It was fought on 28 June 1709. Outnumbered and outgunned, the Swedes were vanquished and their infantry all but annihilated; after two days of resistance the cavalry surrendered. Charles fled to Turkey with about 1,500 horsemen. When news of Poltava spread, the military prestige of the tsar soared as other governments assessed the implications of the Swedish disaster. Sweden itself had to come to terms with the problems posed by a king in exile. Some foreign responses to Poltava were immediate: in Poland, pro-Saxon factions turned on Stanislaus Leszczynski, drove him from the throne and restored Augustus II (1710); the Danes took the opportunity to attack the Swedes in Skania, albeit without success. The next few years were to show that Poltava belonged among that handful of battles in European warfare between 1600 and 1720 which can be deemed to have changed the course of an entire war.


## The Northern War: Part II, 1710–1721

While in Turkey, Charles devoted his energies to persuading the Ottoman government to reopen war against Russia, and in this he was supported by French diplomats. Louis XIV, hard pressed in the War of the Spanish Succession, viewed with alarm the eclipse of the traditional French clients, Poland and Sweden. The key to their recovery seemed to depend on the Russians being restrained. The Turks were responsive to the arguments of Charles and the French, for they too saw long-term dangers in a militarily expansive Russia. In 1711 the sultan declared war on Russia. He chose the moment well, for Peter I was preoccupied with Baltic affairs. Unable to send sufficient forces to deter the large army which the Turks gathered, he quickly signed peace at Prut (22 July 1711) and surrendered Azov. Success against Russia motivated Turkey in its attempt to restore its position in the Balkans, an episode which led to the Treaty of Passarowitz (1718) (see above, pp. 277–8). On the other hand, at Prut the Turks secured nothing for Charles, who felt betrayed; he had wanted them to extract from Peter a guarantee of safe passage for Charles to Sweden.

That was not forthcoming until 1713. In 1712 the Turks declared war on Russia again, but a revolt in Mesopotamia forced them to withdraw from the war and agree with Russia the Treaty of Adrianople (1713). It repeated the terms of Prut, with some additions: peace was guaranteed for twenty-five years; Peter promised to respect the independence of Poland; he recognized the autonomy of the Ukrainian Cossacks; and he promised Charles safe passage through Poland to Sweden. Preparations could now be made, but ironically Charles rejected the Polish route. The Treaty of Utrecht opened up new possibilities, especially the Franco-Austrian settlement of 1714 by which the emperor allowed Charles to travel to Sweden via Hungary, Austria and Germany if he wished. After consultation with his ministers in Stockholm, Charles decided on this route and the preparations were made. He left Turkey in September and was home by the end of the year.

He faced a major crisis, for during his absence Sweden's enemies had been pursuing war vigorously. The Russians invaded Finland, Carelia, Estonia, Ingria and Livonia, threatening Sweden with the loss of the whole of its eastern Baltic possessions. In 1713 Prussia entered the war, seizing Stettin and West Pomerania; it also signed a treaty with Russia guaranteeing their mutual conquests. Denmark went to war with Sweden again, and Hanover had ambitions regarding the Swedish-held ports of Bremen and Verden. In 1715, George of Hanover – now also king of Britain – signed a pact of mutual recognition with Russia along the lines of the Russo-Prussian treaty. However, when he offered to Frederick William I of Prussia the services of a British fleet to protect the Prussian occupation of Stettin, he provoked political problems in London, where the cabinet and parliament protested that George had exceeded his authority.

Charles XII turned to the one power which might assist him, France. In April 1715 he signed an alliance with Louis XIV with the aim of recovering Stettin. However, Louis XIV died later in the year and the regent, the duc d'Orléans, was reluctant to risk being drawn into the Baltic conflict. As was seen above (p. 365), his chief priority was to establish harmonious relations with Britain and the United Provinces in the interests both of establishing international stability in Europe and of securing their support in the event of a succession problem in France. Thus, when Peter I, seeking to explain Russian intentions and calm western fears, went on a second European tour in 1717 which took him to France, the regent signed an accord with the tsar whereby France would use its influence to secure peace in the Northern War. The prospects of an end to war were raised when Charles XII was killed in battle in 1718. After his arrival in Sweden, he had raised another army and in 1717 had gone on the offensive by invading Norway. His aim was to detach it from Denmark in order to secure better terms from his enemies. His campaign continued into 1718, and in December he was with his army besieging the fortress of Fredriksten. During the fighting, on 11 December, he looked over the parapet of a trench and was shot through the head by a bullet from the fortress. Like Gustavus Adolphus he died in battle, but unlike Gustavus he left his kingdom militarily weak and financially bankrupt.

Charles's sister, Ulrica Leonora, was elected queen and she authorized her ministers to seek peace. Overtures were made to Britain, Hanover, Prussia and Denmark, and by the treaties of Stockholm

(20 February 1719 and 1 February 1720), peace was signed with Hanover and Prussia. The former secured Bremen and Verden from Sweden, while Prussia retained part of West Pomerania including Stettin. Peace with Denmark was signed at Copenhagen on 3 July 1720. Sweden kept Wismar and part of West Pomerania, but relinquished Holstein. Sweden also lost its exemption from tolls in the Sound. The final peace was signed with Russia at Nystadt on 30 August 1721. Sweden suffered extensive territorial losses. Russia kept Ingria, Estonia, Livonia, part of Finland and the fortress of Viborg in return for a financial indemnity and a promise not to intervene in Swedish domestic affairs.

The Treaty of Nystadt brought the Northern War to an end and confirmed that strategic changes had taken place in the Baltic. The era of Swedish domination was over. Charles XII's determination to continue fighting had exhausted the financial and economic resources of his kingdom, leaving an immense task of reconstruction to be undertaken. Nevertheless, Sweden remained a considerable power, and should not be written off as being of no further consequence. In place of the former imperium, a balance of power had emerged in the Baltic, although the question of its permanence remained open. At the eastern end, Russia was the principal beneficiary, having secured extensive provinces and ports. The construction of St Petersburg was proceeding, and it was evident that the future history of the Baltic would be influenced to a considerable extent by Russian intentions. Russian success owed much to the military reforms of Peter. He had introduced conscription, constructed a Baltic fleet, established a school of navigation at Moscow in 1701 and a naval academy at St Petersburg in 1715. Whilst Russian forces remained traditional in many respects, they were sufficiently modernized to hold their own against the Swedes, Poles and Turks. The Prussians too could be well satisfied with the outcome of the war. Prussia had chosen its moment of intervention carefully, and had limited its ambitions territorially. Stettin was a rich prize. As one of the most prosperous ports in the Baltic, it enriched the coffers of the king of Prussia, but also provided him with a base from which to launch future military expeditions should circumstances require. Denmark too had preserved its vital interests. The renunciation by Sweden of claims to Holstein removed a major source of conflict, and Denmark's hold on the Sound not only was confirmed, but was rendered even more profitable by the abolition of Sweden's exemption from tolls. The conflict in the Mediterranean, arising out of Spain's attempts to recover its loss of

Italy at Utrecht, came to an end with the Treaty of London (1720). After agreement at Nystadt in 1721, Europe as a whole was in an extraordinary and remarkable condition of peace.

### Responses to War in Poland, Sweden and Russia

The Northern War had repercussions in all the belligerent states, three of which should be noted in the concluding section of this discussion. First there was Poland. The restoration of Augustus II failed to bring stability to the country. On the contrary, he and the Saxon faction inflicted brutal reprisals on his opponents, who formed a defensive Confederation of Tarnogród (1715) with the aim of driving Augustus from the throne. A civil war broke out, and for a time it looked as if the Confederate forces might achieve their aim. Peter I intervened to save Augustus, but demanded a price. Convinced that Poland was irredeemably anarchic, Peter placed it under his 'protection' in 1717 by imposing a settlement on the Polish diet. Augustus II was confirmed as king, but the Saxon army would leave Poland and the diet promised to limit the size of the Polish army. This devastated country achieved respite from civil war only by submitting to *de facto* Russian overlordship.

The constitutional and political complexion of Sweden was changed by the war. A reaction set in against the powers of a monarch who could determine policy alone, even though far distant in Turkey. As a preliminary, Ulrica Leonora abdicated in 1720 in favour of her husband, the prince of Hesse, who assumed the title Frederick I. The Riksdag then followed the example of the English parliament in 1689 and 1714, by defining and limiting the powers of the crown and enhancing those of the Riksdag itself. That body continued to be composed of four estates – nobles, clergy, burghers and peasants – but for a measure to become law, it now required the consent of three estates. Thereby, the lower orders or estates could block 'sectional' legislation by the upper orders. Each estate was presided over by a speaker or chairman elected annually, the speaker of the House of Nobles presiding when the estates met together. Supreme executive, legislative and judicial authority was vested in a Secret Committee of fifty nobles, fifty clergy, twenty-five burghers and (occasionally) twenty-five peasants. The committee initiated legislation, appointed ministers, controlled foreign and domestic policy and acted as a supreme court of appeal. The monarch was reduced to a figurehead. In short, a constitutional revolution occurred in Sweden; it was made necessary by the bitter experience of a long and destructive war.

In Russia, the triumphant Peter I was in no such danger (after Nystadt, the Russian senate hailed him as 'Father of the Fatherland, Peter the Great, and Emperor of all Russia'); on the contrary, it was he who imposed radical change on his subjects. Even during the war he had imposed reforms on an astonishing scale, and continued to do so to the end of his reign. As autocrat, he alone created law and decided policy, but to improve their implementation, he supplanted many of the existing administrative procedures with new ones. At the centre, in 1711, he created a small executive council, the Senate, through which he ruled. For the administration of the country he adopted Swedish models. In 1718 he created the first administrative college, and by the time of his death in 1725 ten were in existence. Sweden was also the inspiration behind his reform of provincial administration. In 1708 Russia was divided into eight provinces (eleven in 1718), which in turn were subdivided into counties. These were the basic units in which taxation was collected, the principal innovation being the introduction of a poll tax in 1717. This proved an immense undertaking, for nobody knew how many subjects Peter had. He ordered a census which, in the face of much popular resistance, was driven through by force. The poll tax was fully operative by 1724. Municipal government and administration were brought under central control. In 1721 a college was set up to oversee all the municipalities; it was based in St Petersburg, whose functions as capital city were expanding. Justice was reorganized, the country being divided into eleven judicial areas corresponding to the provinces; courts were established in these areas, but were subject to a central College of Justice founded in 1719. Reform extended to economic affairs. A College of Manufactures was created in 1719 to support selected industries, especially those serviceable to war.

One institution which Peter was determined to subject to state authority was the church. His personal religious commitments were probably as serious as those of most of his subjects, and like Louis XIV in France and Joseph I in Austria, he could not abide religious divergence. He subjected the Old Believers to unremitting persecution, driving them to Siberia and beyond. Yet in his attitude to the reformed Orthodox church bequeathed by Nikon, he was equally resolute that it should be turned into a branch of the state. To that end he issued the Ecclesiastical Regulation in 1721. It laid down in

**Figure 15**  Church of the Trinity, Moscow

minute detail the duties of monastic and parish clergy, and required them to take an oath of loyalty to the state. It abolished the office of patriarch, replacing it with a bureaucratic institution, the Holy Synod, which served as a Ministry of Religious Affairs under another name. Composed of three bishops and nine clergy or monks, its members were nominated by Peter and its meetings were chaired by a state bureaucrat, the Chief Procurator. The Regulation forbade the foundation of any new monasteries or convents, and women under the age of fifty were debarred from becoming nuns. The Regulation met remarkably little resistance from the church, chiefly because the new measures did not touch on liturgy or doctrine. The Orthodox church adopted an attitude of acceptance towards the Regulation, and adapted itself to the environment which it created.

There is no question that many of Peter's reforms were expedients in response to war, but it would be a mistake to go no further in their interpretation. Modern scholarship stresses the emergence in Peter's mind of a political philosophy which places him among the forerunners of the Enlightened Despots of the later eighteenth century. He developed a concept of the state as an entity which, while comprising people and land, was superior to both; the state had its instruments of action (the governmental and administrative bodies created by Peter) and its servants, from the tsar down through the ranks of bureaucrats. It could be likened to a well-designed and efficiently run machine whose purpose was to organize and exploit the human and material resources of Russia, to the end that the country could overcome any challenges which it encountered. Modern scholarship also insists, however, that for all Peter's immense expenditure of energy, the results rarely matched the intention. Most reforms overlaid rather than replaced older habits. Russia remained overwhelmingly rooted in tradition and resistant to change. Nevertheless, this does not invalidate the earlier proposition, that the ideas underlying the Petrine programme constituted much more than pragmatic reactions to problems created by war; after all, some aspects of reform – for example, the legal – had nothing to do with war, but were essential to the good ordering of the state. The point may also be made that, in spite of the forces of inertia which frustrated many of his plans, and his abiding reliance on an often brutal coercion to effect change, Peter did inspire others with his vision; he was by no means alone in the wilderness. Leading aristocratic families such as Sheremetov and Golitsyn, and service nobility such as Krekchin and Saltykov, espoused the tsar's political philosophy; so did bureaucrats who served in organs of central and provincial administration. If any physical creation exemplified Peter's concept of the state, it was St Petersburg. Just as Versailles was the embodiment of Louis XIV's vision of France, so was St Petersburg the incarnation of a certain ideal of Russia. Its buildings were western in style; it was cosmopolitan (foreigners were not confined to the suburbs); it made no claims to religious significance; it was given over to government and commerce; it was the main Russian naval base in the Baltic; and it had lively secular entertainments in its theatres and music halls. Peter could not refashion Russia as a whole, but in St Petersburg he created a city which invited his successors to preserve the incentive towards constant reform. Yet we should be wary of contrasting too strongly St Petersburg and Moscow, or of depicting Moscow as representing the old and St Petersburg the new. Moscow continued to flourish and, as was stated above, it was the seat of a new school of mathematical and navigational studies. In many respects St Petersburg complemented rather than supplanted Moscow as the embodiment of Russia. It exemplified that theme in Petrine thought which sought to add the best of the new to the best of the old.

# Conclusion

The Interlude between the first and second parts of this book sum-marized the main themes of European history down to 1660; what should be stressed with regard to the decades between 1660 and 1720? Warfare lost none of its prominence in those years. The scale on which wars were fought continued to rise; so did attendant prob-lems of finance, the provision of ordnance and the maintenance of supplies. Lines of intricate defensive systems were built in strategically significant zones of Europe, many being in border regions; their location heightened the importance of frontiers in peace negoti-ations, and the acquisition or loss of relatively small areas of territory could totally alter a state's possession of chains of fortifications. The adjustments which states made to the pressures of war varied according to circumstance. In their respective lists of priorities, they had to decide on the importance of such issues as the size of the army or navy, recruitment of soldiers, the type and quality of weapons, financial reform and changes in the administration of the state.

The causes of wars lost none of their variety after 1660, a factor which rendered peace-making all the more difficult. Some wars were begun deliberately, some were accidental, while others began as op-portunistic adventures as states exploited each other's vulnerability. Dynastic claims continued to trigger war, and ideological consider-ations still played their part. Domestic affairs influenced the commit-ment of governments to war. This was especially the case of Britain and Ireland where, as a consequence of the 'Revolution' of 1688, William III propelled the kingdoms into the forefront of European conflict. In eastern Europe it was little short of impossible to distinguish foreign from civil war. The conflicts in Poland, Russia, the Ukraine and the Ottoman Empire interwove the domestic and the international to a such a degree that distinctions are rendered meaningless; and since civil conflict was endemic for long periods in eastern Europe, it is equally problematic to identify periods of peace as against war. In a sense, the very instability of eastern Europe was an effective deterrent against excessive intervention by central and western European states. The experience of Sweden was an object lesson. This country, whose armies earlier in the century had carried all before them, foundered in Poland and on the vast plains of Russia and the Ukraine. Warfare in eastern Europe made different technical demands from war in the west, and armies successful in one arena were not necessarily so in another. The Austrian Habsburgs appreciated this, and limited their ambitions in the east. They drove the Turks from Hungary, but refrained from any mission to 'liberate' the Balkans.

Another characteristic of the post-1660 decades was a resurgence of religious intolerance, much of it orchestrated by governments. The later chapters of this book have evoked state persecution of Protestants and Jansenists in France, Catholics and dissenters in Britain and Ireland, Old Believers in Russia, Protestants in Austria, Bohemia, Moravia and Silesia, and Catholics in Saxony. Moreover, penal legislation usually existed alongside popular religious tensions which could explode into such violent episodes as the Popish Plot in England. This widespread trend doubtless is to be explained by the continuing political suspicion shown by governments towards religious minorities and the effects of warfare in which the temptation for one country to foment religious dissidence and rebellion in that of an enemy was irresistible; the harsh socio-economic conditions of the late seventeenth century also contributed to a climate of religious conflict and persecution, and the desire by some governments to fulfil an ideal of the mono-confessional state played its part. However, although religious persecution was common, it did not go unchallenged. Some governments were practising a pragmatic religious toleration by the late 1600s (the United Provinces and Brandenburg–Prussia did so), and in the cosmopolitan ports of the Baltic, North Sea and Mediterranean, religious exclusivism was rare. Many German cities were multi-confessional, and upheld the kind of religious toleration that the imperial or free cities of the Holy Roman Empire had established in the sixteenth century. Thus, Frankfurt was predominantly a Lutheran city, yet Catholic churches and monasteries were permitted. Heidelberg possessed Calvinist, Lutheran and Catholic congregations. Moreover, if the journals recorded by English travellers on the continent are anything to go by, a climate of opinion was emerging which was beginning to make a connection between religious toleration and a flourishing economy. Edward Browne who travelled widely in Germany in the 1670s, Thomas Penson who went to the Netherlands in 1690, and Ellis Veryard who travelled through the Netherlands, France, Spain, Italy and the Levant at the end of the century, observed that towns and regions which practised religious toleration were notably more prosperous than those which demanded religious conformity; and to their empirical and critical eye, causative links existed between these conditions.[1] On a more abstract plane, a figure such as Pierre Bayle, the son of a French pastor, who personally experienced persecution from Catholic and Protestant alike, advocated religious toleration and freedom of conscience as estimable principles in themselves. He used his *Dictionnaire historique et critique* (1697) as a vehicle for the propagation of such views and exerted a palpable influence on Enlightenment thought in the next century.

The activities of the state after 1660 continued along lines already apparent earlier in the century. The intervention by governments in the lives of their subjects continued unabated, especially in the realm of finance and its administrative apparatus. Escalating costs of war compelled governments to continue extracting money from their subjects in the form of direct and indirect taxes (in which regard, new types of tax were devised), voluntary and forced loans, manipulations of the currency and other time-honoured devices. Bureaucracies steadily expanded, notably in Prussia and Russia, and although they remained elementary by comparison with the later eighteenth and nineteenth centuries, they were unmistakable harbingers of the future. 'Absolute' monarchs in France, Spain, parts of Germany and Scandinavia still made exclusive claims to sovereignty and the powers that accompanied it, but took care to collaborate as much as possible with the social, and increasingly the economic, elites whose consent was a practical, if not theoretical, prerequisite to effective rule. Just as religious intolerance found its critics, so did 'absolute' monarchy. In the France of Louis XIV, Jansenists regarded his sovereign claims to be grossly inflated, while, within Louis's own court, the duc de Saint Simon, whose memoirs are the most detailed and perceptive, if subjectively prejudiced, account of court and government, experienced growing disillusion with absolute monarchy as practised by the Sun King. Perhaps the most thorough-going critique of contemporary monarchic practice, and even ideology, emerged in England, where John Locke's *Two Treatises of Government* (1690), published in the aftermath of '1688', placed the monarch firmly in a contractual relationship with his subjects. To Locke, whose ideas rapidly acquired currency on the continent and in the American colonies, such notions as 'sovereignty belongs to the king alone', 'the king is answerable only to God', 'subjects may not resist the will even of an unjust monarch' could no longer be tolerated. If monarchic or, indeed, any form of government were to flourish in the next century, it must discard absolutist claims and language, and acknowledge not only that it had obligations to its subjects, but that it was answerable to them for its conduct. European monarchs of all hues had always acknowledged the first of these assertions, but not the second; it was to the challenge of the second that they would have to respond in future.

In the realm of ideology, that response increasingly looked to the sciences for inspiration. Influenced by the kinds of scientific changes referred to in this book, monarchic regimes and their servants came to think of the state in scientific terms: as an entity whose legitimacy and effectiveness rested on the extent to which it corresponded to models of the universe derived from Newtonian science. In itself, there was nothing novel about taking the universe as the source of an analogy of the state: this had been a favourite theme of sixteenth-century French writers. However, the Newtonian universe was not that of the sixteenth century, and an analogy based upon the Newtonian model was very different from its predecessors. Now, the behaviour of objects in the universe was conditioned, not by the constant intervention of God and angels, but by forces of gravity acting between the objects themselves. As an analogy of the state, it implied a political theory close to that propounded by Locke, for a modern kingdom could be seen as a micro-universe wherein the monarch, rather like a star orbited by satellites, but endlessly dependent on their mutual gravitational forces, had legitimate expectations of his subjects, but was answerable to them for his own conduct. By acknowledging such a 'contract', monarchic or, indeed, any form of government could be explained as 'natural' or 'scientific'. Like the Lockian contract theory to which they corresponded, 'scientific' images of the state were not easily compatible with older ideologies based on religion, history, law and custom, and, as the eighteenth century progressed, tensions between the traditional and the 'scientific' were to transpire. In the particular historical context of the late 1600s and early 1700s, however, modern science provided a rich source of arguments and correspondences with which to legitimate modern regimes in modern terms.

This book terminates around the year 1720, and while there is a certain arbitrariness in so doing, the choice can be justified on several counts. One is by reference to international relations. By this time, statesmen were seeking to reorder Europe around treaties of peace which, taken together, constituted a comprehensive settlement of the continent. Utrecht (1713), Passarowitz (1718), London (1720), Nystadt (1721), and their accompanying treaties, incorporated most of Europe into their provisions, and aspired to create an international context defined by principles of balance and restraint. The main contours of peace settlements were, of course, dependent on the outcomes of wars, but also were fashioned by the skills of negotiators. One thread running through the later chapters of this book has been that of peace congresses, their organization and conduct. This is a subject that deserves closer investigation, but perhaps sufficient indications have been given to confirm that, between 1660 and 1721, European statesmen were becoming increasingly sophisticated in their handling of congresses, and conceived them not just as occasions to resolve particular conflicts, but as forums wherein a new international order gradually could be constructed. The search for, and preservation of, such an order was being maintained also by diplomatic contact on a more systematic basis than before. Although diplomatic services remained small and primitive by comparison with those of the present day, they testified to a growing conviction that the regular exchange of ambassadors, envoys, residents and other categories of representative could help to defuse international tensions. The statesmen of the early 1700s made commendable progress towards the goal of universal peace, for without suggesting that Europe after 1720 enjoyed decades of undiminished bliss, it did regulate its international affairs with less recourse to war than previously. Major conflicts certainly occurred – the Wars of the Polish Succession (1733–8) and Austrian Succession (1740–8), and the Seven Years War (1756–63) – but a noticeable curtailment of the incidence of warfare was achieved.

The domestic strategies espoused by governments also support the contention that by 1720 a new era was opening. Most countries were now giving the highest priority to socio-political stability and economic prosperity within the state after the agitation of the preceding few decades; it was a task requiring habits of self-restraint. Nowhere was this more true than in Britain and Ireland. The mid-1680s and early 1690s forced upon those kingdoms a number of substantial constitutional adjustments whose consequences, with their considerable adversarial potential, threatened to revive socio-political instability down to 1715 and beyond. Although the fiscal burden of war forced the crown to turn the British and Irish parliaments into permanent assemblies, by the turn of the century relations between those two bodies were tense. The British parliament claimed primacy over its Irish counterpart, including the right to legislate for Ireland. The Irish parliament denied the claim, and although neither side gave way on the question of principle, the British assembly generally refrained from asserting its 'right' in the interest of avoiding a crisis. Both crown and the two parliaments sought to moderate the political atmosphere of the 1690s and early 1700s by avoiding courses of action which, by their nature, would lead to conflict. By this time, nascent political parties – Tories (who defended the established Anglican Church and prerogatives of the crown) and Whigs (who advocated toleration for all Protestants, and upheld the interest of the individual in civil and ecclesiastical affairs) – had emerged; and in Robert Walpole, First Lord of the Treasury, Britain had a political leader whose exercise of power and management of parliament have earned him the attribute of being the first prime minister. Party discipline and the manipulation of the British and Irish parliaments by the government helped to tranquillize the tenor of political life, and in their different ways the governments of France, Sweden, Spain, the United Provinces, and indeed most European states, were seeking to do likewise.

The years around 1720 may be seen as pivotal in another, although admittedly somewhat amorphous, sense. A generation of intellectuals was coming to maturity which was not only critical of many political, religious and economic assumptions of the seventeenth century, but was working towards new principles upon which to found European civilization. Such writers as Montesquieu, Swift and Voltaire were subjecting received social, religious and political attitudes to radical reassessment, and advocating the abandonment of some hitherto axiomatic truths. The famous thesis advanced by Paul Hazard in 1935[2] still has much to commend it: that between the 1680s and 1710s, the 'European mind' underwent a transformation as it loosened its ties to a classical past, embraced philosophical and religious scepticism, and advocated socio-political values based on scientific and rationalist systems of thought. By the 1720s, a growing band of commentators was calling for a Europe in which social hierarchies would be governed by moral criteria, not accidents of birth, Christianity would be based on humility and reason, not dogma and tradition, law would be rooted in nature, not the power of political factions, and economic prosperity would be disseminated among the many, not limited to the few. Hazard's thesis doubtless now looks over-schematic, and many of the features which he attributed to the 1680s and the decades immediately following can also be detected in earlier periods, but its broad intent remains persuasive: to demonstrate that by 1720 a tide of radical socio-political criticism was rising in Europe and would, in due course, lead to a fundamental reorientation of European intellectual life. This latter phenomenon, which we now call the Enlightenment, expressed itself through novels, plays, poetry, music and painting as well as epoch-making political and economic treatises, but its first manifestations were appearing by the 1720s. This new movement was to urge Europeans to question all tradition and have confidence in the power of reason to construct a new and enlightened Europe; and, by implication, it called on them to leave behind much of what had formed the character of the Europe of the seventeenth century.

# European Rulers

## Papacy

| Pope | Life | Reign |
| --- | --- | --- |
| Clement VIII | 1536–1605 | 1592–1605 |
| Leo XI | 1535–1605 | 1605 |
| Paul V | 1552–1621 | 1605–21 |
| Gregory XV | 1554–1623 | 1621–23 |
| Urban VIII | 1568–1644 | 1623–44 |
| Innocent X | 1574–1655 | 1644–55 |
| Alexander VII | 1599–1667 | 1655–67 |
| Clement IX | 1600–69 | 1667–69 |
| Clement X | 1590–1676 | 1670–76 |
| Innocent XI | 1611–89 | 1676–89 |
| Alexander VIII | 1610–91 | 1689–91 |
| Innocent XII | 1615–1700 | 1691–1700 |
| Clement XI | 1649–1721 | 1700–21 |

## Holy Roman Empire

| Emperor | Life | Reign | Relationship to predecessor |
| --- | --- | --- | --- |
| Charles V | 1500–58 | 1519–56 | Grandson of Maximilian I |
| Ferdinand I | 1503–64 | 1556–64 | Brother |
| Maximilian II | 1527–76 | 1564–76 | Son |
| Rudolf II | 1552–1612 | 1576–1612 | Son |
| Matthias | 1557–1619 | 1612–19 | Brother |

## Holy Roman Empire (*cont.*)

| Emperor | Life | Reign | Relationship to predecessor |
|---|---|---|---|
| Ferdinand II | 1578–1637 | 1619–37 | Cousin |
| Ferdinand III | 1608–57 | 1637–57 | Son |
| Leopold I | 1640–1705 | 1658–1705 | Son |
| Joseph I | 1678–1711 | 1705–11 | Son |
| Charles VI | 1685–1740 | 1711–40 | Brother |

## France

| King | Life | Reign | Relationship to predecessor |
|---|---|---|---|
| Henri IV | 1553–1610 | 1589–1610 | Distant cousin to Henri III |
| Louis XIII | 1601–43 | 1610–43 | Son |
| Louis XIV | 1638–1715 | 1643–1715 | Son |
| Louis XV | 1710–74 | 1715–74 | Great-grandson |

## Spain

| King | Life | Reign | Relationship to predecessor |
|---|---|---|---|
| Philip III | 1578–1621 | 1598–1621 | Son of Philip II |
| Philip IV | 1605–65 | 1621–65 | Son |
| Charles II | 1661–1700 | 1665–1700 | Son |
| Philip V | 1683–1746 | 1700–24, 1724–46 | Distant cousin |

## Portugal

| King | Life | Reign | Relationship to predecessor |
|---|---|---|---|
| Philip III of Spain | | | |
| Philip IV of Spain | | | |
| John IV | 1604–56 | 1640–56 | None |
| Alfonso VI | 1643–83 | 1656–83 | Son |
| Peter II | 1648–1706 | 1683–1706 | Brother |
| John V | 1689–1750 | 1706–50 | Son |

## England, Scotland, Ireland

| Monarch | Life | Reign | Relationship to predecessor |
|---|---|---|---|
| James I/VI | 1566–1625 | 1603–25 | Second cousin to Elizabeth I |
| Charles I | 1600–49 | 1625–49 | Son |
| Charles II | 1630–85 | 1660–85 | Son |
| James II | 1633–1701 | 1685–88 | Brother |
| William III and | 1650–1702 | 1688–1702 | Nephew |
| Mary II | 1662–94 | 1688–94 | Daughter |
| Anne | 1665–1714 | 1702–14 | Sister of Mary II |
| George I | 1660–1727 | 1714–27 | Distant cousin |

## Denmark

| King | Life | Reign | Relationship to predecessor |
|---|---|---|---|
| Christian IV | 1577–1648 | 1588–1648 | Son of Frederick II |
| Frederick III | 1609–70 | 1648–70 | Son |
| Christian V | 1646–99 | 1670–99 | Son |
| Frederick IV | 1671–1730 | 1699–1730 | Son |

## Sweden

| Monarch | Life | Reign | Relationship to predecessor |
|---|---|---|---|
| Charles IX | 1550–1611 | 1604–11 | Brother of John III |
| Gustavus II Adolphus | 1594–1632 | 1611–32 | Son |
| Christina | 1626–89 | 1632–54 | Daughter |
| Charles X | 1622–60 | 1654–60 | Cousin |
| Charles XI | 1655–97 | 1660–97 | Son |
| Charles XII | 1682–1718 | 1697–1718 | Son |
| Ulrica | 1688–1741 | 1718–20 | Sister |

## Poland (kings elected)

| King | Life | Reign | Relationship to predecessor |
|---|---|---|---|
| Sigismund III | 1566–1632 | 1587–1632 | |
| Wladislaus IV | 1595–1648 | 1632–48 | Son |
| John Casimir | 1609–72 | 1648–68 | Brother |
| Michael Wisniecki | 1640–73 | 1669–73 | None |
| John III Sobieski | 1624–96 | 1674–96 | None |
| Augustus II [i] | 1670–1733 | 1697–1704 | None |
| Stanislaus Leszczynski | 1677–1766 | 1704–9 | None |
| Augustus II [ii] | | 1710–33 | |

## Russia

| Tsar | Life | Reign | Relationship to predecessor |
|---|---|---|---|
| Fedor I | 1557–98 | 1584–98 | Son of Ivan IV |
| Boris Godunov | 1552–1605 | 1598–1605 | Brother-in-law |
| Fedor II | 1589–1605 | 1605 | Son |
| Dmitri | ? | 1605–6 | Unknown [claimed to be half-brother of Fedor I] |
| Basil Shuisky | d.1612 | 1606–10 | Distant relative of Fedor I |
| Michael Romanov | 1596–1645 | 1613–45 | None |
| Alexis | 1629–76 | 1645–76 | Son |
| Fedor III | 1661–82 | 1676–82 | Son |
| Ivan V | 1666–96 | 1682–96 | Joint tsars; brother and |
| Peter I | 1672–1725 | 1682–1725 | half-brother of Fedor III |

## Ottoman Empire

| Sultan | Life | Reign | Relationship to predecessor |
|---|---|---|---|
| Mehmed III | 1566–1603 | 1595–1603 | |
| Ahmed I | 1589–1617 | 1603–17 | Son |
| Mustafa I [i] | 1591–1639 | 1617–18 | Brother |
| Osman II | d.1622 | 1618–22 | Son of Ahmed I |
| Mustafa I [ii] | | 1622–23 | |
| Murad IV | 1611–39 | 1623–39 | Nephew of Mustafa I |
| Ibrahim I | 1615–48 | 1639–48 | Brother |

## Ottoman Empire (*cont.*)

| Sultan | Life | Reign | Relationship to predecessor |
|--------|------|-------|------------------------------|
| Mehmed IV | c.1641–91 | 1648–87 | Son |
| Suleiman II | 1641–91 | 1687–91 | Brother |
| Ahmed II | 1642–95 | 1691–95 | Brother |
| Mustafa II | 1664–1703 | 1695–1703 | Son of Mehmed IV |
| Ahmed III | 1673–1736 | 1703–30 | Brother |

# Significant Dates

| Year | Western Europe | Central and southern Europe | Northern and eastern Europe |
|---|---|---|---|
| 1598 | *France*: Edict of Nantes *Spain*: death of Philip II, succession of Philip III | | *Russia*: Boris Godunov tsar |
| 1600 | English East India Co. founded | | |
| 1602 | Dutch East Indies Co. founded | | |
| 1603 | *England*: death of Elizabeth I, succession of James I (James VI of Scotland) | | |
| 1604 | *England/Spain*: Peace of London *England*: Hampton Court Conference | | |
| 1605 | *England*: Gunpowder Plot | *Rome*: Paul V elected pope | *Russia*: death of Boris Godunov |
| 1606 | | | *Russia*: Basil Shuisky tsar |
| 1607 | First English colonies in Virginia | | |
| 1608 | France and United Provinces sign Treaty of the Hague | *Holy Roman Empire*: Evangelical Union formed | |

| 1609 | *Spain/United Provinces*: twelve-year truce *England/Ireland*: end of Nine Years War; beginning of Plantation of Ulster | *Holy Roman Empire*: Catholic League formed; Jülich–Cleves crisis *Bohemia*: Letter of Majesty *Italy*: Galileo first uses telescope | |
|------|------|------|------|
| 1610 | *France*: Henri IV assassinated, succession of Louis XIII | *Italy*: Galileo publishes *Siderius nuncius* | |
| 1611 | *England*: Authorized Version of the Bible | | *Sweden*: death of Charles IX, succession of Gustavus Adolphus |
| 1612 | | *Holy Roman Empire*: death of Rudolf II, succession of Matthias | |
| 1613 | | | *Russia*: Michael Romanov tsar |
| 1614 | | *Holy Roman Empire*: Treaty of Xanten | |
| 1615 | *France/Spain*: marriages of Louis XIII to Anne of Austria and Philip [IV] of Spain to Elisabeth of France | | |
| 1617 | | | *Sweden/Russia*: Peace of Stolbova *Ottoman Empire*: death of Ahmed I, succeeded by Mustafa I |
| 1618 | | *Bohemia*: Defenestration of Prague, beginning of Thirty Years War | *Russia/Poland*: war ends in truce *Ottoman Empire*: Mustafa I deposed, replaced by Osman |

| 1619 | | *Holy Roman Empire*: death of Matthias, Ferdinand II elected emperor | |
|------|---|---|---|
| 1620 | *France*: Béarn united to France; beginning of Huguenot rebellion | *Bohemia*: battle of White Mountain *Spain/Italy*: Spanish troops occupy Valtelline | |
| 1621 | *Spain/France*: Treaty of Madrid *Spain/United Provinces*: end of twelve-year truce; war renewed *Spain*: death of Philip III, succession of Philip IV | *Rome*: Gregory XV elected pope | |
| 1622 | *France*: Peace of Montpellier | | *Ottoman Empire*: Osman deposed, Mustafa I restored |
| 1623 | | *Rome*: Urban VIII elected pope | *Ottoman Empire*: Mustafa I replaced by Murad |
| 1624 | *France*: Richelieu becomes principal minister | | |
| 1625 | *England/France*: marriage of Charles [I] and Henriette-Marie of France *England*: death of James I/VI, succession of Charles I | | |
| 1626 | *France/Spain*: Treaty of Monzón | | |
| 1627 | *France*: siege of La Rochelle begins | *Italy*: Mantuan succession crisis | |
| 1628 | *England*: Buckingham assassinated *France*: La Rochelle surrenders | | |

| 1629 | *France*: Peace of Alès | *Holy Roman Empire*: Edict of Restitution; Peace of Lübeck | *Poland/Sweden*: Truce of Altmark |
|------|------|------|------|
| 1630 | *France/Holy Roman Empire*: Treaty of Ratisbon | | |
| 1631 | *France/Sweden*: Treaty of Bärwalde | *Italy*: Treaty of Cherasco *Holy Roman Empire*: Swedish victory at Breitenfeld | |
| 1632 | *France/Lorraine*: Treaty of Liverdun | *Holy Roman Empire*: Swedish victory at Lützen, death of Gustavus Adolphus *Italy*: Galileo publishes his *Dialogue* | *Sweden*: Christina becomes queen *Poland*: death of Sigismund III, succeeded by Wladislaus IV |
| 1633 | | *Germany/Holy Roman Empire*: League of Helibronn created *Italy*: trial of Galileo | |
| 1634 | | *Holy Roman Empire*: Wallenstein assassinated; imperial army defeats Swedes at Nördlingen | *Poland/Russia*: peace *Poland/Ottoman Empire*: truce |
| 1635 | *France/Spain*: France declares war on Spain | *Holy Roman Empire*: Peace of Prague | *Poland/Sweden*: peace |
| 1636 | *France/Holy Roman Empire*: Ferdinand II declares war on France *France*: rising of Croquants | | |
| 1637 | | *Holy Roman Empire*: death of Ferdinand II, election of Ferdinand III | |
| 1638 | *France*: birth of Louis XIV | | |
| 1639 | *France*: revolt of Nu-pieds | | *Ottoman Empire*: death of Murad, succeeded by Ibrahim |

| 1640 | *Spain*: revolts of Catalonia and Portugal<br>*Portugal*: John IV crowned king | *Holy Roman Empire*: Frederick-William becomes elector of Brandenburg | |
|------|------|------|------|
| 1641 | *England*: the Grand Remonstrance | | |
| 1642 | *France*: death of Richelieu, Mazarin enters royal council<br>*England*: Charles I wins victory at Edgehill | | |
| 1643 | *France*: death of Louis XIII, succession of Louis XIV; battle of Rocroi | | |
| 1644 | *England*: Charles I's army defeated at Marston Moor | *Holy Roman Empire*: negotiations begin in Westphalia<br>*Rome*: Innocent X elected pope | |
| 1645 | *England*: Laud executed; Charles I defeated at Naseby | *Austria/Ottoman Empire*: Peace of Vasvar | *Denmark/Sweden*: Peace of Brömsebro<br>*Russia*: death of Tsar Michael, succeeded by Alexis |
| 1647 | *United Provinces*: death of Frederick Henry, prince of Orange, succeeded by William II as stadtholder | *Italy*: revolts in Sicily and Naples | |
| 1648 | *Spain/United Provinces*: Spain recognizes Dutch independence<br>*France*: beginning of Frondes | *Holy Roman Empire*: Peace of Westphalia | *Denmark*: death of Christian IV, succeeded by Frederick III<br>*Ukraine*: rising of Cossacks<br>*Ottoman Empire*: Ibrahim succeeded by Mehmed IV |

| | | | |
|---|---|---|---|
| 1649 | *England/Ireland*: execution of Charles I; Cromwell invades Ireland *France*: Treaty of Rueil | | *Russia*: law code |
| 1650 | *Scotland*: battle of Dunbar *United Provinces*: death of William II *France*: Fronde of Princes begins | | |
| 1651 | *France*: majority of Louis XIV *England*: defeat of Charles II at Worcester; Navigation Act | | |
| 1652 | *France*: end of Parisian Fronde *Spain*: Barcelona retaken by Philip IV *England/United Provinces*: war begins | | |
| 1653 | *France*: Fronde at Bordeaux ends *England*: Cromwell becomes Lord Protector *United Provinces*: Johan de Witt becomes Grand Pensionary of Holland | | |
| 1654 | *England/United Provinces*: Peace of Westminster | | *Sweden*: Queen Christina abdicates, succession of Charles X |
| 1655 | *England/France*: Treaty of Westminister | *Rome*: Alexander VII elected pope | *Poland*: invaded by Rákóczy and Charles X of Sweden |
| 1656 | *Portugal*: death of John IV, succession of Alfonso VI | | *Ottoman Empire*: Venetian fleet defeats Turks in Dardanelles; |

| | | | |
|---|---|---|---|
| | | | Mehmed Köprölü becomes grand vizier |
| 1657 | *England/France*: alliance against Spain *England*: parliament offers crown to Cromwell | *Holy Roman Empire*: death of Ferdinand III | *Denmark/Sweden*: war begins |
| 1658 | *England*: death of Cromwell | *Germany/Holy Roman Empire*: League of the Rhine; Leopold I elected emperor | *Denmark/Sweden*: Treaty of Röskilde |
| 1659 | *France/Spain*: Treaty of the Pyrenees | | |
| 1660 | *France/Spain*: marriage of Louis XIV and Maria Teresa *England*: restoration of Charles II; foundation of Royal Society | | *Sweden/Denmark*: Peace of Oliva *Sweden*: death of Charles X, succession of Charles XI |
| 1661 | *France*: death of Mazarin; personal reign of Louis XIV begins *England*: Robert Boyle, *The Sceptical Chemist* | | |
| 1662 | *England/France*: Charles II sells Dunkirk to Louis XIV *France/United Provinces*: alliance *England*: Royal Society receives charter | | *Russia*: Copper Riots in Moscow |
| 1664 | *France*: East and West Indies Companies founded *England/United Provinces*: English seize New Amsterdam (New York) | *Austria*: battle of St Gotthard; Peace of Vasvar | |

| | | | |
|---|---|---|---|
| 1665 | *England/United Provinces*: war begins<br>*England*: plague in London<br>*Spain*: death of Philip IV, succession of Charles II | | *Denmark*: absolute monarchy confirmed |
| 1666 | *England*: fire of London<br>*France/England*: France declares war on England<br>*France*: Academy of Sciences founded | *Austria*: *Kommerzkollegium* founded | |
| 1667 | *France/Spain*: War of Devolution begins<br>*England/United Provinces*: Peace of Breda<br>*United Provinces*: 'concept of harmony' | *Rome*: Clement IX elected pope | *Russia*: rising of Stenka Razin |
| 1668 | *France/Austria*: secret treaty to partition Spanish empire<br>*France/Spain*: Treaty of Aix-la-Chapelle<br>*Spain/Portugal*: Peace of Lisbon | | |
| 1669 | *France*: Northern Company founded | | |
| 1670 | *England/France*: secret Treaties of Dover<br>*France*: Levant Company founded | *Rome*: Clement X elected pope<br>*Hungary*: Leopold I defeats rebels; *Kuruc* movement begins | |
| 1671 | *France/England*: secret treaty of mutual support | | *Russia*: execution of Stenka Razin |
| 1672 | *France/United Provinces*: Louis XIV invades republic; de Witt murdered; William III becomes stadtholder | | |

| 1673 | *Dutch War*: Spain joins war against France | | |
| 1674 | *England/United Provinces*: Peace of Westminster | | *Poland*: John III Sobieski elected king |
| 1675 | *France*: 'papier-timbré' revolt | *Dutch War*: defeat of Sweden at Fehrbellin | |
| 1676 | *Dutch War*: discussions begin in Nijmegen; French naval victory at Palermo | *Rome*: Innocent XI elected pope *Hungary*: Treaty of Warsaw between *Kuruc* movement and France | *Russia*: death of Tsar Alexis, succession of Fedor III |
| 1678 | *Dutch War*: Peace of Nijmegen *England/United Provinces*: Treaty of the Hague *England*: Popish Plot affair begins | | |
| 1679 | *Dutch War*: Treaty of Saint Germain between France, Sweden, Brandenburg | | |
| 1680 | | *France/Germany/ Spain*: Reunions continue | |
| 1681 | *United Provinces/ Sweden*: alliance to guarantee treaties of Westphalia and Nijmegen | | |
| 1682 | *France*: Assembly of clergy adopts Gallican articles | | *Russia*: death of Tsar Fedor III, succession of Ivan V and Peter I as co-tsars |
| 1683 | *France*: death of Colbert *France/Spain*: Spain declares war on France | *Austria*: Vienna besieged by Turks | |

|  |  |  |  |
|---|---|---|---|
|  | *United Provinces/ Sweden*: Treaty of the Hague |  |  |
| 1684 |  | *France/Germany/ Spain*: truce of Ratisbon *Italy*: Pope Innocent XI forms Holy League against Turks |  |
| 1685 | *France*: Edict of Fontainebleau revokes Edict of Nantes *England*: death of Charles II, succession of James II; Monmouth and Argyll rebellions |  |  |
| 1686 |  | *Germany*: League of Augsburg created *Hungary*: Charles V of Lorraine takes Buda from Turks |  |
| 1687 | *England*: James II issues Declaration of Indulgence; Isaac Newton publishes *Principia mathematica* | *Hungary*: Habsburgs become hereditary kings; battle of Mohács | *Ottoman Empire*: Venetians take Athens; Mehmed IV replaced by Suleiman II |
| 1688 | *England*: 'Glorious Revolution' | *France/Germany*: War of League of Augsburg begins *Brandenburg–Prussia*: death of Frederick William, succession of Frederick | *Ottoman Empire/ Holy League*: Belgrade taken by Holy League |
| 1689 | *England/Ireland*: Bill of Rights; James II lands in Ireland | *Germany*: England and United Provinces join League of Augsburg *Rome*: Alexander VIII elected pope | *Russia*: Regent Sophia overthrown by Peter I |
| 1690 | *Ireland*: battle of the Boyne |  |  |
| 1691 | *Ireland*: battle of Aughrim; Treaty of Limerick | *Rome*: Innocent XII elected pope | *Ottoman Empire*: Turks capture Belgrade; |

| | | | |
|---|---|---|---|
| | | | Suleiman II replaced by Ahmed II |
| 1694 | *England*: death of Mary II; Triennial Act | | |
| 1695 | | | *Ottoman Empire*: Ahmed II replaced by Mustafa II |
| 1696 | | | *Russia*: death of Tsar Ivan V, Peter I rules alone and takes Azov |
| | | | *Poland*: death of John III Sobieski |
| 1697 | Peace of Ryswick | | *Poland*: Frederick-Augustus of Saxony elected as Augustus II |
| | | | *Ottoman Empire/ Holy League*: battle of Zenta |
| | | | *Russia*: Peter I goes on tour of western Europe |
| 1698 | *Spanish Succession*: first treaty of partition between Louis XIV and William III | | |
| 1699 | | | *Ottoman Empire/ Holy League*: Peace of Carlowitz |
| 1700 | *Spanish Succession*: second treaty of partition; death of Charles II of Spain, succeeded by Philip V (duc d'Anjou) | *Rome*: Clement XI elected pope | *Russia/Ottoman Empire*: Peace of Constantinople; Northern War begins |
| 1701 | *Spanish Succession*: France seizes barrier forts; anti-French alliance formed | Brandenburg–Prussia becomes kingdom of Prussia | |
| | | *Holy Roman Empire/ Britain/United Provinces*: Treaty of the Hague | |

| 1702 | *England*: death of William III, succeeded by Anne War of the Spanish Succession begins | | |
|---|---|---|---|
| 1703 | | *Hungary*: Rákóczy revolt begins | *Russia*: Peter I founds St Petersburg *Ottoman Empire*: Mustafa II replaced by Ahmed III |
| 1704 | *Spanish Succession*: battle of Blenheim | | *Poland*: Augustus II deposed, Stanislaus Leszczynski elected king |
| 1705 | | *Holy Roman Empire*: death of Leopold I, succession of Joseph I | |
| 1706 | *Spanish Succession*: battles of Ramillies and Almanza | | *Sweden/Saxony*: Treaty of Altranstädt |
| 1707 | *England/Scotland*: parliamentary union | *Austria/Sweden*: Convention of Altranstädt | |
| 1708 | *Spanish Succession*: battle of Oudenaarde | | *Russia/Sweden*: battle of Holowczn |
| 1709 | *Spanish Succession*: battle of Malplaquet | | *Russia/Sweden*: battle of Poltava *Poland*: Stanislaus Leszczynski deposed |
| 1710 | | | *Poland*: Augustus II restored |
| 1711 | | *Hungary*: Peace of Szatmár *Holy Roman Empire*: death of Joseph I, succeeded by Charles VI | *Russia/Ottoman Empire*: Peace of Prut |

| | | | |
|---|---|---|---|
| 1713 | Peace of Utrecht | *Prussia*: death of Frederick I, succession of Frederick-William I *France/Rome*: bull *Unigenitus* issued | *Russia/Ottoman Empire*: Peace of Adrianople |
| 1714 | *Britain*: death of Queen Anne, succession of George I | *France/Holy Roman Empire*: Peace of Rastadt | |
| 1715 | *Britain*: rising of Jacobites *France*: death of Louis XIV, succession of Louis XV | | *Poland*: Confederation of Tarnogród |
| 1716 | *France/Britain*: alliance | | |
| 1717 | *Spain/Italy*: Triple Alliance of France, Britain, United Provinces to deter Spain in Italy | | *Ottoman Empire*: Eugene of Savoy takes Belgrade |
| 1718 | | | *Sweden*: death of Charles XII *Austria/Hungary/ Venice/Ottoman Empire*: Peace of Passarowitz |
| 1719 | *Spain/Italy*: France declares war on Spain | | *Northern War*: first treaty of Stockholm |
| 1720 | *Spain/Italy*: Treaty of London | | *Northern War*: second treaty of Stockholm; Treaty of Copenhagen |
| 1721 | | *Rome*: Innocent XIII elected pope | *Northern War*: Peace of Nystadt |

# Further Reading

Given the number and variety of the subjects covered in this book, a comprehensive bibliography is impractical. The following recommendations therefore are limited to major works which have appeared, generally in the English language, over the past twenty years or so. Most contain excellent bibliographies which can be consulted to supplement this present list. Major advances in the dissemination not only of bibliographical information, but of primary source material in history, have been made in recent years via the Internet. The websites of many university history departments contain links which can be explored with profit. An excellent bibliographical guide to most branches of history is available at the website of the Institute of Historical Research, University of London: http://www.history.ac.uk. Electronic databases and electronic journals are available on the Internet, but often through subscription. However, many academic and large public libraries provide access to such sources.

## General and Regional

Asch, R. G. and Birke, A. (eds), *Princes, Patronage and the Nobility: The Court at the Beginning of the Modern Age, c. 1450–1650* (Oxford, 1991).

Aston, T. (ed.), *Crisis in Europe, 1560–1660: Essays from Past and Present* (London, 1965).

Bergin, J. (ed.), *The Seventeenth Century: Europe, 1598–1715* (Oxford, 2000).

Bideleux, R. and Jeffries, I., *A History of Eastern Europe: Crisis and Change* (London, 1997).

Black, J., *The Rise of the European Powers, 1679–1793* (London, 1990).

Bonney, R., *The European Dynastic States, 1494–1660* (Oxford, 1991).

Chaunu, P., *La Civilisation de l'Europe Classique* (Paris, 1984).

Cipolla, C. M. (ed.), *The Fontana Economic History of Europe: The Sixteenth and Seventeenth Centuries* (London, 1974).

Clark, S., *State and Status: The Rise of the State and Aristocratic Power in Western Europe* (Cardiff, 1995).

Davis, N. Z. and Farge, A. (eds), *A History of Women*, vol. III: *Renaissance and Enlightenment Paradoxes* (London, 1993).

De Vries, J., *The Economy of Europe in an Age of Crisis, 1600–1750* (Cambridge, 1976).

Kamen, H., *Early Modern European Society* (London, 2000)

Kamen, H., *European Society, 1500–1700* (London, 1984).

Kiernan, V. G., *State and Society in Europe, 1550–1650* (New York, 1980).

Kirby, D., *Northern Europe in the Early Modern Period: The Baltic World, 1492–1772* (London, 1990).

Koenigsberger, H. G., *Estates and Revolutions: Essays in Early Modern European History* (Ithaca, NY, 1971).

Le Roy Ladurie, E., *Times of Feast, Times of Famine: A History of Climate since the Year 1000* (New York, 1971).

Lockyer, R., *Habsburg and Bourbon Europe, 1470–1720* (London, 1974).

McKay, D. and Scott, H. M., *The Rise of the Great Powers, 1648–1815* (London, 1983).

McNeill, W. H., *Europe's Steppe Frontier, 1500–1800* (Chicago, 1964).

Miller, J. (ed.), *Absolution in Seventeenth-century Europe* (London, 1990).

Munck, T., *Seventeenth-century Europe, 1598–1700* (London, 1990).

*New Cambridge Modern History* (13 vols, Cambridge, 1957–1971).

Parker, G. and Smith, L. M. (eds), *The General Crisis of the Seventeenth Century* (London, 1978).

Rabb, T. K., *The Struggle for Stability in Early Modern Europe* (Oxford, 1975).

Scott, T. (ed.), *The Peasantries of Europe from the Fourteenth to the Eighteenth Centuries* (London, 1998).

Shennan, J. H., *Liberty and Order in Early Modern Europe: The Subject and the State, 1650–1800* (London, 1986).

Spellman, W. M., *European Political Thought, 1600–1700* (London, 1998).

Tapié, V-L., *The Age of Grandeur: Baroque and Classicism in Europe* (London, 1960).

Treasure, G., *The Making of Modern Europe, 1648–1780* (London, 1985).

Ward, W. R., *Christianity under the Ancien Régime, 1648–1789* (Cambridge, 1999).

Wigley, T. M. L., Ingram, M. J. and Farmer, F. (eds), *Climate and History: Studies in Past Climates and their Impact on Man* (Cambridge, 1981).

Zagorin, P., *Rebels and Rulers, 1500–1650* (2 vols, Cambridge, 1982).

## International Relations and War

Anderson, M. S., *War and Society in Europe of the Ancien Régime, 1618–1789* (London, 1988).

Asch, R. G., *The Thirty Years War: The Holy Roman Empire and Europe, 1618–48* (London, 1997).

Barrie-Curien, V., *Guerre et pouvoir en Europe au XVIIe siècle* (Paris, 1991).

Bély, L., Bérenger, J. and Corvisier, A., *Guerre et paix dans l'Europe du XVIIe siècle* (2 vols, Paris, 1991).

Black, J., *European Warfare, 1660–1815* (London, 1994).

Black, J., *A Military Revolution? Military Change and European Society, 1550–1800* (London, 1991).

Black, J., *The Origins of War in Early Modern Europe* (Edinburgh, 1987).

Bussmann, K. and Schilling, H. (eds), *1648: War and Peace in Europe* (2 vols, Munich, 1999).

Childs, J., *Armies and Warfare in Europe, 1648–1789* (Manchester, 1982).

Childs, J., *The British Army of William III, 1689–1702* (Manchester, 1987).

Childs, J., *The Nine Years War and the British Army, 1688–1697: The Operations in the Low Countries* (Manchester, 1991).

Corvisier, A., *Armies and Societies in Europe, 1494–1789* (Bloomington, Ind., 1979).

Downing, B. M., *The Military Revolution and Political Change: Origins of Democracy and Autocracy in Early Modern Europe* (Princeton, NJ, 1992).

Duffy, M., *The Military Revolution and the State* (Exeter, 1980).

Frost, R. I., *The Northern Wars: War, State and Society in Northeastern Europe, 1558–1721* (London, 2000).

Limm, P., *The Thirty Years War* (London, 1984).

Osiander, Andreas, *The States System of Europe, 1640–1990: Peacemaking and the Conditions of International Stability* (Oxford, 1994).

Parker, G., *The Military Revolution: Military Innovation and the Rise of the West, 1500–1800* (Cambridge, 1988).

Parker, G., *The Thirty Years' War* (London, 1984).

Polisensky, J. V., *The Thirty Years War* (London, 1971).

Polisensky, J. V., *War and Society in Europe, 1618–1648* (London, 1978).

Rotberg, R. I. and Rabb, T. K. (eds), *The Origins and Prevention of Major Wars* (Cambridge, 1989).

Steinberg, S. H., *The 'Thirty Years War' and the Conflict for European Hegemony, 1600–1660* (London, 1966).

Tallett, F., *War and Society in Early Modern Europe, 1495–1715* (London, 1992).

## Sciences and Learning

Butterfield, H., *The Origins of Modern Science* (London, 1950).

Cohen, I. B. (ed.), *Puritanism and the Rise of Modern Science: The Merton Thesis* (New Brunswick, 1990).

Drake, S., *Galileo* (Oxford, 1981).

Fantoli, A., *Galileo: For Copernicus and for the Church* (South Bend, Ind., 1994).

Feingold, M., *The Mathematician's Apprenticeship: Science, Universities and Society in England, 1560–1640* (Cambridge, 1984).

Finocchiaro, M. A., *The Galileo Affair: A Documentary History* (London, 1989).

Hahn, R., *The Anatomy of a Scientific Institution: The Paris Academy of Sciences, 1666–1803* (Berkeley, Calif., 1971).

Hall, A. R., *The Revolution in Science, 1500–1750* (London, 1983).

Harman, P. M., *The Scientific Revolution* (Lancaster Pamphlets, London, 1983).

Henry, J., *The Scientific Revolution and the Origins of Modern Science* (London, 1997).

Hunter, M., *The Royal Society and its Fellows, 1660–1700: The Morphology of an Early Scientific Institution* (2nd edn, Oxford, 1994).

Hunter, M., *Science and Society in Restoration England* (Cambridge, 1981).

Middleton, W. E. K., *The Experimenters: A Study of the Accademia del Cimento* (Baltimore, Md, 1971).

Ornstein, M., *The Role of Scientific Societies in the Seventeenth Century* (Chicago, 1928 [New York, 1975]).

Porter, R. and Teich, M. (eds), *The Scientific Revolution in National Context* (Cambridge, 1992).

Redondi, P., *Galileo: Heretic* (London, 1988).

de Ridder-Symoens, H. (ed.), *A History of the University in Europe*, vol. II: *Universities in Early Modern Europe (1500–1800)* (Cambridge, 1996).

Stroup, A., *A Company of Scientists: Botany, Patronage, and Community at the Seventeenth-century Parisian Royal Academy of Sciences* (Berkeley, Calif., 1990).

Sturdy, D. J., *Science and Social Status: The Members of the Académie des Sciences, 1666–1750* (Woodbridge, 1995).

Wallace, W. A., *Galileo and his Sources: The Heritage of the Collegio Romano in Galileo's Science* (Princeton, NJ, 1985).

Westfall, R. S., *Never at Rest: A Biography of Isaac Newton* (Cambridge, 1980).

## Britain and Ireland

### England and Wales

Aylmer, G. (ed.), *The Interregnum: The Quest for Settlement, 1646–1660* (London, 1972).

Aylmer, G., *Rebellion or Revolution? England from Civil War to Restoration* (Oxford, 1987).

Baxter, S. B., *William III* (London, 1966).

Beddard, R. (ed.), *The Revolutions of 1688* (Oxford, 1991).

Black, J., *A System of Ambition? British Foreign Policy 1660–1793* (London, 1991).

Bliss, R. M., *Restoration England, 1660–1688* (Lancaster Pamphlets, London, 1985).

Bradshaw, B. and Morrill, J. (eds), *The British Problem, c. 1534–1707: State Formation in the Atlantic Archipelago* (London, 1996).

Brewer, J., *The Sinews of Power: War, Money and the English State, 1688–1783* (London, 1989).

Carlin, N., *The Causes of the English Civil War* (Historical Association Studies, Oxford, 1999).

Clark, J. C. D., *English Society 1688–1832: Ideology, Social Structure and Political Practice during the Ancien Regime* (Cambridge, 1985).

Clark, J. C. D., *Revolution and Rebellion: State and Society in England in the Seventeenth and Eighteenth Centuries* (Cambridge, 1986).

Collinson, P., *The Religion of Protestants: The Church in English Society, 1559–1625* (Oxford, 1982).

Coward, B., *The Stuart Age: A History of England 1603–1714* (London, 1980).

Fincham, K. (ed.), *The Early Stuart Church, 1603–1642* (London, 1993).

Fletcher, A. J., *The Outbreak of the English Civil War* (London, 1981).

Fletcher, A. J. and Roberts, P. (eds), *Religion, Culture and Society in Early Modern Britain* (Cambridge, 1994).

Foster, A., *The Church of England, 1570–1640* (London, 1994).

Glassey, L. K. J. (ed.), *The Reigns of Charles II and James VII & II* (London, 1997).

Haley, K. H. D., *Politics in the Reign of Charles II* (Historical Association Studies, Oxford, 1985).

Harris, T., Seaward, P. and Goldie, M. (eds), *The Politics of Religion in Restoration England* (Oxford, 1990).

Hill, B., *The Early Parties and Politics in Britain, 1688–1832* (London, 1996).

Hill, C., *The Century of Revolution, 1603–1714* (London, 1980).

Hill, C., *God's Englishman: Oliver Cromwell and the English Revolution* (London, 1979).

Hill, C., *The World Turned Upside Down: Radical Ideas during the English Revolution* (London, 1974).

Hirst, D., *England in Conflict, 1603–1660: Kingdom, Community, Commonwealth* (London, 1999).

Holmes, G., *The Making of a Great Power: Late Stuart and Early Georgian Britain, 1660–1722* (London, 1993).

Hoppit, J., *A Land of Liberty? England 1689–1727* (Oxford, 2000).

Hughes, A., *The Causes of the English Civil War* (Basingstoke, 1991).

Hutton, R., *Charles II: King of England, Scotland and Ireland* (Oxford, 1989).

Jones, J. R., *The Anglo-Dutch Wars of the Seventeenth Century* (London, 1996).

Jones, J. R., *Britain and Europe in the Seventeenth Century* (London, 1966).

Jones, J. R., *Country and Court: England 1658–1714* (London, 1978).

Jones, J. R. (ed.), *The Restored Monarchy, 1660–1688* (London, 1979).

Kenyon, J. P., *The Civil Wars of England* (London, 1988).

Kenyon, J. P. (ed.), *The Stuart Constitution, 1603–1688: Documents and Commentary* (Cambridge, 1966).

Kishlansky, M., *A Monarchy Transformed, 1603–1714* (London, 1996).

Lindley, K., *The English Civil War and Revolution: A Sourcebook* (London, 1998).

Miller, J., *Charles II* (London, 1991).

Miller, J., *James II: A Study in Kingship* (Hove, 1978).

Mullett, M., *James II and English Politics 1678–1688* (Lancaster Pamphlets, London, 1994).

Ohlmeyer, J. H., *Civil War and Restoration in the Three Stuart Kingdoms* (Cambridge, 1993).

Richardson, R. C., *The Debate on the English Revolution Revisited* (Manchester, 1989).

Russell, C., *The Causes of the English Civil War* (Oxford, 1990).

Russell, C., *The Fall of the British Monarchies* (Oxford, 1995).

Scott, J., *England's Troubles: Seventeenth-century English Political Instability in European Context* (Cambridge, 2000).

Sherwood, R., *Oliver Cromwell: King in All but Name, 1653–1658* (Stroud, 1997).

Smith, D. L., *The Stuart Parliaments, 1603–1689* (London, 1999).

## Scotland

Buckroyd, J., *Church and State in Scotland 1660–1681* (Edinburgh, 1981).

Ferguson, W., *Scotland's Relations with England: A Survey to 1707* (Edinburgh, 1977).

Goodare, J., *State and Society in Early Modern Scotland* (Oxford, 1999).

Goodare, J. and Lynch, M. (eds), *The Reign of James VI* (East Linton, 2000).

Houston, R. A., and Whyte, I. D. (eds), *Scottish Society, 1500–1800* (Cambridge, 1989).

Levack, B. P., *The Formation of the British State: England, Scotland and the Union, 1603–1710* (Oxford, 1988).

MacDonald, A. R., *The Jacobean Kirk, 1567–1625: Sovereignty, Polity and Liturgy* (St Andrews, 1998).

Mitchison, R., *Lordship to Patronage: Scotland 1603–1745* (Edinburgh, 1990).

Stevenson, D., *The Scottish Revolution, 1637–1644: The Triumph of the Covenanters* (Newton Abbot, 1973).

Stevenson, D., *Revolution and Counter-revolution in Scotland, 1644–1651* (London, 1977).

Stevenson, D., *Union, Revolution and Religion in Seventeenth-century Scotland* (Aldershot, 1997).

Young, J. R., *The Scottish Parliament, 1639–1661: A Political and Constitutional Analysis* (Edinburgh, 1996).

## Ireland

Canny, N. P., *Kingdom and Colony: Ireland in the Atlantic World, 1560–1800* (Baltimore, Md, 1988).

Connolly, S. J., *Religion, Law and Power: The Making of Protestant Ireland, 1660–1760* (Oxford, 1992).

Corish, P. J., *The Catholic Community in the Seventeenth and Eighteenth Centuries* (Dublin, 1981).

Fitzpatrick, B., *Seventeenth-century Ireland: The War of Religions* (Dublin, 1988).

Foster, R. F., *Modern Ireland, 1600–1972* (London, 1988).

Maguire, W. A. (ed.), *Kings in Conflict: The Revolutionary War in Ireland and its Aftermath, 1689–1750* (Belfast, 1990).

Moody, T. W., Martin, F. X. and Byrne, F. J. (eds), *A New History of Ireland*, vol. III: *Early Modern Ireland, 1534–1691* (Oxford, 1976).

Ohlmeyer, J. (ed.), *Ireland from Independence to Occupation, 1641–1660* (Cambridge, 1995).

Ó Siochrú, M., *Confederate Ireland, 1642–1649* (Dublin, 1999).

Simms, J. G., *War and Politics in Ireland, 1649–1730*, ed. D. W. Hayton, and G. O'Brien (London, 1986).

Stevenson, D., *Scottish Covenanters and Irish Confederates: Scottish–Irish Relations in the Mid-Seventeenth Century* (Belfast, 1981).

Stradling, R. A., *The Spanish Monarchy and Irish Mercenaries: The Wild Geese in Spain, 1618–1668* (Dublin, 1994).

Wheeler, J. C., *Cromwell in Ireland* (Dublin, 1999).

## Italy

Burke, P., *The Historical Anthropology of Early Modern Italy: Essays on Perception and Communication* (Cambridge, 1987).

Hanlon, G., *Early Modern Italy, 1550–1800* (London, 2000).

Hanlon, G., *The Twilight of a Military Tradition: Italian Aristocrats and European Conflicts, 1560–1800* (London, 1997).

Johns, C. M. S., *Papal Art and Cultural Politics: Rome in the Age of Clement IX* (New York, 1992).

Johns, C. M. S., *Papal Art and Cultural Politics: Rome in the Age of Clement XI* (New York, 1993).

Koenigsberger, H. G., 'The Revolt of Palermo in 1647', in H. G. Koenigsberger (ed.), *Estates and Revolutions: Essays in Early Modern European History* (Ithaca, NY, 1971), 253–77.

Krautheimer, R., *The Rome of Alexander VII, 1655–1667* (Princeton, NJ, 1985).

Magnuson, T., *Rome in the Age of Bernini* (2 vols, Stockholm, 1982).

Nussdorfer, L., *Civic Politics in the Rome of Urban VIII* (Princeton, NJ, 1992).

Prodi, P., *The Papal Prince. One Body and Two Souls: The Papal Monarchy in Early Modern Europe* (Cambridge, 1987).

Sella, D., *Italy in the Seventeenth Century* (London, 1997).

Southorn, J., *Power and Display in the Seventeenth Century: The Arts and their Patrons in Modena and Ferrara* (New York, 1988).

Villari, R., *The Anti-Spanish Revolt in Naples* (Cambridge, 1991).

## Spain and Portugal

Allen, P. C., *Philip III and the Pax Hispanica, 1598–1621* (New Haven, Conn., 2000).

Darby, G., *Spain in the Seventeenth Century* (London, 1994).

Elliott, J. H., 'The Decline of Spain', *Past and Present*, 20 (1961), 52–75.

Elliott, J. H., *Imperial Spain, 1469–1716* (London, 1963).

Elliott, J. H., 'A Question of Reputation? Spanish Foreign Policy in the Seventeenth Century', *Journal of Modern History*, 55 (1983), 475–483.

Elliott, J. H., *Richelieu and Olivares* (Cambridge, 1984).

Elliott, J. H., *Spain and its World, 1500–1700* (London, 1989).

Hanson, C. A., *Economy and Society in Baroque Portugal, 1668–1703* (London, 1981).

Hargreaves-Mawdsley, W. N., *Eighteenth-century Spain, 1700–1788: A Diplomatic and Institutional History* (London, 1979).

Kamen, H., *Philip V of Spain: The King who Reigned Twice* (New Haven, Conn., 2001).

Kamen, H., *Spain, 1469–1714: A Society of Conflict* (London, 1983).

Kamen, H., *Spain in the Later Seventeenth Century, 1665–1700* (London, 1980).

Lynch, J., *The Hispanic World in Crisis and Change, 1598–1700* (Oxford, 1992).

Parker, G., *The Army of Flanders and the Spanish Road, 1567–1659: The Logistics of Spanish Victory and Defeat in the Low Countries* (Cambridge, 1972).

Stradling, R. A., *The Armada of Flanders: Spanish Maritime Policy and European War, 1568–1668* (Cambridge, 1992).

Stradling, R. A., *Europe and the Decline of Spain: A Study of the Spanish System, 1580–1720* (London, 1981).

Stradling, R. A., *Philip IV and the Government of Spain* (Cambridge, 1988).

Stradling, R. A., *Spain's Struggle for Europe, 1598–1668* (London, 1994).

Thompson, I. A. A., *War and Society in Habsburg Spain* (Aldershot, 1992).

## France

Beik, W. H., *Absolutism and Society in Seventeenth-century France: State Power and Provincial Aristocracy in Languedoc* (Cambridge, 1985).

Bergin, J., *Cardinal Richelieu: Power and the Pursuit of Wealth* (London, 1985).

Bergin, J., *The Making of the French Episcopate, 1589–1661* (London, 1996).

Bergin, J., *The Rise of Richelieu* (London, 1991).

Bluche, F., *Louis XIV* (Oxford, 1990).

Blunt, A., *Art and Architecture in France, 1500–1700* (2nd edn, London, 1970).

Bonney, R., *The King's Debts: Finance and Politics in France, 1589–1661* (Oxford, 1981).

Bonney, R., *The Limits of Absolutism in Ancien Régime France* (London, 1995).

Bonney, R., *Political Change in France under Richelieu and Mazarin* (Oxford, 1978).

Briggs, R., *Communities of Belief: Cultural and Social Tensions in Early Modern France* (Oxford, 1989).

Briggs, R., *Early Modern France, 1560–1715* (Oxford, 1977).

Campbell, P. R., *Louis XIV, 1661–1715* (London, 1993).

Collins, J. B., *The State in Early Modern France* (Cambridge, 1995).

Holt, M. P., *The French Wars of Religion, 1562–1629* (Cambridge, 1995).

Knecht, R. J., *Richelieu* (London, 1991).

Lossky, A., *Louis XIV and the French Monarchy* (New Brunswick, 1994).

Lublinskaya, A. D., *French Absolutism: The Crucial Phase, 1620–1629* (Cambridge, 1978).

Lynn, J. A., *Giant of the Grand Siècle: The French Army, 1610–1715* (Cambridge, 1997).

Lynn, J. A., *The Wars of Louis XIV, 1667–1714* (London, 1999).

Major, J. Russell, *From Renaissance Monarchy to Absolute Monarchy: French Kings, Nobles and Estates* (London, 1994).

Mettam, R., *Government and Society in Louis XIV's France* (London, 1977).

Mettam, R., *Power and Faction in Louis XIV's France* (Oxford, 1988).

Moote, A. L., *Louis XIII, the Just* (London, 1989).

Mousnier, R., *Peasant Uprisings in Seventeenth-century France, Russia and China* (London, 1971).

Parker, D., *The Making of French Absolutism* (London, 1983).

Pillorget, R. and Pillorget, S., *France baroque, France classique, 1589–1715* (2 vols, Paris, 1995).

Roosen, W. J., *The Age of Louis XIV: The Rise of Modern Diplomacy* (Cambridge, Mass., 1976).

Rowen, H. H., *The King's State: Proprietary Dynasticism in Early Modern France* (New Brunswick, 1980).

Shennan, J. H., *Louis XIV* (London, 1986).

Sonnino, P., *Louis XIV and the Origins of the Dutch War* (Cambridge, 1988).

Sonnino, P. (ed.), *The Reign of Louis XIV: Essays in Celebration of Andrew Lossky* (London, 1990).

Sturdy, D. J., *Louis XIV* (London, 1998).

Wolf, J. B., *Louis XIV* (New York, 1968).

## Dutch Republic/United Provinces

Alpers, S., *The Art of Describing: Dutch Art in the Seventeenth Century* (London, 1983).

Haak, B., *The Golden Age: Dutch Painters of the Seventeenth Century* (London, 1984).

Haley, K. H. D., *The Dutch in the Seventeenth Century* (London, 1972).

Israel, J. I., *Dutch Primacy in World Trade* (Oxford, 1989).

Israel, J. I., *The Dutch Republic and the Hispanic World, 1606–1661* (Oxford, 1982).

Israel, J. I, *The Dutch Republic: Its Rise, Greatness and Fall, 1477–1806* (Oxford, 1995).

Price, J. L., *Culture and Society in the Dutch Republic during the Seventeenth Century* (London, 1974).

Price, J. L., *The Dutch Republic in the Seventeenth Century* (London, 1998).

Price, J. L., *Holland and the Dutch Republic in the Seventeenth Century: The Politics of Particularism* (Oxford, 1994).

Rowen, H. H., *Johan de Witt: Grand Pensionary of Holland* (Princeton, NJ, 1978).

Rowen, H. H., *John de Witt: Statesman of the 'True Freedom'* (Cambridge, 1986).

Schama, S., *The Embarrassment of Riches: An Interpretation of Dutch Culture in the Golden Age* (London, 1987).

Tex, J. den, *Oldenbarnevelt* (2 vols, Cambridge, 1973).

Vries, J. de and Woude, A. van der, *The First Modern Economy: Success, Failure and Perseverance of the Dutch Economy, 1500–1815* (Cambridge, 1997).

## Sweden and Denmark

Hatton, R. M., *Charles XII of Sweden* (London, 1968).

Lockhart, P. D., 'Denmark and the Empire: A Reassessment of the Foreign Policy of King Christian IV, 1596–1648', *Scandinavian Studies,* 62 (1992), 390–416.

Lockhart, P. D., *Denmark in the Thirty Years War, 1618–1648: King Christian IV and the Decline of the Oldenburg State* (Selinsgrove, 1996).

Lockhart, P. D., 'Religion and Princely Liberties: Denmark's Intervention in the Thirty Years War, 1618–1625', *International History Review,* 17, no. 1 (1995), 1–22.

Roberts, M., *Essays in Swedish History* (London, 1967).

Roberts, M., *Gustavus Adolphus* (London, 1973/1992).

Roberts, M., *Gustavus Adolphus: A History of Sweden, 1611–1632* (2 vols, London, 1953, 1958).

Roberts, M., *Sweden as a Great Power, 1611–1697: Government, Society, Foreign Policy* (London, 1968).


## Germany

Benecke, G., *Society and Politics in Germany, 1500–1750* (London, 1974).

Gagliardo, J., *Germany under the Old Regime, 1600–1790* (London, 1991).

Holborn, H., *A History of Modern Germany* (2 vols, London, 1965).

Hughes, M., *Early Modern Germany, 1477–1806* (London, 1992).

Koch, H. W., *A History of Prussia* (London, 1987).

Sagarra, E., *A Social History of Germany, 1648–1914* (London, 1977).

Scribner, R. and Ogilvie, S. (eds), *Germany: A New Social and Economic History* (2 vols, London, 1996).

Theibault, J., *German Villages in Crisis: Rural Life in Hesse-Kassel and the Thirty Years War, 1580–1720* (Atlantic Highlands, 1995).

Vierhaus, R., *Germany in the Age of Absolutism* (Cambridge, 1998).

Wilson, P. H., *German Armies: War and German Politics, 1648–1806* (London, 1998).


## Austrian Habsburg Lands

Barker, T. M., *Double Eagle and Crescent: Vienna's Second Turkish Siege in its Historical Setting* (Albany, 1967).

Birely, R., *Religion and Politics in the Age of Counter-Reformation: Emperor Ferdinand II, William Lamormaini S.J. and the Formation of Imperial Policy* (Ithaca, NY, 1981).

Evans, R. J. W., *The Making of the Habsburg Monarchy: An Interpretation* (Oxford, 1979).

Evans, R. J. W., *Rudolf II and his World: A Study in Intellectual History, 1576–1612* (Oxford, 1973).

Evans, R. J. W. and Thomas, T. V. (eds), *Crown, Church and Estates: Central European Politics in the Sixteenth and Seventeenth Centuries* (New York, 1991).

Fucíková, E. et al., *Rudolf II and Prague: The Court and the City* (London, 1997).

Ingrao, C. W., *The Habsburg Monarchy, 1618–1815* (Cambridge, 1994).

Ingrao, C. W., *In Quest and Crisis: Emperor Joseph I and the Habsburg Monarchy* (West Lafayette, 1979).

Kann, R. A., *A History of the Habsburg Empire, 1526–1918* (Berkeley, Calif., 1974).

Kann, R. A., *A Study in Austrian Intellectual History: From Late Baroque to Romanticism* (New York, 1960).

McKay, D., *Prince Eugene of Savoy* (New York, 1977).

Mann, G., *Wallenstein* (London, 1976).

Pamlényi, E., *A History of Hungary* (London, 1975).

Seton-Watson, R. W., *A History of the Czechs and Slovaks* (London, 1965).

Spielman, J., *Leopold I of Austria* (New Brunswick, 1977).

Stoye, J., *The Siege of Vienna* (London, 1964).

Sugar, P., Hanák, P. and Frank, T. (eds), *A History of Hungary* (Bloomington, Ind., 1990).

Wheatcroft, A., *The Habsburgs: Embodying Empire* (London, 1995).

Wilson, P. H., *The Holy Roman Empire, 1495–1806* (London, 1999).

## Poland

Davies, N., *God's Playground: A History of Poland in Two Volumes.* Vol. I: *The Origins to 1795* (Oxford, 1981).

Fedorowicz, J. K. (ed.), *A Republic of Nobles: Studies in Polish History to 1864* (Cambridge, 1982).

Kaminski, A., *Republic vs Autocracy: Poland–Lithuania and Russia, 1686–1697* (Cambridge, Mass., 1993).

Potichnyi, P. (ed.), *Poland and the Ukraine: Past and Present* (Toronto, 1980).

## Turkey and the Balkans

Coles, P., *The Ottoman Impact on Europe* (London, 1968).

Inalcik, H. and Quataert, D., *An Economic and Social History of the Ottoman Empire*, vol. II: *1600–1914* (2 vols, Cambridge, 1994–7).

Jelavich, B., *History of the Balkans*. Vol. I: *Eighteenth and Nineteenth Centuries* (Cambridge, 1983).

Parry, V. J. et al., *A History of the Ottoman Empire to 1730: Chapters from 'The Cambridge History of Islam' and 'The New Cambridge Modern History'* (Cambridge, 1976).

Shaw, S. J. and Shaw, E. K., *History of the Ottoman Empire and Modern Turkey* (2 vols, Cambridge, 1976–7).

## Russia and the Ukraine

Anderson, M., *Peter the Great* (London, 1978).

Blum, J., *Lord and Peasant in Russia from the Ninth to the Nineteenth Century* (Princeton, NJ, 1961).

Bushkovitch, P., *Religion and Society in Russia: The Sixteenth and Seventeenth Centuries* (Oxford, 1992).

Crummey, R. O., *Aristocrats and Servitors: The Boyar Elite in Russia, 1613–1689* (Princeton, NJ, 1983).

Dukes, P., *A History of Russia, c.882–1996* (3rd edn, London, 1998).

Dukes, P., *The Making of Russian Absolutism, 1613–1801* (London, 1990).

Dunning, C. S. L., *Russia's First Civil War: The Time of Troubles and the Founding of the Romanov Dynasty* (Baltimore, MD, 2001).

Fuller, W. C., *Strategy and Power in Russia, 1600–1914* (New York, 1992).

Hoetzsch, O., *The Evolution of Russia* (London, 1966).

Hosking, G., *Russia: People and Empire, 1552–1917* (London, 1997).

Hughes, L., *Russia in the Age of Peter the Great* (London, 1998).

Keep, J. L. H., *Soldiers of the Tsar: Army and Society in Russia, 1462–1874* (Oxford, 1985).

Kivelson, V. A., *Autocracy in the Provinces: The Muscovite Gentry and Political Culture in the Seventeenth Century* (Stanford, 1996).

Longworth, P., *Alexis, Tsar of all the Russias* (Oxford, 1992).

Magocsi, A., *A History of the Ukraine* (Toronto, 1996).

Pipes, R., *Russia under the Old Regime* (London, 1974).

Porshnev, B. F., *Muscovy and Sweden in the Thirty Years War, 1630–1635* (Cambridge, 1996).

Raeff, M., *Understanding Imperial Russia: State and Society in the Old Regime* (New York, 1984).

Skrynnikov, E. G., *The Time of Troubles: Russia in Crisis, 1604–1618*, trans. H. Graham (Gulf Brieze, Florida, 1988).

Subtelny, O., *Ukraine: A History* (Toronto, 1988).

# *Notes*

---

## Chapter 1     The Context of 1600

1   S. F. M. Grieco, 'The Body, Appearance, and Sexuality', in N. Z. Davis and A. Farge (eds), *A History of Women*, vol. III: *Renaissance and Enlightenment Paradoxes* (London, 1993), 73–4.

2   Racine to La Fontaine, Uzès, 11 Nov. 1661, *Racine: Lettres d'Uzès* ed. J. Dubu (Nîmes, 1991), 2.

3   H-J. Martin, *Livre, pouvoirs et société à Paris au XVIIe siècle (1598–1701)* (2 vols, Paris, 1969), ii. 1,064.

4   The circles were: Austria, Bavaria, Burgundy, Electoral Rhine, Franconia, Swabia, Upper Rhine, Lower Rhine–Westphalia, Upper Saxony, Lower Saxony. Bohemia was not a circle, even though it was part of the empire.

5   Charles V abdicated both as emperor and king of Spain in 1556; his son Philip succeeded as Philip II of Spain; Charles's brother, Ferdinand, followed him as emperor.

6   For the Habsburg imperial succession, 1519–1740, see the list on pp. 397–8.

7   The sessions met December 1545 – March 1547; May 1551 – April 1552; January 1562 – December 1563.

8   The word Huguenot (originally *Eyguenet*) is an adaptation of the German word *Eidgenossen*, or confederate.

## Chapter 2     Central and Southern Europe, 1600–1635

1   Hussites were followers of John Huss (*c.* 1369–1415), rector of the University of Prague and critic of the church; his death by burning at the stake initiated the Hussite Wars in Bohemia.

2 The Treaty of Zsitvatorok was the first occasion that a sultan negotiated with a Christian ruler as an equal; hitherto all 'treaties' between the Turks and Christian governments had, on the Turkish side, been issued as autonomous proclamations.

3 The children were: (i) Ferdinand III (1608–57); (ii) Maria Anna (1610–65) = Maximilian of Bavaria; (iii) Cecilia Renata (1611–44) =Wladislaus IV of Poland; (iv) Leopold William (1614–62), regent of the Netherlands.

4 The ecclesiastical electors and Ferdinand of Styria attended in person; the electors of Saxony, Brandenburg and the Palatinate sent representatives.

5 R. J. W. Evans, *Rudolf II and his World: A Study in Intellectual History, 1576–1612* (Oxford, 1973), 201; C. W. Ingrao, *The Habsburg Monarchy, 1618–1815* (Cambridge, 1994), 38; R. W. Seton-Watson, *A History of the Czechs and Slovaks* (London, 1965), 116.

6 By the Peace of Westphalia (1648), Charles-Louis was restored to the Palatinate, but Bavaria was promoted to an electorate. Maximilian thus kept his electoral vote, and the number of electors rose from seven to eight.

7 The figures for Spanish Italy in 1600 are: Naples, 3,320,000; Milan, 1,240,000; Sicily, 1,130,000; Sardinia, 330,000 (P. Chaunu, *La civilisation de l'Europe classique* [Paris, 1984], 56).

8 Y-M. Bercé et al., *L'Italie au XVIIe siècle* (Paris, 1989), 63.

9 He wrote his name various ways: Waldstein, Valdstyn or Valdstejn; the German form 'Wallenstein' is commonly used.

10 The Treaty of Passau (1552) ended many years of warfare in Germany; the Peace of Augsburg (1555) took it as its point of reference in its territorial and religious settlements.

11 M. Roberts, *Sweden as a Great Power, 1611–1697: Government, Society, Foreign Policy* (London, 1968), 140.

12 M. Roberts, *Gustavus Adolphus* (London, 1973/1992), 109.

## Chapter 3   Central and Southern Europe, 1635–1648

1 The opera *La Muette de Portici* (presented in Britain as *Masaniello*) by Daniel Auber (1828) is a good example.

2 Guise was a descendant of the Anjou family which had ruled Naples from the thirteenth century to 1443, when the house of Aragon acquired the kingdom through conquest.

3 P. Chaunu, *La civilisation de l'Europe classique* (Paris, 1984), 56–7.

## Chapter 4    Western Europe, 1600–1665: Spain and France

1  P. Chaunu, *La civilisation de l'Europe classique* (Paris, 1984), 60.
2  J. H. Elliott, *The Count-Duke of Olivares: The Statesman in an Age of Decline* (London, 1986), 86.
3  Olivares held the title of 'count' by inheritance, but had that of 'duke of San Lúcar' conferred on him by Philip IV. He requested, and received, from the king the right to use the compound title, and was commonly referred to as the Count-Duke (*el Conde-Duque*).
4  G. Mutto, 'The Spanish System: Centre and Periphery', in R. Bonney (ed.), *Economic Systems and State Finance* (Oxford, 1995), 257.
5  Ibid.
6  Quoted in Elliott, *The Count-Duke of Olivares*, 196–7; and H. Kamen, *Spain 1469–1714: A Society of Conflict* (London, 1983), 211.
7  The forces would be composed as follows: Castile 44,000 men; Catalonia 16,000; Portugal 16,000; Naples 16,000; Spanish Netherlands 12,000; Aragon 10,000; Milan 8,000; Valencia 6,000; Sicily 6,000; Mediterranean and Atlantic islands 6,000 (J. H. Elliott, *Imperial Spain, 1469–1716* (London, 1963), 326).
8  Quoted in R. Pillorget and S. Pillorget, *France baroque, France classique, 1589–1715* (2 vols, Paris, 1995), i. 1518.
9  In round figures, the value of Spanish imports of precious metals between 1621 and 1660, measured in ducats, were:

| 1621–5 | 32.5 millions | 1641–5 | 16.5 millions |
| 1626–30 | 30 millions | 1646–50 | 14.1 millions |
| 1631–5 | 20.5 millions | 1651–5 | 8.75 millions |
| 1636–40 | 19.5 millions | 1656–60 | 4 millions |

(Source: Elliott, *Imperial Spain*, 175).

10  In 1589, Henri de Navarre (Henri IV) had a younger brother Charles, who died in 1590; next in line of succession was Henri II, duc de Condé.
11  A *parlement* was primarily a law court; it was a corporation of lawyers, not an elected body, and should not be confused with the 'parliament' familiar to the English-speaking world.
12  J. A. Lynn, *Giant of the Grand Siècle: The French Army, 1610–1715* (Cambridge, 1997), 42–3, 50, 55.
13  R. Bonney, 'The Secret Expenses of Richelieu and Mazarin, 1624–1661', *English Historical Review*, 91 (1976), 828–9.
14  Pillorget and Pillorget, *France baroque, France classique*, i. 312.
15  R. Mousnier, *La vénalité des offices sous Henri IV et Louis XIII* (2nd edn, Paris, 1971), 362–3.

16  'Croquant' – a clod-hopper – was a term of abuse for a peasant; during the rising at La Couronne in 1636, a crowd of 'croquants' killed an artisan who had shouted the word at them.

## Chapter 5   Western Europe, 1603–1660: Britain and the United Provinces

1  L. Stone, *The Crisis of the Aristocracy, 1558–1641* (Oxford, 1965), 97–115.

2  Ibid., 166–74.

3  At the beginning of a reign, parliament usually voted 'tonnage and poundage' to the monarch for life, but in the case of Charles I it voted the duty only on an annual basis. Since parliament did not meet between 1626 and 1628, Charles did not have formal parliamentary consent.

4  They were: (1) communicants should kneel, not sit, to receive communion; (2) Easter and Christmas must be observed; (3) confirmation must be introduced; (4) communion might be administered to the dying in their houses; (5) a child must be baptized on the first Sunday after its birth.

5  A. G. Dickens, *The English Reformation* (London, 1964), 308.

6  The (Thirty-nine) Articles of Religion had been adopted by the Convocation of the Church of England in 1562, 'for the avoiding of the diversities of opinions, and for the establishing of consent touching true religion'.

7  Rupert was the son of Frederick V, elector of the Palatinate, and his wife Elizabeth, daughter of James I of England.

8  Over 20,000 were collected by George Thomason (d. 1666), a bookseller. They passed into royal possession and were given to the British Museum by George III in 1762. The 'Thomason Tracts' constitute an outstanding source on the intellectual agitation of the period.

9  This assembly later was dubbed 'the Barebones Parliament', although it never referred to itself as a 'parliament', wishing to distinguish itself from its predecessor.

10  It is difficult to identify a precise date at which the Provinces became independent. The Union of Utrecht (1579), which brought 'rebel' provinces together, comes closest, but Spain did not acknowledge the independence of the republic until 1648.

11  Seven provinces were represented in the Estates General: Friesland, Gelderland, Gröningen, Holland, Overijssel, Utrecht and Zeeland; an eighth province, Drenthe, also formed part of the republic, but was not represented in the Estates General.

12  The stadtholders originated as governing representatives of the overlords of the Netherlands, the dukes of Burgundy and, in the sixteenth century, the kings of Spain.

13  A. R. Myers, *Parliaments and Estates in Europe to 1789* (London, 1975), 128–9.

14  J. I. Israel, *The Dutch Republic: Its Rise, Greatness and Fall, 1477–1806* (Oxford, 1995), 328.

15  M. 't Hart, 'The Emergence and Consolidation of the "Tax State", II: The Seventeenth Century', in R. Bonney (ed.), *Economic Systems and State Finance* (Oxford, 1995), 286–7.


## Chapter 6   Northern Europe, 1618–1660: Scandinavia, Russia and Poland

1  R. Bonney (ed.), *Economic Systems and State Finance* (Oxford, 1995), 455.

2  Strictly speaking, the term 'Russia' is anachronistic, for the state in question at this period was the Grand Duchy of Muscovy; in the interests of simplicity, however, 'Russia' will be used.

3  M. Roberts, *Gustavus Adolphus* (London, 1973/1992), 109.

4  G. Parker, *The Military Revolution: Military Innovation and the Rise of the West, 1500–1800* (Cambridge, 1988), 53–4.

5  See note 2 above.

6  The Zemsky Sobor ('assembly of land') was created by Ivan IV in 1550. It was composed of an upper house or duma (nobles, clergy and high state officials) and a lower house (gentry and merchants).

7  In the Orthodox hierarchy, a metropolitan came above an archbishop, but below a patriarch.

8  R. Mousnier, *Peasant Uprisings in Seventeenth-century France, Russia and China* (London, 1971), 157–9.

9  E. Melton, 'The Russian Peasantries, 1450–1860', in T. Scott (ed.), *The Peasantries of Europe from the Fourteenth to the Eighteenth Centuries* (London, 1998), 233; Mousnier, *Peasant Uprisings*, 175.

10  Melton, 'Russian Peasantries', 234–5.

11  The word Ukraine means 'borderland' (*y-Krai*: on the frontier); this is significant historically given the competition between Russia, Poland and the Ottoman Empire for control of the Ukraine.


## Interlude

1  For example. J. H. Shennan, *Government and Society in France, 1461–1661* (London, 1969), 62–70, argued against the thesis and concluded (p. 69) that 'current historical ideas about a mid-century crisis lead in

mutually exclusive directions. That being so, it becomes impossible to support the theory of a general European crisis . . . .'

2   Published as M. Roberts, *The Military Revolution, 1560–1660* (Belfast, 1956); the occasion was his professorial inaugural lecture at Queen's University, Belfast. It is reprinted in M. Roberts, *Essays in Swedish History* (London, 1967), 195–225.

## Chapter 7   Central and Southern Europe with the Ottoman Empire, 1648–1720

1   When Ahmed I died in 1617, he was succeeded by his brother Mustafa. Within a few months the *Divan* deposed him and recognized his nephew Osman as sultan. In 1622 Osman was assassinated. Mustafa was restored, but replaced again in 1623 by another younger brother, Murad. Murad's reign lasted until 1639, but he too was succeeded by a brother, not a son: Ibrahim, who ruled until 1648. Three of Ibrahim's sons then ruled: Mehmed IV (1648–87), Suleiman II (1687–91), and Ahmed II (1691–5). At this stage, the succession of brothers was broken when the throne went to a son of Mehmed IV, Mustafa II (reigned 1695–1703), but he too was succeeded by a brother, Ahmed III (reigned 1703–30) (see list of European Rulers, pp. 400–1).

2   After his death in 1661, Mehmed Köprölü was followed by his son Ahmed (served 1661–76); another son, Mustafa, was grand vizier 1689–91, and a cousin, Hussein served 1697–1702.

3   The palatine was the king's chief representative in Royal Hungary.

4   In Croatia, the ban was the equivalent of the Hungarian palatine.

5   He is commemorated in music by the famous Rákóczy March, composed by a Hungarian gypsy in 1809 and popularized by Berlioz's *Marche Hongroise*.

## Chapter 8   Western Europe, 1660–1720: France and Spain

1   Nicolas Fouquet, the *surintendant des finances*, also was a member until he was arrested later in 1661 and charged with corrupt administration of finances; he was imprisoned for life.

2   In addition to the *parlement* of Paris, the others, with dates of their creation, were: Toulouse (1443), Grenoble (1453), Bordeaux (1462), Dijon (1477), Rouen (1499), Aix (1501), Rennes (1554) and Pau (1620); as France annexed neighbouring territory, Metz (1633) and Besançon (1676) were added.

3 The kings of France claimed to possess the divinely given power of curing scrofula by touching sufferers; the monarchs of England claimed the same power.

4 R. F. E. Ferrier and J. A. H. Ferrier, *The Journal of Major Richard Ferrier, M.P., while Travelling in France in the Year 1687* (Camden Miscellany, London, 1895), 26. 'Monsieur' was the king's brother, Philippe, duc d'Orléans; the 'dauphiness' was Marie Anne Christine of Bavaria, wife of the dauphin, Louis.

5 D. J. Sturdy, *Louis XIV* (London, 1998), 53.

6 Nobility whose titles came through the tenure of senior legal offices.

7 No official title was given to the body in 1666; that of 'Academy of Sciences' only slowly crept in.

8 H. Kamen, *Spain in the Later Seventeenth Century, 1665–1700* (London, 1980), 134–7; H. Kamen, *Spain 1469–1714: A Society of Conflict* (London, 1983), appendix 2.

9 Strictly speaking, Philip V ruled twice: he abdicated in 1724 in favour of his son Luis I, but Luis died later in the year; reluctantly Philip V returned to the throne and ruled until his death in 1746.

10 There were nine councils at the beginning of Philip V's reign: the royal council and the councils of state, Castile, the Inquisition, the Indies, orders, war, finance, Aragon.

## Chapter 9   Western Europe, 1660–1720: Britain, the United Provinces and War

1 This was an acronym, the ministers being Clifford, Ashley, Buckingham, Arlington and Lauderdale.

2 As contained in the 'Act for the better discovering and repressing of Popish recusants', 1606.

3 They were: Thomas Osborne, earl of Danby; William Cavendish, earl of Devonshire; Richard, Lord Lumley; Charles Talbot, earl of Shrewsbury; Henry Compton, bishop of London, Henry Sydney and Edward Russell, younger sons of their respective families. The first five were all members of the House of Lords, Compton in his capacity as a bishop; but Compton was also the son of a peer, the earl of Northampton.

4 The provinces of Holland, Gelderland, Overijssel and Utrecht were in favour; Zeeland, Friesland and Gröningen were against.

5 J. A. Lynn, *The Wars of Louis XIV, 1667–1714* (London, 1999), 111.

6 The Elector Charles II had been a Calvinist; Philip William was a Catholic; thus the balance in the imperial electoral college swung even further in favour of the Catholic Habsburgs.

7 Of the 224 members of the Irish House of Commons, 218 were Catholic.

8   This is according to the old calendar then in use. The battle is now celebrated by the Orange Order in Northern Ireland and elsewhere on 12 July.

9   The main treaties which together constituted the Peace of Utrecht were: (a) 11 April 1713 between France, Britain, Portugal, Prussia and Savoy; (b) 13 July 1713 between Spain, Britain and Savoy; (c) 4 November 1713 between France and the United Provinces; (d) 26 June 1714 between Spain and the United Provinces; (e) 6 March 1714 between France and the emperor (signed at Rastadt, not Utrecht); (f) 7 November 1714 between France and the Holy Roman Empire (signed at Baden, not Utrecht); (g) 6 February 1715 between Spain and Portugal (signed at Utrecht).

## Chapter 10   Northern Europe, 1660–1721: Scandinavia, Russia and Poland

1   R. Bonney (ed.), *Economic Systems and State Finance* (Oxford, 1995), 460.

2   His title was king *in* Prussia, not king *of* Prussia (although the latter formulation commonly was used). This was to indicate that the rights of his Prussian subjects were not affected by the change.

3   The cult of Razin continues to the present day; 'Stenka Razin' is the most popular of all Russian folk songs.

## Conclusion

1   E. Brown[e], *An Account of Several Travels through a Great Part of Germany...* (London, 1677); 'Penson's Short Progresse into Holland, Flaunders and France with Remarques written by Tho. Penson, Arms Painter, Anno Dom. 1690' (British Library, Harleian MS 3516); E. Veryard, *An Account of Divers Choice Remarks...Taken in a Journey through the Low Countries, France, Italy, and Part of Spain...as also a Voyage to the Levant* (London, 1701).

2   *La crise de la conscience Européenne, 1680–1715* (Paris, 1935).

# Index